D1144741

A NOTE ABOUT THE AUTHOR

Tim Wu is an author, policy advocate, and professor at Columbia University, best known for coining the term "Net Neutrality." In 2006, *Scientific American* named him one of fifty leaders in science and technology; in 2007, *01238* magazine listed him as one of Harvard's 100 most influential graduates; in 2013, *The National Law Journal* included him in "America's 100 Most Influential Lawyers"; and in 2014 and 2015, he was named to the "Politico 50." He formerly wrote for *Slate,* where he won the Lowell Thomas gold medal for Travel Journalism, and is a contributing writer for *The New Yorker.*

ALSO BY TIM WU

The Master Switch

THE ATTENTION MERCHANTS

THE ATTENTION MERCHANTS

From the Daily Newspaper to Social Media,
How Our Time and Attention is Harvested and Sold

TIM WU

ATLANTIC BOOKS
London

First published in 2016 in the United States of America by Alfred A. Knopf, a division of Penguin Random House LLC, New York, and distributed in Canada by Random House of Canada, a division of Penguin Random House Limited, Toronto.

First published in Great Britain in e-book and hardback in 2017 by Atlantic Books, an imprint of Atlantic Books Ltd.

1 2 3 4 5 6 7 8 9 10

A CIP catalogue record for this book is available from the British Library.

Hardback ISBN: 978 1 78 2394822
Trade paperback ISBN: 978 1 78 2394839
E-book ISBN: 978 1 78 2394846

Printed in Great Britain by TJ International Ltd, Padstow, Cornwall

Atlantic Books
An Imprint of Atlantic Books Ltd
Ormond House
26–27 Boswell Street
London
WC1N 3JZ

www.atlantic-books.co.uk

For Sierra

CONTENTS

INTRODUCTION   Here's the Deal   3

PART I   **MASTERS OF BLAZING MODERNITIES**

CHAPTER 1   The First Attention Merchants   11

CHAPTER 2   The Alchemist   24

CHAPTER 3   For King and Country   37

CHAPTER 4   Demand Engineering, Scientific Advertising,
              and What Women Want   51

CHAPTER 5   A Long Lucky Run   65

CHAPTER 6   Not with a Bang but with a Whimper   73

PART II   **THE CONQUEST OF TIME AND SPACE**

CHAPTER 7   The Invention of Prime Time   85

CHAPTER 8   The Prince   95

CHAPTER 9   Total Attention Control,
              or The Madness of Crowds   108

CHAPTER 10   Peak Attention, American Style   123

CHAPTER 11   Prelude to an Attentional Revolt   144

CHAPTER 12   The Great Refusal 151

CHAPTER 13   Coda to an Attentional Revolution 170

PART III **THE THIRD SCREEN**

CHAPTER 14   Email and the Power of the Check-in 183

CHAPTER 15   Invaders 191

CHAPTER 16   AOL Pulls 'Em In 198

PART IV **THE IMPORTANCE OF BEING FAMOUS**

CHAPTER 17   Establishment of the Celebrity-Industrial Complex 217

CHAPTER 18   The Oprah Model 227

CHAPTER 19   The Panopticon 237

PART V **WON'T BE FOOLED AGAIN**

CHAPTER 20   The Kingdom of Content: This Is How You Do It 255

CHAPTER 21   Here Comes Everyone 267

CHAPTER 22   The Rise of Clickbait 276

CHAPTER 23   The Place to Be 289

CHAPTER 24   The Importance of Being Microfamous 303

CHAPTER 25   The Fourth Screen and the Mirror of Narcissus 308

CHAPTER 26   The Web Hits Bottom 318

CHAPTER 27   A Retreat and a Revolt 328

CHAPTER 28   Who's Boss Here? 335

EPILOGUE   The Temenos 340

Acknowledgments 345

Notes 347

Index 387

THE ATTENTION MERCHANTS

HERE'S THE DEAL

In 2011, the Twin Rivers school district in central California faced a tough situation. The district, never wealthy, was hit hard by the housing crisis of the early 2000s and the state government's own financial meltdown. By the 2010s, schools were cutting not only extracurricular activities but even some of the basics, like heat. One day in winter, a student posted a picture of a classroom thermostat reading 44 degrees Fahrenheit.

Such were the circumstances when the Twin Rivers board was approached by a company named "Education Funding Partners." EFP offered a tantalizing new way to help solve the district's financial problems, using what it called "the power of business to transform public education." Acting as broker, the firm promised that it could bring the district as much as $500,000 in private money per year. And, EFP stressed, its services would cost nothing. "EFP is paid solely out of corporate contributions," the pitch explained, "essentially providing a free service to districts."

To gain this free bounty, the board didn't actually have to do anything. It needed only to understand something: that the schools were already holding an asset more lucrative than any bake sale. That asset, simply stated, was their students, who by the very nature of compulsory education were a captive audience. If the schools could seize their attention for the purpose of educating them, why not sell off a bit of it for the sake of improving the educational experience? Specifically, EFP was proposing that Twin Rivers allow corporate advertising within the schools. Moreover, EFP explained, it would bundle students from Twin Rivers with those in other school districts around the nation so as to appeal to bigger brands—the Fortune 500 companies—with deeper pockets.

If EFP was promising the district free money, its pitch to corporate advertisers was no less seductive: "Open the schoolhouse doors," it said, promising "authentic access and deep engagement with audiences in the school environment." Advertisers have long coveted direct access to the young, who are impressionable and easier to influence. Establishing a warm association with Coca-Cola or McDonald's at an early age can yield payoffs that last a lifetime—or, in the lingo, "drive purchase decisions and build brand awareness." That in essence is what EFP offered its clients: "an unparalleled system for engagement in the K–12 market"—a chance to mold the consumers of the future.

Twin Rivers soon began to see the light. "We need to be innovative about the assets we have and learn how to bring in more revenue," said a spokeswoman. In other parts of the country, the prospect of opening schools to commercial advertising had prompted public debate. Not so in Twin Rivers, where the administrators seemed to regard signing the deal, which they did in 2012, as a matter of duty. "In these challenging economic times," said the chief business officer, "our students are counting on us to find ways to make our resources stretch further than ever before." EFP, for its part, promised all messaging would be "responsible" and "educational." With that, the school doors were thrown open.

Twin Rivers is only one of the many school districts in the United States—mostly in poor or middle-class areas—that have begun to rely on selling access to their students as an essential revenue source. Some schools plaster ads across student lockers and hallway floors. One board in Florida cut a deal to put the McDonald's logo on its report cards (good grades qualified you for a free Happy Meal). In recent years, many have installed large screens in their hallways that pair school announcements with commercials. "Take your school to the digital age" is the motto of one screen provider: "everyone benefits."

What is perhaps most shocking about the introduction of advertising into public schools is just how uncontroversial and indeed logical it has seemed to those involved. The deals are seen as a win-win, yielding money that it would be almost irresponsible to refuse. Yet things were not always this way. There was once a time when, whether by convention or technological limitation, many parts of life—home, school, and social interaction among them—were sanctuaries, sheltered from advertising and commerce. Over the last century, however, we have come to accept a very different way of being, whereby nearly every bit of our lives is commercially exploited to the extent it can be. As adults, we are hardly ever unreachable; seldom away from a screen of some kind; rarely not being solicited or sold to. From this perspective, the school administrators are merely giving students a lesson in reality, exposing them to what is, after all, the norm for adults. But where did the norm come from? And how normal is it?

This book explains how our current state of affairs came to be. It is the consequence of the dramatic and impressive rise of an industry that barely existed a century ago: the Attention Merchants. Since its inception, the attention industry, in its many forms, has asked and gained more and more of our waking moments, albeit always, in exchange for new conveniences and diversions, creating a grand bargain that has transformed our lives. In the process, as a society and individually, we have accepted a life experience that is in all of its dimensions—economic, political, social, any way you can think of—mediated as never before in human history. And if each bargain in isolation seems a win-win, in their grand totality they have come to exert a more ambiguous though profound influence on how we live.

Who exactly are the attention merchants? As an industry, they are relatively new. Their lineage can be traced to the nineteenth century, when in New York City the first newspapers fully dependent on advertising were created; and Paris, where a dazzling new kind of commercial art first seized the eyes of the person in the street. But the full potential of the business model by which attention is converted into revenue would not be fully understood until the early twentieth century, when the power of mass attention was discovered not by any commercial entity but by British war propagandists. The disastrous consequences of propaganda in two world wars would taint the subsequent use of such methods by government, at least in the West. Industry, however, took note of what captive attention could accomplish, and since that time has treated it as a precious resource, paying ever larger premiums for it.

If the attention merchants were once primitive, one-man operations, the game of harvesting human attention and reselling it to advertisers has become a major part of our economy. I use the crop metaphor because attention has been widely recognized as a commodity, like wheat, pork bellies, or crude oil. Existing industries have long depended on it to drive sales. And the new industries of the twentieth century turned it into a form of currency they could mint. Beginning with radio, each new medium would attain its commercial viability through the resale of what attention it could capture in exchange for its "free" content.

As we shall see, the winning strategy from the beginning has been to seek out time and spaces previously walled off from commercial exploitation, gathering up chunks and then slivers of our un-harvested awareness. Within living memory it was thought that families would never tolerate the intrusion of broadcasting in the home. An earlier generation would find it astonishing that, without payment or even much outcry, our networks of family, friends, and associates have been recruited via social media to help sell us things. Now, however, most of us carry devices on our bodies that constantly find ways to commercialize the smallest particles of our time and attention. Thus, bit by bit, what was once shocking became normal, until the shape of our lives yielded further and further to the logic of commerce—but gradually enough that we should now find nothing strange about it.

This book shares with my previous one, *The Master Switch,* the basic objective of making apparent the influence of economic ambition and power on how we experience our lives. As in that book, I'd like to pose at the outset the cynic's eternal question: What difference does the rise of the Attention Merchants make to me? Why should I care? Quite simply because this industry, whose very business is the influence of consciousness, can and will radically shape how our lives are lived.

It is no coincidence that ours is a time afflicted by a widespread sense of attentional crisis, at least in the West—one captured by the phrase "homo distractus," a species of ever shorter attention span known for compulsively checking his devices. Who has not sat down to read an email, only to end up on a long flight of ad-laden clickbaited fancy, and emerge, shaking his or her head, wondering where the hours went?

While allowing that many of us are perpetually distracted, spend too much time on social media or watching television, and consequently consume more advertising than could ever serve our own useful purposes, the cynic may still ask: But isn't it simply our choice to live this way? Of course it is—it is we who have voluntarily, or somewhat voluntarily, entered into this grand bargain with the attentional industry, and we enjoy the benefits. But it is essential that we fully understand the deal. Certainly some of our daily attentional barters—for news, good entertainment, or useful services—are good deals. But others are not. The real purpose of this book is less to persuade you one way or the other, but to get you to see the terms plainly, and, seeing them plainly, demand bargains that reflect the life you want to live.

For the history also reveals that we are hardly powerless in our dealings with the attention merchants. Individually, we have the power to ignore, tune out, and unplug. At certain times over the last century, the industry has asked too much and offered too little in return, or even been seen to violate the public's trust outright. At such moments, the bargain of the attention merchants is beset with a certain "disenchantment," which, if popular grievance is great enough, can sometimes turn into a full-fledged "revolt." During those revolts—of which there have been several over the last century—the attention merchants and their partners in the advertising industry have been obliged to present a new deal, revise the terms of the arrangement. We may, in fact, be living in such a time today, at least in those segments of the population committed to cord-cutting, ad-avoiding, or unplugging. We are certainly at an appropriate time to think seriously about what it might mean to reclaim our collective consciousness.

Ultimately, it is not our nation or culture but the very nature of our lives that is at stake. For how we spend the brutally limited resource of our attention will determine those lives to a degree most of us may prefer not to think about. As William James observed, we must reflect that, when we reach the end of our days, our life experience will equal what we have paid attention to, whether by choice or default. We are at risk, without quite fully realizing it, of living lives that are less our own than we imagine. The goal of what follows is to help us understand more clearly how the deal went down and what it means for all of us.

PART I

MASTERS OF BLAZING MODERNITIES

Since the rise of capitalism, it has been known that capturing someone's attention could cause him to part with some money. Even before that, there was paid spectacle, like the modern theater. But as recently as the late nineteenth century, the first real industries of attention capture were still embryonic, though by then, printed matter like books and broadsheets had joined live spectacle as mental fodder created for profit.

From the 1890s through the 1920s, there arose the first means for harvesting attention on a mass scale and directing it for commercial effect, thanks to what is now familiar to us in many forms under the name of advertising. At its inception it was as transformative as the cotton gin. For advertising was the conversion engine that, with astonishing efficiency, turned the cash crop of attention into an industrial commodity. As such, attention could be not only used but resold, and this is where our story begins.

CHAPTER 1

THE FIRST ATTENTION MERCHANTS

In the summer of 1833, with *The New York Times* and *The Wall Street Journal* both decades from their first editions, New York City's leading newspaper was *The Morning Courier and New York Enquirer,* a four-page daily with circulation of just 2,600 in a city of almost 300,000.[1] At 6 cents, it was something of a luxury item, which was just as well, since like several of its rivals, including *The Journal of Commerce,* it was aimed at the city's business and political elite. Most New Yorkers, in fact, did not read newspapers at all; "they went their way, if not entirely unaware of their presence, at least untouched by their influence," as one historian put it. "There was little or nothing about these papers to attract the average reader."[2]

In this sluggish market a young man named Benjamin Day thought he spied an opportunity. A print shop proprietor who had once worked at a newspaper, the twenty-three-year-old Day decided he'd try publishing a paper of his own. The venture was risky, for his motives were different from those of many other newspapermen of his time. Day did not have a particular political agenda, nor was he a rich man subsidizing a vanity press for the presentation of his views. As one might gather from a painting of him scowling in a tall stovepipe hat, Day saw himself as a businessman, not a journalist. "He needed a newspaper not to reform, not to arouse, but to push the printing business of Benjamin H. Day."

Day's idea was to try selling a paper for a penny—the going price for many everyday items, like soap or brushes. At that price, he felt sure he could capture a much larger audience than his 6-cent rivals. But what made the prospect risky, potentially even suicidal, was that Day would then be selling his paper at a loss. What Day was contemplating was a break with the traditional strategy for making profit: selling at a price higher than the cost of production. He would instead rely on a different but historically significant business model: reselling the attention of his audience, or advertising. What Day understood—more firmly, more clearly than anyone before him—was that while his readers may have thought themselves his customers, they were in fact his *product*.

It wasn't, of course, as if newspapers had never tried advertising as a revenue source. Since the first dailies in the early eighteenth century, there had been forms of advertising or paid notices. But the line between news and advertising could be blurry, and so it's hard to identify the first true advertisement. (In 1871, *The New York Times* would assign the distinction—in English at least—to a publication announcement of the heroic poem "Irenodia Gratulatoria" in 1652.) Indeed, the earliest newspapers "treated advertising as a form of news . . . presumably because it was considered interesting to readers." Unlike the persuasive, rhetorical advertisements to come, early ads were purely informational. Most were what we'd call classifieds—lost items, things for sale, job openings, and private notices of various kinds.

Day's idea was not to offer such a notice board but rather to sell his readers' attention en bloc to more substantial advertisers. But for such undifferentiated attention to be valuable to anyone, he would have to amass a giant readership. That would mean making the *New York Sun* alluring to the broadest segment of society—by any means necessary.

The *New York Sun* first appeared on September 3, 1833: all text and in smaller format than the broadsheets, to save on costs. Day did it all—he was "proprietor, publisher, editor, chief pressman, and mailing clerk." For the paper's first issue, he took the unusual step of filling it with advertisements from businesses he had never solicited. You might say that he ran advertisements, in effect, to try and find advertisers. Such could also be understood from his statement on the front page: "The object of this paper," he wrote, "is to lay before the public, at a price within the means of every one, ALL THE NEWS OF THE DAY, and at the same time afford an advantageous medium for advertising." His plan for delivering on the promise of such a broad readership was to feature stories from which no one could look away.

"MELANCHOLY SUICIDE—a Mr. Fred A. Hall . . . put an end to his life on Sunday last by taking laudanum," read the first headline in the very first issue. Young Mr. Hall, the story revealed, was about to be shipped off to Indonesia by his father to end a romance. Unable to bear the separation, he took his life. "He was about twenty-four years of age, of engaging manners and amiable disposition, and one whose loss, even under less affecting circumstances, would have been deeply lamented."

The first issue of the *Sun* told also the story of William Scott and Charlotte Grey. Scott was jailed for assaulting Grey, his female companion. Brought before the magistrate, Scott was offered release on one condition: that he promise to marry Grey, the injured party. "Mr. Scott cast a sheep's eye towards the girl, and then looking out of the window, gave the bridewell a melancholy survey. [He] was hesitating which he should choose—a wife or prison. The Justice insisted on an immediate answer. At length he concluded that he 'might as well marry the critter,' and they left the office apparently satisfied."

On its first day, the *New York Sun* reportedly sold about three hundred copies. It was a start, but still a money-loser; to get it off the ground Day would have to do much better. He continued to find his best stories at New York's police court, with its "dismal parade of drunkards and wife beaters, con men and petty thieves, prostitutes and their johns." Copying a British publication, therefore, he hired a man called George Wisner (for $4 a week) just to cover the court, creating quite possibly "the first full-time news reporter in U.S. history." Day's man went to court every day, returning with a wealth of lurid or comic material from the proceedings, such as the following testimony from "a little curly-pated fellow by the name of John Lawler," who was brought before the court on a charge of kicking over the mead stand belonging to Mary Lawler, the complainant:

MAGISTRATE: Well, let's hear your story. Do you know the boy?
COMPLAINANT: The boy, did you say? Indeed, sir, divil a bit o'boy is here about the baste, nor man neither, barring he drinks brandy like a fish. (loud laughter)

MAGISTRATE: Did you ever see him before?

COMPLAINANT: Indeed, I guess I did. Many years ago he was my husband, but your honor sees, I gave him a divorce. That is, ye see, I gave him a bit of paper stating that I would live with him no longer. (laughter)

PRISONER: It's no such thing, yer honor. She used to go off with other men, so I sold her for a gill of rum.

Unlike other papers, the *Sun* also offered detailed coverage of New York's slave trade, including stories of captured runaways (despite having abolished slavery in 1827, New York still honored the property rights of slave state residents) and of the misery of slave marriages sundered by the auction block. Though otherwise apolitical and nonpartisan, the *New York Sun,* mainly owing to Wisner, took a consistent principled stand in favor of abolition. "We believe the day is not far distant," the *Sun* said, "when the clanking of slavery's chains will be heard no more—and Americans stand before the world practicing, as well as preaching, the glorious doctrine that *all* men are created free and equal."

Such stories gained Day the audience and attention he sought. Within just three months, he was selling thousands of copies a day, threatening the established papers. The more copies he printed, however, the more money he lost based on the penny price alone.[3] So it all depended on the advertising revenue, which was growing as well. At some magical moment during that first year, it happened: the lift generated by paid advertising exceeded the gravity of costs. And at that point, like the Wrights' aeroplane, the *New York Sun* took flight, and the world was never really the same again.

By the end of 1834, the *New York Sun* claimed five thousand readers a day, making it the city's leading paper. Day had wanted only to bolster his modest income, but he wound up proving that newspapers could work as a freestanding business. The *Sun*'s success showed that a paper need not serve as a party organ, need not rely on a rich patron to fund its losses. For their part, rival papers could not at first fathom how the *Sun* was able to charge less, provide more news, reach a larger audience, and still come out ahead. What Day had figured out was that newsstand earnings were trivial; advertising revenue could make it all happen.

Besides striking it rich, Day accomplished something else, too. For even more than the business model, the long-term social consequences of a newspaper for the masses were profound. Large numbers of people taking in daily news gave rise to what Jürgen Habermas has called a "public sphere"[4]—a more quotidian term for this effect is "public opinion," but by whatever name, it was a new phenomenon, and one dependent on the nascent but growing attention industry.

Unfortunately for Day, the competition eventually figured out how he was doing it. And soon his business model faced copycats. One of them, the *New York Transcript,* an evening paper, became an early ancestor of ESPN by focusing on sports coverage, which at the time was limited to horse races and prizefights. But the greatest challenge came from *The Morning Herald,* another penny paper first published in 1835 by a former schoolmaster named James Gordon Bennett. Severely cross-eyed, Bennett was a strange man—a shameless braggart who promoted himself as a paragon of gentility while also feeding the public's appetite for the lurid and debauched. One historian would call him "a flagrant charlatan—but always a charlatan who accomplished his ends." In his paper's second issue Bennett announced that his mission was "to give a correct picture of the world . . . wherever human nature and real life best displays their freaks and vagaries."

From the beginning, *The Herald* established a specialty in the coverage of violent death. By one count, it reported in its first two weeks "three suicides, three murders, a fire that killed five persons, an accident in which a man blew off his head, descriptions of a guillotine execution in France, a riot in Philadelphia, and the execution of Major John André half a century earlier." Bennett would pioneer on-the-scene crime reporting, beginning with his sensational account of the murder of Helen Jewett, a prostitute killed with a hatchet and left on a burning bed. Bennett was let in to see the naked corpse:

It was the most remarkable sight I ever beheld. . . . "My God" I exclaimed, "how like a statue!" The body looked as white, as full, as polished as the purest marble. The perfect figure, the exquisite limbs, fine face, the full arms, the beautiful bust, all surpassed, in every respect, the Venus de Medici. . . . For a few moments I was lost in admiration of the extraordinary sight. . . . I was recalled to her horrid destiny by seeing the dreadful bloody gashes on the right temple.

When not chronicling death in its many forms, Bennett loved to gain attention for his paper by hurling insults and starting fights. Once he managed in a single issue to insult seven rival papers and their editors. He was perhaps the media's first bona fide "troll." As with contemporary trolls, Bennett's insults were not clever. He attacked the older, 6-cent *Courier and Herald* and its portly editor, respectively, as "bloated" and "big-bellied." The *Sun*'s editors he condemned as the "garbage of society," and the paper as "too indecent, too immoral for any respectable person to touch, or any family to take in." Taking notice of its support for the complete abolition of slavery, he blasted it as a "decrepit, dying penny paper, owned and controlled by a set of woolly-headed and thick-lipped Negroes."

As politicians, professional wrestlers, and rappers know well, trash-talking remains an effective way of getting attention, and it worked well for Bennett. Like those practitioners of the art in our own time, he did not hesitate to tout his own magnificence. His *New York Herald,* he proclaimed, "would outstrip everything in the conception of man," for he was making *The Herald* into "the great organ of social life, the prime element of civilization, the channel through which native talent, native genius, and native power may bubble up daily, as the pure sparkling liquid of the Congress fountain at Saratoga bubbles up from the centre of the earth, till it meets the rosy lips of the fair."

Bennett's blend of murder and highfalutin beatdown was evidently worth a penny to many, and in less than a year, *The Herald* claimed a circulation of seven thousand, drawing roughly even with the *Sun*. The race was on to see which paper—and which kind of appeal—would harvest the most attention in New York.

In the ensuing contest we can observe a very basic and perhaps eternal dynamic of the attention industries. We've already seen the attention merchant's basic modus operandi: draw attention with apparently free stuff and then resell it. But a consequence of that model is a total dependence on gaining and holding attention. This means that under competition, the race will naturally run to the bottom; attention will almost invariably gravitate to the more garish, lurid, outrageous alternative, whatever stimulus may more likely engage what cognitive scientists call our "automatic" attention as opposed to our "controlled" attention, the kind we direct with intent.[5] The race to a bottomless bottom, appealing to what one might call the audience's baser instincts, poses a fundamental, continual dilemma for the attention merchant—just how far will he go to get his harvest? If the history of attention capture teaches us anything, it is that the limits are often theoretical, and when real, rarely self-imposed.

In the case of the *New York Sun,* however, there is little evidence of even theoretical limits. For in reacting to its new competitors, the paper readily discarded what we would consider the paramount journalistic ethic, that of being bound by facts.

In 1835, not long after the launch of *The Herald,* the *Sun* ran a headline story, styled as a reprint from an Edinburgh newspaper, of "astronomical discoveries" by the famous scientist Sir John Herschel. Herschel, son of another famous astronomer, had in fact moved to the Cape of Good Hope in 1834 to build a new telescope. From the Southern Hemisphere, the *Sun* reported, "[he] has obtained a distinct view of objects in the moon, fully equal to that which the unaided eye commands of terrestrial objects of the distance of a hundred yards."[6] Over the next several weeks, a five-part series reported all that Herschel had discovered: the moon was covered with great seas and canyons, pillars of red rock and lunar trees, unlike any other, save the "largest kind of yews in English churchyards, which they in some respects resemble." But Herschel's greatest discovery was life on the moon, or more precisely: large, winged creatures, which when not borne aloft could pass for humans:

> Certainly they *were* like human beings, for their wings had now disappeared, and their attitude in walking was both erect and dignified. . . . They averaged four feet in height, were covered, except on the face, with short and glossy copper-coloured hair, and had wings composed of a thin membrane, without hair, lying snugly upon their backs. We scientifically denominated them as Vespertilio-homo, or man-bat; and they are doubtless innocent and happy creatures, notwithstanding that some of their amusements would but ill comport with our terrestrial notions of decorum.

The depiction of the moon, and one with life on it (not just life, but unicorns and flying man-bats with insistent libidos), was, apparently, widely accepted, in part thanks to the scientific style of the correspon-

dent, the pretense that the story was reprinted from a respectable Edinburgh journal, and the impossibility of replicating with the naked eye
the findings of the world's largest telescope. The series was, understand-
ably, a sensation, and the initial runs of the newspaper sold out, with
crowds surrounding its offices, hungrily awaiting the next installment.
When the dust settled, the *New York Sun,* founded just two years prior,
had driven its circulation to a very precise-sounding 19,360, sailing past
not only the other New York dailies but even the London dailies founded
decades earlier, to take its place as the most widely read newspaper in the
world.

Having decisively demonstrated that a business could be founded on
the resale of human attention, Benjamin Day became the first attention merchant worthy of the title. There might have been good reason
to doubt the circulation claims of a newspaper that had just reported
the discovery of life on the moon. But it cannot be denied that the *Sun*
succeeded or that the model Day conceived would spawn generations of
imitators, from radio networks and broadcast television to Google and
Facebook.

———————

Posters had been around since 1796. But no one had ever seen the likes of
those that began to appear in Paris in the late 1860s, some of them seven
feet high, with beautiful, half-dressed women gamboling over fields of
vibrant color. "Luminous, brilliant, even blinding," one journalist wrote,
marveling at the "vivid sensations and intense emotions, rapidly blunted,
[only] to be revived again." Contemporaries marveled at what was happening to the Paris cityscape. It was "the education of everyone through
the retina . . . instead of the bare wall, the wall attracts, as a kind of
chromolithographic salon."

The new posters were the invention of Jules Chéret, an aspiring artist and onetime printer's apprentice who'd spent seven years in London
studying lithography, then a relatively new technique by which images
were rendered in oil on soft limestone. Bringing the latest in British technology back to Paris and adding some of his own innovations, Chéret
began to produce by commission an altogether new species of commercial art.

Before Chéret the poster had usually been a block of text, sometimes with a small illustration—not unlike the title page of a book, only larger. We can usefully think of the mass-produced poster as an early screen—though a static version, to be sure—the phenomenon now so ubiquitous in our lives. The giant Parisian poster wasn't the first mass-produced poster; it was, however, a technological and conceptual innovation.* For despite being static, the Parisian posters evoked a sense of frantic energy in their bright, contrasting colors, and beautiful, half-dressed women—elements that made them nearly impossible to ignore. There were always, of course, arresting sights to behold in art and nature. But the posters were commercial and scalable. "A master of blazing modernities," as one critic called him, Chéret could print thousands of them, producing their mesmeric effects on millions of passersby. As such, his posters are the second milestone in the industrialized harvesting of attention.[7]

The neuroscience of attention, despite having greatly advanced over the past few decades, remains too primitive to explain comprehensively the large-scale harvesting of attention. At most it can shed light on aspects of individual attention. But there is one thing scientists have grasped that is absolutely essential to understand about the human brain before we go any further: our incredible, magnificent power to ignore.

Have you ever found yourself speaking to someone at length only to realize they haven't heard a single thing you've said? As remarkable as our ability to see or hear is our capacity to disregard. This capacity, along with the inherent need to pay attention to something at any given moment, has dictated the development of the attention industries.

Every instant of every day we are bombarded with information. In fact, all complex organisms, especially those with brains, suffer from information overload. Our eyes and ears receive lights and sounds (respectively) across the spectrums of visible and audible wavelengths;

---

* In technique if not technology, Chéret did have a precedent. In Japan, a few decades earlier, advertisers had begun block-printing large posters featuring beautiful women, albeit more fully clad than their French counterparts. Historians of design have described the influence of Japanese prints on Chéret and his imitators. See Stephen Eskilson, *Graphic Design: A New History*, 2d. ed. (New Haven: Yale University Press, 2012), 59–61.

our skin and the rest of our innervated parts send their own messages of
sore muscles or cold feet. All told, every second, our senses transmit an
estimated 11 million bits of information to our poor brains, as if a giant
fiber-optic cable were plugged directly into them, firing information at
full bore. In light of this, it is rather incredible that we are even capable
of boredom.

Fortunately, we have a valve by which to turn the flow on or off at
will. To use another vernacular, we can both "tune in" and "tune out."
When we shut the valve, we disregard almost everything, while focusing on just one discrete stream of information—like the words on this
page—out of the millions of bits coming in. In fact, we can even shut
out everything external to us, and concentrate on an internal dialogue,
as when we are "lost in thought." This ability—to block out most everything, and focus—is what neuroscientists and psychologists refer to as
paying attention.[8]

We ignore so much stuff for a simple reason: if we didn't, we'd quickly
be overwhelmed, our brains flooded until they seized up. Depending
on the kind of information, it takes our brains some amount of time to
process it, and when we are presented with too much at once we begin
to panic, like a waiter who has too many orders shouted at him at once.

But our capacity to ignore is limited by another fact: we are always
paying attention to *something*. If we think of attention as a resource,
or even a kind of currency, we must allow that it is always, necessarily,
being "spent." There is no saving it for later. The question is always, what
shall I pay attention to? Our brains answer this question with varying
degrees of volition, from "shhh—I'm reading this" to letting our minds
wander in the direction of whatever might draw it in, whether in the
corner of our screen or along some road we are walking. That is where
the attention merchant makes his opportunity. But to succeed he must
motivate us to withdraw our attention from where it is and surrender it
to something else. It needn't be a thoughtful calculation.[9]

This puts us in a position to understand the success and significance
of the Parisian posters. With their bold and contrasting colors—fields of
yellow, red, and blue that tend to spill over onto each other, the posters
were practically impossible to ignore. The attention-grabbing effect of
bright colors was, at the time, understood only intuitively, but it has since
been described by brain scientists. The depiction of exuberant women

in some state of undress perhaps requires less comment, but that they appear to be moving is significant. The impression of motion is achieved by painting multiple versions of the same dancer, each in a slightly different attitude, as in a well-known poster for the Folies-Bergère. Taking these in rapidly in sequence creates the impression of flip-book or Mutoscope. In an early ad for Vin Mariani, the woman is almost running off the poster, skirts trailing, as she pours a glass.

But there is more to the posters' allure. Significantly, they catch the viewer on his way somewhere, the "in between" moments of the day that are in the interstices of our more purposeful mental engagements. That is, times when one might be bored, waiting for a streetcar, or simply strolling around, looking for something to catch the eye. The attentional habit of gazing at the world with nothing better to do has doubtless been a human practice since the species emerged. But its exploitation for commercial purposes is relatively new.

What used to be thought of as the "reptilian core" of our brains—let's now simply speak of those neural circuits governing behavior that seems reflexive, like flinching at a loud noise—should not be underestimated where the harvesting of attention is concerned; for once you recognize the triggers, you begin to see them everywhere: the flashing signs employed by vendors, those bouncing icons on your computer screen, the little pictures of cats or sexy women attached to Internet links. All of these stimuli set off neural responses that cause us to engage, whether we mean to or not. Flipping through a book of classic posters is instructive, for it is almost a catalogue of attention triggers. Motion, color, critters of every kind, sexualized men and women, babies and monsters seem to work best on us. It was the achievement of the late nineteenth century's poster pioneers to recognize these responses and put them to profitable use—a lesson that neither advertisers nor their eventual imitators in government would ever forget.

————————

At first the Parisian posters were welcome and admired. At the height of Jules Chéret's success, the Third Republic awarded him the Legion of Honor, France's highest civilian decoration. But he was prolific, and so were his imitators, resulting in an all-out "poster craze" that spread through Europe and the Americas. There were soon dozens of French poster artists, including those now more famous for fine art, like Henri de Toulouse-Lautrec, whose can-can dancers sitting on the laps of customers are unmistakable.[10] At the start of the twentieth century, however, perhaps with foresight, Chéret and other artists began to abandon the business, while Toulouse-Lautrec died from a combination of alcoholism and syphilis. Despite this loss of artistry, the poster craze continued, overspreading the city without limit.

Industries, unlike organisms, have no organic limits on their own growth; they are constantly in search of new markets, or of new ways to exploit old ones more effectively; as Karl Marx unsympathetically observed, they "nestle everywhere, settle everywhere, establish connexions everywhere."[11] Soon, the posters came to define Paris; by one contemporary account, the city was "hardly more than an immense wall of posters scattered from the chimneys down to sidewalks with clusters of squares of paper of all colors and formats, not to mention simple inscriptions."

Eventually it was too much; the novelty was no more. Here for the first time, but certainly not the last, attention harvesting, taken too far, engendered a vehement social reaction; the proliferation of commercial art and its displacement of other things began to drive people crazy. As the famous adman David Ogilvy once put it, "I have a passion for landscape, and I have never seen one improved by a billboard. Where every prospect pleases, man is at his vilest when he erects a billboard."

In Paris the same aesthetic objections were made: critics said that the advertising poster was destroying her reputation as the world's most beautiful city. Groups including the Society for the Protection of the Landscape and Aesthetics of France, and Les Amis de Paris (Friends of Paris), gained followings by declaring war on the "ugly poster." Sometimes decrying advertising as "unhygienic" or comparing it to prostitution, they proclaimed their goal to make Paris "more beautiful—materially and morally."[12]

Let us pause here to remark a major recurrent dynamic that has shaped the course of attention industries: "the revolt." Industries may have an inherent tendency to "nestle everywhere," but when the commodity in question is access to people's minds, the perpetual quest for growth ensures that forms of backlash, both major and minor, are all but inevitable. The minor version I shall refer to as the "disenchantment effect"; this describes what happens when a once entrancing means of harvesting attention starts to lose its charm. Our ability to ignore things is adaptive; with enough exposure it can make us indifferent to any stimulus, until, say, a poster that was once arresting becomes one we can see through as if it did not exist. It is because of this effect that the attention merchant's approach is always trending in the direction of going too far, almost to the point, sometimes even reaching it, of causing shock.

But the revolts can also take another, more dramatic form that is central to our story. When audiences begin to believe that they are being ill-used—whether overloaded, fooled, tricked, or purposefully manipulated—the reaction can be severe and long-lasting enough to have serious commercial consequences and require a significant reinvention of approach. Almost like a financial bubble bursting, a mass public revolt can reconfigure the industry or inspire regulatory action. That is what happened in Paris, where the anti-poster movement began to lobby the city to impose restraints on where advertisements might be placed, to impose taxes on posters to limit their spread, and to ban billboards along the train tracks. Since it was France, the issue was always stated as an aesthetic concern, but as so often, behind aesthetic concerns there was something deeper at work. Every time you find your attention captured by a poster, your awareness, and perhaps something more, has, if only for a moment, been appropriated without your consent. Perhaps that feeling of violation was what Ogilvy felt when he wrote that "when I retire from Madison Avenue, I am going to start a secret society of masked vigilantes who will travel around the world on silent motor bicycles, chopping down posters at the dark of the moon. How many juries will convict us when we are caught in these acts of beneficent citizenship?"

Indeed as we shall see, behind such impassioned backlash is very often an awareness that the exploitation of human attention is in some deeper way the exploitation of our persons. Buffeted by constant intrusions, we sometimes reach the point of feeling we've had enough, and that feeling is ultimately one the attention industries cannot ignore. In Paris, the municipal authorities did indeed take aggressive action, restricting the placement of posters, which they came to view as a blight, a weed in need of containment. Those limits still exist and are perhaps one reason visitors continue to find the city beautiful.

CHAPTER 2

THE ALCHEMIST

With his round spectacles, thin mustache, and balding pate, he must have often gone unnoticed. Except for the fuchsia boutonniere he always wore, he was indifferent to self-adornment—"my limit on shoes is $6.50," he once allowed.[1] Perhaps it was just as well, since he was something of "a timid introvert," a nervous fellow, to judge by the dried licorice root he chewed on during idle moments. There were few other self-indulgences; "he allowed himself virtually no diversions, no sports, music, politics, books, plays."[2]

Claude C. Hopkins was perhaps an unlikely figure to revolutionize the business of harvesting and using human attention, but that is what he did in the early twentieth century, when he became one of advertising's greatest innovators. Still in its infancy, this new form of communication was, as we have said, the means by which attention could be converted into cash, for Hopkins was a particular master of the art of using attention to create demand for new products. As adman Drayton Bird writes, "If the advertising business ever produced a full-blown genius, Claude Hopkins may have been the man."[3]

Hopkins was born in 1866 in a small town in Michigan. His mother was Scottish, his father a newspaperman from a long line of Freewill Baptist ministers. Claude was subject to a strict evangelical upbringing, by the lights of which, as he would write, "seemingly every joy in life was a sin." When his father abruptly abandoned the family, Hopkins, aged ten, became the sole wage earner, laboring as a boy janitor, delivering papers, and selling silver polish. At age seventeen, he followed family tradition and found work at the church as a religious instructor and unordained minister. "I was destined to be a clergyman," he wrote. "My given names were selected from the Who is Who of clergymen."

If Hopkins had remained true to this vocation, our story would be different. But in his late teens he began to have a crisis of faith and came to "consider the harmless joys of life which had been barred to me." He made up his mind to quit the ministry, preaching to his congregation of nearly eight hundred one last sermon, a heretical jeremiad "against hell fire, against infant damnation, against the discipline I knew. It even questioned the story of the creation and of Jonah and the whale." The congregants left in stunned silence, and the next day his mother disowned him. Hopkins was now irrevocably an outsider, a status that he seemed to relish for reasons perhaps only he knew.

Hopkins left home to seek his fortune, though by his own often unreliable account, he was not after wealth or fame, merely the freedom for what he loved most, which was hard work. "I have always been an addict to work," he would recall. "I love work as other men love play. It is both my occupation and my recreation." Indeed after working through a series of menial jobs, Hopkins was hired as a "scheme man" for a company selling carpet sweepers, as writers of early advertisements were known long before copywriting acquired the glamour of a David Ogilvy or Don Draper. The new man's talent was discovered when he conceived of an advertisement picturing Santa Claus employing the Bissell Carpet Sweeper. "What article can you buy at the same cost that will contribute so much genuine, lasting pleasure and comfort to the recipient as a Bissell Sweeper?[4] It will be a constant reminder of the giver for ten years or more." The fallen preacher had found his life's true calling.

His early career as a preacher may seem an incongruous footnote to the one that would make his name, but it is in fact quite significant if considered in the larger history of attention capture. Before the nineteenth century, human attention was a largely untapped resource in relation to its eventual commercial and political applications. One reason was the lack of advertising such as we would recognize it today. Yes, there have always been commercial notices and signs; the Greeks and Romans used them to indicate wares for sale, as did merchants in China. Some of the graffiti covering the walls of Pompeii, preserved by the eruption of Vesuvius, turn out to be advertisements for erotic services. But as we shall see, there is a crucial difference between this sort of signage and the industrialized capture of attention.

Attention in our sense of it was not vital for commerce as it has become. In a manner that still holds for some professions, like medicine, or for small businesses, merchants typically relied on a good reputation or a network of custom to attract business. As for advertising, it "was thought to be the work of the vulgarian; it was also thought useless."[5] Nor did the State, with the occasional exception of particular kings and emperors—the first two Napoleons, for instance—find it useful to seek regular access to the public mind. Before the democratic age ushered in by the nineteenth century, most political powers had no need to influence the governed.

This is not to say that there were no regular claimants on human attention, only that commercial and political ones hadn't yet arrived. When they did, however, they were met by one that had stood for centuries. With its combination of moral injunctions as well as daily and weekly rituals, organized religion had long taken human attention as its essential substrate. This is especially true of monotheisms, whose demands for a strict adherence to the one true God naturally promote an ideal of undivided attention. Among early Christians, for example, total attention to God implied ceaseless prayer. The early Church father Clement of Alexandria wrote of the "Perfect Christian" as one who "prays throughout his entire life, endeavoring by prayer to have fellowship with God."[6] Likewise the desert monastics of the fourth century took as their aim "to maintain there as near as possible a ceaseless vigil of prayer, punctuated only by the minimal interruption for food and sleep."[7]

Such an aspiration to monopolize the attention of believers was hardly abandoned after Christianity's early days. Some 1700 years later, John Wesley, the founder of Methodism, prescribed various means for keeping the mind attuned to God, such as the practice of thinking of him immediately upon waking, right before falling asleep, for at least an hour during the day, and before taking any important action. (This discipline shares some similarity with the Jewish practice of offering *brachot,* or blessings, at various routine moments, such as before eating or drinking, or more exceptional ones, as when thunder is heard, among other practices codified in the Mishnah in the third century CE.)

To be sure, it isn't as if before the twentieth century everyone was walking around thinking of God all the time. Nevertheless, the Church was the one institution whose mission depended on galvanizing attention; and through its daily and weekly offices, as well as its sometimes central role in education, that is exactly what it managed to do. At the dawn of the attention industries, then, religion was still, in a very real sense, the incumbent operation, the only large-scale human endeavor designed to capture attention and use it. But over the twentieth century, organized religion, which had weathered the doubts raised by the Enlightenment, would prove vulnerable to other claims on and uses for attention. Despite the promise of eternal life, faith in the West declined and has continued to do so, never faster than in the twenty-first century.[8] Offering new consolations and strange gods of their own, the commercial rivals for human attention must surely figure into this decline. Attention, after all, is ultimately a zero-sum game. But let us not get too far ahead of the story.

If you'd attended the Chicago World's Fair in 1893, you might have spotted him. Far from the Ferris wheel and main concourses, Clark Stanley stood before his booth in an elaborate cowboy outfit, a beaded leather jacket with a colorful bandana, his hair worn long with a prominent goatee and mustache. Behind him, his booth crawled with rattlesnakes. Apparently comfortable with the reptiles, Stanley handled the creatures like pets, petting them and draping them around his neck. "I am not the least afraid of being bitten" he reported. "In fact, I have been bitten hundreds of times."

While spectators watched, Clark would reach into a sack, pluck out a fresh snake, asphyxiate it with ether, and plunge it into a pot of boiling water. As he did so, fatty remnants of the snake rose to the top, which Clark skimmed and, on the spot, mixed into an elixir. The resulting potion he called "Clark Stanley's Snake Oil Liniment" and sold to onlookers. The Snake Oil, Clark boasted, had the power to cure many ailments: it was "good for man and beast."

Of Stanley's life we have only his own account, which he called *The Life and Adventures of the American Cowboy,* by Clark Stanley Better Known as the Rattlesnake King, a slim volume that functioned both as an autobiography and advertising brochure. By his account he was born in central Texas in the 1850s and hit the cattle trail at age fourteen. After more than a decade as a cowboy, he was invited one day to visit the Hopi Indians to witness their secret snake dance. Befriending the medicine man, who was impressed with Stanley's Colt revolver and "fancy shooting," he was invited to live with the Indians and learn their secrets, including, most precious of all, "the secret of snake oil" that was entrusted to him alone.

How much of this story is true we may never know, but what we do know for certain is that, at the time, Clark Stanley the Rattlesnake King was among the most successful advertisers in America, forming a part of the growing "patent medicine" industry. His snake oil liniment was only one of dozens of products, like "Lydia Pinkham's Herb Medicine" or "Kickapoo's Indian Sagwa," that were sold through advertising and traveling shows and promised quick cures for nearly any ailment. Yet patent medicine's most important influence was not on medicine but on advertising. As the industry grew, its pressing advertising needs drew many of the nation's most creative and talented copywriters, who would come up with some of modern advertising's most important techniques. It was also through the sale of patent medicine that advertising first proved conclusively its real utility, as a kind of alchemy, an apparently magical means of transforming basically useless substances into commercial gold.

It should be no wonder, then, that sometime in the 1890s, the restless Claude Hopkins made his way to Racine, Wisconsin, to become the advertising manager of Dr. Shoop's Restorative, a patent medicine outfit that specialized in nerve tonics and other nostrums.[9] As he later explained, "The greatest advertising men of my day were schooled in the medicine field. It is sometimes hard to measure just what advertising does. Not so in a medicine. Advertising must do all."

Like the Parisian posters, patent medicine advertisers understood the importance of using startling images and evocative words to turn the head. The Snake Oil Liniment advertisements featured Clark Stanley's enigmatically captivating face framed between a cowboy hat and goatee; here was an early instance of the stylized visages that were typical of early branding and which persist in the likes of Aunt Jemima and the Quaker Oats Quaker man—surrogates, perhaps, for the humans whose reputation had been, in a preceding age of commerce, the cornerstone of trustworthiness. "CLARK STANLEY'S SNAKE OIL LINIMENT" is whimsically spelled out in letters formed of snakes, with encouraging claims of efficacy on either side: "A Wonderful, Pain-Destroying Compound" and "The Strongest and Best Liniment for cure of all pain and lameness." An ad for another medicine, "Kickapoo's Indian Sagwa" similarly evokes the power of exotic remedy with the image of a Native American clutching the bottle and wearing a serenely knowing expression.[10]

But their secret was to be more than merely eye-catching: the medicine ads brazenly promised to make wishes come true.* And what more basic and seductive human wish than to be cured of one's infirmities? Clark Stanley described his snake oil as good for "rheumatism, neuralgia, sciatica, lame back, lumbago, contracted muscles, toothache, sprains, swellings, etc." Some patent medicines, like "The Elixir of Life" sold by a Dr. James W. Kidd, of Fort Wayne, Indiana, went so far as to promise immortality, deliverance from the greatest fear of all. In an advertisement for the elixir, Dr. Kidd reports that he "is able, with the aid of a mysterious compound known only to himself . . . to cure any and every disease that is known to the human body."[11]

The power of promising cure, let alone eternal life, would have been only too familiar to Claude Hopkins, the former preacher. His copy for Dr. Shoop's, now over a century old, is worth reading carefully, as it follows a still familiar formula of anticipating doubts and the likelihood that the sufferer may have been let down many times before. One might even detect the influence of Matthew's Gospel, specifically the story of "a certain woman, which had an issue of blood twelve years, And had suffered many things of many physicians, and had spent all that she had, and was nothing bettered, but rather grew worse" (9:25–26). Hopkins may have had the parable in mind when he wrote

> Some sick one may say:—"But I've tried about all medicines, consulted many physicians, and spent a great deal of money. Nothing can help me."
>
> Tell him that the physician who compounded this remedy knows better than he. This physician, who by thousands of bedsides has watched his remedy cure the most difficult cases, knows best what it will do.

---

* In early advertising jargon, the technique of making convincing promises to the buyer is known as "reason-why" or "hard-sell" advertising.

Dr. Shoop knows that he has discovered the way. He has solved the problem after the arduous labor of a lifetime. He knows it because he has made thousands of successful tests—made them in large hospitals, where the results were public; made them through many other physicians who confirm his opinion. And in his private practice he has successfully treated more than one hundred thousand patients suffering from chronic troubles.

Dr. Shoop has seen his treatment cure in many thousand cases where all other treatments failed. And he has never known his remedy to fail in any disease told of in this book, where any other treatment afterward succeeded.

A few more signal tricks rounded out the medicine advertising approach. Perhaps chief among these was the "secret ingredient." Every patent medicine needed something to set it apart from all the others making similar claims, some kind of mysterious element that was not and perhaps could not be fully explained. It fired the imagination, feeding hope where reason offered thin gruel. Carbolic smoke; swamp root; baobab fruit; and in the case of Clark Stanley's liniment, the secret was, of course, the magic of snake oil itself.[12]

It is easy to ascribe the success of such hokum to the gullibility of another age, until we stop to reflect that the techniques successfully used to sell patent medicine are still routinely used today. The lotions and potions of our times inevitably promise youthfulness, health, or weight loss, thanks to exotic ingredients like antioxidants, amino acids, miracle fruits like the pomegranate and açaí berry, extracted ketones, or biofactors. There is scarcely a shampoo or lotion for sale that does not promise an extraordinary result owing to essence of coconut, or rosemary extracts, or another botanical. As devotees of technology we are, if anything, more susceptible to the supposed degree of difference afforded by some ingenious proprietary innovation, like the "air" in Nike's sports shoes, triple reverse osmosis in some brands of water, or the gold-plating of audio component cables. For all our secular rationalism and technological advances, potential for surrender to the charms of magical thinking remains embedded in the human psyche, awaiting only the advertiser to awaken it.

––––––––––

Hopkins did work wonders—for Dr. Shoop's at least. Advertisers like Clark Stanley had relied on their own traveling roadshows and advertisements in major periodicals, like the relatively new *Ladies' Home Journal* or *Harper's* magazine. To create a national campaign for the small regional brand, Hopkins took inspiration from the success of two former peddlers, Aaron Montgomery Ward and Richard Sears, whose mail-order catalogues (Montgomery Ward's and Sears's) built a thriving business on the back of a federally subsidized carrier. Thus did the U.S. Post Office first become a platform for commercial harvesting of attention. Hopkins began to post more than 400,000 pamphlets for Dr. Shoop's every day, reaching millions with this pioneering effort at "direct mail" advertising, or what we now call "spam."

If Hopkins ever suffered from uncertainty, he never expressed it. "I had a proposition which no reasonable person could refuse. As most people are reasonable, I knew that most people in need would accept it. My offer was impregnable." But Dr. Shoop's would not hold on to Hopkins for long. As his fame as a scheme-man spread, Hopkins was lured to Chicago by a wealthy promoter named Douglas Smith. Smith had bought the rights to a Canadian germicide (Powley's Liquid Ozone), which he renamed Liquozone, and he offered Hopkins a share of the profit if he could do for Liquozone what he had done for Dr. Shoop's, but on an even grander scale.

Once again, Hopkins used the mails to flood the nation with pamphlets. Given the margins—Liquozone cost next to nothing to make—and the size of mailings, he did not need to persuade many that his product could relieve a host of ailments, both minor (like dandruff) as well as fatal (including malaria, anthrax, diphtheria, and cancer). In another stroke of genius, Hopkins pioneered the idea of a free sample. "Do as millions have done—stop doubting—give Liquozone a test."[13] The average consumer who did so would go on to spend 91 cents on the medicine before realizing its uselessness.[14]

By the early 1900s, Hopkins could also sense the beginnings of a mounting reaction and hostility toward patent medicines, which, after all, typically didn't do what they claimed, apart from some narcotic or placebo effects. Business continued booming but skepticism was rising among the suckers. Such was Hopkins's genius, however, that his work now began riding the growing backlash like a riptide: his product would be advertised as the *anti*–snake oil. Liquozone was the real thing. In the words of his direct mail literature:

> We wish to state at the start that we are not patent medicine men, and their methods will not be employed by us. . . . Liquozone is too important a product for quackery.[15]

By 1904, Hopkins and Smith saw revenues of $100 million (in current dollars), having sent out five million free samples. Liquozone even expanded to European markets, proving the new advertising approach lost nothing in translation. In promising to alleviate all of life's sufferings, Hopkins was speaking a universal language.

By 1905, thanks to Liquozone, Claude Hopkins had become America's leading scheme man, and a wealthy one besides. For all his odd ways, he had built his success on a deep understanding of human desire. Unfortunately for him and Liquozone, the backlash Hopkins had begun to sense was about to arrive in full force.

In 1900, Samuel Hopkins Adams, a crime reporter at the *New York Sun,* was yearning to make his mark. Approaching the age of thirty he had made for himself a perfectly fine middle-class life, but after nine years at the *Sun* he was growing restless. "Newspaper reporting is a good job for five years," he would later write, "but after that a man should move along."[16]

Like many reporters at the time, Adams wanted to do a different kind of writing, one that would expose important truths and change the world, a mission that called for pieces of greater length than the usual news story. It is a common enough mid-career urge: having taken care of life's immediate needs, some of us yearn to chase villains, right wrongs, fight on the side of the angels. In contemporary parlance, we'd say Adams became an investigative reporter. In the far more evocative term of that era, he had decided to become a "muckraker." "He believed in morality and Puritan righteousness," his biographer would write. "What Adams lacked was a subject." This he would now find in patent medicine.

By the turn of the century, the industry was generating annual revenues of $45–$90 million, approximately $1.3–$2.9 billion adjusted for inflation, in a nation of just 85 million. Despite its inherent fraudulency, however, it escaped scrutiny for a variety of reasons.

For one, there was no regulatory state of the kind we now take for granted—no FDA to test medicines before they were sold to the public. Efforts to charge sellers of potions with violating common law had largely failed: their promises were gratuitous, and quaffing a product was an assumption of risk by nineteenth-century legal standards. In addition, the press had long displayed little interest in offending an industry that was perhaps its greatest single source of advertising revenue.* That changed in 1905, when the editor of *Collier's Weekly,* one of the new muckraking magazines, commissioned Adams to investigate mischief in the patent medicine business. Adams took on the subject with the fervor of a man finding his life's calling. Undertaking an extremely thorough investigation, Adams relied on some of the skills he'd picked up as a crime reporter. "Find out where the foe is before you strike," he said. "Don't hit out with your eyes shut."[17] He purchased many patent medicines, including Hopkins's Liquozone and Clark Stanley's Snake Oil, and hired chemists to analyze them.

On October 7, 1905, *Collier's* published his exposé under the hard-hitting title "The Great American Fraud."[18] The cover, itself a masterpiece of attention capture, was terrifying. It featured a shadowed skull, with bags of money behind it, patent medicine bottles for teeth, and on its forehead the indictment:

THE PATENT MEDICINE TRUST:
PALATABLE POISON FOR THE POOR

Accusing the entire industry of fraud, Adams opened his story this way:

GULLIBLE America will spend this year some seventy-five millions of dollars in the purchase of patent medicines. In consideration of this

---

* An exception was *The Ladies' Home Journal,* which had stopped taking medicine ads by 1892. Its editor, Edward Bok, also revealed that the going rate for patent medicine endorsements in Washington, D.C., was seventy-five dollars for a senator and forty dollars for a congressman.

sum it will swallow huge quantities of alcohol, an appalling amount of opiates and narcotics, a wide assortment of varied drugs ranging from powerful and dangerous heart depressants to insidious liver stimulants; and, far in excess of all other ingredients, undiluted fraud. For fraud, exploited by the skillfulness of advertising bunco men, is the basis of the trade.

The article went on to detail the pernicious ingredients of the patent medicines, the deaths and addictions users suffered, the complicity of a press dependent on advertising revenue, and numerous other shady business practices. The exposé ran to eleven articles, and unfortunately for Douglas Smith and Claude Hopkins, the third was entirely dedicated to Liquozone, which Adams called a particularly noxious offender for "the prominence of its advertising and the reckless breadth of its claims."

Liquozone, concluded Adams, is "a fraud which owes its continued existence to the laxity of our public health methods and the cynical tolerance of the national conscience." Even the name was a sham. "Liquid oxygen doesn't exist above a temperature of 229 degrees below zero," pointed out Adams. "One spoonful would freeze a man's tongue, teeth and throat to equal solidity before he ever had time to swallow." Douglas Smith was accused of creating an "ingenious system of pseudoscientific charlatanry." For his part, Hopkins had buttressed Liquozone's claims with dozens of endorsements by doctors. Adams rebutted each one, either on the merits or by showing the endorser did not exist or was in fact a veterinarian.

Naturally, Adams also commissioned a chemical assay, which showed that Liquozone was nothing more than highly diluted sulfuric acid with coloring added. Perhaps his most impressive, if inhumane, undertaking was to test Liquozone's curative claims on laboratory animals. Guinea pigs were infected with anthrax, half of them treated with Liquozone, the other half serving as the control group. Within twenty-four hours all of the guinea pigs, treated and untreated, were dead. When repeated with diphtheria and tuberculosis, the experiment produced similar results.[19] The lab concluded that Liquozone not only "had absolutely no curative effect but did, when given in pure form, lower the resistance of the animals, so that they died a little earlier than those not treated."

Coming in a more trusting age, when such revelations had greater power to shock, Adams's article caused an astonishing outcry. A variety of actors, including various women's organizations, and a crusading physician named Harvey Washington Wiley, began to push for legislation, long stalled in Congress, to impose basic labeling rules for foods and medicines. In 1906, Upton Sinclair's *The Jungle* encouraged demands for industry reform generally, with its depiction of nauseating and immoral practices in the meat industry. By that time President Theodore Roosevelt had joined the campaign; he'd later give a speech praising *Collier's Weekly* for having "hit the patent medicine concerns very hard and greatly reduced the amount they spent in advertising."[20] Roosevelt added his weight to the assault on Congress, and the Food and Drugs Act was finally passed that year, despite strong congressional reluctance amid fierce industry lobbying.

The regulation took a particular form that has proven influential to this day. Rather than banning patent medicines or their advertising, it imposed a "truth in labeling" requirement that made "misbranding" illegal and also required that any "dangerous" ingredients be listed. As understood by the government, this criminalized any false claims about potential therapeutic benefits. These new laws, along with advances in legitimate medicine, marked the beginning of the collapse of the patent medicine industry. The end did not come all at once. But even more than legislation, the precipitating factor was the public disenchantment with industry advertising. Even those who dared violate the new law with false claims met with a stony public, desensitized to tricks that had once been so seductive and had already been pushed to the logical extreme by Hopkins. Once the bubble popped, the astonishing alchemy that had made worthless decoctions into precious elixirs could never work again. Thus did Snake Oil go from being a cure-all to a byword for fraud. The ultimate effect was eventually to drive nearly all producers out of business. After peaking in 1907, this once mighty American industry began a death spiral, finally to become a fringe business by the 1930s.

We can also see patent medicine as a victim of its own success. In some version, folk medicines had been around for centuries, and when their claims were more modest, and their advertising less importunate, they may have delivered some of what they promised at least by virtue of the placebo effect, which, as scientists have shown, can be quite significant.

But the industry had caught the spirit of late nineteenth-century capital-ism, and for patent medicine, this translated into too great a fraud, too much profit, too much damage to public health. And so the industry col-lapsed of its own weight. But the means that it had invented for convert-ing attention into cash would live on in other forms, finding new uses in the hands of both government and other commercial ventures.

Few of the patent medicine sellers would enjoy second acts. Clark Stanley, the Rattlesnake King, continued with Snake Oil for a time but eventually fell afoul of the new laws. A Rhode Island prosecutor, acting on behalf of the Bureau of Chemistry, indicted him for violating the Food and Drugs Act in 1916. The bureau tested a sample of Snake Oil and found it to contain "a light mineral oil (petroleum product) mixed with about 1 percent fatty oil (probably beef fat) capsicum, and pos-sibly a trace of camphor and turpentine."[21] As the government charged, Snake Oil was "falsely and fraudulently . . . represented as a remedy for all pains and lameness . . . when, in truth and in fact, it was not."

In 1907, in the aftermath of the *Collier's* piece, passage of the new law, and the collapse of Liquozone, Hopkins, who remained ultimately a sensitive soul beneath his stoic exterior, suffered a serious breakdown. Exposed as a fraud, his business in ruins, Hopkins was, according to one acquaintance, "disgraced and disheartened." He decided to give up all forms of salesmanship and never to "enter the vortex of advertising again." Instead, he planned to use his writing skills to become an author. "I intended to keep busy, but I would write in the future for fame and not for money."[22] After consulting a French doctor, Hopkins retreated to a cottage on the shores of Lake Michigan to convalesce. As he would tell it, "I basked in the sunshine, sleeping, playing, and drinking milk." And that might have marked the end of Hopkins's advertising career—but for events taking place thousands of miles away.

CHAPTER 3

FOR KING AND COUNTRY

Shortly after noon on August 3, 1914, Lord Herbert Kitchener was pacing the decks and working himself into a rage. He was anxious to return home to colonial Egypt, but the steamer meant to take him there was still docked in Dover, its departure already delayed an hour, when a man from Downing Street scrambled aboard. That messenger was clutching a letter from the prime minister, a letter that would not only postpone Kitchener's trip home but also set him on an unexpected course to become one of the pivotal figures in the story of mass attention capture.[1]

Kitchener was himself no stranger to attention. In 1911, he'd been appointed the king's vice-consul in Egypt, becoming de facto ruler of the land of the pharaohs. By then he was already Britain's best known military officer, a living embodiment of colonial rule. Sir Arthur Conan Doyle wrote of him, "He was in a very special sense a King-Man, one who was born to fashion and control the Great Affairs of Mankind." And with his erect posture, large mustache, and taste for full dress uniform, he very much looked the part.[2]

The message from Prime Minister Herbert Asquith ordered the indispensable Kitchener back to London for a meeting of the War Council. The next day, Britain would declare war on the German Empire. There wasn't much choice, since Germany had defied a British ultimatum to end its occupation of Belgium. Unfortunately, however, the United Kingdom's military was in no shape for a major ground war. "No one can say my colleagues in the Cabinet are not courageous," said Lord Kitchener later. "They have no Army and they declared war against the mightiest military nation in the world." It was with some misgivings, then, that Kitchener accepted the appointment as secretary of state for war.[3]

In August 1914, the British had an able, professional fighting force of just eighty thousand regulars—small enough, the late German chancellor Otto von Bismarck had once joked, to be arrested by the German police. With reserves, the army numbered a few hundred thousand, many of whom were stationed overseas, mainly in India. Germany, meanwhile, had been on a war footing for years. Its Imperial Army of nearly 4.5 million (including reserves) was undefeated, with numerous impressive victories over the last several decades. Having just overrun Belgium, it was on its way into France and seemed unstoppable.[4]

Foreseeing a much longer war than his colleagues did, one with heavy losses, Kitchener took the highly realistic view that Britain needed to do something it had never done before: raise a huge army of a million men at least. With conscription ruled out by tradition and policy, however, Kitchener had the idea to make a direct and personal appeal to the British public. And thus began the first state-run attention harvest, or what historians would later call the "first systematic propaganda campaign directed at the civilian population."[5]

———————

In our times, the idea of a government-run mass recruiting campaign does not sound especially controversial. But in 1914 it was unprecedented, not just in Britain, but anywhere. "That the State should advertise itself was an idea which occurred to few before the war," concluded an official British history, "and which, had it been brought before the notice of the general public, would have seemed to them repellent."[6]

Remember that, for much of human history, rulers did not feel any particular need for public attention, and, indeed, usually tried to avoid it. Apart from rituals such as triumphal entry into the lands of a new subject people, dating back to the Romans, and the Royal Progress, the jaunt first undertaken in medieval times to "show the sacred body of the prince," kings and queens once depended on the mystique of inaccessibility as an expression of power.

Before the democratic age, only the Church, as discussed, systematically sought and used access to the mind of the people. In fact, the very word "propaganda" originally had a strictly ecclesiastical meaning of propagating the faith. As Mark Crispin Miller writes, "It was not until 1915 that governments first systematically deployed the entire range of modern media to rouse their population to fanatical assent." The entry of the State into the game—with its vast resources and monopoly on force—would be spectacularly consequential.[7]

Kitchener was aware of his own celebrity as a living icon of British imperial power. Within a week of his new appointment, every newspaper carried an appeal from him that also appeared on posters across the nation:

Your King and Country Need You
A CALL TO ARMS

An addition of 100,000 men to His Majesty's Regular Army
is immediately necessary
in the present grave National Emergency.
Lord Kitchener is confident
that this appeal will be at once responded to
by all those who have the safety of our Empire at heart.

Whether the trick was provoking a sense of duty or subtle fears of German invasion or simply presenting the image of the great man himself, the initial August appeal was extraordinarily successful. Within a month, an astonishing 30,000 men a day were signing up at recruitment offices. By October, over 750,000 had joined the British Army, creating, in two months, an infantry larger than America's current active force. Lord Kitchener now had his army.

But just as soon as they'd raised an army, Kitchener and the Recruiting Committee realized that they still had a problem. Facing an enemy of over six million and the prospect of heavy losses, Britain would need a steady stream of new recruits as hostilities progressed.[8] Yet the drive, which had been so successful initially, seemed to be losing steam. Those intimate personal appeals of Lord Kitchener's, which had proved so compelling at first, were now apparently being ignored. Something more was needed to keep recruitment in the minds of the public.

The answer was a transition from Kitchener's occasional appeals to a more systematic, and totalizing approach to government propaganda. A special Parliamentary Recruiting Committee was created in the fall of 1914 to run a "permanent 'information' campaign"—an institutionalized effort to develop ways of keeping the recruitment emergency foremost in the minds of Britons. The campaign's most useful tool turned out to be a French invention we have seen before, the giant illustrated advertisement. Beginning in the final months of 1914, the country was blanketed in government war posters, and by 1916, the recruitment authority would calculate that it had printed nearly 12.5 million of them. By the war's end, it would print some 54 million. The London *Times* reported on January 3, 1915, that these posters were to be seen "on every hoarding, in most windows, in omnibuses, tramcars and commercial vans. The great base of Nelson's Column is covered with them. Their number and variety are remarkable. Everywhere Lord Kitchener sternly points a monstrously big finger, exclaiming 'I Want You.'"[9]

The finger reference is to the most famous of the ubiquitous posters, in which the field marshal points directly at the viewer, with the caption "Your country needs YOU." In the words of one recruit, who doubtless spoke for many, "It was seeing the picture of Kitchener and his finger pointing at you—any position that you took up, the finger was always pointing to you." Like all effective posters, this one proved nearly impossible to ignore.[10]

Also in the fall, the authorities began to conduct what they called "aggressive open-air propaganda" in the form of massive parades and rallies. One staged in the fall of 1914 in Brighton was perhaps typical. There, the military paraded through the seaside town, with horses dragging giant artillery guns through the streets, and the band whipping up the crowd with martial tunes. The ensuing rally culminated in a stirring speech by Rudyard Kipling, who, deploying rhetoric for its original ancient purpose, played upon deep-seated fears of German domination:[11]

Have no illusions. We are dealing with a strong and magnificently equipped enemy, whose avowed aim is our complete destruction. The violation of Belgium, the attack on France and the defense against Russia, are only steps by the way. The German's real objective, as she always has told us, is England, and England's wealth, trade and worldwide possessions.

If you assume, for an instant, that the attack will be successful, England will not be reduced, as some people say, to the rank of a second-rate power, but we shall cease to exist as a nation. We shall become an outlying province of Germany, to be administered with that severity German safety and interest require.

If we are to win the right for ourselves and for freedom to exist on earth, every man must offer himself for that service and that sacrifice.[12]

George Coppard, whose wartime diaries would later be published, described how he signed up at age sixteen following much the same sort of rally at Croydon. "This was too much for me to resist, and as if drawn by a magnet, I knew I had to enlist right away."[13]

Seeing the necessity to keep innovating, the government did have a few more inspired ideas. For example, it built a small fleet of specialized "cine-motor vans," which were equipped to screen films conducive to enlistment on large walls around the country—the drive-in movie was thus born not of romance but existential threat. In 1918, on the fourth anniversary of the war, the government would distribute a special, sealed message from the prime minister to be read aloud at 9 p.m. sharp at more than four thousand cinemas, music halls, and theaters. By such means—at a time when "broadcast" still referred to a crop sowing technique—the prime minister reached an estimated 2.5 million people at once, an unheard of audience at the time.[14]

Mainly, though, it was no single invention that marked the government's effort so much as its massive scale and organization.[15] In this, the British anticipated an insight that would be expressed by the French philosopher Jacques Ellul halfway through the twentieth century: to succeed, propaganda must be total. The propagandist must utilize all of the technical means and media available in his time—movies, posters, meetings, door-to-door canvassing in one century, social media in another, as the rise of ISIS attests. Where there is only sporadic or random effort—a planted newspaper article here, a poster or a radio program there, a few slogans sprayed on walls—this modern form of attention capture does not bear its once unimagined fruit.[16]

Even the most successful and adaptive efforts to harvest attention can come up short. In fact, by the nature of the crop, most do. Ultimately the military would have to resort to conscription to meet its manpower needs. Still, Kitchener's recruitment drive was almost certainly the most successful in history. Out of 5.5 million men of military age at the start of the war, about half had enlisted voluntarily by late September of 1915, this despite staggeringly high casualties in the early years. To heed the call was to accept a great chance of death or serious injury, a roughly 50/50 chance. That Lord Kitchener's campaign managed to achieve by persuasion what other countries achieved by legal coercion was a lesson lost on no one. Just as the patent medicine advertisements had demonstrated that attention could be converted into cash, the first propaganda drives showed it was also convertible into other forms of value, like compliant service even unto death. The British example would come to be copied by others for the rest of the century: by governments in the Soviet Union, communist China, and Nazi Germany; and elsewhere, as we'll see, by commercial actors. As the historians M. L. Sanders and Philip Taylor wrote, "The British Government was responsible for opening a Pandoran box which unleashed the weapon of propaganda upon the modern world."[17]

As for Lord Kitchener, who started things, he would never make it back to his beloved Egypt or even see the end of the war. In June 1916, en route to a diplomatic summit in Russia, his armored cruiser hit a series of mines laid by a German submarine possibly tipped off by a spy in the war secretary's office. Kitchener perished with his staff and more than six hundred crewmen. Sir Arthur Conan Doyle, by then also part of the British propaganda effort, wrote in memoriam: "Amid the desolate waters of the Orkneys, he left behind him the memory of something vast and elemental, coming suddenly and going strangely, a mighty spirit leaving great traces of its earthly passage."[18]

———————

The very first country to try out the British propaganda techniques was not one synonymous with mind control, but rather the Land of the Free, which, in 1917, would abandon its neutrality to enter the war. Long before Americans began borrowing British television shows, they were borrowing propaganda techniques. However, like nearly every American imitation of a British original, the American version would be much bigger.

George Creel was a newspaperman and a devout Wilson supporter who had played a key role in the messaging of Woodrow Wilson's 1916 reelection campaign. He was a partisan who was never anything but passionate and energetic; one journalist wrote of him, "What Sunday is to religion, Creel is to politics. Creel is a crusader, a bearer of the fiery cross." In 1917, as Wilson prepared to declare war on the German Empire (breaking his campaign promise), Creel proposed to Wilson that the administration should adopt a "progressive" alternative to wartime press censorship. He argued that the United States could use modern scientific advertising techniques to "arouse ardor and enthusiasm" for the war.

Wilson, who felt indebted to Creel anyway, was so taken with Creel's idea that, about a week after asking Congress to declare war, he placed Creel in charge of a new "Committee on Public Information," the first institutionalized federal propaganda agency in American history. Animated by his new role, Creel, the true believer, would never seem to be afflicted by any qualms about the use of propaganda. He cheerfully called the job "a plain publicity proposition, a vast enterprise in salesmanship, the world's greatest adventure in advertising."[19] To run America's first propaganda campaign, Wilson, by executive order, granted him a broad and unspecified authority. In his sunny way, Creel would take that authority and run with it, going to extremes that must be described as alarming.

In 1917, the United States remained intensely divided over the merits of entering a war that had already claimed millions of lives and enormous resources, with no end in sight. To many it also seemed, essentially, a contest between European powers for European territory. And so many Americans, especially those of German or Irish descent, saw no particular reason for their country to take the side of the British. Wilson and Creel were both all too familiar with these objections. Indeed, Wilson had just won reelection on a neutrality platform, which Creel had explained and justified in a bestseller published during the campaign entitled *Wilson and the Issues*.[20] There was no stronger case for staying out than the one these two men had made.

Nonetheless, when Wilson changed his view, George Creel underwent the kind of abrupt reversal that only certain men infinitely glad to be of use could manage. There was no longer room for divided opinion, he declared, for America was now endangering itself with "voices of anger and confusion" and "the pull and haul of opposed interests." For Creel, it would not be enough to achieve a "mere surface unity." Rather the entire citizenry now needed to share "a passionate belief in the justice of America's cause."

A "war-will"—a concept borrowed from nationalist writers, denoting a surrender of the individual to the greater will of the nation—was the new necessity. Creel wrote that this "*war-will,* the will-to-win, of a democracy depends on the degree to which each one of all the people of that democracy can concentrate and consecrate body and soul and spirit in the supreme effort of service and sacrifice." If the language sounds familiar, it should. Benito Mussolini would later describe his own project as the creation of "an objective Will transcending the individual and raising him to conscious membership of a spiritual society."[21] Leni Riefenstahl's Nazi propaganda film *Triumph of the Will (Triumph des Willens)* would likewise glorify a collective will in spiritual terms. But for the time being, Creel was alone in hailing the fascist virtue of "weld[ing] the people of the United States into one white-hot mass instinct with fraternity, devotion, courage, and deathless determination."

To be fair, Creel's nationalism and his conception of a "war-will" was a far cry from the more malevolent strain that would arise later. "In no degree was the Committee an agency of censorship, a machinery of concealment or repression," he insisted. "Its emphasis throughout was on the open and the positive." But if he was a second-rate fascist, as a propagandist he was of the first rank. For, as he averred, what he practiced was "Propaganda in the true sense of the word, meaning the 'propagation of faith.'"[22]

Following the British example, Creel sought a massive and totalizing seizure of the nation's attention. For this, a flood of government communication was necessary, for he understood that "to conduct as well as accommodate this torrent he needed to command every possible sluice, the broader the better."[23] Toward this end there was "no medium of appeal that we did not employ. The printed word, the spoken word, the motion picture, the telegraph, the cable, the wireless, the poster, the signboard—all these were used in our campaign to make our own people and all other peoples understand the causes that compelled America to take arms."

Within a year of its founding, Creel's committee had twenty domestic subdivisions, and reported staff of 150,000; it may have been the fastest-growing government bureaucracy in world history. It did more of everything, faster, channeling the age's spirit of mass production. The committee produced more posters, speeches, pamphlets, press releases than any other entity. "In addition to newspapers and magazines, county fairs, movies, classrooms, post office walls, churches, synagogues, union halls—virtually every physical interface with the public—was a venue for a CPI message." The argument for war was made "overwhelmingly powerful by dint of sheer volume, repetition, and ubiquity." In the burgeoning battle for human attention, Creel's approach was the equivalent of carpet-bombing.

Because Creel's committee kept meticulous records, we have some measure of how many people he reached. The U.S. government printed 75 million pamphlets and books (compare with *USA Today,* which has a subscription of 1.6 million). It introduced the "Four Minute Man" program, in which ordinary citizens were asked to give pro-war speeches, four minutes in length, at movie theaters while the reels were being changed. The more than 75,000 volunteers delivered a total of 755,190 speeches, reaching a very precisely estimated 134,454,514 people.[24]

Under Creel, too, the American government joined forces with the movie business to screen some of the first American propaganda films. A special division of the committee produced features like *Pershing's Crusaders* and *America's Answer to the Hun,* both of which enjoyed solid ticket sales. Early on, Creel had made clear to the private film industry, just then in the midst of relocating to Hollywood, that any productions "prejudicial" to the war effort would be suppressed. After some prodding, the studios began to see both the patriotic and commercial potential of patriotic "hate" films, like *Wolves of Kultur,* which came out in fifteen episodes. But the greatest hit of all was *The Kaiser, the Beast of Berlin.* Sadly, no prints survive, but we do have this news report on the reaction to the film in the Midwest:

Fourteen thousand people the largest number that ever saw a motion picture in Omaha in one week saw *The Kaiser* [*The Beast of Berlin*] at the Auditorium in that city last week. . . . Wild cheering marked every show when the young captain socked the Kaiser on the jaw. Patriotic societies boosted the picture because of its aid in stirring up the country to war. Street car signs were used; huge street banners swung over the crowds in the downtown district, and a truck paraded the streets with the Kaiser hanging in effigy and a big sign "All pro-Germans will be admitted free." None availed himself of the invitation.[25]

Finally, there was the American version of the giant Kitchener poster that had been so important to the British effort. Lacking a living personification of the cause, however, the Pictorial Arts Division substituted the allegorical Uncle Sam pointing his finger and declaring "I want YOU for the U.S. Army," for what would surely be the most indelible instance of the recruitment genre.[26] In another poster reading "Destroy This Mad Brute," Germany appears as a giant crazed gorilla; this King Kong *avant la lettre,* clutches in one arm a beautiful woman naked to the waist—the ravaged Belgium—and in the other hand, a club emblazoned with the word *Kultur.* The appeal is right to the male amygdala, the brain's seat of violent emotions, shown in functional MRI to light up at such primal horrors.

Some 700,000 Americans volunteered for the armed forces, even though, unlike the British, the American army, from nearly the beginning, relied on conscription. Not all of Creel's success, however, is owing to its superb attention capture and effective messaging. Acting under the authority of the new Espionage and Sedition Acts, federal prosecutors removed, silenced, or scared off the committee's natural competitors, namely, antiwar dissenters. In the summer of 1918, Eugene Debs, founder of the Socialist Party, tried to expose what he called a campaign to apply "the brand of treason to the men who dare to even whisper their opposition" to the war. At a speech in Canton, Ohio, he told the crowd, "You are fit for something better than slavery and cannon fodder. You need to know that you were not created to work and produce and impoverish yourself to enrich an idle exploiter. You need to know that you have a mind to improve, a soul to develop, and a manhood to sustain." Afterward, the U.S. attorney for Northern Ohio charged him with ten counts of violating the Espionage Act, for which Debs was sentenced to ten years in prison. In an opinion written by Justice Oliver Wendell Holmes, the great progressive hero, the U.S. Supreme Court upheld Debs's conviction without dissent.[27]

The outlandish success of the British and American propaganda campaigns left their mark on the rest of the century, setting a new standard for what was possible in manipulating the public to adopt a strong viewpoint about a matter where opinion had been divided before. The effect on those who lived through it seemed to depend very much on something deep within one's character. Some who found the experience alarming determined never to let such a thing happen again. Others found the wild success of British and American propagandizing nothing less than inspiring.

Walter Lippmann, a progressive journalist, co-founder of *The New Republic,* and a power within the Wilson administration, had been among those who pressured Wilson to take the nation to war. During the war he worked at the Creel Committee, and witnessed firsthand its power to whip the country into a fanatical assent. Despite his own initial support for the war, the ease with which the Creel Committee had succeeded turned him into something of a lifelong cynic.

What Lippmann took from the war—as he explained in his 1922 classic *Public Opinion*—was the gap between the true complexity of the world and the narratives the public uses to understand it—the rough "stereotypes" (a word he coined in his book). When it came to the war, he believed that the "consent" of the governed had been, in his phrase, "manufactured." Hence, as he wrote, "It is no longer possible . . . to believe in the original dogma of democracy; that the knowledge needed for the management of human affairs comes up spontaneously from the human heart. Where we act on that theory we expose ourselves to self-deception, and to forms of persuasion that we cannot verify."[28]

Any communication, Lippmann came to see, is potentially propagandistic, in the sense of propagating a view. For it presents one set of facts, or one perspective, fostering or weakening some "stereotype" held by the mind. It is fair to say, then, that any and all information that one consumes—pays attention to—will have some influence, even if just forcing a reaction. That idea, in turn, has a very radical implication, for it suggests that sometimes we overestimate our own capacity for truly independent thought. In most areas of life, we necessarily rely on others for the presentation of facts and ultimately choose between manufactured alternatives, whether it is our evaluation of a product or a political proposition. And if that is true, in the battle for our attention, there is a particular importance in who gets there first or most often. The only communications truly without influence are those that one learns to ignore or never hears at all; this is why Jacques Ellul argued that it is only the disconnected—rural dwellers or the urban poor—who are truly immune to propaganda, while intellectuals, who read everything, insist on having opinions, and think themselves immune to propaganda are, in fact, easy to manipulate.

All this, in Lippmann's view, helped explain why the British and American governments were able, with such surprising speed, to create a "war-will." They presented a simple, black-and-white stereotype by which to understand the war, used every resource of the state to thoroughly propagate that view, and then prevented any dissenting analysis from reaching anyone with a sympathetic stereotype as to what the war was about. That "public opinion" had been so easy to manufacture left Lippmann an abiding pessimist about democracy's dependence on it.

Lippmann's orientation was shared by prominent progressives in the American judiciary, who, witnessing the rough treatment of dissenters like Debs, began to think twice about what had been done in the name of progressivism. Among the first to express himself was the famed lower-court jurist Judge Learned Hand, who'd been among the few during the war to squash an indictment under the Espionage Act.[29] After the War, as prosecutors continued to arrest and jail socialists and anarchists for their views, the most prominent progressives on the Supreme Court, Justices Holmes and Louis Brandeis, underwent a transformation. In a series of dissents and concurrences, renowned for their eloquence, the two outlined the case for stronger speech protections in the Constitution. Justice Brandeis, as if in apology for the Court's behavior during the war, would in 1927 write a memorable paean to the value of liberty of speech in his famous concurring opinion in *Whitney v. California:*

Those who won our independence believed that the final end of the State was to make men free to develop their faculties, and that, in its government, the deliberative forces should prevail over the arbitrary. They valued liberty both as an end, and as a means. They believed liberty to be the secret of happiness, and courage to be the secret of liberty. They believed that freedom to think as you will and to speak as you think are means indispensable to the discovery and spread of political truth; that, without free speech and assembly, discussion would be futile; that, with them, discussion affords ordinarily adequate protection against the dissemination of noxious doctrine; that the greatest menace to freedom is an inert people; that public discussion is a political duty, and that this should be a fundamental principle of the American government.[30]

Yet others had nearly the opposite reaction, responding to propaganda's dramatic success not with dismay but enthusiasm, in the sense of glimpsing a grand opportunity. Among them was the young, Vienna-born Edward Bernays, the nephew of Sigmund Freud. Residing in the United States, and just twenty-four at the start of the war, he was making his living as a journalist turned press agent. To create publicity for his clients, Bernays was already employing his uncle's idea of a human nature driven by unconscious desires. (According to legend, Sigmund Freud gave him his *General Lectures* in exchange for a box of cigars.) During the war Bernays worked, like many journalists, on the Creel Committee, and like Lippmann, he emerged with a sense of the futility of democracy. But unlike Lippmann, Bernays drew from the experience a belief in the necessity of enlightened manipulation. Otherwise, he wrote, the public "could very easily vote for the wrong man or want the wrong thing, so that they had to be guided from above." As he saw it, "the conscious and intelligent manipulation of the organized habits and opinions of the masses is an important element in democratic society."

But Bernays's real passion was for manipulation on behalf of business interests. As he later recalled, "I decided that if you could use propaganda for war, you could certainly use it for peace." He would devote the rest of his influential career as the self-described "father of public relations" to the use of propaganda techniques on behalf of commercial clients. In his words, the wartime triumph had "opened the eyes of the intelligent few in all departments of life to the possibilities of regimenting the public mind."[31] And that "business offers graphic examples of the effect that may be produced upon the public by interested groups."

With the government campaigns as proof-of-concept for what a mass advertising campaign might achieve, corporate America soon caught Bernays's enthusiasm. There was something about the British and American use of advertising for official purposes that cleansed the practice of its tainted reputation. Applied to a high common purpose it could no longer be deemed a mere prop of charlatanry. "Advertising has earned its credentials," concluded *Printer's Ink,* the advertising trade magazine, "as an important implement of war."[32]

The losers of the war were also important witnesses to British and American propaganda efforts, from which they too sought to learn. Erich Ludendorff, a lead German general during the attack on Belgium, reflected that "before the enemy propaganda we were like a rabbit before a snake." Another German war veteran, while in prison, wrote a tract admiring British propaganda as "marvelous," praising its simple presentation of "negative and positive notions of love and hatred, right and wrong, truth and falsehood," thereby allowing "no half-measures which might have given rise to some doubt." The fan was Adolf Hitler, and given his chance, he thought he could do even better.

CHAPTER 4

DEMAND ENGINEERING, SCIENTIFIC

ADVERTISING, AND WHAT WOMEN WANT

All around you people are judging you silently.

—J. WALTER THOMPSON ADVERTISEMENT,
WOODBURY'S BEAUTY PRODUCTS, 1922

T he advertising man is the enfant terrible of the time, unabashed
before the eternities," wrote S. N. Behrman in *The New Republic*
in 1919. "He does not conceal his awareness of the fact that he is the cornerstone of the most respectable American institutions; the newspapers
and magazines depend on him; Literature and Journalism are his hand
maidens. Even war needs him, to say nothing of Swift and Company."[1]

What a difference a world war makes.

In the immediate aftermath of the war, from 1918 to 1920, with
advertising redeemed in the public eye and private consumption once
again rising, American and European business began to spend wildly
on advertising, doubling industry revenue in just two years. By 1930,
that spending had increased by a factor of ten; and in the process a truly
international industry was born, as the profits and powers derived from
using access to the public mind became clear, once and for all.[2]

The new confidence of the industry was captured in a 1923 manifesto
entitled *Scientific Advertising*. "The time has come when advertising has
in some hands reached the status of a science," it boasted. "It is based on

fixed principles and is reasonably exact. The causes and effects have been analyzed until they are well understood. We know what is most effective, and we act on basic law." Nothing, in advertising, was now left to chance: "Every course is charted. The compass of accurate knowledge directs the shortest, safest, cheapest course to any destination."[3]

The New Republic had described the typical advertising man as "young, good-looking, sartorially perfect, with sleek hair and parti-colored shoes." The author of the *Scientific Advertising* manifesto, however, was none of these things. He was Claude C. Hopkins, whom we last saw on the shores of Lake Michigan. The onetime preacher and patent medicine scheme-man had been reinvented as a top-drawer adman and the most influential copywriter of his era. Rescued from convalescence by Albert Lasker, the president of Chicago's Lord & Thomas, Hopkins had adopted his winning patent-medicine techniques to sell everyday products like cigarettes, orange juice, and toothpaste, proving the old patter could work astonishingly well for a broader range of merchandise than anyone might have expected. His success helped transform the copywriter from low-level functionary to the mystical master behind the scenes, the creative wizard who could turn unknown new products into national bestsellers. He had, however, not changed his own presentation, still wearing the round spectacles and the boutonniere, nervously chewing on his licorice root and introducing himself, with his slight lisp, as "Thee Thee Hopkins." Not quite what one might imagine for the first avatar of *Mad Men*'s Don Draper, but a force to be reckoned with all the same.[4]

Hopkins, now influential, was fond of speaking for the entire industry. "From our desks we sway millions," he once commented in a speech, explaining what advertising had become.

> We change the currents of trade. We populate new empires, build up new industries and create customs and fashions. We dictate the food that the baby shall eat, the clothes the mother shall wear, the way in which the home shall be furnished. . . . Our very names are unknown. But there is scarcely a home, in city or hamlet, where some human being is not doing what we demand.[5]

Hopkins's gifts notwithstanding, the truly significant actors of the 1920s were not just the admen but the firms themselves, a new generation of large, big-city agencies that grew to maturity as the brokers and engineers of the new attention economy. These new institutions would, in the century to follow, function as private laboratories of attention capture and demand generation, whether it was in Chicago at Lord & Thomas, New York's enormous new firms J. Walter Thompson, BBDO, and McCann Erickson, or London-based firms like WS Crawford, and others in Paris and Tokyo. On behalf of their clients, they bought what attention was for sale—mostly the audiences of print media—and determined how to use it for maximum effect.

Scale and accumulated expertise are what set the new firms apart from their predecessors. Just as the industrial revolution had transformed manufacture, and Ford's assembly lines pursued a never-ending quest for more efficient methods of mass production, so, too, did the new firms transform the casually intuitive and improvisational approach that had once been advertising into a machine for mass attention capture. Their campaigns were unending and exhaustive, like the British and American propaganda campaigns, which to some extent had solved the already recognized problem of disenchantment. As soon as one approach stopped working, a new one would be launched, in the ideal case stabilizing sales indefinitely.

The efforts of this industry, moreover, were helping remake the economies of the world's wealthiest nations. In the United States the average household went from spending a mere $79 per year on durable goods at the turn of the century to $279 by the 1920s ($1,900 and $6,700 in present value). Total consumption expenditures increased by 25 percent from 1923 to 1929. The effect was a transformation into what were later called "consumer societies" as mass production reached nearly every aspect of daily life.[6]

So just what was "scientific advertising," this buzzword of the day? It was, upon inspection, really just a dressed-up term for a few basic approaches.[7] The first was creating the desire for products that otherwise might not exist—then known as "demand engineering." The second was the relatively new discipline of "branding"—creating loyalty for some maker, like Cadillac or Coca-Cola, by creating the impression, valid or not, that something truly set it apart from others like it. The third technique involved the first deployment of "targeted" advertisements—addressed to the yet mysterious but increasingly sought-after new creature known as the female consumer.

None of this was rocket science. Take "demand engineering," which while sounding arcane, in practice relied on just a few simple devices. Among the simplest was the method that had worked for patent medicine. Also known as "reason-why" advertising, this approach presented the product as the miraculous cure to some existing problem.[8]

Consider Claude Hopkins's campaign for a new invention called orange juice, which presented it as an elixir for infants. A doting mother is pictured seated with a rosy-cheeked newborn, a posture for nursing, but this mother is feeding her baby with a spoon. "Orange juice is regularly prescribed for the diet of tiny babies because physicians know its purity and food value." In another advertisement, a "DR. WILEY" says "Oranges . . . Are Better Than Medicine." The consumer is informed that "practically every well-known physician advises orange juice for the diet of little children—even tiny babies." Later, with the discovery of "Vital Amine C" (what we now call vitamin C), orange juice would acquire its magic ingredient, and a daily glass would become necessary for everyone's good health. "You need orange juice every day."[9]

The similarities with patent medicine advertising run deep, for the link between orange juice and the health of infants was based on nothing and ultimately proved to be highly dubious. Today the American Academy of Pediatrics strongly cautions against feeding babies orange juice, because it "could risk having juice replace breast milk or infant formula in the diet," resulting in malnutrition; in addition, "excessive juice consumption may be associated with diarrhea, flatulence, abdominal distention, and tooth decay." These side effects may have been unknown in the 1920s, but so was any proof of a supposed health benefit. While not as dangerous, orange juice was no more an elixir than Liquozone had been.[10]

As consumerism grew, it also became possible to sell products solving problems that were hardly recognized as such, let alone matters of life and death. Demand was engineered by showing not so much that the product would solve the problem but that the problem existed at all. Bringing subconscious anxieties to the fore was the inspired brilliance behind the great campaigns for mouthwash and toothpaste, two products largely unknown before the 1920s.

"Halitosis—Makes you Unpopular" was the headline of Listerine's campaign. Originally a disinfectant, invented for medical usage on the battlefield, the brown liquid had also been marketed as a floor cleaner. But in the 1920s, under new management, the manufacturer presented it as a cure for a devastating problem countless Americans were unwittingly afflicted with. "No matter how charming you may be or how fond of you your friends are, you cannot expect them to put up with halitosis (unpleasant breath) forever. They may be nice to you—but it is an effort."[11]

The ominously clinical-sounding "halitosis" was a largely unheard of word when Listerine introduced it. But they rightly gauged the human psyche and the tenor of the times by stirring fears about a problem everyone encounters in others from time to time without comment. Directing this kind of scrutiny to it can't help but make one wonder about one's own breath (as you yourself may now be doing). The campaign was a masterpiece of demand engineering, and between 1922 and 1929, the Listerine company's annual earnings rose from $115,000 to over $8 million.[12]

"Just run your tongue across your teeth," read another classic newspaper ad, in big print, offering an irresistible challenge. "You'll feel a film— that's what makes your teeth appear 'off color,' and invites decay and gum troubles." Here was Hopkins's most famous campaign, which brilliantly tapped into another subconscious fear, that of decay and aging. For this problem, Pepsodent, a new "film-removing dentifrice," was just what the doctor ordered.[13]

The manipulation of public fears for profit did not go unnoticed. In 1926, the newly founded *Time* magazine declared:

> The omnipotent buying public carries in its mind only a dim conception of the part played in its daily life by this enormous new pseudoscience, advertising. How did that tube of Pepsodent toothpaste, for instance, reach your bathroom shelf? . . . It got there, obviously, because somehow Lord & Thomas had at least made you suspect that of all toothpastes Pepsodent is the one most imperative to your health and happiness. You may not remember but somewhere you read that you had a film on your teeth and that gritty Pepsodent was the thing which would polish that film away.[14]

Nevertheless, the public was generally satisfied with what it was being sold. And Hopkins was more than satisfied. As part owner of the toothpaste company he made a killing, though perhaps the former preacher couldn't enjoy that kind of success. He wrote that he considered his Pepsodent campaign a form of public service. "So the commercial aspect has been largely hidden in the altruistic. . . . The advertisements breathe unselfishness and service." And while he allowed, "I made for myself a million dollars on Pepsodent," he would complain about the difficulty of finding ways to spend the money.[15]

It is right to pause here to acknowledge that the psychological premises of these and other advertisements may owe something to Sigmund Freud, who was coincidentally at the height of his productivity and whose books, especially *The Interpretation of Dreams* and *The Psychopathology of Everyday Life*, were widely available in translation. Indeed, it is often argued that Freud's elucidation of the unconscious must have driven the new techniques of advertising over the 1910s and 1920s. This is a central contention, for instance, of the 2002 documentary series *The Century of the Self*, which gives great credit to Freud's nephew Edward Bernays of the Creel Committee for introducing appeals to the unconscious mind to product marketing.

The simple narrative of Freud's nephew transforming American advertising is an appealing stereotype, in Lippmann's sense of the term; but, alas, the historical record does not bear it out. Of course, one can't deny that Freud's ideas were in the air; and one can hardly prove that advertisers were not unconsciously drawing on them. But the facts suggest that the leading advertising firms of the time, to the extent they tipped their hand, put their faith in Freud's American competition, the behavioral school of psychology. Its main objective would surely have sounded like the name of the game to men like Hopkins: "the prediction and control of behavior."[16]

"Whenever one of us goes to the theatre or picks a necktie, we are responding to definite laws," wrote Stanley B. Resor, president of New York's J. Walter Thompson and perhaps the most influential proponent of behavioral science. "For every type of decision—for every sale in retail stores—basic laws govern the actions of people in great masses." Resor was serious enough about the discipline to hire John B. Watson, the famous author of the 1913 *Behaviorist Manifesto*. Watson was more ethologist than psychologist, more concerned with hardwired human traits and conditioned responses than the Freudians, who were more interested in the individual psyche and its personal experience. For Watson, unlike Freud, mental states and moods were irrelevant. "The time seems to have come," he said, "when psychology must discard all reference to consciousness." Instead, he pursued a unitary theory of animal response, for the behaviorist "recognizes no dividing line between man and brute."[17]

Watson believed that humans, like other animals, could be conditioned to respond in predictable ways, and his most famous experiments were conducted on human infants. In the one on "Little Albert," a human version of Pavlov's experiments on dogs, Watson induced a phobia of rats in an eleven-month-old. He did so by striking a metal bar with a hammer behind the baby's head every time a white rat was shown to him. After seven weeks of conditioning, the child, initially friendly to the rodent, began to fear it, bursting into tears at the sight of it. The child, in fact, began to fear anything white and furry—Watson bragged that "now he fears even Santa Claus."*[18]

At J. Walter Thompson, Watson was, in some sense, given a chance to perform his experiments on a larger population. As he maintained, "To make your consumer react, it is only necessary to confront him with either fundamental or conditioned emotional stimuli." Soon Resor made Watson an "ambassador-at-large" and an account executive. When not advising on campaigns, he traveled America and the globe to sell executives on scientific advertising, and on his firm, which possessed all the tools necessary to control the minds of the public. As he said it plainly in one speech: "Since the time the serpent in the Garden of Eden influenced Eve and Eve in turn persuaded Adam, the world has tried to find out ways and means of controlling human behavior. In advertising, we call the process selling."[19]

We have said that creating demand for new products was the first great goal of the early advertising industry. Otherwise, as Resor once

---

* The baby's mother, employed as a wet nurse at the hospital where the experiment was conducted, was paid $1 for her troubles.

explained, "the achievements of American mass production would fall of their own weight." The second great objective realized in the 1920s was the engineering of reputation, also known as branding.

Brands hardly existed before mass production; in a prior age, it was the reputation of the individual merchant that did the work, much as it still does today for doctors, accountants, and other professionals. But by the 1920s, advertisers came to understand that a reputation, once necessarily earned, could now be manufactured like a war-will or any consumer good. And so over the early part of the century, American and European firms invested millions to create associations with names that previously had no broad connotations, names like "Cadillac," "Kraft," "Lucky Strike," "Heinz," "Coca-Cola," and so on. The fact that all of these remain familiar and enjoy enviable sales nearly a hundred years on shows how that initial investment, if properly husbanded, can pay dividends indefinitely.

Theodore MacManus was the dean of this soft-sell approach, credited with building brands like Cadillac, Dodge, Chrysler, and General Electric. Born in Buffalo, New York, and raised as a devout Catholic, MacManus mostly frowned on the harder-edged reason-why approaches favored by his Protestant rivals. As for Claude Hopkins, his main intellectual rival, MacManus viewed him as an unscrupulous con artist who seemed to believe that "all men are fools." Hopkins's way, thought MacManus, was not only contemptuous but bad for the client, for it "yielded glittering advertising successes which shortly become business failures."

MacManus's alternative was an advertising of iconography. He built up his brands to be trusted, even revered. He sought not so much to persuade customers but to convert them; to create a lasting loyalty. In his hands, the Cadillac meant something, and its drivers were meant to identify with their vehicles. He famously wrote an advertisement telling Cadillac's drivers that, as the greatest car in the world, Cadillac necessarily bore the "penalty of leadership." For to become a "standard for the whole world" was also to be "a target for the shafts of the envious few." Still, quality will out: "That which is good or great makes itself known, no matter how loud the clamor of denial. That which deserves to live— lives." For the Dodge brand, MacManus invented a new word: "dependability." He claimed to believe that "while men may be fools and sinners, they are everlastingly on the search for that which is good."[20]

MacManus's "suggestive" style was an advertising that "implants thoughts not by force but by infiltration." He aimed to create the impression that "the man manufacturing the product is an honest man, and that the product is an honest product, to be preferred above all others." The projection of a "substantial and more or less virtuous character" did depend on some blandishments, such as beautiful illustrations; but otherwise he saw himself as simply delivering the unvarnished Truth. To that, the honorable advertising executive could add the newly discovered powers of propaganda, an accelerant to the natural process by which that Truth is duly recognized.

Whether MacManus truly believed in the inherent goodness of all that he sold is impossible to know, but his writings in the voice of Cadillac or Dodge Motors, for example, have the undeniable ring of authenticity. And of course, MacManus was a company man, not an agency man; he was not required to sing the praises of whoever walked through the door. As a loyal employee of the General Motors company during its rise to greatness, he was after all promoting what were, in the 1920s, among the best cars on earth. His position, then, came with a license to indulge in poetic praise that the seller of toothpaste might not enjoy.

Perhaps we'll never know his mind. He did promise his clients, with no apparent Faustian anxiety, that "we have found a hothouse in which a good reputation can be generated, as it were, over night. In other words, the thing for which men in the past have been willing to slave and toil for a lifetime, they can now set out to achieve with semi-scientific accuracy and assurance of success, in periods of months instead of years." Perhaps the most impressive proof of his theory is that, to this day, "Cadillac" is a general superlative (as in Cadillac health plan), even to those who don't esteem it as the finest car money can buy.[21]

––––––––––

During this period it also struck businessmen, as if all at once, that if America was becoming a consumer society, most of this new purchasing of household goods was being done by the lady of the house. "In the purchase of things for personal use," declared one authority in 1921, "men do very little on their own initiative." Companies, run mostly by men, therefore, came to see cracking the code of the female consumer as the key to commerce. As an advertisement in *Printer's Ink* put it, "The proper study of mankind is man . . . but the proper study of markets is women." To men of industry, however, the promised land was mostly a terra incognita.[22] Hence, advertising's third major development was a great new effort to appeal to women—through what would later be called "targeted" advertisements.

A famous early advertisement for Woodbury soap, crafted by a woman named Helen Lansdowne, typified the new approach. When she was given the account, the product had long been sold by patent medicine principles. Its advertisements had a branding visage, consisting of the mustachioed Dr. John Woodbury, the dermatologist who invented it in 1877. The face, which was also stamped into each bar, was accompanied by the slogan "a pure antiseptic toilet soap—for the skin, scalp, and complexion." Some versions tried for the softer touch with the tag line "Women should be beautiful." But the grim Dr. Woodbury still loomed large, producing a rather creepy dissonance.[23]

The ineffectiveness of the old Woodbury's advertisements reflected a clueless dependence on a series of broad stereotypes for advertising to women. "Women as a whole are more suggestible than men," declared the contemporary textbook *Advertising, Its Principles and Practice.* "They are more easily influenced by their emotions." Robert E. Ramsay, the author of *Effective Direct Advertising,* wrote that "women are more responsive to appeals made by illustration and by use of color than men are." Whatever the validity of such claims, they didn't exactly have women figured out.[24]

Lansdowne went in an entirely different direction. In her advertisement, a dashing clean-shaven man in white tie is pictured with his arm wrapped around a beautiful woman, whose hand he holds. His cheek rests against her temple; he appears enthralled, while she stares pointedly at the viewer, her skin aglow.

"A Skin you love to touch," reads the copy. "You, too, can have the charm of a radiant, velvety skin."

A good deal of Woodbury's soap was sold on the strength of this concept, which, however simple, captured something that had eluded the imaginations of copywriters like Hopkins and MacManus. No, it isn't sex. The "Skin" advertisements are sometimes described as the first to make use of it, but the French posters of the late nineteenth century alone prove that simply isn't true. What is really most notable about this marriage of word and image is that, unlike the traditional ads, which offer a cure for a problem—new snake oil in old bottles—Lansdowne's advertisement holds out the promise of a better life. It sells the reader on herself, a new self, better than the old. Here was an innovatively oblique way of pushing the product by connecting it to the consumer's deepest yearning to be beautiful and desired. Lansdowne's promise may not have exhausted the full range of female aspirations, but the ones she chose to fulfill have hardly been improved upon, at least for selling facial soap. Still, other such promises of fantasies fulfilled began to be made by Woodbury and other purveyors of various crèmes and unguents, for instance, that using them would vault one into the glamorous purlieus of high society.

On the strength of her Woodbury's advertisements and other achievements, Landsowne, after the war, was asked to run a new Women's Editorial Department at J. Walter Thompson in New York, the largest firm in the United States and the most obsessed with scientific advertising. (Its president, Stanley Resor, also asked for Helen's hand in marriage.) This amounted to a "scientific" or at least institutionalized effort to develop the art and science of targeting women by designating an entire department to understand their wants and needs.

The new department was staffed entirely by women—"Lady Persuaders"—who were physically segregated from the rest of editorial, with their own office space, accounts, and even distinct style manual; they were asked to wear hats to distinguish themselves from female secretaries. Helen Lansdowne identified as a suffragette and hired for her staff many leaders of the women's suffrage movement, like Frances Maule, a prominent New York activist. Maule, who became the department's most frequent public speaker, declared, on behalf of the department, that it was time to jettison the "good old conventional 'angel-idiot' conception of women" and remember "the old suffrage slogan—that 'Women Are People.'"[25]

As people, however, they were subject to some of the same sorts of manipulation that worked on the general population. One type of targeted advertisement, like the Woodbury soap advertisements and countless others, in which the right soap or treatment or crème would, the advertisements seemed to suggest, land one at fancy dinner parties, surrounded by admiring men, or otherwise make one the belle of an actual or figurative ball. As the president of the advertising trade association later explained, "When advertising invests a prosaic article like soap with the sentiment of feminine attraction, it adds color and perfume to a menial thing. It also stirs in women the renewed desire to be comely, [and] appeals to a deep-seated hope."

Demand engineering, too, found itself refitted for women consumers, as the "whisper" or "scare" campaigns, which warned of a social disgrace or judgment, from which the product at hand offered deliverance. Consider J. Walter Thompson's 1922 advertisement for P&G's laundry detergent targeting mothers. The copy reads, "If little Molly should be in an accident, what would the neighbors think of those 'clean' underclothes? Molly's underclothes are supposedly clean, but actually they are gray and untidy." Targeting the unwed, Listerine would retrofit its wildly successful "halitosis" campaign. In the "poor Edna" series, it is Edna's stale breath, which of course no friend would tell her about, that has left her lovelorn, or in the enduring expression coined for the campaign, "often a bridesmaid but never a bride."[26]

> Edna's case was really a pathetic one. Like every woman, her primary ambition was to marry. Most of the girls of her set were married—or about to be. Yet not one possessed more grace or charm or loveliness than she. And as her birthdays crept gradually toward that tragic thirty-mark, marriage seemed farther from her life than ever. . . . That's the insidious thing about halitosis (unpleasant breath). You yourself, rarely know when you have it. And even your closest friends won't tell you.

And sometimes the power of the suffragette movement itself was harnessed to sell to women. Imagine a floor cleaner with a feminist agenda; that is precisely what Old Dutch Cleanser claimed to be: a "Champion of Women's Rights," among which it included "freedom from household drudgery" and "the right to a clean home and the leisure to enjoy it." By similar logic, an advertisement for Shredded Wheat argued that the cereal was a "Declaration of Independence" from cooking. Here, then, in the Women's Editorial Department, we witness the birth of a nexus between products and the individual, one that serves advertisers to this day. Going far beyond the question of usefulness or even quality as a matter of brand development, advertisers began to imbue products with traits and associations that consumers could identify with.

The Women's Editorial Department at J. Walter Thompson was also responsible for pioneering a final technique that made its way into all advertising by the end of the 1920s. Both Helen Lansdowne and Stanley Resor believed that women were in particular likely to notice and imitate the behavior of the rich, high-born, and famous. And so, over the 1920s, they took a rarely used practice—the paid endorsement—and turned it into a mainstay for women's products, from which it later spread to all products. Resor explained the strategy this way at an executive meeting. "The desire to emulate is stronger in women than in men," he said. "Lombroso, the celebrated psychologist, explains it in terms of woman's ability to excite her imagination with external objects. It enables her to become princess or movie queen by using the cold cream or toilet soap they recommended."[27]

Of course the power of celebrities and stars to capture attention was hardly new, much less an invention of advertising. By the 1910s, upstart film studios like Famous Players (later to become Paramount) and United Artists had built themselves on the unusual power of big stars like Charlie Chaplin or Mary Pickford to attract large audiences. Lord Kitchener, as we have seen, leveraged his personal fame to coax a great many young British males to an early death. And when Henry Luce founded *Time* magazine in 1923, he drove circulation with endless stories and pictures of famous and powerful men, like President Calvin Coolidge and Benito Mussolini, a Luce favorite, who was featured eight times before the war. ("Remarkable self-control, rare judgement," wrote *Time* of Il Duce in the 1920s, "and an efficient application of his ideas to the solving of existing problems.")[28]

Advertisers themselves had, in limited ways, been using celebrity endorsements—as early as the nineteenth century, Pears' soap billed itself as the choice of the royal family. But the testimonials for patent medicines from renowned "doctors" as well as grateful patients had queered the practice of testimonials for the most part. And so it took a bit of daring for J. Walter Thompson Company, at Lansdowne's direction, to resurrect it for Pond's cold cream, originally marketed not as a beauty product but as a spot remover.

Alva Belmont, famous for marrying and divorcing one of the Vanderbilts, was the first to endorse Pond's, in exchange for a $1,000 donation to the National Woman's Party; her 1924 testimonial is an odd mixture of advocacy and cold cream. "Mrs. Belmont not only has given lavishly to women's causes from her colossal fortune, has been and is a tremendous worker, but also is particularly interested in woman's special problem of how to keep her force and her charm through middle life and later." Pond's cold cream turned out to be the answer to both problems.[29]

Later ads relied on Alice Roosevelt Longworth (eldest daughter of Theodore Roosevelt), Gloria Morgan Vanderbilt (who had married another Vanderbilt), and later European royals and aristocrats, like the Queen of Romania, Lady Diana Manners (reputedly the most beautiful young woman in England), and most popular of all, Princess Marie de Bourbon of Spain, who was quoted as saying, "Happily . . . no woman's skin need fade if she faithfully uses Ponds' Wonderful Two Creams."[30]

Through its variously "scientific" techniques like demand engineering, branding, or targeting, the advertising industry had become an increasingly efficient engine for converting attention into revenue. It did so by beginning its now familiar practice of giving consumers, particularly women, a constantly receding ideal to strive after. Perhaps social practice had always done so, but now new strategies of attention capture were doing so in the service of commerce, an infinitely more insatiable and unyielding force than social convention.

Ultimately despite the role that many of the "Lady Persuaders" also played in the women's rights movement, their work at J. Walter Thompson tended mainly to reinforce the condescending biases and stereotypes they had once been at pains as activists to undo. Frances Maule, once in advertising, opined that whether they knew it or not, women usually suffered from a sense of "unimportance, insignificance, [and] inadequacy." Successful advertisements for soap or cold cream worked by promising a remedy for such emotions, so that by buying the product a woman might achieve that " 'grand and glorious feeling' which we are seeking all the time." The president of the advertising trade association described the effect more cynically: "It is an illusion, of course . . . still it is a means to that end and its proper use [is] a very desirable practice."[31]

CHAPTER 5

A LONG LUCKY RUN

George Washington Hill owned two dachshunds: one was named Lucky; the other was named Strike. He was born in 1884, the son of Percival Hill, president of the American Tobacco Company. The father gave the son the Lucky Strike brand to manage as his own, and Hill took to it the way some take to a sports team. He smoked Luckies incessantly, and his Rolls-Royce had packs of them taped to the rear windows. "I would not call him a rounded man," said Albert Lasker. "The only purpose in life to him was to wake up, to eat, and to sleep so that he'd have strength to sell more Lucky Strikes."[1]

In 1925, the elder Hill died, leaving the American Tobacco Company entirely in the hands of George Washington, who was determined to make Lucky Strike, his pet brand, America's leading cigarette, and to spend as much as necessary to do it. Whatever the merits of the product, his money was good, and he believed in the power of advertising. By 1931 he would be spending nearly $20 million per year on it, up from $400,000 in 1925; it was at the time an unprecedented outlay, and possibly the most spent on advertising a single product up until that time.[2]

Both in its rich success and a number of its excesses, the Lucky Strike campaign of the late 1920s would mark a kind of culmination of advertising's might and arrogance at decade's end. Hill's man for the job was

Lasker of Lord & Thomas, the firm that had rescued Claude Hopkins from patent medicine's collapse and then largely absorbed his methods of the hard sell. (An aged Hopkins was by this point retired, living in a forest mansion and writing his memoirs.) To round out the team, Hill also hired Edward Bernays, who had just released his most acclaimed work, *Propaganda,* espousing his ideas of how the techniques government had developed during the war could now be applied to the purposes of business. The two got down to work, though not always together.

What might make Lucky Strike stand out? In 1917, the brand had gotten its start with an idea conceived by Hopkins.[3] "It's toasted" was the slogan, the "secret" step supposedly yielding a better flavor. In the mid-1920s, Lasker built on the concept with a campaign borrowing from patent medicine's playbook: the brand was presented as a health tonic—specifically, a cure for the problem of sore throats caused by most cigarettes. With a new claim that toasting "removes harmful irritants that cause throat irritation," including "harmful corrosive acids," the Lucky Strike slogan became: "Your throat protection—against irritation—against cough." There was even a secret process involved: "the 'TOASTING' process includes the use of the Ultra Violet Ray . . . heat purifies and so 'TOASTING'—that *extra, secret process*—removes harmful irritants that cause throat irritation and coughing."[4] To drive home the hygienic benefit, Lasker ran a "precious voice" campaign, with testimonials from opera stars and other singers. What could be more persuasive than the Metropolitan Opera's lead soprano attesting that she smoked Luckies to protect her livelihood?[5]

The testimonials were, of course, paid for, but it is still startling that Lasker was able to coax the singers into the effort. Even by the late 1920s, there were inklings that cigarettes might be bad for you. So, to preempt the truth, Lasker deployed another old patent medicine trick: he tried to co-opt medical authority. The American Tobacco Company sent doctors free cartons of Luckies in exchange for a vague nod that they might be less abrasive than other brands.[6] Whether or not the doctors knew what they were agreeing to, Lord & Thomas went ahead with ads that portrayed them as, in effect, touting the health benefits of smoking Lucky Strikes. One advertisement features a doctor in a white coat holding up a packet, with the copy: "20,679 physicians say 'LUCKIES are less irritating' . . . Your throat protection."[7]

To sell the smoking of cigarettes as a healthful habit had a certain genius to it and might have had a long fruitful run, but at some point George Washington Hill, like so many others, got converted to the feminine principle of the 1920s. He decided, abruptly, that the real secret to Lucky Strike's success would be persuading women to smoke them, especially in public. In his diary, Bernays recalled the day that the boss had this epiphany. "Hill called me in. 'How can we get women to smoke on the street? They're smoking indoors. But, damn it, if they spend half the time outdoors and we can get 'em to smoke outdoors, we'll damn near double our female market. Do something. Act!' "[8]

In the late 1920s, it was still taboo for women to smoke in public; in some cities, including, for a brief while, New York, it was even against the law.[9] But to the monomaniacal Hill, the idea was sheer commercial opportunity. "It will be," he told Bernays, "like opening a new gold mine right in our front yard."

Good soldiers both, Lasker and Bernays soon caught the spirit of women's liberation, or at least noticed its utility. Lasker allowed that, after his wife had been asked to refrain from smoking in a restaurant, he was determined "to break down the prejudice against women smoking." But it was Bernays, the public relations man, who took more seriously the idea of a commercial cause in social-activist clothing. He was in fact a critic of advertising in the Hopkins mold, and believed that ideally one should seek to make it obsolete. "The old-fashioned propagandist," wrote Bernays, "using almost exclusively the appeal of the printed word, tried to persuade the individual reader to buy a definite article, immediately." In contrast, Bernays believed it possible to create demand at an even more fundamental level, by changing customs and norms. He asked:

> What are the true reasons why the purchaser is planning to spend his money on a new car instead of on a new piano? Because he has decided that he wants the commodity called locomotion more than he wants the commodity called music? Not altogether. He buys a car, because it is at the moment the group custom to buy cars. The modern propagandist therefore sets to work to create circumstances which will modify that custom.

The skilled propagandist could be not merely an engineer of demand, then, but a maker of manners, bringing a multiplier effect to the commercial use of attention capture.

Bernays sought to overthrow the taboo against women smoking outside the home by framing it as an abridgement of their freedom. Relying on some back-of-the-envelope Freudian analysis, including the idea of cigarettes as phallic objects and a source of oral satisfaction, he presented smokes as vital to a fuller life. And he hired a group of attractive women to march in the 1929 New York City Easter Day Parade, brandishing their Lucky Strikes, or "torches of freedom."[10] He had paid Ruth Hale, a prominent feminist, to sign the letter inviting the women to the march. "Light another torch of freedom! Fight another sex taboo!" it thundered.[11]

The historical record is somewhat muddled as to the real effect of the stunt, precisely because of Bernays's natural tendency to take credit as the mysterious puppet master behind the scenes.[12] Perhaps seduced by an irresistible story, many have accepted his version of events, in which the "Torches of Freedom" parade marks a kind of social turning point. No less astute a critic of propaganda than Noam Chomsky allows that Bernays's "major coup, the one that really propelled him into fame in the late 1920s, was getting women to smoke."[13]

It is of course impossible to assign—or deny—definitive credit for something as complex as a change in social norms. Suffice it to say that contemporary reporting of the "Torches of Freedom" event was relatively thin. *The New York Times* buried its account of the protest halfway through its story on the presumably more urgent subject, the Easter Parade itself: "About a dozen young women strolled back and forth [on Fifth Avenue] while the parade was at its peak, ostentatiously smoking their cigarettes. . . . One of the group explained that the cigarettes were 'torches of freedom' lighting the way to the day when women would smoke on the street as casually as men."[14] *The Washington Post* would not mention the demonstration until 1991, by which time the event had gathered significance by reason of the story's propagation; in the end, Bernays's signal triumph may have been the particularly good job he did capturing the attention of historians.

·   ·   ·

At roughly the same time that the boss called in Bernays, Lasker was also tasked with engineering greater demand among women for Lucky Strike. This was the beginning of the "Reach for a Lucky" campaign. Far cruder and more conventional than Bernays's effort, it also likely sold more cigarettes to women than all the torches of Easter. Lasker started from advertising's most tried and true premise, borrowed from patent medicine: cigarettes needed to be a cure for *something*—if not sore throats, then what? Noticing that women often expressed concern about their weight, he came up with the idea of selling Lucky Strike as a remedy for excess weight, a diet aid. The original slogan "Reach for a Lucky instead of a Bon-Bon" soon became "Reach for a Lucky instead of a sweet," and would long be remembered simply as "Reach for a Lucky."[15]

In a typical ad, a glamorous flapper is puckering up, blowing smoke perhaps, with her eyes shut tight; the copy reads, "To keep a slender figure, no one can deny . . . Reach for a Lucky instead of a sweet." A number of others invoke "The Shadow which pursues us all"; in these, a matronly silhouette ominously frames the profile of a lithe young woman. For good measure, Lasker added Hopkins's coda to nearly all these ads: "It's toasted."

Lasker may never have been at J. Walter Thompson, much less the Women's Department, but his imitation of their approach worked wonders. Sales of Luckies exploded, increasing by 8.3 billion units in 1928 alone. As other brands followed suit, rates of smoking among women tripled from the 1920s to the mid-1930s.

In this way, George Washington Hill got what he wanted. By the end of the decade, Lucky Strike had overtaken Camel as the nation's leading cigarette for no evident reason than its advertising spending. To succeed, propaganda must be total. But along the way, the campaign crossed some lines, resorting to the sort of dangerous misrepresentations that had made patent medicines so successful. Just as before, the success had been based purely on advertising, and won at the expense of public health. Perhaps predictably, then, "Reach for a Lucky" and campaigns like it began to provoke a wave of public resentment that would reach full force by the beginning of the 1930s. For the American Tobacco Company, it would begin when the Federal Trade Commission called in Hill and Lasker to have a talk about those medical testimonials.

By 1928, Claude Hopkins, now in retirement, would announce that his trade had reached its own end of history. "Human nature does not change," he wrote, and the principles of scientific advertising "are as enduring as the Alps." Nothing bolstered this assertion like the institutional sophistication of the modern agency itself, which had ably sold itself, apart from much else. No longer peddling primitive space ads in penny papers, the advertising executive was now deftly marrying word and image across the spectrum of print media on behalf of burgeoning giants of manufacture and service, wielding the power of life and death over consumer products.[16] As the 1920s closed, advertising had grown itself from a dubious activity and negligible industry into a major part of the economy. American companies went from spending an estimated $700 million in 1914 to almost $30 billion a year by 1929, then about 3 percent of gross domestic product.[17] Advertising was now as big as many of the industries it served.

With Stanley and Helen Landsdowne Resor, now married and at the head of it, J. Walter Thompson was, by that time, the largest agency in the world.[18] The firm leased space in the art deco Graybar Building attached to the Grand Central Terminal in New York (a block from Madison Avenue), completing its move to the center of American corporate life.

The rewards to those who had made the climb were ample indeed. The Resors acquired both a mansion in Connecticut and a vast ranch in Jackson Hole, Wyoming, where they hired the pioneer of modern architecture Ludwig Mies van der Rohe to build their vacation home, his first American commission.[19] As for Albert Lasker, the president of Chicago's Lord & Thomas, his estate on five hundred acres included a working farm, an eighteen-hole golf course, and a movie theater, among its twenty-six structures.[20] Even the abstemious former preacher Claude Hopkins was eventually moved to acquire a pile in the Michigan wilderness, as well as an oceangoing yacht. His wife, writes David Ogilvy, persuaded him "to employ an army of gardeners on their estate, and to buy splendid Louis XVI furniture. She filled their vast house with an endless procession of guests. Her cook was famous. And she played Scarlatti to Hopkins for hours at a time."

.   .   .

With its acquired wealth and grandeur, the industry began to see itself differently, in a way more attuned with its origins, which its cloak of science had served to conceal. No, not the origins in patent medicine, redolent of swindle and charlatanism—that lineage advertising was glad to have disowned, even if it would never disown the methods. Rather, it was now that advertising began to see itself in the image of the original propaganda body, the Church; its work as a mission; and its masters as capitalism's new priestly class. The agencies were educating the masses, doing a sort of missionary work on behalf of the great new companies fulfilling the broadest needs and deepest desires of the nation. President Coolidge captured the new image in a 1926 speech: "Advertising ministers to the spiritual side of trade. It is a great power that has been entrusted to your keeping which charges you with the high responsibility of inspiring and ennobling the commercial world. It is all part of the greater work of regeneration and redemption of mankind."[21]

Many of the most talented copywriters, as we've seen, came from families steeped in organized religion. Some saw surprisingly little difference between the two callings. In *The Man Nobody Knows,* a 1925 bestseller by adman Bruce Barton, himself the son of a Methodist preacher, Jesus Christ is depicted, not ironically but with earnest reverence, as an early advertising man and small-business owner, managing his team of disciples who "mastered public attention" and came up with winning slogans such as "the meek shall inherit the earth." Barton reached even deeper when he wrote that "advertising" was a force "as old as the world . . . 'Let there be light' constitutes its charter. All Nature vibrates with its impulse. The brilliant plumage of the bird is color advertising addressed to the emotions."

Whether or not advertising was as exalted a purpose as some had proclaimed, by the end of the 1920s it had unquestionably changed the tenor of daily life across the industrialized world. For it was then that a conspicuous feature of modern existence, albeit one that we are all now well used to, was born: namely, the fact of being constantly cajoled and sold to, the endless stream of appeals that take such effort to ignore, promising as they do the answers to all our problems, the satisfaction of all our yearnings. Now is when advertising was first woven into the fabric of most Americans' lives, as bit by bit the major brands planted themselves in the collective consciousness, like so many mighty trees—as if Cadillac or Coca-Cola could never have been just names but were somehow imbued with meaning from the beginning of time. The built environment created by advertising began to seem like a natural ecosystem; the incessant barrage of commercial propositions became a fact of life.

It is therefore all the more stunning to imagine that the industrialization of human attention capture as we know it had really only begun. The possibilities of electronic media and the Internet still lay in the future. Thanks to the rise of advertising, the world seemed cluttered with come-ons, but these were still confined to newspapers, magazines, posters, billboards, and leaflets. And yet unbeknownst to most of those making the most grandiose claims for advertising, some of its best days were already behind it.

When, in 1932, Claude Hopkins died of heart failure, at the age of sixty-six, *The New York Times* described him as "the man who had written $100 million worth of copy." Despite his success, however, when Hopkins was near death, he claimed with his peculiar piety that "money means nothing to me, save that my Scotch instinct rebels at waste."[22] He had also ended his autobiography on a strange note: "The happiest are those who live closest to nature, an essential to advertising success." It was an odd sentiment from one foremost in the effort to replace nature with advertising. Perhaps the old preacher had one further prophecy in him.

CHAPTER 6

NOT WITH A BANG

BUT WITH A WHIMPER

In 1926, Stuart Chase and Frederick Schlink met in a Greenwich Village speakeasy and over the conversation found that they agreed about many things. Chase was an accountant and former investigator at the Federal Trade Commission; Schlink, a standards engineer, had worked in the National Laboratories. Although following markedly different professions, both men were near zealots for the scientific method and its power to expose truths that might be contrary to popular opinion. They also shared, above all, an implacable contempt for the advertising industry, and what they regarded as the massive fraud it was perpetrating on the American public.[1]

The two would later use the following parable to capture their view of the inherent tension between truth and advertising:

Two men are discussing the merits of a famous brand of oil. Says one, "I know it must be good; it sells a million dollars worth a year. You see their advertisements everywhere." But the other says, "I do not care how much it sells. I left a drop of it on a piece of copper for 24 hours, and the drop turned green. It is corrosive and I do not dare to use it."

. . . The first speaker followed the crowd, but his friend disregarded the fact of bigness and went after the facts of chemistry. As a result, he arrived at a precisely opposite course of action from the common one. Sometimes the crowd is right; often it is wrong. It remains for science to read the balance.[2]

That evening, Chase and Schlink decided to collaborate on what would become a manifesto: *Your Money's Worth: A Study in the Waste of the Consumer's Dollar.* As they wrote:

> Consumers make their blunder-ing way, so many Alices in the Wonderland of salesman-ship; they buy not what they freely want, but what they are made to want. In the office of the advertising agency, human psychology is an open book. There is no strand or chord of it upon which the advertiser has not learned to play. . . . But there is just a chance that the gentlemen who run this unparalleled side show may be putting on the acts a little too fast; just a chance that the superlatives have almost reached the limits of registering on the brain; that the sheer multiplicity of brand names dizzies the spectator instead of seducing him. . . . In that hope this book has been written, but its authors have not deluded themselves with the belief that the triumph of science is inevitable.[3]

Both encapsulating and amplifying an emergent disenchantment with the high-handedness of advertising, *Your Money's Worth* would become a bestseller, known in its time as the *Uncle Tom's Cabin* of the consumer movement, and, along with the Depression, it sparked another major revolt—another period of consumer resistance. The authors knew their success owed in part to a perspective that was, in their words, "in no sense revolutionary." Chase and Schlink were no critics of the free market, private property, or any other defining feature of American capitalism. Indeed, it was in the defense of the market's integrity that they attacked advertising, which, with its misleading and deceptive claims, and manufactured demand for relatively needless products, was distorting the economy to the nation's detriment. In the wake of the book's success, in 1929 the authors founded Consumers' Research Incorporated, which aimed to be the world's first scientific consumer product testing service. The new organization produced a confidential newsletter—the *Consumers' Research General Bulletin*—which supplied its subscribers with secret reviews of products and product claims, based on rigorous testing.[4]

Chase and Schlink's ventures were, in fact, only the leading edge of a broad-based assault that would ultimately figure in advertising's near collapse. Over the 1930s the movement collected a range of fellow travelers, among them academics like Rexford Tugwell, the Columbia University economist and member of Franklin D. Roosevelt's Brain Trust, who opined that nine tenths of advertising was simple economic waste; as well as members of various women's groups, like the League of Women Shoppers. It was fitting perhaps, after so much targeting of them by advertisers, that women were widely viewed as the heart of the movement. The average woman was outraged, *Business Week* reported, to find that "the soap which made her so popular at the dance was made with a little creosol . . . recommended by the Government for disinfecting cars, barns and chicken yards."[5]

Some of the most intense new critics of advertising were internal. In 1928, Theodore MacManus, who had so famously branded Cadillac, Dodge, and Chrysler, decided he'd had it. Writing in *The Atlantic,* he denounced both his own industry and the whole of modern civilization: "Advertising has gone amuck," he wrote, "in that it has mistaken the surface silliness for the sane solid substance of an averagely decent human nature." A serious Catholic, he blamed the American brand of Protestantism for creating a "Nadir of Nothingness" in which people worshipped consumer goods as "brightly packaged gifts of the gods."[6]

Helen Woodward, a copywriter of prominence, wrote a popular book lamenting the emptiness of what she'd done with her life. She offered a professional confession: "In the advertising business we thought ourselves important. We thought we knew what we were doing; we had our plans for next week or next year. The realization came to me with a slow shock that I was nothing, we were nothing. We were feathers all of us, blown about by winds which we neither understood nor controlled."

The darkest was the work of James Rorty, another former copywriter, who wrote *Our Master's Voice: Advertising* (1934), in which he described the job's effect on the soul. The adman, he wrote, "inevitably empties himself of human qualities. His daily traffic in half-truths and outright deceptions is subtly and cumulatively degrading. No man can give his days to barbarous frivolity and live. And ad-men don't live. They become dull, resigned, hopeless. Or they become daemonic fantasts and sadists." In one poetical passage reminiscent of "The Hollow Men," T. S. Eliot's 1925 cry of despair for Western civilization following the Great War, Rorty memorializes his former colleagues thus: "they are dead men. Their bones are bakelite. Their blood is water, their flesh is pallid— yes, prick them and they do not bleed. Their eyes are veiled and sad or staring and a little mad. From them comes an acrid odor—they do not notice it, it may be only the ozone discharge of the machine itself."[7]

Advertising had not come so far so fast to take these attacks lying down. The International Advertising Association pronounced *Your Money's Worth* a work of "communist propaganda." The purpose of the consumer movement, another critic charged, was "to overthrow capital-ists, but to have the overthrowing done by an army of embattled con-sumers and housewives rather than by the traditional revolutionary agent—Marx's proletariat."

They also bit the hand that fed them, attacking the new consumer clubs as efforts to foment socialism among gullible females. "Women's clubs have put aside Oriental travel and the poetry of Edna St. Vincent Millay as topics for discussion," wrote one condescending critic, "and are now clamoring for speakers on 'Consumer Education.' Editors of women's magazines find that their readers want fewer recipes for sum-mer salads and more information on consumer goods specification or social consciousness."[8]

But despite the brave and defiant front, advertising was in serious trouble. Like all American industry, it was damaged by the Depression. In addition to consumer resentment, it was also meeting a rising new skepticism among clients, the producers of goods and services who, fac-ing their own declining fortunes, began to wonder whether advertis-ing was really as effective as they had once thought; whether it wasn't, perhaps, just a waste of money. With the economy as a whole in utter collapse, advertising outlays shrank over the 1930s to almost one third of what they had been by the end of the 1920s; several firms folded, and consumption's former high priests and priestesses were among those left jobless. Trying to salvage some business, the remnants of the industry fell back to hard-selling patent medicine techniques that only confirmed the worst claims of critics.[9]

The consumer movement, meanwhile, kept up a relentless onslaught over the early 1930s, with the publication of still more books, includ-ing *100,000,000 Guinea Pigs* (on food and drug advertising) and *Skin Deep* (an attack on the cosmetic industry), as well as *Eat, Drink and Be Wary, Guinea Pigs No More,* and *The Popular Practice of Fraud,* all of them encouraging a growing sense that neither advertisements nor manufacturers were to be trusted. The combined effect raised an inter-esting question—just what use, if any, was advertising to the economy? Let's consider it for a moment.[10]

In classical economics, sellers supply products to consumers who want them, and the price is set by the intersection of supply and demand. But of course this model, which still dominates market analysis, leaves out plenty of details. For instance: How do consumers actually find out—or "discover" in today's marketing parlance—what products exist in the first place? Even in an information-rich world, one sometimes doesn't hear about things for one reason or another, and you cannot demand, much less buy, something you don't even know about. How often have you discovered a film or a novel that you love years after its release?

Nor can the competition envisioned by classical economics and driven by differences in price and quality work unless people actually find out about the prices and quality differences that various producers offer. If I don't know that fifteen minutes can save me 15 percent or more on my car insurance, how does competition contribute to efficiency? Put another way, if a price falls in the market and no one hears it, it doesn't make a sound.

Information cannot be acted upon without attention and thus atten-tion capture and information are essential to a functioning market economy, or indeed any competitive process, like an election (unknown candidates do not win). So as a technology for gaining access to the human mind, advertising can therefore serve a vital function, making markets, elections, and everything that depends on informed choice operate better, by telling us what we need to know about our choices, ideally in an objective fashion.

That, at least, is the ideal. The trouble, of course, is that most com-panies don't care so much about market efficiency as maximizing profit; and so advertising rarely stops at the presentation of objective information meant to aid the competitive process.[11] After all, what makes people "want" a product in the first place? There are some things, like a mother's milk, and basic comforts that one might be born wanting; but for such items advertising is hardly necessary. Most other products in the contemporary economy are what one might call acquired tastes. No one is born wanting 4K television, a purse branded by Hermès or Louis Vuitton, or the odor eliminator product Febreze. For the advertisers, by far the most valuable function of advertising, then, is the shaping or creation of demands that would not otherwise exist.* We have seen ample examples in the creation of demand for orange juice, toothpaste, mouthwash, the Cadillac automobile, or cigarettes (among women), and in the 1920s advertising executives described this as their function. "The achievements of American mass production would fall of their own weight," Stanley Resor observed, "without the mass marketing machinery which advertising supplies."

At its worst, as Chase and Schlink argued, advertising actually tries to attack and distort the mechanisms of choice, by presenting information that is either completely false (as in some patent medicine advertising), or deceptive, by, for example, failing to disclose important truths (like the fact that cigarettes cause cancer). And when advertising confuses, misleads, or fools customers, it does not aid the market process, or indeed any process premised on informed choice, but instead defeats it.

Branding, which grew to such heights in the 1920s, was subject to a slightly different criticism. As economist Edward Chamberlin, in his 1933 work *The Theory of Monopolistic Competition,* alleged, the creation of strong brand loyalties, having little to do with intrinsic value, was a calculated effort to foster irrational attachments by which a brand might survive competition from other brands that were as good or better. The most effective brand advertising, after all, does not try to convince you to make a choice, but rather to convince you that there *is* no choice—that Coca-Cola is *the* cola, that Camel is *your* cigarette, or that Harley-Davidson is the *only* motorcycle one would consider. It can succeed if

---

* Some economists contest the idea that demand can be created by advertising, despite the empirical evidence. Whether "wants" can be created may just depend on how you define them. One might be said to be born wanting "beautiful things," and advertising merely identifies for you what is beautiful. Or one can more easily say that advertising shapes or creates demand.

it manages to make the brand part of your identity: One might feel the same loyalty to Miller the beer as a resident of Wisconsin feels to the state. True brand advertising is therefore an effort not so much to persuade as to convert. At its most successful, it creates a product cult, whose loyalists cannot be influenced by mere information: companies like Apple, Hermès, and Porsche are among those that have achieved this kind of immunity to competition, at least among their true believers. What is offered to adherents is not merely a good product (though often it is), but something deeper and more deeply fulfilling—a sense of meaning that comes with the surrender of choice.

The harms of advertising are aptly attested by the Lucky Strike campaign of the late 1920s and '30s. The massive amounts spent on cigarette advertising had spurred demand for a dangerous product and deterred switching between brands, while also preventing cheaper newcomers from making much headway. The result was an oligopoly of branded cigarettes—Camels, Lucky Strike, and so on—that has lasted for decades, and, of course, no few cancerous lungs.[12]

As advertising suffered through its comeuppance, much the same fate awaited Lucky Strike, when its "Reach for a Lucky" slogan attracted the attention of the Federal Trade Commission. (The confectionery industry, displeased with tobacco's displacement of their product, might have had something to do with this scrutiny.) The FTC had taken particular note of the claims that cigarettes soothed the throat, along with the dubious doctor's endorsements and paid testimonials; it also cast a jaundiced eye on the suggestion that cigarettes were a weight-loss aid. Finding both the testimonials themselves and the failure to disclose the payment for them deceptive, the commission insisted that Hill stop claiming that Luckies would help anyone lose weight.[13]

Unfortunately, the commission's actual power over deceptive advertising, legally ambiguous at best, was definitively quashed by a skeptical Supreme Court in 1931, just as Lucky's campaign was firing on all cylinders. Consequently, Hill and Lasker were back to their old tricks, if somewhat more cautious, now peddling their claim more by implication than outright assertion. A new version of the ad from later in the 1930s shows a slender and beautiful woman on the edge of a diving board, surrounded by a plumper silhouette. "IS THIS YOU FIVE YEARS FROM NOW?" it asks. "When tempted to over-indulge, Reach for a Lucky instead."[14]

But the humbling of the FTC and general sense of outrage yielded a legal reform movement whose goal was to control the excesses of advertisers and their clients. At the Agriculture Department (the FDA's ancestor), Rexford Tugwell, the economist, was appointed an assistant secretary with a mandate to improve consumer protection. Like others in FDR's government, he felt the 1906 Food and Drugs Act had not been strong enough to prevent unscrupulous practices. So the administration introduced a bill that pushed for legislators to impose tough rules over advertising.[15]

As originally conceived, the so-called Tugwell Bill was very tough indeed. It combined the concepts of false labeling and false advertising, designating as the latter anything that was clearly untrue, or that, by "ambiguity or inference," created a false impression. The law also barred advertisements from purporting that a product could cure any of a long list of diseases. Products falsely labeled or advertised would be subject to seizure by the Department of Agriculture; their promoters subject to criminal prosecution.[16]

Such strong medicine would have effectively outlawed many of the techniques that the advertising industry had adopted over the 1910s and 1920s. Though the softer brand advertising would have been unaffected, much of reason-why advertising's arsenal, the entire patent medicine approach included, would have been finished. If Hill and Lasker had persisted with the Lucky Strike campaign as it stood, they might both have landed in prison. And many of today's most familiar infomercials claiming the miraculous benefits of this or that would be illegal.

Unlike patent medicines, however, the advertising industry, though bloodied, was more than equipped to defend itself; and its side was joined by the fledgling pharmaceutical industry, already practiced in government relations, and determined to protect what it called the "sacred right of self-medication." Rexford Tugwell became the target of claims that he was a communist agent trying to import socialism: "The world knows that he has visited Russia and has found its institutions acceptable," charged one industry flack, and now "he believes that packaging and advertising constitutes economic waste that should be prevented."

Advertising also cleverly enlisted newspapers to its cause, even issuing threats to pull most of its business were the bill to pass; as the historian Inger L. Stole points out, the American media almost entirely declined to cover the controversy. Sensing their very viability was at stake, the newspapers, food producers, and drug manufacturers formed a tight phalanx with the advertising industry, doing everything they could, even funding front groups, until they were sure the Tugwell Bill would go down in flames.[17]

In 1938, a far weaker law was passed; the Federal Trade Commission regained its powers to oversee advertising through a ban on "unfair or deceptive acts or practices," which referred only to factually untrue statements, not the potential inferences targeted by Tugwell. The new law reflected "a five-year effort to render such protections painless for business interests"; and many at the time argued, like Milton Handler, a law professor at Columbia, that it did not go far enough: "While the [new law] represents a sincere attempt to stem the avalanche of false and misleading advertising, it is no more than a first, and unfortunately, inadequate step in that direction. Unless buttressed by clarifying amendments broadening its prohibitions and implementing it with effective sanctions, it will not effect an abiding solution of the vexing problem of false and misleading advertising."[18]

The industry, albeit humbled, had survived, and mostly unregenerate. In the end it was left with the grim awareness that it had worse problems than government. In Depression-era America, advertising's pitches were falling on deaf ears, or at least, on the ears of people now lacking the means to buy all those items great and sundry on which they had frittered away so much money just a few years before.[19]

Something had to change, and it would. But few in late 1930s advertising could have predicted it would be an explosion in the supply of usable attention. This happened thanks to two new inventions, the first one whose potential most doubted and the second whose potential they could scarcely imagine. A whole new attention economy would soon be born, and advertising would cling to it for dear life.

PART II

THE CONQUEST OF TIME AND SPACE

The first thirty years of the twentieth century demonstrated that attention could be harvested on a mass scale and converted into unprecedented levels of commerce and military might. It is therefore remarkable that this effort—which seemed at the time so pervasive, to the point of inflaming critics and whole movements—was, in retrospect, so circumscribed in time and place. To see where and when attention was being harvested, one had only to see where advertising (or propaganda, its noncommercial twin) was to be found. For however inescapable and multifarious it may have seemed at the time, advertising before 1930 was confined to the oldest of media, those from the nineteenth century or earlier—newspapers, magazines, billboards—and the oldest of the major communication networks, the mail system. It had as yet no purchase on the new media of the twentieth century, which were only beginning to transform the lives of those who heard and watched them—the movies, radio, and soon, television. Furthermore, there remained a divide between the highly commercialized public sphere and the traditional private one. A newspaper or leaflet might be brought inside, but otherwise the family home was shielded from the commercial bombardment to which one was subjected in public. This, however, was soon to change.

As global advertising crashed in the 1930s, along with the rest of the economy, the industry was in existential crisis, and desperate to renew itself. With advertising's usefulness now in question, the old channels of attention could no longer generate enough revenue to keep the advertising business viable. So it began to search for others, and its search led it into what turned out to be human attention's mother lode. By means of new technologies, advertising and its master, commerce, would enter what had been for millennia our attention's main sanctuary—the home.

CHAPTER 7

THE INVENTION OF PRIME TIME

In 1928, Walter Templin, the new general manager of Pepsodent toothpaste, was looking for an idea, anything that might save the company, which was on the verge of collapse.

Just a few years earlier, thanks to Claude Hopkins's inspired "tooth film" campaign, Pepsodent had reigned as king of the dentrifices. But by the late 1920s, the product had suffered from bad, if accurate, publicity. Unlike our toothpastes, Pepsodent didn't contain fluoride or appropriate cleaning agents. Its vaunted "clean" feeling was produced by an abrasive ingredient that was, according to one Columbia University chemist who tested it, "hard and sharp enough to cut glass."[1] Furthermore, he found that "Mucin placque [technical term for the 'film'] cannot be digested from teeth by any advertised use of 'Pepsodent.'"[2]

Another problem was that Pepsodent's initial success had lured in competitors, so that there were more than one hundred brands of toothpaste on the market by the late 1920s. Some were admittedly even worse: Tartaroff, for example, which claimed to turn teeth "into gems of pearl-like beauty," in fact whitened them by burning off enamel with hydrochloric acid.[3] But Pepsodent was also losing market share to better alternatives, like the upstart Colgate, "the ribbon dental cream," which promised a "safe" dentifrice with a "delicious flavor." (A "man is known by the teeth he keeps.")[4] By 1928, Hopkins's brainchild was on the verge of going out of business.

But Templin, a Canadian who had relocated to Chicago, had an idea. Like many in the 1920s, he was entranced by the invisible miracle of radio broadcast. In fact, before Pepsodent, he'd run a radio set manufacturer. Might there be some way of promoting Pepsodent on the airwaves? But how?

———————

In the 1920s, the idea of advertising on radio was controversial if not contemptible. Even *Printer's Ink* had opined that "the family circle is not a public place, and advertising has no business intruding there unless invited."[5] Radio, moreover, was in a utopian phase, and its destiny seemed to be the uplift of the human condition, not selling toothpaste.* As the future president Herbert Hoover had put it in 1922, "It is inconceivable that we should allow so great a possibility for service, for news, for entertainment, for education, and for vital commercial purposes to be drowned in advertising chatter."[6] Some even doubted that radio could be an effective advertising platform, based on failures of ad-supported cinemas in the 1910s. As Samuel "Roxy" Rothafel, owner of New York's largest movie theater, said, "If you try to sell some brand of shoes or anything else over the radio you'll have no radio audience."[7]

At the time, companies with designs on radio's audiences stalked them indirectly, by sponsoring content. Gillette, for example, underwrote a lecture series on the "history of the beard." Most, however, sponsored a musical act like *La Palina Hour,* named after La Palina cigars, or the Clicquot Club Eskimos, a banjo ensemble presented by a popular ginger ale (the "Eskimos" played their banjos in full parkas before their studio audiences).

So perhaps a Pepsodent orchestra? But another toothpaste had gotten there first—the Ipana Troubadours played swing but dressed like Spanish bullfighters. Among the nondental ensembles, listeners could also enjoy the Goodrich Zippers, the Silvertown Cord Orchestra (featuring the Silver Masked Tenor); the Sylvania Foresters; the Champion

---

* On the idealistic days of the early radio, see *The Master Switch,* chapter 2.

Sparkers; the Fox Fur Trappers; the Ingram Shavers; the Yeast Foamers' Orchestra; the Planters Pickers; and, of course, the Freed-Eisemann Orchestradians. The field, suffice to say, was fairly crowded.

One evening in 1928, at a friend's home in Chicago, at 7 p.m. to be exact, Templin heard something quite different on the radio, something along the lines of:

"Dell me 'dis one ding—is you a democrat, or is you a ree-publican?"
  "Well, I was a democrat . . ."
  "mm hmmm"
  "Bu' I believ' I done switched ovah to da republicans now."
  "Who is da man who's runnin' in dese heah elect'n times, explain dat to me."
  "Herbert Hoover. Versuvius Al Smith."
  "Wha' is da difference?"
  "Da one of dem is a mule. And da otha' is an elephant."

Two white actors, Freeman Gosden and Charles Correll, speaking in "Negro" voices, were telling a story that never ended—a "serial"—in fifteen-minute installments. It was carried by a local station, one of the countless independents that existed in the early days of the medium.* Little did Templin or anyone else realize that his discovery of *Amos 'n' Andy*—the ancestor of the sitcoms and other broadcast entertainment that captivated so many for so long—was to revolutionize the business of capturing and selling attention.

The characters, Amos and Andy, were two Southern blacks who'd moved from Georgia to Chicago, only to be perpetually confused and confounded by modern urban life. Andy, voiced by Correll, was the older, brash and overconfident, "absolutely convinced that he had the answers to everything."[8] Amos, meanwhile, was earnest and simple—as later promotional materials read: "It's 'Ain't dat sumpin'?' when he's happy or surprised."[9] Originally from Richmond, Virginia, Gosden, who played

---

* The show debuted in January 1926 as a two-man comedy series, *Sam 'n' Henry,* on Chicago's WGN. In March 1928, the show moved to the *Chicago Daily News*'s radio station, WMAQ, where it was reinvented as *Amos 'n' Andy.* See Jeffrey L. Cruikshank and Arthur W. Schultz, *The Man Who Sold America: The Amazing (but True!) Story of Albert D. Lasker and the Creation of the Advertising Century* (Boston: Harvard Business Review Press, 2010).

Amos, was the son of a Confederate soldier. The show, he said, was based on his experiences of being raised by a black nanny alongside a black boy named Snowball.

When *Amos 'n' Andy* had come on, Templin noticed something peculiar at this friend's house: the entire family stopped what it was doing to gather around the radio and listen intently for the show's entire duration. Radio, he rightly concluded, could not only capture attention, it could do so inside the customer's home. It could cause a whole family to ignore one another and listen in rapt silence.

We have spoken of the mind's impressive ability to shut the door to the outside world; but while *Amos 'n' Andy* was on, people were apparently glad to fling it wide open. The rapt attention was different from what the musical acts had. Templin recognized that this was an astonishing power, if it could only be harnessed.

His idea was to take the *Amos 'n' Andy* show to the NBC radio network, with Pepsodent as sponsor. Kenneth Smith, now head of Pepsodent, and the other executives seemed to like the idea, perhaps because it seemed connected to the old tradition of advertising toothpaste in print using stylized black men with shiny white teeth. (In fact, it was around this time that an English company launched the Darkie brand, with a smiling black man as its logo.)[10]

But outside Pepsodent, the idea met immediate resistance. As *Broadcasting* magazine later recounted, "Other advertisers laughed at [Pepsodent's] foolhardy ignorance of radio." The conventional wisdom, wrote the magazine, was that "people won't listen to talk on the radio. They'd rather talk themselves."[11] When Templin went to NBC, its managers offered him a choice: the Vincent Lopez orchestra, or Jesse Crawford, the organist. When Templin insisted on *Amos 'n' Andy,* and in "six quarters" (fifteen minutes, six days a week), the network was unresponsive.

A subsequent attempt to sell *Amos 'n' Andy* to the new CBS network was no more successful. Informed that the show was a "daily blackface act," then President H. C. Cox said, "Do you mean to tell me that you believe an act can go on a network at the same time every day in the week, five days in succession?" The answer was yes. "I think you should go back to Chicago," said Cox. "It's very plain to see that you know nothing about radio."[12]

Even within Pepsodent some had their doubts, arguing that *Amos 'n'*

Andy's dialogue format was too simple. They proposed a longer, more elaborate blackface program, with a chorus and an orchestra—a sort of minstrel competitor to the Eskimos or Troubadours. Ultimately, however, after nine months of wrangling, NBC agreed to take the order, for an enormous sum, over $1 million, and introduce its first sponsored serial program—indeed probably the first network "show" that wasn't musical or educational. It agreed to sell thirteen weeks at 7 p.m. on its farm team Blue network, which, given Pepsodent's dire financial straits, was effectively a bet on Pepsodent itself. "Never in the history of radio," said one commentator, "had there been such an order as that."[13]

Amos 'n' Andy would be the same show it was before, with two changes. First, the characters would move from Chicago to Harlem. And second, as a concession to the tradition of musical acts, NBC introduced a theme song. Adding what seems now a further coat of racism, the music director chose "The Perfect Song," the theme from *The Birth of a Nation*, D. W. Griffith's 1915 hit film glorifying the Ku Klux Klan.

And of course the sponsor's message had to be right. Pepsodent and Lord & Thomas hired, on an exclusive basis, an announcer with an exceptionally mellow voice named Bill Hay, who pronounced at the end of every *Amos 'n' Andy* segment this message:

"Use Pepsodent Toothpaste Twice a Day—See Your Dentist at Least Twice a Year."[14]

In August of 1928 as the series launched on NBC, Amos 'n' Andy were making their move to Harlem:

AMOS: Heah we is goin' to New York—we don't know whut we goin' do.
ANDY: Dat IS right too. Yo' know, I been thinkin' 'bout dis heah thing. We was crazy to come heah.

Templin had gotten his way, but after the first run, *Amos 'n' Andy* looked to Pepsodent like a mistake. Despite high hopes, listenership was low and there was little noticeable effect on sales. Realizing he had nothing to lose, however, Templin doubled his bet, spending one of Pepsodent's last millions on the program.

For whatever reason, the second time was the charm. By the end of 1929, *Amos 'n' Andy* had become a craze, and the first bona fide hit serial in broadcast history—and the first show people refused to miss, arranging their time around it. No less a cultural arbiter than *The New Yorker* was now remarking both the show's quality and the phenomenon: "*Amos 'n' Andy* have gone beyond all control. The radio has never had a more amusing feature, nor one that has created so much havoc."[15]

The audiences, astounding at the time, are still impressive by today's standards. While measurements were crude in those days, by 1931, *Amos 'n' Andy* is believed to have attracted some 40 million listeners each and every evening—with some episodes reaching 50 million—this out of a population that was then 122 million. It was a result unprecedented for any entertainment product, the equivalent of having today's Super Bowl audiences each and every evening—and with just one advertiser.

Having seized their audience, the sponsor's messages soon grew longer, and soon were indistinguishable from the old hard-sell advertising copy, albeit written to be heard, not read:

> As we have told you repeatedly, Pepsodent Tooth Paste today contains a new and different cleansing and polishing material. We want to emphasize the fact that this cleansing and polishing material used in Pepsodent Tooth Paste is contained in no other tooth paste. That is very important. It is important to us, because Pepsodent laboratories spent eleven years in developing this remarkable material. It is important to the public, because no other cleansing and polishing material removes film from teeth as effectively as does this new discovery. What's more, this new material is twice as soft as that commonly used in tooth pastes. Therefore it gives great safety, greater protection to lovely teeth. Use Pepsodent Tooth Paste twice a day—See your dentist at least twice a year.[16]

In our fragmented age, it is only a few times a year when even a quarter of the entire nation listens to or watches anything at once. But during the height of the *Amos 'n' Andy* craze, that happened every day, and consequently the 7 p.m. time slot, according to contemporary reports, began to influence the schedule of everything. Hotels, restaurants, and movie theaters would broadcast the show for their patrons. Fearing displacement, movie theaters advertised the installation of radios to broadcast *Amos 'n' Andy* at 7 p.m., before the newsreels and features.

We have yet to ask an obvious question: Just what, exactly, was so enrapturing about *Amos 'n' Andy*? It was not necessarily the patter and gags. Despite *The New Yorker*'s enthusiasm, another early critic panned the show's national debut in the *New York Sun:* "Their lines are not good and there is no pretense of whatever to carry out the illusion of comedy. It is a straight dialogue between two common-place 'darkies' and is without even the saving asset of a well thought-out situation . . . on first acquaintance they hardly attract a second glance."[17] Indeed, there were other regional radio minstrel shows in the 1920s, not much funnier, and none reached an audience anything close to that of *Amos 'n' Andy*. It seems that what gripped so much attention, what kept millions coming back, were the show's elaborate and suspenseful plot lines. *The New Yorker* again: "For Amos 'n' Andy . . . have finally mastered the trick of creating suspense. With half a dozen plots running through their sketches, they hold the dramatic tension in a way to arouse the admiration of Professor Baker." In particular, much of the show turned on the romance between the earnest Amos and Ruby Taylor, whom he'd met in Chicago. Later, the focus was on the engagement of know-it-all Andy and the bossy divorcée Madam Queen. Nowadays we might say that *Amos 'n' Andy* resembled a soap opera—but as we shall see, it was really soap operas that copied *Amos 'n' Andy*.

Subsequent commentators would remark the obvious appeal of reinforcing stereotypes that justified the second-class social status of blacks. (The NAACP did register complaints, but these had no effect on NBC at the time.) As one historian, Erik Barnouw, wrote in 1966, "In retrospect it is easy . . . to see the stories and *Amos 'n' Andy* as part of the ghetto system. All of it was more readily accepted and maintained if one could hold onto this: 'they' were lovely people, essentially happy people, ignorant and somewhat shiftless and lazy in a lovable, quaint way, not fitting in with higher levels of enterprise, better off where they were."[18]

But there was also great empathy stirred in some hearts, rather like that provoked by *Uncle Tom's Cabin* in antebellum America. As one listener wrote in fan mail, "We have been inspired by the high aims and rigid honesty of Amos, and we have all been close to tears at times when real trials and tribulations beset either of our beloved friends."

The wild success of *Amos 'n' Andy,* and similar shows to follow it, marked something profound, though in a sense quite unexpected. And it represents a turning point in our story, for three different reasons.

First, while NBC might have originally considered itself a way to demonstrate the excellence of RCA's radios, after *Amos 'n' Andy* it was now clearly and irresistibly in the business of selling the attention of enormous audiences to those who could pay for and use it. The broadcaster thus definitively became an attention merchant, in the model pioneered by Benjamin Day at the *New York Sun.* Some ironies would be papered over: never mind that a sponsor had had to beg to buy the airtime (at a premium) in order to show NBC just how much attention radio could theoretically capture and sell the next time; the attention was now and ever after the broadcaster's product to develop and to resell to the highest bidder. Needless to say, there would never be a backward glance to the days when the network existed to sell the hardware![19]

Second: the power of *Amos 'n' Andy*—an entertainment offering—to bring in giant audiences willing to hear advertising effected an unlikely merger between the business of entertainment producers and that of advertisers. Before this point, received wisdom had it that advertising and entertainment did not mix. Books had never enjoyed much success selling ads in their pages; and the experiments with inserting advertising into films had also failed, most dramatically in the 1910s, when a series of silent movie theaters based on advertising, as opposed to box office sales, went bankrupt. But *Amos 'n' Andy* and its successors managed to thread the needle, creating a business model by which any medium could, to use a later vernacular, "sell eyeballs."

The proof was in the pudding, in the sense that the show did save Pepsodent toothpaste, at least for a while. Sales increased more than twofold between 1929 and 1930. Emboldened, Templin doubled down on his bet, sponsoring in 1931 *The Rise of the Goldbergs,* another fifteen-minute serial, this one about a Jewish family living in the Bronx.* And so the epic battle for the attention of America's white Protestant majority would

---

* Amazingly, a loose remake—or at least a show with the same title—was launched for television in 2013.

be waged and won thanks to the chance discovery of its fascination with the perceived hilariousness of blacks and Jews.

Third, and perhaps most momentous: here also began a race for the conquest of time and space that continues to this day. *Amos 'n' Andy* demonstrated that an industry could, in effect, wholly "own" a part of the day—in this case, seven p.m., every day, across the land. And it could do so in spaces once inviolable, inconceivable. For with this show, selling had definitively breached the barrier between public and private space. What the agents of commerce could long do "out there" they could now also do "in here," and no one was grumbling, at least not yet.

Having planted the flag in the evening hours, broadcasters would proceed to colonize other parts of the day laden with attention as yet un-reaped. Soon they would find success with daytime soap operas, targeting women at home with little to do, thanks to all the modern conveniences they had been sold. Using the basic serial template of *Amos 'n' Andy,* soap opera plots centered on family relationships among the white middle class, the target consumer. Early soap operas were thus even more natural selling tools than minstrel shows were. As one contemporary boasted, "The transition from commercial announcements to the story can be practically painless, and a great deal of actual selling can be done in the story itself."[20]

The methods used in daytime radio were more overt than those of prime time. The most respected and trusted characters would testify during the show about the merits of, say, Pillsbury's new cake mixes. In one episode of the soap opera *Today's Children,* for example, the trusted housewife character, "traditional but open to modern ideas," visits Pillsbury's kitchen. She exclaims, "The thing that impressed me so much was the orderliness of the kitchen—jest like my kitchen." Of Pillsbury she said, "They're always makin' and testin' new recipes . . . they served this cake at luncheon—never have put anythin' in my mouth so delicious . . . I got the recipe."

As Irna Phillips, inventor of the first radio soap operas, explained: "sincerity, honesty, genuineness—true values. If the woman listener is made conscious of these standards in the story itself, how little effort it would take to make her conscious of these same standards with the product advertising." In *Fortune* magazine, Phillips revealed her own recipe for engaging female listeners. "You appeal to," she said, "(1) the instinct for self-preservation, (2) sex, (3) the family instinct, or (4) all three together if you can manage."

———————

The invention of "Prime time"—the attentional habit of turning on the radio (later, the television) at the designated hour each and every evening of the year—was a momentous cultural as well as commercial innovation at a point when the two categories were drifting steadily closer. For it transformed not only the industries equipped to capture attention, but also the lives of those whose attention was now there for the taking. We have already remarked how who we are can be defined, at least in part, by what we attend to—how much more so this is when what we attend to is determined less by our volition and more by ambience. When we speak of living environments and their effects on us, then, we are often speaking too broadly—of the city, the countryside, and so on. Our most immediate environment is actually formed by what holds our attention from moment to moment, whether having received or taken it. As William James once put it, "My experience is what I agree to attend to."

With the establishment of prime time, daytime, and other new zones of attention, we see in effect another feature of the modern self emerge. Insofar as we are influenced, even formed, to some degree, by whatever we pay attention to, the novel fact of an entire population listening to the same show at the same time every day could not help but create a new degree of shared awareness, even shared identity. Prime time was (and to a lesser degree remains) a massive ritual of collective attention, a force drawing people together.

During World War I, George Creel had envisioned welding the American people into one white-hot mass instinct with fraternity, devotion, courage and deathless determination."[21] God and country had always had special tools for achieving this, the ultimate ones being threats of eternal damnation and external force, respectively. But the attention merchants had no access to such threats, or need for them; they would compel us with carrots, not sticks. They would rely on the power of entertainment to weld audiences into a saleable product. The approach, ultimately, would prove no less effective.

CHAPTER 8

THE PRINCE

William S. Paley, president and chairman of the Columbia Broadcasting System, was of a type lost to our times, when vice has ceased to pay virtue its natural tribute, hypocrisy. He was simultaneously well mannered and insatiably hedonistic, cultivating the finest things and the fanciest of friends while maintaining a quiet, understated demeanor. "His strivings were nearly invisible," wrote an associate, "his actions always veiled in gentility."[1] His several marriages, each to a beautiful socialite, never interfered with his sexual conquests. Paley was, in short, a playboy of the old school. And due to timing, coincidence, and some level of innate talent, he would become a primary, and perhaps the prime, merchant of the twentieth century's definitive attention industry, broadcasting.

Paley's entry into it was close to a chance occurrence. Born rich, he had, by age twenty-seven, graduated from college and taken a secure place in the family business, which sold La Palina cigars. His classmates had seen him as destined to do little more than live off his parents' money and chase women and the other pleasures of the bon vivant. But something happened while he was serving as the advertising manager for the family cigar company: he, like so many others, became entranced by radio. The family had decided to advertise on the new medium, whereupon Paley devised the idea of "La Palina girl," a glamorous and sultry singer who was depicted as the only female guest at an all-male gathering of smokers, whom she would amuse with her wisecracks and song. While producing the show, Paley fell in love with La Palina girl—the miraculous sensation of coming up with a hit. While no *Amos 'n' Andy,* his show did drive sales of the family cigars from 400,000 to one million a day—making it "one of radio's earliest spectacular achievements."

So smitten was he that Paley started cajoling his father for a toy, almost as another rich kid might ask for a sports car, and soon, crossing the Atlantic, Samuel Paley would be telling a fellow passenger, "I just bought the Columbia Broadcasting System for my son." As an investment, it seemed foolish at best. The network had long been available to NBC and its boss, David Sarnoff, but it was so tiny (sixteen part-time, low-wattage stations) and NBC so powerful that Sarnoff had written it off as worth neither buying nor destroying. Columbia was an outsider with a limited following, and concerning its first programming, a reviewer in *Radio Broadcast* was brutal. "Probably not a dozen people in the country, beside ourselves, heard it. No one not paid to do so, as we are, could have survived it." Thus, still in his late twenties, Paley became an unlikely captain of what looked like a sinking ship. With his "cocktail slouch" he seemed, according to a contemporary, "just a rich man's son, another angel with ten fingers to burn."

But Paley was easy to underestimate, as he soon showed. In the late 1920s, the business worked this way: network shows were produced either by the networks themselves—so-called public interest, or "sustaining" shows—or by other businesses that "sponsored" a show, the way Pepsodent sponsored *Amos' n' Andy.* The broadcast schedule at most affiliated stations was therefore a combination of these sustaining programs, for which they paid the network a licensing fee, and the sponsored shows, plus whatever fare the local station itself might put on. NBC and CBS lost money producing the sustaining shows, but the idea was to make up the difference with the substantial advertising proceeds from the sponsored shows, of which a small portion went to the affiliates.

In 1928, Paley made a bold offer to the nation's many independent radio stations. The CBS network would provide any of them *all* of its sustaining content *for free*—on the sole condition that they agree to carry the sponsored content as well, for which they would, moreover, receive a handsome check. In short, Paley was offering a full slate of programming, and paying stations to take it—an apparent win-win deal, considering they were often desperate to fill their hours anyhow.

In just three months, Paley shocked the broadcast world by signing twenty-five new affiliates. CBS, once a kind of joke, became larger than either of NBC's Red or Blue networks* in just one fiscal quarter. Paley understood that, under the guise of a giveaway, he was in fact buying audiences on the cheap (a trick similar to that of the American penny press of the 1830s). With his requirement of carrying the full CBS schedule, he had also begun a trend toward homogenizing and nationalizing the content of radio. That would eventually become a cause for complaint, but at the time it was an insuperable competitive advantage: NBC, in contrast, was stingily charging its affiliates to license its sustaining programs, while also driving a hard bargain, on a show-by-show basis, over their share of proceeds from running the sponsored shows—to say nothing of setting very exacting technical requirements to become an NBC station. With CBS and Paley everything was free and easy, good times for all, and so stations were happy to join up.

Paley never understood the technical side of radio well, but he understood from the beginning the very particular and unusual business of being an attention merchant. By that time, there were large new industries, like film, in the relatively straightforward business of selling content. Broadcasting, however, was still in a nebulous state, somewhere between a public service and a business. Officially, radio stations were trustees of the public airwaves and were required, by federal law, to conduct their broadcasting "in the public interest."[2] Accordingly, some stations were noncommercial, and the commercial stations were required to broadcast some programs that were public minded. Nonetheless Paley understood that radio was quickly becoming a business, that amassing a giant audience was key, and that broadcasting would become enor-

---

* From the 1920s, NBC ran two networks: the Red and the Blue. The Red had previously been AT&T's network, until 1926 when AT&T effectively exited the industry, as described in *The Master Switch,* pp. 78–81. In 1942, American antitrust officials ordered NBC to divest the Blue network, which became a third network, the American Broadcasting Company, or ABC.

mously profitable by growing the network and by offering skillful programming. Yet before any of this would work, he would first need to sell advertisers on the possibilities of broadcasting itself.

Over the 1920s and 1930s, CBS produced a series of pamphlets emphasizing the power of broadcasting to reach into the minds of its listeners. One entitled *You Do What You're Told* argued that since people tended to obey human voices, radio advertising would be more compelling than existing print forms. Radio, according to the pamphlet, "presents the living voice of authority," giving it the "supple power to move people and mold them, to enlist them and command them."*

"Here you have the advertiser's ideal—the family group in its moments of relaxation awaiting your message," said CBS. "Nothing equal to this has ever been dreamed of by the advertising man." It is, as we shall see, one thing to sell access to the minds, quite another to predict reliably the audience's frame of mind; and by dictating the moment of infiltration, radio claimed to do just that. At the time and place of CBS's choosing, the audience would be "at leisure and their minds receptive."

The attention merchant's business model was always a bit sinister and easily misunderstood. Among those who never fully seemed to grasp it was Paley's chief rival, radio's incumbent chieftain, David Sarnoff. Sarnoff ran both NBC and the mighty Radio Corporation of America, corporate owner of the NBC network, as well as America's leading seller of radio sets, and later televisions.[3] He had been in the forefront of establishing radio broadcasting itself (as a means of selling radio sets), and the founding of the National Broadcasting Company in 1926, as a "machinery which will insure a national distribution of national programs, and a wider distribution of programs of the highest quality."†

From his palatial offices atop New York's Rockefeller Center, Sarnoff ruled unchallenged, a daunting, if vain and brutal, figure. He did truly have a knack for seeing around the corner, even if he was in the habit of falsifying documents after the fact so as to enhance his reputation for precognition. But for a self-proclaimed visionary, he certainly had his blind spots. Perhaps because of his empire's stake in selling the hardware,

---

* It is worth remembering that we, who now swim in a sea of voices transmitted, recorded, and even synthesized, are conditioned to exhibit less of this reflex.

† Sarnoff's astonishing career is chronicled in *The Master Switch*, chapters 5, 9, and 10.

he never seemed either to fully grasp or appreciate NBC's true mission as an attention merchant. Perhaps he simply didn't like the association with advertising and its hucksters. "We're the pipes," Sarnoff liked to tell his associates, sounding like an industrialist of a previous generation. His success in broadcasting, though considerable, was never premised on catering to audiences, but rather on domination pursued by overwhelming force, lobbying for helpful laws or imposing tough technical standards on affiliates, with the ultimate aim of burying or buying his competitors. As historian David Halberstam put it, "He was not a man of entertainment, he was instead a poet of technology, he understood and loved the instruments themselves, genuinely loved touching them, loved the smell and language of the lab." One might add, he loved the game of war and of building empire.

The contrast between Paley and Sarnoff is deeper and more interesting than it may first appear. Both men were Russian Jews, though from different generations. Sarnoff, schooled in a Minsk yeshiva to be a Talmudic scholar, was brought to America a penniless immigrant; he grew into a gruff and domineering self-made man. "There was no mistaking what David Sarnoff wanted," said longtime NBC executive David Adams. "There was no bullshit." Paley, by contrast, had acquired position, together with polish, as a birthright. Yet he was no snob, quite at ease with admen, entertainers, and Protestants, three groups whom Sarnoff held in varying degrees of contempt. Compared with Sarnoff's commands, Paley's were more like agreeable offers.

Paley was well aware of his rival; and in retrospect, everything he and CBS did was, in one way or another, intended to exploit David Sarnoff's weaknesses. When it came to "talent," for example, Sarnoff was indifferent or hostile to the entertainers who performed on his network. He wouldn't even listen to *Amos 'n' Andy,* his most successful program. An almost comically serious person, he hated comedians, and once said, "If comedy is the center of NBC's activities, then maybe I had better quit."

Paley, meanwhile, loved to flatter and mingle with stars of both Hollywood and CBS. A natural programmer, he had a knack for guessing which entertainers had the ineffable charm to hook an audience, not just once but to make them tune in compulsively. "There were other men who were good businessmen," writes Halberstam, "and others who were deft salesmen, but the feel for talent, that was something else, and it was essential in so public and volatile a profession as broadcasting." Paley's ear was good enough to notice talent from the briefest exposure, so he was always ahead of everyone else. "He could, in 1931, go on a shipboard cruise and by chance hear the records of a then unknown singer and know instantly that the singer was big, very big, and send back a cable telling his subordinates to sign Bing Crosby immediately." To be fair, he didn't place that great a bet: Crosby was given the unenviable task of running opposite *Amos 'n' Andy.*

Not every contrast with Sarnoff worked to Paley's advantage. Unlike his rival or early broadcasting's other important figures, Paley, as mentioned, had no feel for technology, whose future he could barely see into the following week. He never, for instance, understood the potential of FM radio, seeing it merely as a threat to AM. And when it came to television, his myopia would prove prodigious. Seeing the early screens, he assumed they would remain too small to attract home consumers. By the mid-1930s, with television already showing serious potential in Europe, Paley shook his head and succeeded in personally lobbying the FCC to slow it down or block it. Frank Stanton, longtime CBS executive, explained that "Bill did not want television, for he thought it would hurt radio." At the time, Paley "didn't see any profit in TV at all."

———————

By the early 1930s Paley's CBS had reached profitability, and was in a position to take a real run at NBC's dominance. He had earlier hired Edward Bernays, author of *Propaganda,* as an adviser. Bernays suggested that CBS distinguish itself from NBC by emphasizing the superior quality of its programming—the theory of the "Tiffany Network" was thus born—and in that way exploit Sarnoff's weakness in matters of taste.[4] Whether or not the idea was truly Bernays's—one must always ask—as a strategy it served many goals at once.

The race between the penny papers in the 1830s may have given the impression that, among attention merchants, the race always goes to the most lurid and shocking. That does tend to be true over the short term, but over longer spans of time, the matter is more complex. The most successful know how to bear downwind, to get moving, but also the delicate art of bearing back upwind to sustain the audience; a continual diet of the purely sensational wears audiences out, makes them seek some repose. *The New York Times* and *The Wall Street Journal,* for example, both beat out their rivals in the late nineteenth century not by being more sensational, but less, while steering shy of being tedious most of the time. Similarly, the Tiffany strategy was aimed for the network to sustain itself by entering the ranks of respectability.

A second advantage of the strategy was in appeasing progressive critics, who argued, with some reason, that radio, once imagined as a public service, had been hijacked by commercial interests. Broadcast radio was, in its early days, thought of as a miracle of science, a sacred and blessed realm that ought be free from commercial intrusion. It was to be for the education, entertainment, and enlightenment of the public, and should always deliver "the best of everything" as John Reith of the BBC put it. But over the late 1920s and early 1930s the commercial radio network, embodied by NBC and CBS, had pulled radio very far from that original conception, and resistance was growing. Paley wisely understood that if CBS was going to profane the sacred, it had better do it well. The trick was getting the programming just right.*

Programming—the blending of various forms of content to maximize audiences and thereby the value of what networks could sell to advertisers—turned out to be as much an art as a science. The radio networks had originally seen themselves more like carriers of whatever the commercial sponsors wished to present, but Paley took a more active role as the master mixologist, trying to optimize the lineup. Having done a turn in advertising as a young man, he understood the challenge and proved a born talent. He had "a gift of the gods, an ear totally pure." And like some prodigal sons, the Prince Hal type, once vested with real responsibility he would surprise everyone, probably even himself. For as Halberstam writes, "He was a sensualist, who unlike most sensualists, had intense inner discipline."[5]

To his lasting credit, over the 1930s, Paley went very far toward showing that network radio could use its economies of scale to do great things besides making money. The total commercialization of broadcasting,

---

* By the 1940s, the critics, who remained unappeased, briefly took over the Federal Communications Commission and published a report (known as the Blue Book) that condemned the commercialization of radio and demanded that stations failing to serve the public interest have their licenses revoked.

as many scholars have opined, was neither inevitable nor salutary; and it was in large measure Paley's knack for pursuing it with real flair that allowed it to happen without further public outcry. Among his offerings were shows that managed to be both popular and highbrow, a blend matched at the time only by Britain's BBC, and since then unmatched on American airwaves until the founding of National Public Radio in the 1970s. In an early, well-publicized coup, Paley signed the New York Philharmonic to a series of unsponsored concerts. He also signed off on a show named the Columbia Workshop for experimental drama, which featured avant-garde verse plays by well-regarded poets like W. H. Auden, Archibald MacLeish, and others.

In 1938, Paley put on the air a young New York director and actor named Orson Welles. Delighting both critics and audiences, Welles's *Mercury Theatre on the Air* presented new takes on classics, like Shakespeare's *Julius Caesar,* which Welles reimagined as a commentary on the rise of fascism. It was on the same program that Welles would pull his legendary *War of the Worlds* prank. Finding H. G. Wells's novel ill-suited to a traditional performance, Welles and his producer, the actor John Houseman, presented it as a series of dramatized news bulletins, describing an ongoing alien invasion of the United States. It famously caused some panic among listeners who missed the show's disclaimers.*

Paley's programming was, of course, not all so elevated. He knew intuitively how to mix and match high and low, balancing the demands of prestige with those of keeping people awake. Ultimately, it was his sponsored content mainly that filled in the low end and the middle. Seeing that comedians went over well on radio, Paley found Jack Benny, who became "Your Canada Dry Humorist," and also signed the couple George Burns and Gracie Allen. For the female listener (daytime radio), CBS aired a show named *The Voice of Experience,* essentially an advice program, sponsored by Kreml medicinal products. When soap operas became a hit on NBC, CBS profitably programmed half a dozen of its own, including *Just Plain Bill* and *Big Sister,* each with a sponsor like Wonder Bread or Rinso laundry soap.

---

* There is some disagreement on the extent of panic. See Jefferson Pooley and Michael J. Socolow, "The Myth of the War of the Worlds Panic," *Slate,* October 28, 2013 (panic exaggerated); *Radiolab, War of the Worlds,* season 4, episode 3 (panic chronicled).

Knowing how to keep the pot simmering without boiling over in public protest, Paley proactively set limits on CBS's advertising; among them, he cut its share of airtime to 10 percent and banned commercials considered offensive. At the risk of giving him too much credit, one could say that such policies not only kept critics at bay but also showed a shrewd awareness of the attention merchant's eternal dilemma: too little advertising and the business can't grow; too much and the listener grows resentful and tunes out.

Bernays also convinced Paley that nothing would burnish the CBS brand so much as building its reputation for news coverage. The old propagandist's instinct was shrewd indeed. For news would give Paley license to brag to Congress how diligently CBS was covering public affairs, while at the same time having news coverage made it clear that the network had the power to favor or ignore individual politicians, making CBS a political force to be reckoned with. Ultimately CBS created what was the nation's first broadcast news service to compete credibly with print. Radio news had never really been more than a gesture before the mid-1930s; but on the recommendation of Bernays, Paley hired Ed Klauber, former city editor at *The New York Times,* giving him all the resources he asked for. Klauber set high standards and made radio news, and the CBS brand in particular, respected. CBS also became the first network to hire its own reporters—hundreds of them. Paley's commitment revealed either blind luck or prescience, for as the 1930s wore on, and Hitler, Franco, and Mussolini came to power, the news, always a money loser, would suddenly begin drawing millions of listeners.*

Meanwhile, with its head start and double-barreled broadcasting, NBC would remain ascendant for most of the 1930s. Sarnoff would continue to imagine he had one further advantage, and that was Paley himself, or at least his bon vivant side. In a way that seems strange in our age of twenty-four-hour days and driven CEOs, Paley never let his work get in the way of his truest passion, living the good life. In the early 1930s, he pursued Dorothy Hart, a beautiful socialite, married at the time to John Randolph Hearst, son of the newspaper publisher. After persuad-

---

* Print news did not welcome the competition and used various means to attack radio newscasting throughout the early 1920s. In 1933, Paley brokered a treaty with the major newspapers and wire services (the Biltmore Agreement) that limited radio news to certain times to ensure radio did not compete with morning and evening newspapers.

ing her to divorce Hearst, Paley and Hart were married and became, as one writer put it, "the golden couple on the town."[6] They made themselves regulars at hot spots like New York's 21 Club, where he and other "socialites, financiers, actors, showgirls, singers, writers, sportsmen and tycoons . . . were united in pursuit of pleasure." Yet Paley managed to do these things while building a profitable network. In some ways, then, they were not merely a distraction but part of the image of easy refinement he meant to project for the business.

Sarnoff, meanwhile, remained as dogged as ever. His wife, Lizette, would see few nights on the town, spending most with him at home, as sounding board for his ideas. Sanorff's idea of leisure was limited to classical music—he was too serious about everything to stand for light entertainment. His love of winning would never wane. If Paley, with his easy living, was still able to keep up, it was because of a certain imprecision in the measurement of radio audiences, which was somewhat like guesswork. Unfortunately for him there would soon be a new way of keeping score.

———————

Late in 1936, an MIT professor named Robert Elder presented a new invention at a conference held in the ballroom of the Yale Club of New York. He called it the "Audimeter" and claimed that it could scientifically measure human attention, something no one had done before. The crude prototype had two rolls of paper in a reel-to-reel arrangement and was attached to a radio. When the radio was on, a stylus scratched a line onto the slowly turning scroll, indicating over time which stations the radio had been tuned to, and for how long.[7]

At this moment the penetration of broadcasts was a matter of guesswork, and relative standing of competitors in radio was a matter of little solid evidence. In the absence of even remotely scientific metrics, listeners were sometimes canvassed by phone during the evening hours or asked on air to mail in a postcard to receive some small gift—all this to get some idea of how many had heard the commercials. The success of shows like *Amos 'n' Andy* and its effect on the sales of Pepsodent toothpaste made some difference, of course. It was something else, however, to prove that these were no fluke but something worth paying for.

Among those listening in the ballroom was one man for whom the presentation was nothing short of electrifying. Arthur Charles Nielsen, grandfather of today's data geeks, then ran a market research company that had created the "Nielsen Drug Index" and the "Nielsen Food Index." Favoring direct reporting, he hated any kind of data collection in which "human elements" might influence results. Consequently, he had a low opinion of the various, early means of measuring radio audiences, like the Hooper Ratings, dominant over the 1930s, that depended on telephone polling. He wanted harder metrics: "If you can put a number on it," Nielsen was said to say, "then you know something."

Nielsen bought out Elder and his partner, Louis Woodruff, and six years later he had developed a working prototype of his own "black box"; once installed in the home of a family (who were paid for their trouble), it would measure exactly what they were tuning in to. One by one, Nielson sent out his black boxes (which came to be called "people meters"), each one like a nerve ending into the body public, slowly creating a vast network that would tell him just how Americans were spending their evening hours. Thus were modern ratings born, becoming in the words of one expert "a feedback mechanism to the industry the same way that the human nervous system is to the human body." If the United States would now have a nervous system collecting information on the apportionment of attention, Nielsen would be its brain.

The first Nielsen ratings for radio would not be released until 1947. But even in its early form, quantitative measure of attention capture allowed the broadcaster to put a more accurate value on the airtime he was selling; and this, inevitably, began to transform the business. It would, of course, be a mixed blessing, as we will recognize, we who sometimes allow numbers—from stock prices to political polls to batting averages—a disproportionate influence on our decision making. Indeed, Professor Elder, inventor of the Audimeter, would live to lament the effect. Broadcasting, he later said, "suffers greatly from the misuse of the [ratings], and for that reason I am not too happy about my part in getting it started."[8]

––––––––––––

It is interesting to speculate how the intervening history of the medium might have been different had Nielsen ratings existed when, for example, Bill Paley made his improbable bet on broadcast news, positioning CBS to become its leader in that market in the crucial years of the war. Given the successful history of print news—even of more recently established publications, like *Time*—the viability of broadcast journalism ought to have been somewhat predictable. Yet from the beginning, the medium always seemed so much more naturally suited to entertainment than news* that only in the late 1930s would Paley and others realize certainly what a powerful attraction the rush of world events could be, provided they were presented in the right way. The vital difference, it would turn out, was personality, a presenter who was a star in his own right.

In 1937, Paley had sent a twenty-nine-year-old CBS employee named Edward R. Murrow to Europe. As a director of operations, his job was to collect suitable material from news outlets there for rebroadcast in the United States. When, however, Hitler invaded Austria, Murrow was pressed into service as a reporter. At this he proved a natural, becoming the first bona fide star of broadcast news. He had an almost constitution-ally serious disposition and his deep voice seemed to match the gravity of the events. He was, as Paley would later say, "the right man in the right place."

Murrow's broadcasts revealed the medium's matchless power of imme-diacy. Giving his listeners a visceral, emotional sense of being there, it was as if he had created a means of teleportation. Every broadcast he began with "This . . . is London" and then simply described what he had seen that day. "Tonight, as on every other night, the rooftop watchers are peering out across the fantastic forest of London's chimney pots. The anti-aircraft gunners stand ready. I have been walking tonight—there is a full moon, and the dirty-gray buildings appear white. The stars, the empty windows, are hidden. It's a beautiful and lonesome city where men and women and children are trying to snatch a few hours sleep underground."[9]

Murrow had a novelist's sense for telling details; here's how he described London after the evacuation of children to the countryside. "For six days I've not heard a child's voice. And that's a strange feeling. No youngster shouting their way home from school. And that's the way

---

* One might argue that FDR's fireside chats, which garnered audiences as large as any of the most successful entertainments, were an indication to the contrary. But for all the attention they captured, these were perceived less as news than moral uplift, and at any rate, sui generis.

it is in most of Europe's big cities now. One needs the eloquence of the ancients to convey the full meaning of it. There just aren't any more children."[10]

The journalistic approach, while objective, was not neutral. The war was not a subject that he thought deserved a balanced presentation of both sides. His aim was to convey the experience of the British, and he insisted on knowing it firsthand; while most reporters retreated to bunkers during Nazi bombardments, Murrow, despite the obvious peril, stood on the roof to capture the sounds and feeling of London under attack. Later, when the tide of war was turning and the RAF began to bomb Berlin, he would join the British on bombing missions. His first flight, in 1943, was aboard a British Lancaster bomber named D-Dog, part of a force of 660. Here he describes the terror of being caught in a German spotlight:

> And then, with no warning at all, D-Dog was filled with an unhealthy white light. I was standing just behind Jock and could see all the seams on the wings. His quiet Scots voice beat into my ears. "Steady lads, we've been coned." His slender body lifted half out of his seat as he jammed the control column forward and to the left. We were going down. D-Dog was corkscrewing. As we rolled down on the other side, I began to see what was happening to Berlin.[11]

By then Berlin was getting its own back from the Allies. But for years it had been under a different kind of bombardment, one entirely invisible from the ground or the air, and even more relentless. The assault was perpetrated by a demagogue whose mesmerizing oratory had been propagated in measures beyond any the world had seen, capturing more human attention than NBC or CBS could dream of, and indeed holding it captive. And so did this demagogue seize his own nation before his mad attempt to seize all the rest.

CHAPTER 9

TOTAL ATTENTION CONTROL,

OR THE MADNESS OF CROWDS

On March 17, 1935, the opening notes of Beethoven's *Eroica* Symphony filled the air across the German Reich. The sound emerged from millions of radio sets in private homes, many of them the *Volksempfänger,* or "people's receiver," a low-priced product designed for the masses. Also blaring were the giant loudspeakers set up by the volunteer Funkwarte (Radio Guard), so that the notes drifted over public squares, factory yards, restaurants, and offices. The stirring strains of heroism likewise found their way into three thousand designated "listening rooms": meeting halls, courtrooms, and schools outfitted with chairs arranged like pews, into which the Radio Guards had herded citizens. All this for the sake of replacing "the anarchic intellectualism of the individual with the organically developed spirituality of the community."

As the orchestra faded, there was a crackling silence, and then a voice announced, "Now speaks the Führer!" Then came another voice, *the* voice, intimately familiar to every German. On this day, Adolf Hitler announced the reintroduction of military conscription, and with it the rebuilding of a standing German army. His words reached an estimated 70 percent of German households, some 56 million people, more than any fireside chat had reached, almost certainly the largest broadcast audience to that point in human history. It seemed literally true, as a Nazi poster put it, that "All of Germany hears the Führer."[1]

Here was the crowning achievement of the Reichsfunk-Gesellschaft, the National Radio Division of the Ministry of Public Enlightenment and Propaganda of the Third Reich. Its reach and power had caused Minister Joseph Goebbels to declare German radio the "towering herald of National Socialism," a force equal to creating a nation with "one public opinion." His broadcast chief bragged that "with the radio we have destroyed the spirit of rebellion." By means of this attention infrastructure, one man could at will reach the minds of the entire nation, whether they cared to hear him or not. As architect Albert Speer said at his war crimes trial, the Third Reich was the first dictatorship "which made the complete use of all technical means for domination of its own country. Through technical devices like the radio and loudspeaker, 80 million people were deprived of independent thought. It was thereby possible to subject them to the will of one man."[2]

The Reichsfunk-Gesellschaft, with the rest of the ministry's apparatus, was designed to smelt an entire people into a single mass consciousness. Other governments—fascist, communist, democratic—had also experimented with efforts to form, in Creel's expression, this "white hot mass." And after the war, both the Soviet Union and the People's Republic of China would conduct vigorously biased and sustained programs of state broadcasting, ultimately reaching more people. But the Third Reich remains unrivaled in its reach into daily life and its power of coercion.

Early in the twentieth century, the Nazis had developed an advanced understanding of how to gain and use access to the minds of the public. It is a fact no less fascinating and relevant for being so depressing to contemplate. For by testing the extremes of what attention capture could accomplish, the Third Reich obliges us to confront directly the relationship between what we pay attention to and our individual freedom. In producing the "people's community" that the Nazis referred to as *Volksgemeinschaft,* the Nazis effected a shutdown of free thought in the land of Kant, Schiller, and Goethe.

It all began in 1924, in a small prison in southwestern Bavaria, where Hitler described to his lieutenant his great admiration for British propaganda during the First World War. Britain, he mused, had mustered "unheard-of skill and ingenious deliberation"; and "by introducing the German as a barbarian and a Hun to its own people, it thus prepared the individual soldier for the terrors of war and helped guard him against disappointment" and also "increased his fury and hatred against the atrocious enemy."

In short, Britain, he felt, had much to teach Germany, which he considered a complete failure at public relations. He faulted the German Empire, with its "mania for objectivity," for failing to capture the necessary attention. "It was hardly probable that [German efforts] would make the necessary impression on the masses. Only our brainless 'statesmen' were able to hope that with this stale pacifistic dishwater one could succeed in arousing men to die voluntarily."

There is, needless to say, good reason to take Hitler's pronouncements about British and American message control with a grain of salt. Nevertheless, it is true that German propaganda in the First World War tended toward the legalistic, officious, and convoluted. Take Germany's defense of its invasion of Belgium, as articulated by its propaganda official in America in 1914. The main point in his *Saturday Evening Post* commentary is that the relevant peace treaty between Germany and Belgium had, technically, expired. "We were sincerely sorry that Belgium, a country that in fact had nothing to do with the question at issue and might wish to stay neutral, had to be overrun." He goes on to blame the Belgians for not surrendering more quickly—"it would have been entirely possible for Belgium to avoid all the devastation under which she is now suffering." In general, German war propaganda made the elementary error—common among clever people and experts, and familiar to the great ancient orators—of jumping into the complex merits of an issue before having engaged the listener. With their reductive messages and vivid imagery, the British and Americans handily avoided that blunder.

Hitler's entire approach to propaganda might be understood as a reaction to the rationalism for which German thinkers were known. Instead, he had an alarmingly intuitive understanding of how to appeal to a mass audience and to the reptilian core. In *Mein Kampf,* he asks, "To whom has propaganda to appeal? To the scientific intelligentsia, or to the less educated masses? It has to appeal forever and only to the masses!" The strong leader, by "understanding the great masses' world of ideas and feelings, finds, by a correct psychological form, the way to the attention, and further to the heart, of the great masses." Propaganda must "be popular and has to adapt its spiritual level to the perception of the least intelligent. . . . Therefore its spiritual level has to be screwed the lower, the greater the mass of people which one wants to attract."

It can also be understood as a reflection of his time working for the advertising industry. In the early 1910s, while living in Vienna, Hitler made money as a freelancer, drawing advertising posters for products like hair tonic, soap, and "Teddy Antiperspirant foot powder." In *Mein Kampf* he suggests that propaganda need be like advertising, and seek first to attract attention: "A poster's art lies in the designer's ability to catch the masses' attention by outline and color," he writes. It must give "an idea of the importance of the exhibition, but it is in no way to be a substitute for the art represented by the exhibition." Similarly "the task of propaganda lies not in a scientific training of the individual, but rather in directing the masses towards certain facts, events, necessities, etc., the purpose being to move their importance into the masses' field of vision." Those who are "already scientifically experienced or . . . striving towards education and knowledge" are not the subject.

Hitler also intuited a few other basic truths about how we process information: since everything can be ignored, imprinting information in the memory requires a constant repetition of simple ideas. "The great masses' receptive ability is only very limited, their understanding is small, but their forgetfulness is great. As a consequence of these facts, all effective propaganda has to limit itself only to a very few points and to use them like slogans until even the very last man is able to imagine what is intended by such a word." Nuance was nonsense; complexity was a risk: "As soon as one sacrifices this basic principle and tries to become versatile, the effect will fritter away, as the masses are neither able to digest the material offered nor to retain it." One couldn't overstate the intensity of the effort required, for the masses "with their inertia, always need a certain time before they are ready even to notice a thing, and they will lend their memories only to the thousandfold repetition of the most simple ideas."

Finally, Hitler understood the demagogue's most essential principle: to teach or persuade is far more difficult than to stir emotion. And far less welcome: what the audience most wants is an excuse to experience fully the powerful feelings already lurking within them but which their better selves might lead them to suppress.

"The psyche of the great masses is not receptive to anything that is half-hearted and weak. Like the woman, whose psychic state is determined less by grounds of abstract reason than by an indefinable emotional longing for a force which will complement her nature, and who, consequently, would rather bow to a strong man than dominate a weakling, likewise the masses love a commander more than a petitioner and feel inwardly more satisfied by a doctrine, tolerating no other beside itself."

———————

Hitler may have dabbled in advertising, but his real understanding of how to command and use attention came from his career as a popular public speaker in Munich. That career began on October 16, 1919, when the former corporal, now age thirty, gave his first scheduled address, in the basement of a beer hall. At the time, amidst great unrest, the city's many beer halls had become popular venues for political speeches and even rallies of various sizes and political affiliations. Every evening, aspiring polemicists would test their mettle on the bibulous crowd.

Hitler had thrown his lot in with the German Workers' Party (Deutsche Arbeiterpartei, or DAP), a small and somewhat inept organization with only fifty-five members. The DAP was a *völkisch* party, meaning it subscribed to a brand of populism based on a mystical, folkloric link between the Germans and their land. The group's ideal of blood and soil was virulently anti-Semitic. But the DAP was just one of dozens of parties with a similar *völkisch* message and hardly the most prominent one.

Hitler was the little known, second speaker in the evening's lineup, which had attracted a crowd of about one hundred (still more than the organizers had expected). The lengthy opening speech hadn't gotten much of a rise. Then it was Hitler's turn. He had not yet perfected his art, but this would, nevertheless, be a break-out performance—the first time a group of any size had been exposed to his intense, emotionally charged style, punctuated by unwavering certainty and unremitting bile. Hitler later wrote, "I spoke for thirty minutes, and what formerly I had felt in my mind, without knowing it somehow, was now proved by reality. I could speak." After his modestly successful debut, Hitler was invited back, taking his act to larger beer halls, attracting larger crowds, and recruiting more members to the DAP. Finally, in February 1920, he gained headliner status in a large hall, the Hofbräuhaus, with an audience of more than two thousand. Overcoming interruptions by communists, he had by the end gotten the audience shouting and whooping, enraptured by his words. He would return in August to deliver a speech entitled "Why We Are Anti-Semites," which, over the course of its two hours, was interrupted fifty-eight times by wild cheering.

Over the next few years, Hitler would give hundreds of similar speeches, perfecting his performance method. Over time, he developed a winning and invariant structure. He always stood in the same, upright, and serious way, and made the same gestures. His speeches began with a long silence, broken by a soft, almost intimate tone of great personal pain and vulnerability, in which he described his difficult upbringing, service in the war, and despair at Germany's defeat. In a bridge section, he would, with rising fury, begin to assign blame, and denounce all that was wrong in the present. In an incredibly intense finish, he bellowed a flood of unrestrained hatred for Jews, plans for renewed greatness, and, finally, one more great call for German unity.

It was during the Munich years, too, that Hitler first began to conclude his speeches by leading his audiences in a rousing and angry chant. A confidant from those years, Ernst Hanfstaengl, had gone to Harvard, and been impressed with the fight songs used at football games. With Hanfstaengl's guidance, "Fight, Harvard, Fight" thus became "Sieg . . . Heil! Sieg . . . Heil! Sieg . . . Heil! . . . Heil Hitler!"

Even without being Nazis, most of us know the experience of being part of a crowd wild with excitement, and have an intuitive sense that the way our minds process information might change under such circumstances, even to the point that we might come to do something or begin to believe something different. If to pay attention is to open the mind to information, to do so in an animated crowd is to fling the doors wide open. To be exposed to any information is to be influenced, but in crowds the possibilities go well beyond everyday experience. Gustave Le Bon, the first theorist of crowd psychology, held that it is loss of individual responsibility that makes the individual in the crowd more malleable. Freud would say that the superego was supplanted by the will of the crowd, as unconscious wishes rise to the surface and are shared. In any case, we know it when we see it.[3]

Among the more notable historic examples is the reaction to William Jennings Bryan's "Cross of Gold" speech at the Democratic National Convention in Chicago in 1896. A thirty-six-year-old former Nebraska congressman, with no following going into the convention, Bryan managed to win the nomination by delivering a plea for pegging the dollar to silver as well as gold in order to increase the monetary supply and broaden economic opportunity. But Bryan brought the house down not merely with what he said but how he said it. "Upon which side will the Democratic Party fight; upon the side of 'the idle holders of idle capital' or upon the side of 'the struggling masses'?" He ended the speech, famously, with a pantomime of a crown and a cross, saying, "You shall not press down upon the brow of labor this crown of thorns. You shall not crucify mankind on a cross of gold."

A correspondent for *The Washington Post* described the crowd's response:

> Words cannot impart the strange and curious magnetism which filled the atmosphere. Bedlam broke loose, delirium reigned supreme. In the spoken word of the orator thousands of men had heard the unexpressed sentiments and hopes of their own inmost souls. The great mass of humanity threw forth the fiery lava of its enthusiasm like Vesuvius in eruption . . . the stamping of the feet was as the roll of thunder among the echoing Alps, and the hurricane of sound almost caused the steel girders of the roof to tremble with its perceptible volume. Every man in the vast audience climbed upon his chair and, infected by the cyclonic frenzy of the moment, seemed absolutely oblivious to what he did or what he said. . . . The almost lunatical excitement was shown by the incident of one woman, who, standing upon a chair, shouted like a savage, and danced like a savage.

So persuasive was Bryan's performance that the crowd carried him aloft on their shoulders before nominating him. And yet it seems obvious that if the same speech were delivered tonight in your living room you might not even remain awake through the end. In fact, Bryan himself had delivered much the same speech in Nebraska the week before, drawing little attention, never mind acclaim.[4]

Over the last decade or so, scientists have begun to investigate joint attention, confirming the intuition that the brain's attentional faculties do operate differently when one is in a group paying attention to the same thing. They've discovered, for example, that when individuals pay attention jointly to a mental rotation test, each actually solves it faster than if he were working in isolation—amazingly, since each person is working independently. It is therefore only more interesting that humans are not born with the ability to pay joint attention; it develops over the first eighteen months of life, as an infant first learns to follow a parent's gaze and pay attention to what he or she is looking at.[5]

Almost everyone who heard the führer agreed that his speeches were mesmerizing. Hanfstaengl allowed that "what Hitler was able to do to a crowd in 2½ hours will never be repeated in 10,000 years." He gave some credit to biology. "Because of his miraculous throat construction, he was able to create a rhapsody of hysteria." Albert Speer described himself on first hearing Hitler speak as being "intoxicated" and feeling that "all can be changed."

Another contemporary put it this way: "Hitler responds to the vibration of the human heart with the delicacy of a seismograph . . . enabling him, with a certainty with which no conscious gift could endow him, to act as a loudspeaker proclaiming the most secret desires, the least permissible instincts, the sufferings and personal revolts of a whole nation."

Le Bon and Freud are now hardly considered cutting-edge guides to how the mind works, but here, in the words of the enraptured, their ideas seem to shine through.

Alfons Heck would remember attending a Nazi rally as a boy in the 1930s. He was not particularly partial to or interested in Hitler; yet at the conclusion of the führer's speech the boy was transformed: "From that moment on, I belonged to Adolf Hitler body and soul." The rally Heck attended, one of those held annually at Nuremberg, boosted Hitler's oratorical effects with various other elements—lights, giant swastika banners, and marching men—to create what Albert Speer called "total theatre." As one attendant described the experience:

Nothing like it has ever been seen before. The wide field resembles a powerful Gothic cathedral made of light. . . . One hundred and forty thousand people . . . cannot tear their eyes away from the sight. Are we dreaming, or is it real? Is it possible to imagine a thing like that? . . . Seven columns of flags pour into the spaces between the ranks. . . . All you can see is an undulating stream, red and broad, its surface sparking with gold and silver, which slowly comes closer like fiery lava.

As Leni Riefenstahl, the filmmaker who documented the 1935 gathering called the "Rally of Freedom," wrote, "What I witnessed in Nuremberg . . . is one of the most remarkable events I have ever experienced. It was all so gripping and grandiose that I cannot compare it to anything I experienced before as an artist."[6]

––––––––––––

It was in 1933, soon after his appointment as chancellor of Germany, that Hitler began to engineer the institutions for his conquest of German minds through the new Ministry for Public Enlightenment and Propaganda, run by his loyal lieutenant Dr. Paul Joseph Goebbels, then just thirty-six years old. Goebbels, if anything, would exceed Hitler in understanding how to capture attention on a mass scale and what to do with it.

At the core of the Third Reich's attention project was a relatively simple idea: to scale the enrapturing effects of Hitler's speeches so as to influence the whole population. Hitler's speeches were, after all, what had turned a party with just fifty-five members into the Nazi movement and a threat to the entire world. They furnished the effort its spiritual dimension. The technical challenge for the ministry, then, was to project the effects of the rally, which at most reached hundreds of thousands of party loyalists, across the nation of 80 million. Under previous dictatorships, the limits of mass attention had been defined by the size of a physical venue—so that the triumphal parade or mass rally was the outer bound. Using radio and film, however, the ministry saw how such physical limits might be dissolved, making it possible to hold the intimate joint attention of millions.[7]

In August 1933, Goebbels gave a speech outlining his priorities. "The radio," he said, "is the most influential and important intermediary between a spiritual movement and the nation, between the idea and the people." As such, it had to be the center of the Nazi project: "A government that has determined to bring a nation together so that it is once more a center of power in the scales of great world events has not only the right, but the duty, to subordinate all aspects of the nation to its goals, or at least ensure that they are supportive. That is also true for the radio. The more significant something is in influencing the will of the broad masses, the greater its responsibility to the future of the nation."[8]

That radio could be used this way was not an idea that had originated with Goebbels; over the 1920s and 1930s a number of states had depended on it to promote national unity and inspiration. As in other areas of propaganda, Britain was arguably the pioneer: in the 1920s, the BBC was by far the most advanced state-owned radio system in the world, and by 1924, it would first begin broadcasting speeches by King George V—long before the stammering George VI would have to rally the nation to challenge the Third Reich. Likewise, Lenin's regime took over Russian radio soon after the communist revolution, and made Radio Moscow the most powerful station on earth in the 1930s, since its main concern was fomenting revolution abroad. As for the United States, where the radio station was invented, the system there was to remain in private hands, used for advertising, with the exception of the occasional fireside chat.

In 1933 the Third Reich trailed England, and possibly the Soviet Union, but as in so many areas it caught up quickly and outstripped its models, borrowing, in a sense, from both Soviet and Western techniques. Like the Soviets, the German ministry took over every detail of programming, with sole discretion over the content. As chief programmer, Goebbels determined that the right formula for forging the people's community *(Volksgemeinschaft)* was not unrelenting speeches but, rather, light musical entertainment punctuated by political material in place of advertising, and the occasional big event—a speech by Hitler or Goebbels, termed a "national moment." He learned, as the Western attention merchants had learned, that a spoonful of sugar helps the medicine go down. And in this way, exposure to the central themes of the National Socialist Party became part of the daily diet of nearly every German.

To the American scholar Max Lerner, writing in 1933, it was obvious how much the ministry had borrowed from America. "The democratic state . . . evolved a technique of advertising and of high pressure salesmanship, a flamboyant journalism, a radio and a cinema that stamped the same stereotypes on millions of brains . . . the most damning blow the dictatorships have struck at democracy has been the compliment they have paid us in taking over and perfecting our most prized techniques of persuasion and our underlying contempt for the credulity of the masses." In short, the Third Reich had grasped the lessons of 1910s propaganda and 1920s advertising and put them to its own use.[9]

Toward its objective of complete inclusiveness, the ministry introduced, as mentioned, the *Volksempfänger,* or "people's receiver." Easily within the means of the average worker, the radio was marketed extensively; so that by 1942 Germany had increased its radio audience from 4.5 to over 16 million households. The Nazi state matched Britain and America in radio penetration, giving the leadership the sort of intimate access to homes that *Amos 'n' Andy* enjoyed.

There was one feature, however, that had eluded NBC and CBS. Radio can be ignored or turned off; one might even choose to listen to foreign stations. The Propaganda Ministry's answer to such problems was to outfit a small army called the Funkwarte, the Radio Guard, party loyalists assigned to every neighborhood or apartment block to make sure that the radio was being listened to. As Eugen Hadamovsky, head of broadcasting, wrote, the Radio Guard were the "living bridge" between the party and the nation, who created the "human contact between radio and its listeners" and also, later, reported anyone who dared seek alternative sources of information.

The German Radio Division saved its greatest efforts for the "national moments," *(Stunden der Nation),* like the one at the beginning of this chapter, for which the entire nation suspended activity and the Radio Guard herded all the people into listening rooms. The resemblance to congregating for a religious service was no accident but a conscious mimicry of the "total experience of worship in a church." It has been debated whether Nazism constituted a "political religion." Certainly, in keeping with the theory of political religions, it did try to supplant the spiritual authority of the existing churches, Lutheran and, to a lesser degree, Catholic.* One of the prime means of accomplishing this at the popular

---

* In *The 'Hitler Myth,'* Ian Kershaw discusses the *Kirchenkampf,* or "church struggle," the Reich's effort to Nazify the German church, purging it of all individuals who resisted the new ideology of blood and soil in favor of traditional Christian teachings.

level was by imposing regular and compulsory shared attention of the sort that religion has always demanded of its adherents.[10]

————————

The Nazi regime's extreme, coercive demands on attention oblige us to consider the relationship between control over one's attention and human freedom. Take the most elementary type of freedom, the freedom to choose between choices A and B, say, chocolate or vanilla.

The most direct and obvious way authoritarians abridge freedom is to limit or discourage or ban outright certain options—NO CHOCO-LATE, for instance. The State might ban alcohol, for example, as the United States once did and a number of Muslim nations still do; likewise it might outlaw certain political parties or bar certain individuals from seeking office. But such methods are blunt and intrusive, as well as imperfect, which is true of any restriction requiring enforcement. It is therefore more effective for the State to intervene before options are seen to exist. This creates less friction with the State but requires a larger effort: total attention control.

Freedom might be said to describe not only the size of our "option set" but also our awareness of what options there are. That awareness has two degrees. One is conceptual: if you don't know about a thing, like chocolate ice cream, you can hardly ask for it, much less feel oppressed by the want of it. The second degree of awareness comes after we know about things conceptually and can begin to contemplate them as real choices. I may be aware that man has gone into space but the idea that I might choose to go there myself, while conceivable, is only a notion until I find out that Virgin Galactic has started scheduling flights.[11]

To take a more common recent example: in the 1990s, switching to a Mac from a PC seemed implausible. Then, Apple ran an advertising campaign showing how it might be done, and what the advantages of doing so were. Soon, there were many happy Mac users, and Apple's market share grew dramatically. When done well, and on behalf of a worthwhile product, advertising can, in this way, advance human freedom, by showing that choices exist and making them seem real. But advertising can also obscure choices, or (as we have seen) present false ones (e.g., "Use this product or suffer the embarrassing consequences").

Nonetheless the advertiser, unless a monopolist, usually remains within the realm of persuasion among a background of choice. True propaganda, by contrast, aims to obliterate that marketplace and the choices as such, by making them seem unthinkable or nonexistent. Only in rare cases is commercial advertising that powerful.

Stated differently, Hitler was not just selling a choice, but a comprehensive vision of reality. To make such a sale, the message had to be complete, monolithic, without a single crack or weakness. The State, as Hitler put it, must "serve its own truth uninterruptedly," for "as soon as by one's own propaganda even a glimpse of right on the other side is admitted, the cause for doubting one's own right is laid." Alternative views, like alternative choices, had no place in this scheme, in which the purposes and ideas of the individual are subsumed into that of the whole, in keeping with the *Volksgemeinschaft*. That this itself can serve as a kind of carrot is often lost amid liberal idealism, which can overestimate how deep our devotion to choice really runs. Choice may be the cornerstone of individual freedom but, as the history of humanity shows, the urge to surrender to something larger and to transcend the self can be just as urgent, if not more so. The greatest propagandists and advertisers have always understood this.

With total attention control, the Nazi Propaganda Ministry was able to sell a new faith, one vested not in the power of choice but in the glory of something greater and of giving oneself over to it. "There are two ways to make a revolution," Goebbels wrote in 1933. "One can fire at the opponent with machine guns until he recognizes the superiority of those who have the machine guns. That is the simplest way. One can also transform a nation through a revolution of the spirit, not destroying the opponent, but winning him over." This he meant not in the sense of winning an argument, but actually displacing individual thought and all its conflicting impulses. As Goebbels put it, "We want to replace liberal thinking with a sense of community that includes the whole people."[12]

––––––––––––

The Third Reich's propaganda was so extreme, its manipulations so blunt and destructive, and its practitioners so vile that it necessarily left a profound impression on the rest of the century, one even greater than the

British and American campaigns of the First World War. In the immediate aftermath, it was as if three completely different lessons were drawn, one by the Soviet Union (which controlled East Germany), another by West Germany, and a third by the former Allies, including the United States.

As mentioned, the Soviets had a State-controlled media before the war, and in some ways the Nazis had learned from it. After the war, the Soviets would repay the compliment: Stalin and the rest of the Politburo concluded that Soviet propaganda needed to operate at a greater scale, for the Germans had shown what it meant to be truly pervasive. Radio broadcasting, which had been used during the war to mobilize the population, was continued and supplemented with television. The Soviets would never fully match the degree of organizational skill of the Nazis, or the spiritual cultivation—such perhaps are the limits of Marx's materialism. Nonetheless, for decades to come, the State would decide what information would be available at all, as it sought to establish its single and, to a substantial degree, galvanizing truth.

West Germany, chastened by the disgrace of the Nazi state, went to the opposite extreme. The Allied occupiers rebuilding the shattered nation were determined that it should never come under the same sort of attentional control that had made ascendant Nazism possible. They therefore reconstituted the broadcast infrastructure so as to make it notably ill-suited for government or corporate propaganda. Both radio and television were decentralized, the network broken up into independent, nonprofit regional broadcasters. To preserve its independence, broadcast would be funded by licensing fees paid by every household and institution, including municipalities; the undue influence engendered by financial reliance on commercial advertising (as in the U.S.) or State grants (as in the U.K.) was thus avoided.

A similar lesson was drawn in the United States and in other parts of Western Europe but, of course, it could not be implemented as fully in the unvanquished countries, where there wasn't the luxury to start from scratch. Most of the Western powers did become decidedly averse to any large, State-run propaganda projects, even Great Britain and the United States, the original inventors and innovators. What efforts continued were directed at the Red threat overseas (as with Radio Free Europe) or with matters of unambiguous public interest, like fire prevention (the

Smokey Bear ads) or the dangers of drug addiction. Otherwise, even the word "propaganda"—once neutral or positive enough to serve as the title of Edward Bernays's book on corporate public relations—became an unambiguous pejorative. And it is surely no coincidence that during the same interval, over the 1950s, the American First Amendment first came to life and began to be used as a serious check on government's power over speech.

But if official propaganda fell into ignominy, there was no such effect on its commercial cousin, advertising. Indeed government's discontinuation of wartime media messaging, in a sense, left the field more open for business interests, who, just as they had immediately following the previous world war, filled the vacuum. After the war, commercial broadcasters would enjoy both the powers of centralized control and the perennial lure of advertising revenues.[13]

What could possibly go wrong?

CHAPTER 10

PEAK ATTENTION, AMERICAN STYLE

Back in the United States, with the war over, all eyes turned to television, the newest and most exciting invention since radio. And in 1950, Mr. Nielsen's new ratings made it official: the National Broadcasting Company ruled the new medium, with exclusive ownership of the five top-rated shows:

Texaco Star Theater NBC
Fireside Theatre NBC
Philco Television Playhouse NBC
Your Show of Shows NBC
Colgate Comedy Hour NBC

On Tuesdays at 8 p.m., 61.6 percent of the 10 million families with a television were tuned to *Texaco Star Theater*. It began with the four "merry Texaco men" (as they called themselves) singing their catchy refrain, "Tonight we may be showmen, / Tomorrow we'll be servicing your cars." The host was a cross-dressing former vaudevillian named Milton Berle; he called himself "Mr. Television," and his brand of humor did not aim high.[1] Following the Texaco men, Berle burst through the curtains outlandishly costumed, usually in drag, whether as Carmen Miranda, or as Cinderella, or as a bride in white escorted by Fatso Marco,

Berle's shorter sidekick. The setup would then give way to Berle's famous torrent of one-liners.

It was not a particularly high bar for television set by NBC and Berle. But the ratings were a triumph for NBC's overlord, David Sarnoff, who as early as 1923 had prophesied the medium's importance. A firm believer in what would later be called "first mover advantage," he had decided during the 1930s that dominating television would be essential to both RCA (which made the sets) and NBC. The world war had ended but the television war had just begun. And so Sarnoff insisted (via internal memo) that he be referred to as "General" David Sarnoff, the "Father of Television."* Bill Paley, meanwhile, entered the postwar period wishfully thinking that radio would remain the main action; sure enough, CBS's lackluster TV ratings reflected this halfheartedness. But even if he were proved wrong, he would keep the mind-set of a middle distance runner, caring not so much about the fast start as finishing first. Going second and waiting for the lay of the land to reveal itself was always less risky. And still believing that Sarnoff basically misunderstood broadcasting, Paley was confident that he and his deep team of programmers could wipe out NBC's lead when the opportunity came. The subsequent race, over the 1950s, would define for decades what the "second screen"— television—would become.

The migration of the screen into the home of every family was an event of unparalleled significance in the history of the attention industries and their influence over people's lives. The poster had always been a sort of prototype. But the first real screens, those in the motion picture theaters, had a seemingly magical power to capture attention. The filmgoer "feels as if he were passing through life with a sharper accent which stirs his personal energies," wrote the psychologist Hugo Münsterberg in 1916. "Love and hate, gratitude and envy, hope and fear, pity and jealousy, repentance and sinfulness, and all the similar crude emotions . . . help greatly to excite and to intensify the personal feeling of life and to stir the depths of the human mind."[2]

---

* The latter was particularly ironic insofar as its only basis was that he'd personally bankrupted and destroyed television's actual inventors; see *The Master Switch,* chapter 10.

A neuroscientist might say that cinema had always shown the ability to activate our mirror neurons, the brain cells known to light up identically whether we observe someone perform an act or do it ourselves.[3] It happens, too, when an image is close enough to reality to make our brain identify with what it sees. Perhaps this partly explains why, even by contemporary standards, television was adopted quickly.

Early models were too expensive: between $5,000 and up to $20,000 in present dollars for a picture tube encased in wooden cabinetry. So most people first saw TV in a saloon. But from a mere 9 percent of homes in 1950, it was in 72 percent by 1956. Once ensconced in private space, it immediately began to devour time—nearly five hours a day by the end of the decade—causing a mixture of excitement, fascination, and fear.

Given TV's novelty and limited offerings, early audiences were not fickle channel surfers. Contemporary accounts suggest something much more like the deeply immersive experience of motion pictures. Indeed, the lights were usually turned off for viewing, and there was little or no conversation. One only got up to change the channel. "We ate our suppers in silence, spilling food, gaping in awe," said one woman in 1950. "We thought nothing of sitting in the darkness for hours at a stretch without exchanging a word except 'who's going to answer that confounded telephone?'"[4]

We have, to this point, treated all attention paid as more or less the same, which is a reasonable way to broach a complex subject. And it is all the same, insofar as everything that captures it enters our mind the same way. But of course there are differences in *quality* of attention; watching an airplane fly overhead is not as involving as being engrossed in a film. We might half listen to a professor babble, but our ears prick up at the sound of a marriage proposal. The most basic dividing line is likely between *transitory* and *sustained* attention, the former quick, superficial, and often involuntarily provoked; the latter, deep, long-lasting, and voluntary. What matters for present purposes is that selling us things relies mainly on the former—on which the attention merchant thrives—but our happiness depends on balancing the two.

As the immersive power of the movie screen was brought into the home, some could already see that it might be a force for greatness or nothingness. "It is also almost like a giant eye on life itself," wrote the novelist Calder Willingham, "and can easily become the vehicle for masterpieces of a magnitude and power never achieved before in the arts, given the artists to create them and the audience to support them. For this very reason, it would also become the worst cultural opiate in history, buy and corrupt all talent, and completely degrade the sensibility of the country. Everything depends on the use to which television is put."[5]

Just what uses would the attention gathered by television be put to? The next decade would begin to answer that question.

Though dominant in ratings, NBC still clearly suffered from the same weakness in programming that had limited it in radio, mainly because of Sarnoff's indifference to content. When Paley and his team of programmers launched their attack, the strategy would be one that had worked before, that of promoting CBS as the higher-quality alternative—the Tiffany Network—purveyor of the best of the best.

NBC's lackadaisical approach was epitomized by the *Camel News Caravan,* its television news show. The fifteen-minute *Caravan* was hosted by a former actor, John Cameron Swayze, and consisted mainly of his reading out headlines and playing newsreels designed for movie theaters, until delivering his signature sign-off, "That's the story folks," almost the same one used by Porky Pig.[6] The show was not only superficial but also subject to onerous censorship and direction by Camel's owner, the R. J. Reynolds Company. The sponsors preferred upbeat news, and mandated coverage of football (for men) and fashion (for women). They also set out a surprisingly detailed speech code that barred any display of competing brands, pipes, cigars, not to mention "no-smoking signs" as well as actual, living camels. When, in 1952, *Reader's Digest* published a report linking, for the first time, cigarettes and cancer, the ensuing media sensation somehow never reached the *Camel News Caravan.* As one writer put it, "What Camel wanted, Camel got . . . because they paid so much."[7]

Anyone could do better than that, and CBS soon established itself as the leader with *CBS Television News* (later renamed the *CBS Evening News*). In 1951, CBS radio's star, Edward Murrow, appeared on television, perhaps surprising viewers, who had only ever heard his voice. His first show, *See It Now,* was produced by another legend, Fred Friendly, and offered something new—a weekly news analysis, critical in nature, accompanied by clips and delivered by the charismatic Murrow, languorously smoking cigarettes. *The New York Times* generously praised the new competitor, perhaps not yet fully seeing it as such: "A striking and compelling demonstration of the power of television as a journalistic tool . . . in its emotional impact, sensitivity and drama, the commentator's thirty-minute review of the week's news was in all respects a magnificent achievement."[8]

See It Now became deservedly famous in the history of journalism for a series of episodes broadcast in 1954, wherein Murrow decided to challenge American senator Joseph McCarthy's Red Scare—his ceaseless investigations of alleged communists in the U.S. government and other institutions. It was widely and correctly taken as an act of bravery, for McCarthy was vindictive and indeed would try to destroy CBS. But Murrow succeeded in exposing him as a witch-hunter and a bully, and this was partly owing to the power of the medium: the same screen that made Murrow appear serene and dependable made McCarthy, with his strange and craven mannerisms, look like a monster.[9]

There is another dimension to this story that has become clearer with time. McCarthy was basically a typical twentieth-century government propagandist; like Creel, Mussolini, or Goebbels, he used the looming foreign threat to inflame hatred for marginal groups (communists mainly, but also gays) for the sake of amassing power. By exposing him, Murrow and CBS demonstrated not only courage but also the power of the private sector and, in particular, the attention industries, to defeat official propaganda. That had never happened before. And it coincided with the Supreme Court's slow and gradual rediscovery of the First Amendment as a tool to check government controls on free speech.*

Meanwhile, NBC answered its rivals by investing in an unsponsored news program of its own, this one called *The Huntley-Brinkley Report*. Paley, however, was never interested in running a public broadcasting

---

* The Court's progress was admittedly uneven. It had strengthened First Amendment protections in the 1940s in cases like *Taylor v. Mississippi* (1943); yet it remained weak enough that the Court would in 1951 uphold the arrest and conviction of Communist Party leaders in *Dennis v. United States* based on the premise that they intended to overthrow the government. By the middle of the decade the position had softened, and convictions of communists were being overturned, as in *Yates v. United States* (1957). *Dennis* was overruled in 1969.

service; he still wanted only to wrest away the claim NBC had on audiences. In 1952, he struck gold.

Lucille Ball was a forty-year-old radio and B-film actress of modest success, and also a friend of Paley's. Her radio show *My Favorite Husband* became *I Love Lucy* with Philip Morris as its sponsor. Playing on Mondays at 9 p.m., it was an instant hit, within a year soaring past Milton Berle to take the top spot in Nielsen's ratings. In 1953, the show attracted an astonishing average 71.3 percent of audiences, and as an average for an entire season, that figure remains unsurpassed.

What attracted audiences—sometimes over 50 million—to the show was, as everyone agrees, Lucille Ball herself. The show revolved around serial failure: Lucy's desperate wish for a career in show business; she would do anything, no matter how ridiculous, to get her foot in the door. Invariably, for one reason or another, her plots would fall apart. But if her schemes failed, Ball's performance succeeded brilliantly as spectacle. The medium was made for personalities.

An even more unlikely rejoinder to the manic Milton Berle appeared when CBS's programmers found a stone-faced and awkward New York *Daily News* gossip columnist named Ed Sullivan, whose show (originally entitled *The Toast of the Town*) had a shaky start. On first viewing it, even the unerring Paley insisted that Sullivan be temporary. (His evident "anti-talent" would inspire the classic remark that "Ed does nothing, but he does it better than anyone else on television.") But Sullivan's talent wasn't his presence on camera; rather, as with Paley, it was his connections and an eye for the talent of others, and his show gradually took off until it became the most watched on Sunday evenings by a broad margin.

And so it was that CBS and Paley made inexorable inroads, until, by 1955, the rising power had broken NBC's dominance. Not that Paley's lifestyle suffered a whit in the process: in 1947, he had married his second wife, the *Vogue* writer and fashion icon "Babe" Cushing Mortimer, of whom the designer Billy Baldwin said, "So great is her beauty, each time I see her, it is as if for the first time." (Today Babe Paley is perhaps best remembered for her remark that "a woman can never be too thin or too rich.") The two moved into the St. Regis Hotel and spent their weekends in Long Island with friends, who grew to include authors, actresses, and other bon vivants, drawn mainly from the creative classes.

Paley and CBS had done it again, overtaking NBC in five years without breaking a sweat. But this time, however, Sarnoff wasn't content to lose gracefully. In 1953, he would appoint his own star programmer, giving him license to wage total war. As David Halberstam would later write, never had there been a "competition . . . so fierce . . . with weapons so inane."[10]

———————

We can credit these years, the mid-1950s, with the achievement of "peak attention." By that, I mean something quite specific. A historic anomaly, unprecedented and eventually to dissolve, this was the moment when more regular attention was paid to the same set of messages at the same time than ever before or since. The phenomenon resulted from a confluence of the prime-time ritual, the novelty of television, and industry concentration—all combining to create within the Free World the routinely massive audiences previously possible only in fascist and communist regimes. Peak attention would continue through the 1970s, with CBS, NBC, and eventually ABC taking turns at winning the big prize of nearly 60 or 70 million viewers at a time. Nevertheless, the peak of peak attention can be assigned an exact date: Sunday, September 9, 1956, when Elvis Presley made his first appearance on television, on CBS's *Ed Sullivan Show*. Its 82.6 percent share of viewers (out of a U.S. population roughly half of today's) has never been equaled or bettered.

With a great many Americans, sometimes even a majority, watching the same programs, exposed to the same information, every day—or if not exactly the same, the same theme with slight variations—a kind of convergence was inevitable. Sitting in silence, everyone would "receive the same impulses and impressions, find themselves focused on the same centers of interest, experience the same feelings, have generally the same order of reactions or ideas, participate in the same myths—and all this at the same time."[11] That there were three channels to choose from hardly mattered. As the advertising-executive-turned-activist Jerry Mander would write:

It was as if the whole nation had gathered at a gigantic three-ring circus. Those who watched the bicycle act believed their experience was different from that of those who watched the gorillas or the flame eater, but everyone was at the circus.

What was missing was the exaltation of the rally, the thrill of losing oneself in the common experience for as we all watched from our separate living rooms, it was as if we sat in isolation booths, unable to exchange any responses about what we were all going through together. Everybody was engaged in the same act at the same time, but we were doing it alone. What a bizarre situation! [12]

The 1950s would be remembered as a decade of conformity, and while the reasons may be many and complex, one cannot exclude the most salient: the historically anomalous scale of attention capture effected by television, together with the homogeneity of the stuff created to do the capturing. This was, of course, not enforced viewing; there were, as mentioned, three channels, and no facist "Television Guard"—though given the primacy of the ratings champions, most Americans were indeed watching the same shows and the same advertisements most of the time.

Was this propaganda? Certainly, it wasn't experienced that way, and that difference does matter. After all, watching television was voluntary (even if everyone made the same choice); the medium was run not by the State, but private companies, whose goals were commercial, not political. Some of course have contended that shows like *I Love Lucy* did have an underlying social agenda or at least ideology. What must be remembered, however, is that *Lucy* and the other attractions were merely the bait; the effort to persuade came in a different form: a form new to the world, known as the "television commercial."

––––––––––

"The customer is not a moron, she's your wife," wrote David Ogilvy in 1955, expressing, in the vernacular of the times, a buoyant new mentality among American advertising executives.[13] Having nearly collapsed over the 1930s, advertising now found itself, much as it did after World War I, the prime beneficiary of a new medium and a postwar return of consumer spending. Ultimately, the 1950s, if not as individually enriching as the 1920s had been, would be the industry's golden age, as advertising spending quadrupled from 1950 through 1960, from $1.3 billion to

$6 billion, or approximately from $11.5 billion to $54 billion in present value. Advertising was back, ready to feed off of television's bountiful harvest of America's attention. It must have seemed only fair, since every other business was doing the same.

In New York, the embodiment of the new industry was Rosser Reeves, a hard-drinking, hard-sell Virginian, and yet another son of a preacher, who'd made his name as a pioneer of television advertising. The first commercials were primitive—cartoons were common, and it was enough to import the best techniques from print advertising. Reeves soon proved himself the Claude Hopkins of the screen, selling products with claims they would do something for you, thanks to some distinguishing factor. The approach once called "reason-why" advertising was rebranded by Reeves as the "unique selling proposition."* By no surprise, it worked best for medicines. Reeves's television spot for Anacin pain-reliever depicted a hammer striking inside someone's head and promised, based on the unique formula, "fast, fast, fast relief." Reeves even found a way to sell candy as a solution to a problem—M&M's: they "melt in your mouth, not in your hand."[14]

The softer, brand-driven side of advertising made its own comeback, personified by Leo Burnett, a Chicago adman who, working at Cadillac under Theodore MacManus, learned the art of warm associations. Burnett's personal specialty was developing the brand mascot, at which he had no peer. He transformed the Jolly Green Giant, formerly a terrifying ogre, into a beneficent friend, a deity of abundance and protection. "None of us can underestimate the glacier-like power of friendly familiarity" was how Burnett put it, and the Pillsbury Doughboy was his creation as well.[15] Promoting Kellogg's cereals, Tony the Tiger emerged as a sort of eater's id incarnate, announcing with a roar, "They're GRRREAT!" But Burnett's most famous makeover was performed on a human. The Marlboro cigarette had originally been conceived to appeal to women in the late 1920s, with the slogan "Mild as May." When Philip Morris decided to target men instead, Burnett thought that smoking cowboys would

---

* The concept of the "unique selling proposition" followed three requirements: first, the advertisement must propose that the product offer a specific benefit; second, the proposition must be unique and one that competition cannot, or does not, offer; third, the proposal must influence the mass to use or switch over to your product. For more, see Rosser Reeves, *Reality in Advertising* (New York: Alfred A. Knopf, 1961).

efficiently convey masculinity.* *The Economist* would later describe the Marlboro Man as "a mysterious wanderer, a modern Odysseus journeying who knew where; or perhaps a Jungian archetype, ranging the primeval savannah as man had done for most of the past 10,000 years. He was alone by choice in the vastness of the hills and plains, running his cattle and closely encountering wild white horses: alone save for that manly cigarette lodged in his thin, grim lips. Flinty and unconcerned, he would light the next smoke from a flaming stick plunged into his campfire."[16]

Launched in 1955, the Marlboro Man campaign was Burnett's most successful and among the most astonishing campaigns in the history of demand engineering. But upon the cowboy's appearance, Marlboro went from a mere 1 percent of sales to become the fourth bestselling brand in the United States within a year; its sales increased by an astonishing 3,000 percent over that time. Burnett had not modeled the Marlboro Man on himself—he was "rumpled, pillow-shaped, balding and jowly" with "heavy horn-rimmed glasses perched on his spud-like nose."[17] He also proclaimed himself adverse to psychological theory, though he did write that "the cowboy is an almost universal symbol of admired masculinity," and perhaps he had sensed among men in the civilizing 1950s a need for reassurances on that score. In any event advertising was proving that it could project not only "reasons why" but whole mythologies; it was naturally suited to things of the spirit.

If Burnett was trafficking in archetypes, he was not alone; Jungian and Freudian thought had reached the zenith of their influence, both in society and in the advertising industry, where once they had been skeptically brushed off. If ideas of appealing to unconscious desires were once merely in the air, now an array of firms run by professional psychologists offered "motivation research," aimed at the deepest human desires. It is hard to measure, and easy to exaggerate, how effective this analysis was; nonetheless, by 1954 there were at least eight good-sized firms offering it as a billable service. Just as in the good old days, it was under the guise of a science, until, as one reporter put it in 1959, "The difference between an ad man and a behavioral scientist became only a matter of degree."[18]

---

* The earliest Marlboro campaigns went beyond cowboys to include sailors, construction workers, and others, each of whom for some reason had a tattoo on the back of their hands where a stigmata would be, a fact made much of by cultural theorists.

Among the most outspoken, highly paid, and controversial of the new commercial psychologists was Ernest Dichter—"Mr. Mass Motivations," as he was sometimes known. A Freudian from Austria, Dichter made his name and fortune as an advisor to companies with marketing problems. Dichter inhabited, perhaps even created, the image of the Freudian as a man with a pipe, horn-rimmed glasses, and a German accent. For him, nothing was a pipe, everything was a symbol, and his stock in trade was to find them in plain sight, outing encrypted realities as obvious truth with his blunt pronouncements.

Food was especially suggestive to Dichter, who, for instance, asserted that "the wedding cake [is] . . . the symbol of the feminine organ"; and that "the act of cutting the first slice by the bride and bridegroom together clearly stands as a symbol of defloration." When hired by food manufacturers, he began by characterizing a product as "male" or "female" and carrying on from there. Elongated edibles like asparagus he predictably considered male. He theorized that women were uncomfortable eating wieners, being "spellbound and definitely attracted by the meats." He naturally approved of Oscar Meyer's jingle,

> Oh, I wish I were an Oscar Mayer wiener.
> That is what I'd truly love to be
> For if I were an Oscar Mayer wiener
> Everyone would be in love with me.[19]

Most foods in Dichter's mind, however, were female, as was their preparation (except for grilling). But there were also some products for which he could not quite make up his mind. "Some foods are bisexual," he opined, "among them roast chicken and oranges."[20]

Dichter was just as blunt about the purpose of advertising. It was never merely to inform but existed to "manipulate human motivations and desires and develop a need for goods with which the public has at one time been unfamiliar—perhaps even un-desirous of purchasing."[21] His research was conducted through intense, psychotherapy-like sessions with consumers—usually housewives—sometimes several together, which he was the first to call a "focus group." His analysis rarely failed to uncover deep associations, sexual or otherwise, explaining why consumers bought the things they did.[22]

Perhaps Dichter's most famous effort was one of his first, a job he did for Chrysler. The automaker was concerned about sales of its new model, the Plymouth. Chrysler posed two questions to its corporate therapist: "1. Why do most car buyers buy the same make as their last car? 2. What influence do women have on the purchase of cars?"

In response, Dichter did not really answer the questions. Instead, he wrote, "Tell me how a man drives, and I will tell you what kind of man he is." The Plymouth was available as both a convertible and a sedan. After interviewing car buyers, he theorized that men regarded a convertible as a symbolic mistress, offering adventure, excitement, and romance, even if they were more likely to buy a sedan, which "reminded them of the comfort and familiarity of their wives." He therefore recommended both more advertising for convertibles and prominent showroom placement. This, he advised, would fire the male imagination, drawing in the male car buyer, so that he might yet marry the sedan.[23]

The ultimate success of prime-time television at attention capture, as measured in Nielsen ratings and the effects of TV advertising, would shape every subsequent contest in the market for attention; all future claimants would have to mold themselves as an alternative to TV, with profound consequences for those in the new technologies, the attention economy, and necessarily for most of the world. For television was now, as it still in many ways remains, attention's 800-pound gorilla. With the clearest and most engaging access to the public mind, it could exercise the greatest influence and therefore command the lion's share of advertising revenue.

As though awakening at last to the real challenge of programming, Sarnoff put the job in the hands of a former advertising executive named Sylvester "Pat" Weaver, then president of NBC. In Weaver, Paley for the first time faced an opponent with a talent as great as his own, and in some ways deeper. Unlike Sarnoff, Weaver understood the business of both attracting and selling attention. He had cut his teeth in radio at the agency Young & Rubicam, producer of many leading radio shows over the 1930s, and had later moved to the American Tobacco Company to help George Washington Hill sell Lucky Strike. Like Paley, he was a cultural omnivore, comfortable with the highest of the high and lowest of the low, and he had an uncanny gut instinct for what would work and what wouldn't. While still subject to the General's ultimate command, Weaver turned the war into a fair fight.

There are, as we've seen, two ways to win the contest for attention in a free market: the first is to present something more compelling than the competition; the other is to slip into some segment of the public's waking life that remains reserved or fallow. Weaver took the second tack by introducing television to the early morning and late night. Mealtimes were once thought sacrosanct, but he invaded the breakfast hour with news and entertainment that were light enough to go with eggs and toast. The *Today* show premiered in 1952—and included among its on-air performers a chimpanzee named J. Fred Muggs, usually dressed in a diaper. *The New York Times* described the new show as "the latest plan for electronic bondage dreamed up by the National Broadcasting Company," but that didn't stop it from becoming a hit. Weaver then attacked the other end of the day with the *Tonight* show, which played at the previously uncontested 11:30 p.m. slot, and featured the comedian Steve Allen interviewing celebrities.[24]

The genius of these simple ideas is attested by the fact that both formats survive to the present day, in a multitude of guises, but they did play to NBC's unfortunate reputation for crassness. This effect Weaver tried to hedge with what he called "Operation Frontal Lobes," his personal vision of more cerebral content. A prominent example was the show entitled *Wisdom,* featuring interviews of luminaries in the sciences, arts, and politics: Robert Frost, Marcel Duchamp, Frank Lloyd Wright, and Margaret Mead, to name a few. But that was window dressing. The Weaver mission was better exampled by another inspired play for ratings share: the NBC "spectaculars."

The first was the 1955 broadcast of the Broadway musical *Peter Pan,* which attracted 65 million viewers, rivaling anything CBS had done. The "spectacular" concept demonstrated an understanding of the inertia of attentional habits. Weaver saw these special broadcasts as creating "excitement and controversy and washday gossip," by disrupting the "robotry of habit viewing." Thus he made viewers rethink their schedules, while sucking life out of whatever CBS had in the same slot. The success of the spectacular—a one-time event—also had the unintended benefit of making NBC think differently about sports, and in particular, the most important annual American football games. And so NBC decided to invest heavily in promoting its broadcast of the 1958 National Football League championship game. As luck would have it, professional football turned out to be a good match for television, and the contest between the Baltimore Colts and New York Giants, decided in sudden-death overtime, was proclaimed "the greatest game ever played." Attracting 45 million viewers, it established the precedent and template for what would persist as another great attention ritual: the Super Bowl.[25]

But perhaps none of Weaver's innovations would have as much long-term consequence as his introduction of the "magazine" format over his tenure.* Television shows had heretofore been sustained by a single sponsor. Weaver came up with the idea of repeated commercial breaks, during which the advertiser would have a clear one-minute shot at the viewing audience. The network could now sell one show to several advertisers, as well as exercise more control over content. The advertisers, meanwhile, could split the costs and now enjoyed a more direct opportunity to pound their messages home. CBS and ABC quickly copied NBC, and for networks and advertising firms, the commercial break was a bonanza. The losers were the public, whose viewing pleasure was regularly interrupted for a sales pitch, and the writers of television shows, who now needed to produce content that would tease audiences to "stay tuned" through a commercial break.

The magazine format, in fact, only worked because television was uncompetitive enough that the networks could, effectively, raise their prices in tandem—force the viewers to watch more advertising for the same, or even less, entertainment. It is a testament to the market power over their audiences that CBS and NBC had achieved by the 1950s—there was no serious alternative with less advertising, so viewers put up with the intrusion.

Back at CBS, Paley, now facing NBC's advance, was forced into a long-deferred choice—make CBS live up to the highest ideals of what television could be, or commit to win the fight for the highest ratings and

---

* Technically, others had proposed the magazine format as early as 1933, but Weaver brought it to broadcast television, at first in new shows like *Today* and *The Tonight Show*.

largest profits. Some say that his temperament decided the question: high-minded though he liked to be, "he had always hated being number two." He would rack up the largest audiences, whatever it took.[26]

In the summer of 1955, at the height of Weaver's challenge, Paley threw down what would be his great trump card—a quiz show named *The $64,000 Question.* The concept was not original—Louis G. Cowan, the creator, had pioneered the quiz format for radio—but the prize money was unprecedented and impossible to ignore. Like *Amos 'n' Andy,* the show owed its existence to a desperate advertiser—Revlon—looking for something to set them apart and willing to try anything. So they agreed to the massive cash payout—more than half a million in today's dollars. The rest of the work would be done by the timeless spectacle of human nature amid the vicissitudes of fortune.

As the game was structured, the questions, in categories of the contestant's choosing, began at the $64 level, the amount doubling ($64, $128, $256—all the way to $64,000) with each correct response; one incorrect answer and all earnings would be forfeit. The contestant could quit with his winnings at any time; Paley even introduced breaks at the $16,000 and $32,000 levels, forcing players to go home and think about whether to risk losing it all for a chance at the big prize.

Within weeks of its debut, the show knocked *I Love Lucy* out of first place. Such a sudden and staggering seizure of the public mind warrants closer examination. The opening shot panned the audience of ordinary-looking people, and then zoomed in on one face. Over a drum roll, the announcer said, "Our brush salesman from the Bronx, Wilton Jay Singer, who answered his $8,000 question. He's back to tell us whether he'll take his $8,000 or try for $16,000. On his march to the $64,000 question!"

The producers carefully chose likable protagonists as contestants: like Gino, a cobbler from the Bronx, who happened to know everything about opera; Gloria, a twelve-year-old African American, who was a prodigious speller (she would take home $32,000); or Dr. Joyce Brothers, an attractive blond psychologist who knew everything about the sport of boxing. All were sympathetic people, who explained their deliberations carefully and quickly became stars in their own right, thanks to television's remarkable power to confer celebrity with unprecedented speed.

Suspense, the agony of defeat, and above all, vicarious greed—it was an intoxicating cocktail for viewers.* The show also promoted an exciting and somewhat egalitarian sense that perfectly ordinary people had hidden talents. "Everybody's smart at something," as Louis Cowan put it. Thus, with luck, anyone might become incredibly wealthy and famous overnight—the American dream paced as prime-time spectacle. What's more, the bitter taste of failure was sweetened: the losers, so long as they'd reached $4,000, went home with a Cadillac convertible as a consolation prize.[27]

But Paley's big-money contest triggered even more brutal ratings competition, which became all-consuming and desperate. NBC immediately copied the concept several times over, most notably with *Twenty One,* which pitted two contestants against each other. Sponsored by a relaunched patent medicine (Geritol: "America's number one tonic for tired blood!"), *Twenty One* put even more prize money at stake. But its ratings climb against CBS didn't happen until Charles Van Doren—a handsome, deep-voiced, and patrician English instructor at Columbia—showed up to challenge the reigning champion, Herb Stempel of the Bronx. Stempel had a big nose, thick glasses, and an abrasive manner. The producer would later say, "You want the viewer to react emotionally to a contestant. Whether he reacts favorably or negatively is really not that important. . . . Viewers would watch him [Stempel] and pray for his opponent to win."

Like *The $64,000 Question, Twenty One* made theatrical displays of its integrity, such as storing its questions in a local bank vault to ensure their secrecy, putting its contestant in a sealed glass booth, where he could hear no one but the host. In the final showdowns, the suspense of Van Doren's drawn-out deliberation before answering questions drove audiences wild. He finally knocked out Stempel, going home a rich man, with $129,000, and enough celebrity to appear on the cover of *Time* as "Quiz Champ Van Doren."[28]

With NBC's successful challenge for game show supremacy, the ultimate battle of attention capture began to brew. To draw audiences back, Revlon and CBS quadrupled the winnings for *The $64,000 Question,* and consequently, a ten-year-old boy walked off with $224,000 (more than $1.8 million today) for correctly answering some questions about

---

* So much so that the format would be revived in the late 1990s on British and American television as *Who Wants to Be a Millionaire?*

mathematics, science, and electronics. *Twenty One* countered by bringing in another Columbia University affiliate, a graduate student named Elfrida von Nardroff. She had a winsome pixie cut and alluring way of looking up at the ceiling when searching for an answer. Over sixteen weeks she won $220,500. Revlon could afford the prizes, but had the competition continued it might have bankrupted everyone. *Twenty One* and *The $64,000 Question,* moreover, were only the biggest players in a genre that exploded into more than fifteen different quiz shows by 1958, including *Dotto* (connect the dots), *Beat the Clock* (timed stunts by couples), *Dough-Re-Mi* (song identification), *Tic-Tac-Dough* (trivia questions), and many others competing for the same eyeballs.[29]

The quiz show war typifies what had become of attention industries by the late 1950s: competition had taken on an intensity and anxiousness not seen since the penny papers of the 1830s. It must have made one yearn for the relative gentleness of the old radio days, with their mushy ratings, limited advertising, and smaller revenues for broadcasters and advertising firms. A show did not need to prove itself definitively so much as contribute generally to the network's lineup and make the affiliates happy. It was a lower-pressure environment, like a school where every child is average.

That greater intensity came in part from the disappearance of doubts as to advertising's power to drive sales, making audience attention more valuable. While scientific proof of the conversion of attention into sales may have been lacking, the examples of successful campaigns were too numerous to be ignored. Reeves's commercials for Anacin ("Fast, fast, fast relief") correlated with a 200 percent increase in sales over eighteen months. A new brand named Crest stormed the toothpaste battlements with a special ingredient, "fluoride," and a happy boy crying, "Look, Mom! No cavities!" It became the market leader in just four years' time. Television and print ads of the Marlboro Man, as we've seen, turned an obscure woman's cigarette into one of the market leaders in less than a year, and Revlon was widely thought to be saved by *The $64,000 Question.* Of course, it is possible that Crest was just making great toothpaste, or that Marlboro just happened to take off. Certainly, for every successful advertising campaign there were plenty of others that seemed to have no impact. Nonetheless, the number of notable successes was sufficient to set off a feeding frenzy.

With the potential dollar value of television's attention harvest becoming so obvious, any pretenses to a higher purpose that broadcasting once had were eroding quickly. Now it was clear, as an economist put it, that "programs are scheduled interruptions of marketing bulletins." The trend was exacerbated by another increased quantification. The networks began to consider audience attention their "inventory," which was sold using metrics like "gross rating points" or GRP, a formula that estimated the likelihood of people seeing the advertising at least once (the cumulative audience), and the frequency with which the advertising played. On popular prime-time television, all but the highest commercial bidders—America's largest corporations—were priced out of each time slot.

Moreover, as compared with radio or print, there was on television a larger disparity in profit between the "winner" and "loser" of each time slot. Even the cheapest television programs cost far more to make than a radio show, meaning some ratings minimum was needed just to cover costs. The ratings winner, was able, moreover, to charge a premium for its advertising slots. This made the pressure to win even more intense, and also meant that content could not linger to evolve, as it might on radio or in a magazine—it had to pull in its audience or face cancellation.

Much of the broadcast schedule was simply too valuable to be left to chance. Experimenting with a few stations and high ideals might have their place when sponsorships were the norm, when nothing could be accurately measured, and all was a matter of feel, but now, by the late 1950s, every moment of what was called prime time had both fixed costs and a revenue potential to be met or brutally aspired to. Paley, as we've said, liked to win, and CBS did it best. In 1953, the television network would make its first profit; its ratings dominance, once established in 1955, would hold until 1976.[30] Given the nature of the contest, such consistency bears special remark.

What we learn about Paley from this period is, in fact, slightly ambiguous. The most straightforward theory is that, in the end, his competitive instincts ruled. The game of television was audience aggregation, and so that is the game he played to win. He was, therefore, a merchant of attention in the most undiluted sense, not unlike Benjamin Day of the *New York Sun,* who gave audiences exactly what he could tell they wanted. Unlike others, Paley had no real designs to manipulate or enlighten, unless that might improve ratings. His only aim was to harvest as much of his product as he could, in as pure a form as he could, for sale to the highest bidder. As David Halberstam suggested, he "was totally without sentiment: he knew what was good and would sell, what was bad and would sell, and what was good and would not sell, and he never confused one with another."[31]

Another, not entirely inconsistent, view sees Paley as someone who had higher aspirations, who wanted television to be appealing and worthy, but found himself taken captive by a system he helped make. He had, at times, shown undeniably high ideals, and yet, caught in the competition with NBC, it was as if he lost control over his own creation, which took on a will of its own. "Bill Paley had invented the system," wrote one observer, "but now the system was in the process of swallowing him up." The attention merchant faces a constant pressure to build its audiences, and the first casualty is always anything that attracts less than the largest viewership (many believe this is why the first true golden age of television only came in the 2000s, after the rise of commercial-free models). Fred Friendly, who was at CBS for the whole period, took this more charitable view. For Paley and other CBS executives "looked on while programs proliferated which assaulted their sense of taste, and even decency; they seemed incapable of stopping the inexorable flight from quality."[32]

Incapable, or helpless: countless media scholars have pointed out that, as the 1950s progressed, this approach ceded ever more programming control to Arthur Nielsen. Whether they saw it or not, what Paley and Weaver—programming geniuses both—had ultimately wrought was a system for capturing more attention than ever commercially amassed before. Once that system existed, the logic of capitalism, though not decency, dictated it could be used for only one purpose: to make as much money as could be made. That the substrate for this process was the conscious hours of millions of Americans was hardly CBS's or NBC's problem. In a free society, you are free to do things that aren't good for you, whether it be smoke, drink sugary drinks, or watch game shows. Thanks to the erosion of the public interest model, broadcasters were free to air what suited them. But there are always consequences, and broadcasting executives had no luxury of foresight. As David Halberstam writes, "Whereas at the turn of the century, only an occasional door-to-door salesman visited the American home, by the middle of the century a ceaseless stream of the most subtle electronic impulses created by the nation's most richly rewarded hucksters was beamed into this new marketplace, relentlessly selling not just the American dream but an endless series of material products through whose purchase that dream might be more quickly achieved." In this way, for the first time, to be at home and awake was, for most people, to be sold something.

On June 5, 1955, a Tuesday, at 10 p.m., Fred Friendly and Ed Murrow sat and watched CBS's new show, *The $64,000 Question,* which ran just before their program *See It Now.* In the middle of the show, Murrow said, "Fritzo—how long do you think we'll stay in this time period?"[33]

It wasn't long. Later that year, the sponsor, Alcoa, dropped *See It Now,* telling CBS it wanted something different, "perhaps fictional, or 'like the Ed Sullivan program.'" Paley approached Murrow with the idea of retiring *See It Now* from its weekly slot, and making it an occasional special. Paley then sold the now vacant slot to the Liggett & Myers Tobacco Company, which wanted to run a quiz show called *Do You Trust Your Wife?* In 1958, *See It Now* was canceled for good; despite spectacular ratings by present standards, it was simply no match for the game shows or a new fad, westerns like *Gunsmoke.* Jack Gould at the *The New York Times* wrote, "An era in television ended unexpectedly last night," and attributed it to a "tighter TV economy."[34] A columnist for the *New York Herald Tribune* wrote, "The fact that CBS cannot afford [*See It Now*] but can afford *Beat the Clock* is shocking."[35]

Later in 1958, Murrow would deliver his lament for what he felt had befallen television over the decade. Its deep embrace of advertising had resulted in a kind of self-imposed (and sometimes sponsor-imposed) censorship: anything too downbeat, dark, or challenging was being systematically suppressed, for fear of contradicting the upbeat and optimistic commercial messages of television's sponsors.[36] And so while radio, at its best, had forced Americans to confront the horrors of Europe, television was acting as a buffer. "Television in the main insulates us from the realities of the world in which we live. If this state of affairs continues, we may alter an advertising slogan to read: LOOK NOW, PAY LATER, for surely we shall pay for using this most powerful instrument of communication to insulate the citizenry from the hard and demanding realities which must be faced if we are to survive." Alluding to the Cold War, Murrow added that "there is a great and perhaps decisive battle to be fought against ignorance, intolerance and indifference. This weapon of television could be useful."[37]

Without much to do at CBS, Ed Murrow left his lifelong employer and went to work for the John F. Kennedy administration in the early 1960s. But he contracted lung cancer, which weakened him and then spread to his brain. William Paley went to visit Murrow many times as he died. But there was, ultimately, no final reconciliation, at least according to Murrow's friends. He simply could not stand what Paley had done with television.

CHAPTER 11

PRELUDE TO AN ATTENTIONAL REVOLT

From the 1920s through the 1960s, Zenith Radio Company was one of the world's leading technology firms and, like Apple in its early days, something of a maverick. Zenith's innovations were at times brilliantly forward looking: in the 1920s they made the first portable radio, and one of the first car radios using power generated by the vehicle. At other times, however, their projects bordered on the bizarre. In the mid-1930s, for instance, Zenith seriously tested whether it could transmit thoughts to its listeners via radio waves.[1] "On these programs," it said of its telepathy experiments, "the listeners will be taken where no living person has ever been."

Zenith was led by Commander E. F. McDonald, who was the sort of eccentric who sometimes ends up in charge of technology firms. While running Zenith, he embarked on a series of explorations, partly to satisfy his taste for adventure but also as publicity stunts, to bring attention to Zenith. As *Time* would tell:

Back in the '20s, he mushed off on North Pole expeditions (he is called "Ange-kok," Miracle Worker, by the Eskimos); searched for pirates' gold on a Pacific island; sleuthed for old bones around Lake Superior; flew his own glider; raced his bouncing outboard down the

Hudson; mined gold in Mexico. In his spare time, aboard his 185-ft. yacht, Mizpah, he held parties that rattled Chicago tongues.[2]

He was, then, a natural individualist and would remain so, even through the apogee of American conformism.

In the late 1950s, the Commander caught a whiff of discontent brewing among television consumers, an annoyance at having to sit through the new commercial breaks that now interrupted nearly every program since NBC had first introduced them in the mid-1950s. So he ordered Zenith's engineers to devise a way to give people more control over what their televisions were doing—in particular, the power to "tune out annoying commercials." He wanted, we would say, an ad-blocker.[3]

Within a year, McDonald's engineers had come up with various answers to his challenge. Zenith put the most promising one into development, and soon started advertising its new Flash-Matic, mainly in print: "Just think! Without budging from your easy chair you can turn your new Zenith Flash-Matic set on, off, or change channels. You can even shut off annoying commercials while the picture remains on the screen." The Flash-Matic shot visible light at four photo cells, one in each corner of the screen. It was shaped like a revolver, perhaps inspired by the popularity of the western. The idea, according to the inventor, Eugene Polley, was to let the viewer "shoot-out" the ads. Caetlin Benson-Allott writes, "This gunman would be an active, discerning viewer, not just another slack-jawed subject of mass-media propaganda."[4]

Zenith's invention, what we now call a remote control, might not at first seem like one of history's most consequential; it didn't even really block ads, as the Commander had intended, but merely offered a way to mute the set's volume. But great tech oaks have always grown from little acorns. As Polley would remark in 2002, "The flush toilet may have been the most civilized invention ever devised, but the remote control is the next most important."[5]

The real significance of the remote control was in arming a new popular resistance against the industrialized harvest of attention, what McDonald sensed was a rising demand for a way to defend oneself against what had become such easy access to the mind. It was a desire to take back control over one's attention, which had been not so wittingly surrendered to a temptation very difficult to quit. For while America still watched television faithfully, as Nielsen proved every week, the hushed reverence of the early years was already giving way to a much more ambivalent relationship. Cultural critics regularly opined on the lost promise of television, and Orson Welles may have spoken for many when he said in 1956: "I hate television. I hate it as much as peanuts. But I can't stop eating peanuts."[6]

What had American viewers implicitly agreed to? Consent is not always a simple matter, legally or philosophically. And willpower always figures into the complications. Jacques Ellul wrote of the individual: "If he is a propagandee, it is because he wants to be, for he is ready to buy a paper, go to the movies, pay for a radio or TV set. Of course, he does not buy these in order to be propagandized—his motivations are more complex. But in doing these things he must know that he opens the door to propaganda."[7]

Likewise, no one ever bought a TV merely to keep up with the latest shampoos or tobacco products, much less to be persuaded to buy them. But the terms of the attention merchants' contract with the public, which once had seemed so easy and appealing—"free" entertainment in exchange for a moment of your consideration—seemed suddenly to have been revised, and not in the viewers' favor. Pitches were proliferating, and the programs themselves, their narrative logic, seemed more and more contorted to fit the pitches. The sense of being commerce's dupe was setting in.

To be sure, the first remote control was a feeble assertion of self-determination, since to use it was merely to toggle among three stations. Unfortunately, the visible-light technology didn't work very well either. But great movements, like technologies, must start somewhere.

In the summer of 1957, a book entitled *The Hidden Persuaders* appeared and quickly topped the bestseller lists. Its author, Vance Packard, was a muckraker in the old tradition, who felt that it was time to blow the whistle on the advertising game. As he wrote in the introduction, his aim was:

to explore a strange and rather exotic new area of American life . . . the large-scale efforts being made, often with impressive success, to channel our unthinking habits, our purchasing decisions, and our thought processes by the use of insights gleaned from psychiatry and the social sciences. Typically these efforts take place beneath our level of awareness; so that the appeals which move us are often, in a sense, "hidden." The result is that many of us are being influenced and manipulated, far more than we realize, in the patterns of our everyday lives.[8]

Packard's accusations did not have the visceral effect that exposing the exaggerations and outright lies of patent medicine advertising had had earlier in the twentieth century. To accept his claims of designs on our unconscious desires and use of hidden or subliminal messages to turn citizens into slavish consumers required a measure of sophistication, not to mention an awareness of the unconscious. But *The New Yorker* hailed *The Hidden Persuaders* as a "frightening report on how manufacturers, fund-raisers, and politicians are attempting to turn the American mind into a kind of catatonic dough that will buy, give, or vote at their command."[9]

Packard's most compelling chapters revealed advertising's reliance on shadowy figures like the Freudian Ernest Dichter, whom he cast in a very sinister light, which was not hard to do.* Dichter was found running his "Institute for Motivational Research" from a castle overlooking the Hudson River, reachable only by a winding dirt road. Within that castle, odd experiments were performed on children from the neighboring village, who watched television or played with toys as researchers observed them through one-way glass. Indeed, the entire village, according to Packard, was combed for subjects, who were extensively analyzed and used as archetypes.

Perhaps what made Packard's book so successful was showing com-

---

* As years went by, Dichter would also provide fodder for feminist critics, like Betty Friedan, who included an attack of motivational research in *The Feminine Mystique*. Friedan wanted to know why women had returned to being housewives after making gains in independence earlier in the century. She concluded that "the perpetuation of housewifery, the growth of the feminine mystique, makes sense (and dollars) when one realizes that women are the chief customers of American business. Somehow, somewhere, someone must have figured out that women will buy more things if they are kept in the underused, nameless-yearning, energy-to-get-rid-of state of being housewives." (New York: W. W. Norton, 1963; repr. 1997), 299.

mercials to be not merely annoying but extremely effective, and to a degree that most readers would not have suspected. Without necessarily proving the validity of psychological techniques like Dichter's, it stirred a conspiracy consciousness in the public by revealing that, in the advertisers' minds, there was more to their efforts than met the eye. That the industry had been surreptitiously engaged in mind games was perhaps easier to swallow than the simpler truth that even the most straightforward ads—like anything we attend to, in fact—can and do influence our behavior. Viewers of television had conditioned themselves to believe that their choices were still their own, whatever commercials might be telling them to do. Having been given cause to think otherwise must have induced a shock of recognition. For as Ellul wrote of propaganda, those most susceptible to it are often those most confident in their skills of detecting it and therefore think themselves immune to its effects.[10]

Ultimately, in Packard's view, the only real defense was to cultivate mental privacy through the avoidance of advertising. "It is this right to privacy in our minds—privacy to be either rational or irrational," wrote Packard, "that I believe we must strive to protect."[11]

In 1958, as *The Hidden Persuaders* remained a bestseller forty-six weeks after its publication, CBS's two big hits were *Gunsmoke* and a new quiz show named *Dotto*. *Dotto* was a funny little program based on the children's game "connect the dots." As contestants answered questions correctly, dots were connected revealing a face, the identity of which the contestants were to guess.[12]

Everything was going well when, one day, a suspicious standby contestant named Eddie Hilgemeier came across a notebook belonging to Marie Winn, another contestant (while in the communal dressing room, he most likely rummaged through her purse). Inside the notebook were jottings. As he examined the notes, he realized that they were the answers to the exact questions Winn was being asked on stage at that moment, on live television.

Taking the notebook, Hilgemeier confronted the show's producers, who immediately offered him $500 to keep quiet. He declined and was offered $1,500, which he took, but then decided he wanted $5,000. When refused, he spilled the beans. *Dotto* was fixed, he told the New York *Daily News,* its winning contestants coached and supplied with answers. Both the casting and the competitive drama were as scripted as a soap opera. It seems rather obvious when you watch the old recordings: on the *Dotto* episode in question, the attractive reigning champion Marie Winn defeats her dour, overweight opponent with all the theatricality of a professional wrestling match. If the shows were so reliably suspenseful, and the winners always so appealing, surely there was a reason. In fact, even the amounts won were predetermined, budgeted in advance. The truth came out, and *Dotto* was canceled that summer.

Unexpectedly, the fixing scandal did not stop at *Dotto,* but spread like a stain as more and more contestants came out of the woodwork. Even before Hilgemeier's disclosure, Herb Stempel, onetime champion of *Twenty One,* had been saying he had been coached to take a dive in the final dramatic match against Charles Van Doren. He had been dismissed as a sore loser but when Hilgemeier came forward, the authorities connected the dots, until finally scandal spread to the biggest shows of all, *The $64,000 Question* and *Twenty One.* By 1959, Congress had launched an investigation, and called Charles Van Doren to testify. *Twenty One*'s most famous star gave a shattering confession: "I was involved, deeply involved, in a deception. The fact that I, too, was very much deceived cannot keep me from being the principal victim of that deception, because I was its principal symbol. There may be a kind of justice in that. I don't know."[13]

All of the safeguards—the storing of questions in bank vaults, the isolation booths, and the question-sorting machines—were nothing more than an elaborate sham, similar to the tricks a magician uses to distract his audience. The "little people" were winning big, because the big people wanted it that way. Walter Lippmann, who, having worked for the Creel Committee, knew a thing about putting one over on the public, put things this way in 1959:

> Television has been caught perpetrating a fraud which is so gigantic that it calls into question the foundations of the industry. . . . There has been, in fact, an enormous conspiracy to deceive the public in order to sell profitable advertising to the sponsors. It involves not this individual or that, but the industry as a whole . . . there is something

radically wrong with the fundamental national policy under which television operates. . . . There is no competition in television except among competitors trying to sell the attention of their audiences for profit. As a result, while television is supposed to be "free," it has in fact become the creature, the servant, and indeed the prostitute, of merchandizing.[14]

Lippmann voiced a now widespread conviction that the television networks had squandered their power over American attention. Even Pat Weaver, former NBC president, long since fired by David Sarnoff, chimed in, saying that when it comes to television network, management "doesn't give the people what they deserve."[15] At a government hearing, Eric Barnouw, the acclaimed observer of broadcasting, testified. "The real question," he said, "is whether we can afford to have our culture and artistic life become a byproduct of advertising. My answer is that we can't."[16]

———————

In the popular imagination, it is the 1960s, not the 1950s, that was the era of revolt against commerce, conformism, and the power of advertising. But it is clear that before the decade of counterculture had even dawned, the seeds of doubt about the trustworthiness of prominent American institutions had not only been sown and watered but had borne mature fruit. Disillusionment with the second screen—which, in less than ten years' time, had gone from an amusing novelty to an almost natural presence in every home, to become the combine of the most bountiful commercial harvest of attention the world had ever seen—was the harbinger of an even greater disenchantment. But no mere harbinger: in their carelessness, the attention merchants had revealed that their pleasant arrangement with the American consumer was essentially a confidence game. When that was finally clear, the reverberations would be felt for the rest of the century.

CHAPTER 12

THE GREAT REFUSAL

In the spring of 1966, a forty-six-year-old former Harvard instructor named Timothy Leary, wearing a jacket, a tie, and a distant look, strode up the red-carpeted steps of the Plaza Hotel on New York's Fifth Avenue and into the Oak Room for lunch. Waiting for him was a man Leary knew only by reputation: another academic, Marshall McLuhan, almost a decade older, graying a bit, but not yet wearing the mustache that would become his signature in the 1970s.

To their respective followings both men sitting in the ornate oak-paneled restaurant were "gurus," a word just come into currency in the West. McLuhan was a scholar of the media from the University of Toronto who'd become famous thanks to his book *Understanding Media: The Extensions of Man,* which was full of intriguing pronouncements somehow both bold and enigmatic at once (example: "The 'content' of any medium is always another medium"). He was referred to, variously, as the "Guru of the Boob Tube" and the "Oracle of the Electronic Age."

Leary had, at the time, the more traditional claim to guruship. Having been fired from his teaching position at Harvard, he now lived in a fortresslike mansion in upstate New York, where he was overseeing the development of a grand synthesis, part scientific experiment, part new religion. He and a friend from Harvard, Professor Richard Alpert, who was likewise defrocked and later would take the name Ram Dass, called their project the "International Federation for Internal Freedom." The two men had successfully attracted a large band of devoted followers and their ambitions were grand. As one of them, a British doctor named Michael Hollingshead, explained, "We felt satisfied that our goal was Every Man's, a project of Every Man's private ambition. We sought for that unitary state of divine harmony, an existence in which only the sense of wonder remains, and all fear gone."[1]

Among other things, Leary and his followers were deeply committed to what might fairly be termed an attentional revolution. They wanted the public to block out the messages of the mainstream media and other institutions, which they saw as little more than tools of mass manipulation. Instead the Federation was setting forth on an inward voyage, with a bit of help: to reconfigure the public mind and its priorities, Leary believed in the great potential of taking psychedelic drugs—like LSD—still legal then.

By the time of his lunch with McLuhan, Leary was growing in fame and wanted to bring his ideas to a broader audience; his great ambition was to reach the young, now understood to be broadly disillusioned with how things were and looking for something different. As he would describe it, "For the first time in our history, a large and influential sector of the populace was coming to disrespect institutional authority," giving rise to a contest between "the old industrial society and the new information society." He believed that McLuhan might be able to tell him how he could reach all the disaffected.[2]

McLuhan was fairly sympathetic to Leary's project. For McLuhan saw the media as having become "extensions of man"—as much a part of us as our skin. To take control of one's media consumption was therefore a form of self-determination, a seizing of one's own destiny. And so after hearing Leary out, he finally gave him some counterintuitive advice: "You call yourself a philosopher, a reformer," said McLuhan. "But the key to your work is advertising." If Leary truly wanted to wean great numbers from the pernicious effects of the existing media, he needed first to reach those people by the media's most pernicious means. Most of all, he needed some kind of a catchy line, and to show him how it was done, McLuhan composed a jingle for him then and there, based on an old Pepsi ad: "Lysergic acid hits the spot / Forty billion neurons, that's a lot."

That meeting, Leary would remember, "got me thinking further along these lines: the successful philosophers were also advertisers who could sell their new models of the universe to large numbers of others, thus converting thought to action, mind to matter." Taking McLuhan's advice seriously, he made a list of the most revolutionary American slogans: "Give me Liberty or Give Me Death" came to him first, and then "A Nation Cannot Exist Half Slave and Half Free," "The Only Thing We Have to Fear Is Fear Itself," and finally "Lucky Strike Means Fine Tobacco" (the latter had been used over the 1940s and 1950s, replacing "Reach for a Lucky Instead of a Sweet"). But he needed his own slogan. Later that day, in the shower, the answer suddenly came to him. All he needed was the right occasion to bring it to a broader audience.

Late in 1966, a "psychedelic artist" named Michael Bowen invited Leary to an event in San Francisco meant to unite various emerging countercultural and "alternative" groups—alienated students, poets, rock musicians, jazz hipsters, and members of biker gangs. His advertising posters billed the event as "A Gathering of the Tribes for a Human Be-In." And so it was on January 14, 1967, in Golden Gate Park that Leary first took his carefully constructed message to a broader audience. His speech centered on the infectious refrain, repeated over and over:

"Turn On, Tune In, Drop Out."

McLuhan's advice worked. Leary's line caught on as well as any advertising slogan and became, effectively, the motto of the counterculture.

Most would take Leary's words as a call to pay attention to where your attention is paid; mind what you open your mind for. If this was not America's first call to attentional revolt—Packard and Lippmann had each issued his own, as we've seen—Leary's proposed a far broader compass of things to ignore, not only messages from television and government but college, work, parents, as well as other sources of authority. He called for a complete attentional revolution.

Some two decades on, Leary would write that "unhappily," his ideas had been "often misinterpreted to mean 'Get stoned and abandon all constructive activity.'"[3] Indeed, in the 1960s it was earnestly asked where one was supposed to go after dropping out. But enough who got the message understood that it referred to something more profound, and were able to connect Leary's prescription with the vision of other social critics.

Among the most influential of these was another guru of the counterculture, Herbert Marcuse of the "Frankfurt School," one of a set of German
philosophers who'd fled the Third Reich in the 1930s. Marcuse believed
that he was witnessing a "Great Refusal"—a term he first coined in the
1950s to describe "the protest against unnecessary repression, the struggle
for the ultimate form of freedom—'to live without anxiety.'"[4]

Like Leary—whom he may have inspired in part—Marcuse tended
to believe that liberation could not be achieved from within the system,
but required its fundamental reconstruction. "Intellectual freedom," he
surmised in 1964, "would mean the restoration of individual thought
now absorbed by mass communication and indoctrination" and also the
"abolition of 'public opinion' along with its makers." And so the youth
movement held out the promise for something never achieved except in
mythology—the radical liberation of the human condition. It was a far
more ambitious aim than anything hoped for even by Karl Marx and
his followers, who simply sought liberation from an unfair economic
system. Marcuse envisioned an end to all forms of repression, whether
social, economic, or technological—a sort of return to the Garden of
Eden. By this Great Refusal, he dared hope, the people might "recognize
the mark of social repression, even in the most sublime manifestations
of traditional culture, even in the most spectacular manifestations of
technical progress." The result would be "solidarity for the human species, for abolishing poverty and misery beyond all national frontiers and
spheres of interest, for the attainment of peace."[5]

But on the way to paradise, where should one direct his attention if
not to the ubiquitous media? What should people be doing with their
lives? For his part, Leary offered an answer from a far older and more
mystical prophetic tradition, locating the proper focus of attention with
things of the spirit. "The wise person devotes his life exclusively to the
religious search," Leary said, "for therein is found the only ecstasy, the
only meaning." This was the ultimate sense of his great exhortation, as
he would explain in one speech: "The message of God never changes. It
may be expressed to you in six simple words: turn on, tune in, drop out."[6]

Leary forecast that enormous resistance would meet those trying
to take his advice. "The directors of the TV studio do not want you to
live a religious life. They will apply every pressure (including prison) to
keep you in their game. Your own mind, which has been corrupted and

neurologically damaged by years of education in fake-prop TV-studio games, will also keep you trapped in the game."[7] He was right in seeing that American commerce, and the attention industries in particular, would view what Leary advocated as a mortal threat. But he seems not to have anticipated that just as he had appropriated the tools of advertising for the promotion of his cause, the side of the advertisers might just as easily appropriate his cause for their purposes.

———————

Before Leary, there was Pepsi. In 1963, Alan Pottasch, a newly hired advertising executive at the Pepsi Cola Company, was sitting in his office, pencil in hand, desperately brainstorming ideas for a challenge he might mount against Coca-Cola, the establishment soft drink par excellence, known then as "the brand beyond competition."

Decades of experience had shown that competing with Coca-Cola was a Sisyphean undertaking. Like other giants of the 1950s, Coke had invested millions in advertising meant to cultivate a fierce brand loyalty. Along the way it had succeeded, as few firms do, in transcending mere persuasion and instead convincing people that Coke was not only the better choice but also somehow the only choice. As historian Thomas Frank explains, "Coke built an unrivaled dominance of the once-localized soft-drink marketplace: it offered a single product that was supposed to be consumable by people in every walk of life—rich and poor, old and young, men and women—and in every part of the country." Coke managed to create a phenomenally low "brand elasticity"—the economist's term for the willingness of consumers to accept a substitute, a matter proven by the fact that Pepsi was similar, cheaper, yet remained unable to build market share.[8]

Coke had succeeded by identifying itself with everything wholesome and all-American, drawing on the deep American self-regard and desire to belong—and somehow making it feel that to drink something else might be vaguely treasonous. At Christmas, it even associated itself with Santa Claus, and in fact the company helped cement the modern image of Santa Claus in the public consciousness as a rotund bearded man with a broad belt, clad in Coca-Cola's red and white.

Pepsi, meanwhile, was the perennial underdog. First bottled in 1893, when it was called Brad's Drink, Pepsi was originally sold as a minor-league patent medicine: the "healthy" cola. The name was a play on its claim to treat dyspepsia, or indigestion. As the trailing brand, Pepsi was willing, early on, to try innovative promotional techniques, like catering to the disenfranchised. Coca-Cola advertised itself as the all-American drink, but by this it meant the white American drink, and so Pepsi in the 1940s briefly experimented with niche marketing by creating an all-black marketing department, known as the "negro-markets" department.[9] Over the 1950s, Pepsi depended entirely on identifying itself not as healthful, or even better tasting, but the cheaper cola, occupying the market niche that generic colas hold today. Its most successful jingle, the one McLuhan borrowed for Leary's psychedelic venture, had gone like this: "Pepsi-Cola hits the spot; 12 full ounces, that's a lot." Truth in advertising: Pepsi was sold in a 12-ounce bottle for 5 cents, the price of 6.5 ounces of Coke. By 1957, when Pottasch joined the company, despite all its efforts Pepsi was being outsold by a factor of nearly six to one, giving a classic demonstration of the power of brand to undermine the concept of choice—but without anyone feeling they had sacrificed any freedoms. They were just choosing Coke, that's all.

Pottasch had begun to persuade his management that selling Pepsi as a cheaper alternative was not, in the long run, a winning strategy. But what else could Pepsi be? Like Leary, Marcuse, and others, Pottasch noticed that there was something going on with the young people, who were listening to different types of music and dressing differently than their parents, and—while this was still the early 1960s—giving some signs of rebellion against the consumer culture constructed over the 1950s. But if Leary or Marcuse sought to ride the swirling social movements to challenge the established social order, Pottasch thought he could employ it to sell Pepsi Cola.

"We made a decision," he later recalled, "to stop talking about the product, and start talking about the user."[10] He thus conceived of marketing Pepsi without reference to its inherent qualities, focusing instead on an image of the people who bought it, or who should be buying it. They were the people of the moment: the young, the rebellious, those who (to borrow a later slogan) "think different." They would be known, in Pottasch's new formula, as "the Pepsi Generation."

The new ads were the picture of vitality: beautiful young people casually dressed, hanging out, and having fun. "Come alive!" the text read, "You're in the Pepsi generation!" Others read, "For a generation really on the move." Printed in 1964, they look nothing like the more staid advertisements of just a year earlier. Following up on popularity it had won among African Americans, Pepsi also ran similar ads with African American models, also building what would become the brand's countercultural bona fides.

"For us to name and claim a whole generation after our product was a rather courageous thing," Pottasch would later remember, "that we weren't sure would take off."[11] But his intuition would prove correct. "What you drank said something about who you were. We painted an image of our consumer as active, vital, and young at heart."[12]

Pepsi, of course, did not create the desire for liberation in various matters from music to sex to manners and dress. Rather, it had cleverly identified with a fashionable individualism. All individualisms, of course, harbor a strain of narcissism, and Pepsi had implicitly understood that, too. For ultimately what the Pepsi Generation were consuming wasn't so much cola as an image of themselves.

Whether Pepsi's approach was truly original is a good question; advertisers are continually claiming to invent things that, on closer inspection, have long existed. But clearly, this campaign had nothing to do with the traditional hard sell, with the product, and what it might do for you, front and center. Pepsi's advertisements and their imitators were in some sense just an even softer version of the soft sell, which pictured an ideal and associated it with the product. Into this category one might put both the "Arrow Man," a dashing figure who wore Arrow shirts in the 1920s, and the Marlboro Man, solitary smoker of the Great Plains. But no one who smoked Marlboros wanted or expected to become a wrangler. The Pepsi difference was to suggest that consuming the product somehow made you into what you wanted to be.

In any case, by the end of the decade the Pepsi Generation campaign would start steadily closing the gap with Coke, reaching comparable market share, even if Coca-Cola remained ahead. Meanwhile, Pepsi kept riding the wave it had caught, engineering an ever fuller embrace of the counterculture, even its psychedelic aspects. The company aired a bizarre television spot in which a young woman wearing a sequined dress dances through a night in New York punctuated by abrupt flashes of lights and sound, resembling an LSD trip, with an occasional Pepsi logo thrown in. But Pepsi had greater success with the "Live–Give" campaign, playing on more appealing countercultural values, like a return to natural, simple pleasures and living in peace. Here was consumption coaxed with an anti-consumerist ethos; it was Pepsi selling the counterculture to mainstream America, as Leary and others had only aspired to do.

Consider a typical spot from 1969 that opens with a toddler atop a horse, followed by a long-haired man drinking water (not Pepsi) from a stream using his bare hands. "There's a whole new way of living," sings a voice, "Pepsi helps supply the drive." Then a rapid succession of images: children frolicking in nature, a young couple walking on the beach, a child milking a cow—ordinary people doing regular, yet fulfilling things. A voice-over goes:

"Recognize it? This is the world you live in. Packed with simple pleasures. Places to see. People to love. And Pepsi-Cola is the one cola that belongs with every happy, hopeful moment you love."

The chorus chimes in with the new slogan: "You've got a lot to live . . . and Pepsi's got a lot to give . . ."

It's a truly remarkable compilation of hippie-era images and values. There are no status symbols, workplaces, or wealth; instead, all that is indulged in are natural, easy pleasures, mainly outdoors. The people are attractive but not unattainably so, and the various races and ages mingle in harmony.

What Pepsi pictured (or co-opted) was essentially Marcuse's imagined earthly paradise—unrepressed joy, activity, and love, a life altogether free of anxiety or oppression. There are no technologies, only Frisbees and flowers; love, both familial and romantic, is experienced without hindrance or implied hierarchies. In essence, Pepsi advertised liberation.

The commercials were famous for their music, which sounded like a mixture of the Beatles and Sesame Street. Here is how the company described them:

Exciting new groups doing out-of-sight new things to and for music. It's youth's bag and Pepsi-Cola is in it. There's a whole new way of livin' and Pepsi's supplyin' the background music . . . It's a radio package that obliterates the generation gap and communicates like a guru.[13]

It is interesting to consider what vision the counterculture of the 1960s and 1970s might have achieved if it could have reversed the commercialization of human attention. Its leaders aspired to an age when commercial television and its advertising would face mass indifference and wilt into irrelevance. Once people had tuned out the "establishment" sources of information, advertising would be recognized as a form of propaganda and carefully avoided. Starved of requisite attention, it would collapse as it nearly did in the 1930s. In its place, the public mind would attend to realities that weren't commercial contrivances—nature, spiritual paths, friends, family, and lovers. Media, if any were needed, would be things like live concerts or perhaps programming in the public interest. A cynic might say the 1960s vision of the alternative future was just sex, drugs, and rock 'n' roll, with, perhaps, some public radio thrown in.

There's little question that the revolt of the 1960s did lead part of a generation away from the attention merchants of the 1950s. But industry calibrated an effective response and perhaps ultimately read the public mood more accurately than any guru. For they had detected the essence of the spirit of liberation: for most people it was not an end of desire (as in some Buddhist sense), or a wish for solitary withdrawal (in a monastic sense), or even, as Leary had hoped, a spiritual longing equal to motivating an inward turn. Rather, after decades of relative conformity and one of ultimate conformity, what had been uncorked was powerful individual desires and the will to express them. Above all, most simply wanted to feel more like an individual. And that was a desire industry could cater to, just like any other.

The most confident among the advertisers knew that the 1960s would not extinguish consumerism, for a simple reason: desire's most natural endpoint is consumption, and advertisers, after honing their art for half a century, knew how to convert all manner of desire into demand for products. And young people's desires were no exception. In fact, as one advertising executive, John Adams, put it in 1971, "They [the hippies] are in the peak acquisitive years, and their relative affluence enables them to consume goods and services at a rate unheard of for their age level."[14]

Marcuse, who was the kind of idealist given to unrelenting pessimism, predicted in 1964 that the promise of liberation would be used for further repression. "Liberty can be made into a powerful instrument of domination,"[15] he argued, for "free election of masters does not abolish the masters or the slaves" and "free choice among a wide variety of goods and services does not signify freedom if these goods and services sustain social controls over a life of toil and fear."[16] This is where an intellectual loses his guruship: leading his followers toward a conceptual bridge too far. If the people wanted liberation, and if Pepsi was selling it, most people seemed to think, why not just buy it from them?

Of course, to succeed at selling a new snake oil, albeit one with a spiritual flavor, advertisers would still need one thing—access to the public mind. That they would have it points to the main reason why the hoped-for attentional revolution of the 1960s and 1970s ultimately failed. It was nothing to do with the message, which was, in fact, powerfully delivered and readily embraced. Rather, the failure was owing to one often unremarked fact: over the 1960s and 1970s, most people simply did not stop watching television.

The public was, the activist-adman Jerry Mander wrote, "as they had been for years, sitting home in their living rooms, staring at blue light, their minds filled with TV images. One movement became the same as the next one; one media action merged with the fictional program that followed; one revolutionary line was erased by the next commercial, leading to a new level of withdrawal, unconcern, and stasis. In the end, the sixties were revealed as the flash of light before the bulb goes out."

Consider that, over the 1960s, the countercultural Beatles, the Rolling Stones, and the Doors would all reach their largest audiences by appearing on *The Ed Sullivan Show*. Ultimately, the habit of prime time proved more powerful than the forces arrayed against it. With their access to the public mind mostly intact, the industries of attention had the opportunity not just to survive but to prosper.[17]

———————

While there had always been those who viewed broadcast television as irredeemable, more moderate elements believed that the medium was essentially neutral; if it had become nothing but an attention harvester, it might yet be reimagined and reprogrammed to serve somewhat loftier goals. Essentially they believed in the potential ascribed to TV early on by those like Murrow, who had said, "This instrument can teach, it can illuminate; yes, and even it can inspire. But it can do so only to the extent that humans are determined to use it to those ends."

Accordingly, by the early 1960s, noncommercial television stations were broadcasting in major cities: WNET in New York, KQED in San Francisco, WGBH in Boston, to name a few. It was Murrow himself who opened WNET in 1962, proclaiming the beginning of a "great adventure." And it was with juvenile audiences that the noncommercial alternatives found their first successes, most notably *Mister Rogers' Neighborhood* and *Sesame Street.*

"I got into television," Fred Rogers once told CNN, "because I hated it so." A soft-spoken aspiring minister who favored cardigans, Rogers had the idea, radical in its time, that children's television ought to be good for children. He had worked at NBC in the early 1950s, and then moved to Pittsburgh to work on a local public show named *The Children's Corner,* which briefly ran on the network.

Children, of course, have less control over their attention than adults, but when they do pay attention, they open their minds more fully to the messages presented. By the early 1950s advertisers had come to understand the commercial potential of reaching children by television. The *Howdy Doody Show,* featuring a clown and a dancing puppet, for instance, was sponsored by Kellogg's, and during every show Howdy Doody would dance around a cereal box. But those were the early days. By the late 1950s, programmers had learned to create shows that in a sense served as advertisements themselves, like The Mickey Mouse Club, which helped nurture enduring attachments to characters like Mickey Mouse, Donald Duck, and other friends. That, in turn, helped drive sales of toys, tickets to Disney's feature films, trips to Disneyland, and so on. And by the late 1950s, toy makers began creating toys specifically designed to be advertised on television: like Mattel's first girl-directed toy, the Barbie doll, whose commercials, which ran during breaks in The Mickey Mouse Club, chronicled glamorous episodes in Barbie's life.

Fred Rogers had fundamentally different ideas as to what the goals of children's television should be. But he could find no lasting place for his ideas in 1950s American commercial television. Instead he got his break in Canada, where the State-run Canadian Broadcasting Company invited him to present *Misterogers* for northern children. On his new show, Rogers invited children into an imaginary world populated mainly by puppets, who spoke to children as friends. When in 1964 Rogers returned to the United States, he relaunched the show in Pittsburgh as *Mister Rogers' Neighborhood.* And so began his new routine: changing his shoes as he came in the door, symbolizing the passage into a different world. Rogers's approach to his audience was highly innovative. He addressed ordinary, even mundane challenges, but ones likely to face his young viewers, like a fear of haircuts or monsters, or a quarrel between siblings.

Sesame Street, public television's second great success, was a self-conscious effort to "master the addictive qualities of television and do something good with them." The show's creators appealed to children by mimicking commercial television's tricks for gaining attention, with techniques like breaking news (narrated by Kermit the Frog), sponsors ("Today is sponsored by the letter E"), and "commercial breaks" featuring favorites like Ernie and Bert. Author Malcolm Gladwell summed it up this way: "*Sesame Street* was built around a single, breakthrough insight: that if you can hold the attention of children, you can educate them."[18]

Public broadcasting was not quite radical, but its growing strength came at a time when America's networks had indeed begun a close flirtation with losing relevance—meaning, young audiences. Most of NBC's, ABC's, and CBS's leading shows were still keyed to the tastes of the 1950s. If we examine CBS, in particular, we see that top shows of the 1960s were "rural" shows like *The Beverly Hillbillies* (about a backwoods family living in Beverly Hills), *Green Acres* (urban socialites take up "farm living"), and *Hee Haw* (a country music variety show). Innocuous, comforting entertainment, to be sure, and still capable of bringing tens of millions to prime time, each and every night, but hardly in sync with countercultural viewers. As ratings began dropping, the whole enterprise began to sag. Commercial television was surviving the late 1960s on sheer inertia—the lasting power of attentional habits is never to be underestimated—and the fact that the backlash, such as it was, was mainly in the younger demographics, and had not reached the whole population.

Buoyed by their success with children, over the late 1960s public broadcasters began to reach directly for countercultural audiences with shows like the *Public Broadcasting Laboratory,* a magazine program produced by Fred Friendly. It debuted with a drama featuring blacks in "white-face," and among *PBL*'s productions was *Inside North Vietnam,* a fairly sympathetic portrayal of the country under American air attack. Another ambitious effort was *The Great American Dream Machine,* an antiestablishment, anti-consumerist variety show, if such a thing could exist. "We're trying to show what a great country this could be," said the producers, "if we got rid of the false values sold to us by hucksters and con men who have contempt for the public."[19]

Meanwhile, in an effort to consolidate and extend the success of college radio, National Public Radio was launched at just about the same time, its first program director a college radio veteran, Bill Siemering. "I was an ordinary-looking Midwestern kind of guy," he said once. "No one ever remembered who I was. So I grew a beard." The debut of NPR's new flagship, *All Things Considered,* ran an hour and twenty-eight minutes, beginning with live coverage of Vietnam protests before turning to a lighter segment on small-town barber shops in "this age of unshorn locks, with shagginess transformed into a lifestyle." Over time, NPR would gain audiences even larger than public television's, proving the older broadcast platform yet had real life in it.[20]

Things might have turned out different for television as a whole, and CBS in particular, had the network not appointed a twenty-five-year-old named Fred Silverman as director of daytime programming in 1963. Silverman would later be acclaimed as "the man with the golden gut." Though hardly a hippie, Silverman had a good ear for what would speak to his generation and countercultural critics. Perhaps, too, he was just young enough to teach himself the Pepsi trick for selling to them.

Silverman's first successes were in children's programming, and his first coup was the unexpected success of *A Charlie Brown Christmas,* in 1965. Commissioned independently, the special was nothing like the typically gauzy 1950s holiday programming, for it was written as a sharp rebuke of the commercialization of Christmas. Rejecting the flashy aluminum Christmas trees then in fashion, Charlie Brown buys a pathetic actual pine sapling that seems to die when the first ornament is attached. The perennial loser and "blockhead" has blown it again. But, then, the other children realize that the sad little spruce captures the true spirit of Christmas. They decorate it into a glorious tree, which their song brings to life. *A Charlie Brown Christmas* proved once again the counterintuitive truth that anti-commercialism could yield great commercial success; and so it did, earning high ratings for CBS and excellent exposure for its sponsor, Coca-Cola.[21] Among other things, Silverman, who also launched Scooby-Doo, cited *Sesame Street* as an influence and proof that a show "can be entertaining and informative at the same time." By the late 1960s, CBS had already canceled its last prime-time game shows and launched *60 Minutes,* an obvious bid to resurrect *See It Now.* Now the show would prove that bracing investigative journalism could, in fact, garner top ratings.

By the late 1960s, some at CBS began to see that incremental adjustments aimed at children would not solve the problem facing television. If the business was to grow again, it had to do things aimed beyond the fan base of *The Lawrence Welk Show.* And so in 1970, Fred Silverman, just thirty-two, was made head of all programming, supported by Robert Wood, the new network president, who was forty-five. The new CBS would challenge many axioms of the attention merchant. Perhaps most importantly, it sought not just the largest audiences, but the "right" audiences. CBS was already the largest network, but the men took seriously what McLuhan called the "dinosaur effect"—the premise that they might be at their largest size right before extinction. The two immediately set about a thorough purge, redirecting the network toward the young, liberated, and socially conscious. Among others, chairman William Paley, now in his seventies, but still active in programming decisions, approved. As he said "You finally have . . . a vision of what is absolutely correct."

Within just two years, commercial television—still by far the heavyweight champion of attention capture—had seen its own revolution of sorts. CBS canceled nearly every show about the rural/urban divide and characters that were "fish out of water." As *Life* magazine wrote in 1971, "Slain were every single one of the hillbillies and their imitative relatives." Also on the block: the once dominant *Ed Sullivan Show.* Now came a whole new kind of program, like *The Mary Tyler Moore Show* (about an unmarried urban career woman), *All in the Family* (centered on the experiences of a working-class bigot living in Queens, New York), and *M*A*S*H* (an antiwar comedy about a field hospital during the Korean War, with regular appearances by blood and death). It was the era of "relevancy," and a CBS press release touted its new shows as appealing to the "now generation."

Silverman's bet was astute and his touch as programmer every bit as fine as Paley's—*Mary Tyler Moore, All in the Family,* and *M*A*S*H* were all big hits, eventually to become icons of television history. By 1974, the network had retaken nine of the top-ten-rated programs, and television itself had successfully made itself "relevant," saving it from a slow sapping of its energies, as its first and most faithful viewership began to age and die. At the same time, Silverman's success also perhaps showed the challenge and limits of reforming the medium according to Murrow's vision; for ultimately the business model remained the resale of human attention, and that reality was encoded in the very nature of all the programs. As Paley had first discovered, sometimes you could make the sale with panache; but if not, it still had to be done. Jerry Mander writes, the reformers believed "that television could communicate their message as well as any other. . . . Intent on changing other people's minds, they did not consider that television might change those who used it."[22]

Even a show as beloved and hilariously subversive as *M*A*S*H* can be understood to exemplify what Marcuse described as the kind of opposition that actually perpetuates the status quo.* Alan Alda starred as Hawkeye Pierce, an irreverent but deeply humane surgeon sick of the military and uptight people in general. Here was a man of the 1950s that any partisan of the counterculture could love. It was an example of a show, as Jerry Madel put it, that let the writers feel "they were still reaching 'the people' with an occasional revolutionary message, fitted ingeniously into the dialogue." At the same time, *M*A*S*H* kept tens of millions of Americans, would-be counterculturals among them, faithfully tuned to commercial television during prime time. If the contest really was, as Leary and others proposed, for the minds of the people, it was lost when America renewed its contract with the attention merchants. The broadcasters had adjusted the terms: now it was free, *relevant* entertainment in exchange for attention. But in the end, everyone would remain easily accessible to advertisers.[23]

As for the advertisers themselves, Pepsi had shown that they could make the adjustment to the new sensibility even more nimbly than the

---

* Marcuse had a particularly arcane term for this dynamic by which a putative form of liberation nonetheless manages to perpetuate existing power structures and prop up "the system." He called it "repressive desublimation."

broadcasters. A gang of hip new "revolutionary" agencies with young staff surged to success with innovative ways of doing things that mimicked the new younger thinking. These agencies—"the creatives"—mounted a serious challenge to the approaches, and the billings, of advertising firms established over the 1910s through 1920s and still dominant through the 1950s.

The best and clearest exemplar was New York's Wells, Rich, Greene, founded in 1966 by thirty-eight-year-old Mary Wells, its president and guiding force. Everything about the agency was timely, including Wells's announcement at its founding that "we are terribly aware of the current sounds and fears and smells and attitudes. We are the agency of today." Even the offices spoke rebellion: as one visitor wrote: "There is a psychedelic 'LOVE' poster in the foyer. The guest chairs are rattan or bamboo and they have baby blue pillows. . . . The receptionist is from Haiti with just the right amount of accent and chocolate thigh. It follows that the girls beyond the white foyer wall are mini-minded, but a couple are wearing pants."

For its slogan, Mary Wells chose one perhaps equally suited to a yoga studio: "love power." The idea, apparently, was to reach consumers with friendliness, and make them *love* the product; it was a 180-degree turn from Claude Hopkins's idea of scaring people into buying things. The approach eventually found its way into Wells's famous "I♥NY" campaign, with the iconic Milton Glaser design.[24]

The new breed of advertisers made it explicit that they were not like the advertisers of old. As a cosmetics ad written by Wells Rich reads, "We're not going to sell you a lot of goo you don't need." Instead, the ad reassured its readers, they were with the buyers, and shared their desires:

> We're young too.
> And we're on your side.
> We know it's a tough race.
> And we want you to win.

The firm infused the same rebellious themes into nearly all of its work. Wells herself instructed the staff to come up with ideas this way: "Consider what you can't do, then do it." Indeed, doing it the unconventional way became reflexive. When, for instance, Philip Morris gave them the account for Benson & Hedges—an old British brand whose main distinction was its length (100 mm)—Wells came up with a strange set of advertisements that focused on the disadvantages of a longer cigarette—being caught in doors, under car hoods, and so on, with the tagline "Benson & Hedges 100's must taste pretty good; look what people put up with to smoke them."

Much of this approach depended on hiring a new generation of creatives. By the late 1960s, agencies were a parade of long hair and miniskirts. Draper Daniels, who had worked on the Marlboro Man at Leo Burnett in 1950s, noted wryly, "Obviously, pink shirts are more creative than white shirts. Paisley shirts are more creative than pink shirts. A blue denim shirt, or no shirt at all, is the ultimate in creativity. Beads or a locket are a sure sign of something close to genius."[25]

The new hires were asked to put their revolutionary ideology acquired in college or graduate school into causes like Pond's cold cream. "The suffragettes who whip into the store for today's Pond's creams," read the new copy, are "a whole new genre of unfettered, free-spirited, savvy women who know how to cut through the phony baloney of the beauty business and get right down to basics." After a while, the trick became obvious enough for even the stodgiest of the 1950s advertisers and companies to get in on the act. Anyone, apparently, could be a hippie, or at least work with that desire for individuality and freedom to book billings.[26]

Perhaps no effort better typified the dexterity of advertising's old guard than the campaign for Virginia Slims. Introduced in 1967 by Philip Morris as a Benson & Hedges spinoff for women, Slims were just as long but even thinner. Leo Burnett's creative department dusted off the old 1920s saw of smoking as women's liberation to produce a version styled for second-wave feminism. Now the "torches of freedom" were being carried by women in floral print minidresses. The jingle ironically casts this return to one of modern advertising's lowest points as the ultimate step in the steady march of progress:

> You've come a long way, baby
> To get where you've got to today
> You've got your own cigarette now, baby
> You've come a long, long way

What was the secret to how the attention industries cheated death yet again, even when the whole zeitgeist of the late 1960s and '70s was seemingly against them? The success may finally be put down to the saving logic of capitalism. For what makes capitalism so powerful is its resilience and adaptability. The game is never lost, only awaiting the next spin of the wheel. As a mode of production, capitalism is a perfect chameleon; it has no disabling convictions but profit and so can cater to any desire, even those inimical to it. In *The Conquest of Cool,* Thomas Frank theorizes that "in the sixties . . . hip became central to the way American capitalism understood itself and explained itself to the public." And so even "disgust with the falseness, shoddiness, and everyday oppressions of consumer society could be enlisted to drive the ever-accelerating wheels of consumption."[27]

It would, however, be unfair to claim in a broad sense that the commercial attention industries "won" the 1960s from their noncommercial antagonists, whether public broadcasters, spiritual seekers, those espousing liberation à la Marcuse, or merely those yearning for a simpler life. For clearly those ideas would leave their lasting mark. Individualism became the dominant American ethos, even of capitalism itself. But in a narrower sense, commerce did win: the counterculture's call for the revitalization of spirituality and social consciousness inspired very few to make a permanent break even from television, the great portal to all that was wrong with society. To the contrary, by the early 1970s, television viewing had increased to an average of six hours per day per household. Perhaps Jerry Mander was right to say that the well-meaning had simply fought the wrong fight, seeking to reform television instead of realizing that it was the problem. What kind of force could take a moment of such disenchantment with its existence and turn it into a moment so ripe with opportunity?[28] Who could turn the world on with its guile?

Many were the hopes that would be chewed up and spit out again, Timothy Leary's among them. By the early 1970s, his dream of a religious awakening under the influence of psychedelics lay in ruins when he was imprisoned on drug charges following the criminalization of LSD. And so by that point, the main public exponents of his ideas—albeit in modified form—were companies like Pepsi, Pond's, and the makers of the grapefruit beverage Squirt, whose slogan was "Turn on to flavor, tune in to sparkle, and drop out of the cola rut."

Ever ready to identify itself with anything unquestionably American, even Coca-Cola, the brand once synonymous with 1950s conformity, would eventually arrive at the same place as everyone else. In 1971, they got another pillar of the establishment, the New York agency McCann Erickson (slogan: "Truth well told"), to express Coke's own version of liberation and love in what would be the brand's most enduring campaign. McCann identified the sweetest and most generous aspirations of the era with the buying of Coca-Cola. The result: a canticle to consumption, to fellowship as commerce—and the best damn commercial of the 1970s:

> I'd like to buy the world a home
> And furnish it with love
> Grow apple trees and honey bees
> And snow white turtle doves
>
> I'd like to teach the world to sing
> In perfect harmony
> I'd like to buy the world a Coke
> And keep it company
> That's the real thing[29]

CHAPTER 13

CODA TO AN ATTENTIONAL REVOLUTION

Coming of age in the 1950s and 1960s, Jonathan Robbin was fascinated by two things: social movements and the power of computers. He belonged to a particular breed of idealist, one that might include Frederick Taylor, George Nielsen, and Jeff Bezos, all of whom came to believe deeply that the world's problems could be solved by better data and management. What Wallace Stegner wrote of his character Rodman, a radical-turned-sociologist, he might have written of Jonathan Robbin: he was "interested in change, all right, but only as a process; and he is interested in values, but only as data."[1] Robbin himself put it this way: "I am interested in the problems of measurement and interpretation . . . understanding how things work and using that information and knowledge for the benefit of humanity."[2] In fact, over his career he would join the not-so-rare species of academic who begins by trying to save the world and ends up trying to cash in.

"Equally at home quoting Baudelaire and R. Crumb," as one observer remarked, Robbin would become a professor at New York University in the 1950s.[3] He would spend the following decade building first-generation computer models to predict things like where urban riots were likely to occur, the same way you might predict the weather.[4] Robbin's models were based on observations of the Chicago School of Sociology, which aimed to understand American communities like ecosystems. Neighborhoods, the sociologists thought, could be seen as super-organisms with lives of their own apart from those of the individuals living in them; they would mature and grow or shrink and disappear over time, like a rainforest.[5]

The aim of better understanding communities dovetailed with "the politics of recognition," a major strain of 1960s and 1970s countercultural thought. Like much else it developed in opposition to the "cookie-cutter" mentality of the 1950s. The rough thesis was that the diversity of the American public needed to be understood and recognized, particularly in the case of groups long left out of the dominant discourse. Along with related liberation movements, the 1970s saw a surge in popular interest in marginalized groups, like women, or subcultures, like African Americans, Latinos, gays, Native Americans, and so on. It all fit the spirit of individualism.[6]

Robbin's models brought computational rigor to the Chicago School's methods, which were empirical and qualitative. At the height of a progressive movement to acknowledge and empower neglected groups— African Americans most prominently—Robbin worked on what he called "cluster analysis," by which one could understand more precisely what kind of people lived in any neighborhood based on the "principle that residents living near each other are likely to have similar demographic, socio-economic and lifestyle characteristics."[7] His public-spirited but academic goal to gain a better understanding of what the nation really looked like.

In the early 1970s, however, perhaps succumbing to boredom, or academic disillusionment, Robbin decided there might be a way to commercialize his work. So he founded Claritas (Latin for "clarity"). A one-man start-up, Claritas was arguably the first firm to exploit the new social science that Robbin and other practitioners called "geodemography." The basic notion was that approaches developed to predict urban crime could also help advertisers improve the marketing of their products.

Robbin had noticed that the politics of recognition had a natural commercial counterpart that might be termed the business of recognition. For decades, most of the twentieth century really, advertisers had aimed their appeals to a great commonality, as imagined, or some might say invented, by advertising itself. The only recognition of distinct identities and desires took the form of trying to understand women buyers (as the Women's Department of J. Walter Thompson was charged to do) or young consumers (as everyone tried to do) and eccentric one-off efforts, like Pepsi's run at black America. But there were never rubrics any more granular than "blacks," "youth," or "Southerners." Members of these groups did have some things in common, yet much was missing.

Working with public census data, and the relatively new Zone Improvement Plan (ZIP) codes created by the Post Office, Robbin would produce his great masterpiece by 1978. He called it the "Potential Ratings in ZIP Markets" system, or PRIZM. PRIZM sorted the entire U.S. population into forty subnations, or "clusters," each with a set of exact geographical locations. With PRIZM, a new reality revealed itself to Robbin: there was no United States, but forty distinctive nations all calling the same continent home.

The notion of distinct social subsets within the borders of one country may seem obvious today. But at the time it gave the lie to an essential premise of marketing and advertising: that Americans were a single people whose demands could easily be served by one set of consumer products. Even those single-variable parameters that had earlier served the limited efforts at more specific targeting were obsolete. "Forget sex. Forget race, national origin, age, household composition, and wealth," wrote business author Michael Weiss, describing PRIZM. "The characteristic that defines and separates Americans more than any other is the cluster."[8]

What defined these forty nations? Based on the census data, Robbin identified thirty-four factors that he determined accounted for 87 percent of the variation across the United States. These did include race, income, and the like, but not acting alone. Rather, such markers tended to aggregate and follow the same pattern in similar places. Robbin programmed his computers to profile tens of thousands of new zip codes, sorting the results into these clusters of like-minded areas, each of which he assigned an evocative name, like the "Bohemian Mix," "Shotguns & Pickups," or "Young Suburbia."

As an early guide to the clusters prepared in the 1980s explains, those who lived in "Young Influential" neighborhoods were the "young, upwardly mobile singles and dual career couples"; mostly they were to be "found in the inner-ring suburb of major cities." As to priorities: they "don't care about good schools, because they don't have children." Rather, "they want a mall with a sushi bar, gourmet cookie shop, travel agency and a psychotherapy center."[9] They read books at twice the rate of the national average, and they tended to vote Republican. By contrast, Claritas found that those living in the "Bohemian Mix" areas, like New York's Greenwich Village, were "an eclectic melange of never-married and divorced singles, young Turks and older professionals, blacks and whites" who held "benefit dances for the Sandinistas." "Squash, racquetball and jogging" were among their typical pastimes.[10]

The initial definition of the forty clusters obviously involved considerable subjectivity on Robbin's part, but from the beginning he expected the clusters to evolve and grow more precise. In his vision of America, traditional demarcations, like state lines, didn't have much meaning; to drive across the nation was to visit not places like Kansas or Iowa, but rather local chapters of clusters like "Shotguns & Pickups," "Gold Coasts," and so on. While some (like "Sharecroppers" or "Industrial") were found in only certain regions, in general the same neighborhoods, as he saw it, repeated across the land, with any local variations being merely cosmetic.

PRIZM was put to one of its first great tests in 1982 with the introduction of Diet Coke. When Coca-Cola launched the new product (slogan "Just for the taste of it!"), its objective was to capture customers new to the growing market for diet soda, while not cannibalizing sales of TaB, its existing diet drink. Introduced in 1963, TaB was a healthy profit center and the country's leading diet beverage. But using Robbin's cluster analysis, Coca-Cola was able to determine that, in fact, just six types of people actually drank it, among them "Money & Brains," "Furs & Station Wagons," "Young Influentials," "Pools & Patios," "Black Enterprise," and "Young Suburbia." And so the company came up with a marketing plan that aimed for everyone else, essentially by inverting the pitch. "We positioned it as a great-tasting soft drink that happens to have one calorie, rather than as a diet drink that tastes great," said its adman, Steve Norcia. "We thought this would broaden its appeal as the first diet soft drink to emphasize sheer pleasure and great taste—not just part of a diet regimen."[11]

Such as it could, Coca-Cola avoided advertising Diet Coke in TaB clusters, and even began mailing TaB drinkers coupons for their preferred cola, so as to neutralize any collateral damage. It was entirely in keeping with the ultimate claim of PRIZM that you could say different things to different people and win them all. And it goes a long way toward explaining the system's later importance in politics.

To this point, with some experimental exceptions, the contest for human attention had been mostly approached as if everyone were roughly the same. But PRIZM revealed how the nation was actually a knowable mosaic of sensibilities and tastes—or even vulnerabilities and deepest desires. Here, at last, was a quantitative version of the shamanistic insight offered by Bernays and Dichter. For the advertising industry, it proposed a vast new horizon of targeted campaigns and additional billings. For the advertisers, it promised a more potent kind of messaging than the old scattershot method. Now, firms could not only tailor ads to their desired consumer but also fine-tune the product itself, so as to be more alluring to his or her specific attention. Here, too, was a way around the perennial attention industry problem of conditioned indifference; it is far more taxing to learn to ignore messages that seem to speak to you specifically.

And so, with the launch of Claritas, the liberating politics of recognition would attain its commercial correlative. Born of a wish for greater empathy and greater understanding of people from all backgrounds, the new system industrialized the project of finding out as much as possible about each and every one of us, not out of regard for anyone's dignity, but so as to know precisely what would catch our attention and make us want things we never knew we wanted.

Where marketing had led, media would follow. And so when cable at last scaled the walls that the networks had erected around television, its offerings would be as varied as the new map of America. And the efforts of those like Fred Silverman to make television more vital and interesting would give way to the commercial will to make it all things to all people, if not in all places.

"It seems that America's youth is about to be served," reported *The New York Times* in 1981. "This week Warner-Amex brings the Top 40 to television, when it inaugurates MTV, a 24-hour all music cable network service." The new service, analysts predicted, "will be popular with companies looking for ways to tap teen purchasing power." And if the "video disco channel" were to succeed in gaining five million subscribers, it might "creat[e] additional demand for video discs, and reducing the need for record companies to send groups on costly national concert tours."[12]

Not for you?

How about sixty and one half hours of sports programming per week on one channel? " 'That,' one man, said, 'is the ghastliest threat to the social fabric of America since the invention of the automobile.' 'No,' he was told, 'it is ESPN, the Entertainment and Sports Programming Network for sports junkies who have to have a fix every time they touch the dial.' "[13] Into the late 1980s, a dozen cable networks launched, each targeted not at the middle, like CBS and NBC, but at some demographic fragment.

Bravo launched in 1980, explicitly targeting lovers of the arts, assumed by its backers to be mostly women (but later to include gay men, when the appeal to two groups would be dubbed "dualcasting").[14] Two years on came BET, Black Entertainment Television, targeting blacks; and the Playboy Channel, targeting not only playboys but all straight men; as the *Times* reported, "Playboy Enterprises Inc. is now trying to transfer its 30-year-old formula—either sexual sophistication, or soft-core pornography, depending on the reader—to video." The network did make an effort to reach women as well, with shows like *Dr. Yes: The Hyannis Affair,* which was described as "a sort of topless *Dynasty*" following "the idle rich, with time on their hands and sex on their minds."[15]

"Audience fragmentation" was the industry term for what the new cable networks were molding themselves to, and it was of a piece with the idea of appealing to clusters through PRIZM. Of course it was never entirely clear whether "fragment" was being used more as a verb or a noun: Were the networks reacting to fragmented audiences, or were they in fact fragmenting them? In retrospect, they were doing both.

There is no doubt that the targeting of audience fragments was a reaction to the programming style of the 1950s, when men like William Paley and Pat Weaver went for the broad middle, when the supreme attention grabber was *I Love Lucy,* and one could capture more than 60 million viewers every week with the same show. This had happened at a time of relatively homogeneous national sensibilities following the great collective effort of winning the Second World War. But as we've seen, broadcasters used their monopoly over the most powerful attention capture technology yet invented to mold that relative sameness into a single, national consumer mass, unified in schedule, attentional habits, and information diet. At the time, nothing could have been better for their business or American business generally.

But what happened in the 1980s was a departure also from 1970s programming, which had turned the countercultural spirit into palatable viewing, mostly for the giant new generational block. Antiestablishment in tone, it nevertheless preserved the network status quo. To be sure, it would take the sort of new paradigm that usually follows advances in technology—in this case, the improvement of signal transmission over coaxial cable, among others—to make possible a truly radical break with the broadcast model.

Technology always embodies ideology, and the ideology in question was one of difference, recognition, and individuality. But commerce bows to none, taking its opportunities wherever they may lie. The logic of cable ultimately did not flow from the zeitgeist but rather from the opportunity it created for a host of upstarts to feast on the attentional harvest once the manna of the networks alone. And once all those newcomers began to contest what had been the broad middle, it began to fall apart, not at once, but from this point onward.

One upstart would even be well funded enough to challenge broadcast on its own terms. In 1986 the Fox Broadcasting Company suddenly appeared on televisions across America, its unstated mission to serve the un-served, at least in terms of entertainment. Its owner was an Australian newspaper magnate, Rupert Murdoch; its chairman and CEO, Barry Diller, a self-styled programming revolutionary himself. Out came a show conceived to be the "anti–*Cosby Show*" (in response to the hugely popular NBC sitcom starring Bill Cosby as a prosperous physician and occasionally befuddled father). *Married . . . with Children* was the chronicle of Al Bundy, an unhappy salesman of women's shoes; his lazy, lubricious, and self-indulgent wife, Peggy; their promiscuous and blazingly stupid daughter, Kelly; and their alienated, sarcastic son, Bud. Two years later, the network was out with another outside-the-box concept: a prime-time cartoon for adults called *The Simpsons*. With mostly yellow characters based on members of the cartoonist Matt Groening's own family, *The Simpsons* was a biting satire of middle-class life in middle America.

In 1996, Fox would make perhaps its most momentous move against the legacy broadcasters when it launched Fox News. Promising to be more "fair and balanced" than its chief cable rival, CNN, as well as network news, Fox in practice catered to conservative viewers who considered other news outlets liberal in bias, to the point of contempt for conservatives' views.[16]

In each case, whether broadcast or cable, Murdoch and Diller chased audiences believed, one way or another, to have fallen through the cracks, who had somehow disdained, or been disdained by, the mainstream. Not every new program worked, needless to say: *Babes,* a sitcom about three overweight sisters sharing an apartment, didn't last long, nor did *Get a Life,* about a thirty-year-old paperboy who moves back in with his parents. But hits like *The Simpsons,* together with the Fox News Channel, with its steady rise of market share, more than made up for the duds.

It was billed as a win-win, an alignment of commercial interests with those of a society now diverse enough to require a variety of choices to meet its full range of interests and sensibilities. Underlying the public-spiritedness was a flattering idea that the viewer should have more sovereignty over his mind and what came into it—should have the right to decide exactly how his attention would be spent, among a variety of real choices represented in the free-market gaggle of cable networks, good old broadcast television, and the new Fox shows. The exercise of that choice was facilitated by the now ubiquitous and reliable remote control, the scepter by which the new sovereign decreed his destiny.

As befits a story of unintended consequences, however, no one fully appreciated where "more choice" would lead. The idealists of the 1960s and 1970s envisioned a thoughtful public who knew what they wanted, and would judiciously select programs that precisely matched their preferences. The ordinary viewer, who formerly had his tastes dictated to him, would now be elevated by democratically inspired offerings. The leading visionaries of cable Ralph Lee Smith (author of *The Wired Nation*) and Fred Friendly both foresaw a new age of true media democracy, when one's attention was truly his own.

In actuality, the spectacle of a fragmented audience would prove nightmarish to many of those well-meaning liberals and progressives who had originally welcomed the idea. If they imagined a paradise of shows like *Sesame Street* or the countercultural *Public Broadcasting Laboratory,* the reality would look more like Fox News, MTV, *Married . . . with Children,* and nonstop sports coverage. While never radically progressive, the great middle, which the networks had held together with semi-coercive prime-time rituals, was at least more easily led toward moderate main-stream values. In some sense what did come to pass fulfilled an earlier prophecy of Friendly's concerning broadcast handled poorly; in 1970 he'd warned the system might "give way to a new Tower of Babel, in which a half-hundred voices scream in a cacophonous attempt to attract the largest audience."[17]

Even more unexpected, in retrospect, was the channel surfing, or put another way, the rise of a far more inattentive, scattered habit of viewing. A generation had passed since the darkened rooms of the 1950s, in which audiences had watched shows, one after another, in hushed awe. By the mid-1980s, *Channels* magazine was among the first to notice a new way of watching TV, which it called "grazing." "People, rather than viewing specific shows or even specific types of shows," the magazine reported, "like to sample in an un-patterned way a wide variety of what the medium offers. Their television diet comes from throughout the full buffet of shows."[18]

When you think of it, channel surfing, or grazing, is a bizarre way to spend your time and attention. It is hard to imagine someone saying to himself, "I think I'll watch TV for three hours, divided into five-to-ten-minute segments of various shows, never really getting to the end of anything." It hardly seems the kind of control Zenith could have had in mind when it first introduced the remote, to say nothing of the sovereign choice that cable's more optimistic backers had dreamed of. However fragmented, attention was still being harvested to be sure, but the captivity was not a pleasant experience.

The profusion of channels and ubiquity of the remote control, followed up by the VCR and its fast-forward function, also meant that, for the first time, television commercials were well and truly avoidable by means easier than the old expedient of getting up and going to the kitchen. As *New York* magazine announced: "1985 is the age of zapping—channel switching on remote controls or fast-forwarding through commercials."[19] For advertisers, this provoked a minor crisis, as their business and rates had long hinged on the fundamental precept of unavoidability. "Conventional wisdom in the advertising industry holds that a certain amount of irritation helps make advertising effective," wrote Rena Bartos of the J. Walter Thompson agency in 1981. "But the erosion of advertising credibility," she warned, may "be undermining consumers' trust in brand name advertised products."[20] Consequently, over the 1980s, the major advertising firms (after introducing fifteen-second commercials) began to suggest, not for the first or last time, that advertising would henceforth need to be more entertaining and engaging—something that people *wanted* to watch.

Of course, people have always wanted accurate information about products, but that's not advertising. The goal was something both persuasive but also entertaining, something that, somehow, would keep the channel surfer's finger still. Or as *New York* explained, the 1980s called for "zap-proof" advertisements, which were, in Madison Avenue's thinking: "animation, sixties-type-musical takeoffs, soft-sell patriotism, [and] MTV-style rock videos."[21]

Pepsi changed its slogan to "The choice of a new generation" and paid Michael Jackson an unprecedented $5 million to dance with children to a song set awkwardly to his "Billie Jean" (lyrics: "You're the Pepsi Generation / guzzle down and taste the thrill of the day / And feel the Pepsi way").*

Print advertising has always been less unpopular than television or radio; for it is more under the control of the reader who can avert the eyes. It can also be beautiful. Some of it became much harder to ignore during the 1980s, like a Calvin Klein campaign starring a fifteen-year-old Brooke Shields, or another picturing two men and a woman sleeping in their (Calvin Klein) underwear after a threesome. And on television, viewers (other than parents) might be less disposed to zap Shields posing provocatively in her Calvin Klein jeans and intoning, "You want to know what comes between me and my Calvins? Nothing." These were a far cry from the old, extremely irritating Anacin advertisements depicting hammers pounding the skull. Whether, in fact, they prevented zapping, however, is hard to know for sure. Fortunately for the advertising industry, it remained impossible to accurately measure whether people were watching commercials or not, saving the enterprise from a true and full accounting.

It was also during this era that the Super Bowl became a showcase for advertising's greatest talents, seeming to prove the point that there were, indeed, commercials that people truly wanted to see. A much lauded

* Michael Jackson's agent approached Coca-Cola first, but the market leader was not interested. "They [Coke] saw anything they would do with Michael," recalls the agent, "as a more targeted, ethnic campaign." Monica Herrera, "Michael Jackson, Pepsi Made Marketing History," *Adweek*, July 6, 2009.

advertisement for Coca-Cola that ran during the 1979 Super Bowl featured an enormous African American football player, Mean Joe Greene, being offered a Coke by a young white boy.[22] And in 1984, Apple Computer ran its "Big Brother" advertisement during the Super Bowl to great acclaim. Directed by *Blade Runner* auteur Ridley Scott, it portrayed a young woman running and smashing a giant screen to save society from a totalitarian overlord. "On January 24th Apple Computer will introduce Macintosh," the advertisement proclaimed. "And you'll see why 1984 won't be like '1984.'" The publicity created by its advertising, at least according to Apple, sold $3.5 million of its new Macintoshes.[23]

In retrospect, the word "remote control" was ultimately a misnomer. What it finally did was to empower the more impulsive circuits of the brain in their conflict with the executive faculties, the parts with which we think we control ourselves and act rationally. It did this by making it almost effortless, practically nonvolitional, to redirect our attention—the brain had only to send one simple command to the finger in response to a cascade of involuntary cues. In fact, in the course of sustained channel surfing, the voluntary aspect of attention control may disappear entirely. The channel surfer is then in a mental state not unlike that of a newborn or a reptile. Having thus surrendered, the mind is simply jumping about and following whatever grabs it.

All this leads to a highly counterintuitive point: technologies designed to increase our control over our attention will sometimes have the very opposite effect. They open us up to a stream of instinctive selections, and tiny rewards, the sum of which may be no reward at all. And despite the complaints of the advertising industry, a state of distracted wandering was not really a bad one for the attention merchants; it was far better than being ignored.

This is ultimately where the Great Refusal had led, not to a bang but a whimper. Faced with a new abundance of choice and a friction-less system of choosing, we individuals, in our natural weak-mindedness, could not resist frittering away our attention, which once had been harvested from us so ceremoniously. And the choices would continue to proliferate. As they did, and the attention merchants' work grew more challenging, the strategies for getting the job done would grow only more various and desperate.

PART III

THE THIRD SCREEN

From the 1970s through the 1990s, despite various challenges and adaptations, television and its associated rituals would remain the primary, indisputably dominant harvester of human attention in the Western world. Few but a handful of futurists could see that a new claimant to attention was looming, all the while quietly gathering strength; fewer still could have imagined this force challenging the most powerful attention combine ever invented. For a long while, the third screen would not really even be in the game. It idled as one of those hobbyist novelties that had yet to find its commercial application, rather as radio did in its early days. But once it had developed its own ways of capturing our attention, the computer would hook us for good. As one might expect of a truly disruptive technology, those methods would be nothing one expected, and quite a different proposition from those of broadcasting or other media. The ambiguity of what the computer was for would remain a disadvantage for years longer than broadcasting had taken to prove itself. But that was perhaps because it could, potentially, do just about anything. That very plasticity would let it take audiences from television in ways other technologies could not.

CHAPTER 14

EMAIL AND THE POWER OF THE CHECK-IN

In 1971, a thirty-year-old computer scientist named Ray Tomlinson, working in the outskirts of Cambridge, Massachusetts, took on an interesting assignment. Working at the government contractors Bolt, Beranek and Newman (BBN), near Fresh Pond, he was asked, roughly, to find something that might make the newly operational Internet useful to people.

In 1969, the earliest version of the Internet (called the ARPANET) had connected fifteen of the nation's leading research networks, including those at universities like UCLA, Stanford, as well as ones in the commercial sector, like IBM, and BBN, where Tomlinson worked. Connecting all of these nodes with one "universal" network was itself a technical achievement that has been widely celebrated. But a computer network alone is like a railroad without trains—it isn't inherently useful. They had built it—but who would come?

The Internet's lack of utility was, in fact, a serious danger to its future throughout the 1970s, a very precarious moment in its history. Fortunately, as a government project, it didn't actually have to make any money (had it been required to, there would have been no Internet). But eventually the Internet would have to prove of some use to someone, or face defunding.

Tomlinson, a classic tinkerer in the style of the early programmers, fooled around with a few ideas, with the help of two early computers in his office; even though right next to each other, they were connected through the early Internet. His main idea was to build some means by which his machines could send files to each other (a predecessor to what became known as the File Transfer Protocol). But as he tinkered, Tomlinson began to think not just about the machines but about the people using them. People could be awfully hard to reach by telephone, he mused. That's when he had a clever idea: why not modify his file transfer program to send messages? There was no grand vision; when asked later why he came up with email, he answered, "Mostly because it seemed like a neat idea."[1]

It happened that the large computers in use at the time already had primitive messaging systems, designed to allow users of the same machine to leave one another notes. Tomlinson merely modified his file transfer program so that people all over the networks could append text files, or messages, to other people's "mailbox" files. By his own description, the invention of email was nothing monumental. "Just a minor addition to the protocol" is how he later described the work that would change how everyone communicates.

The very first email messages were sent by Tomlinson to himself. Unlike the first telegraph transmission—Samuel Morse had famously sent the message "What hath God wrought?"—there wasn't much to the first email. "Most likely the first message was QWERTYUIOP or something similar," Tomlinson remembers. In later interviews he would explicitly deny that it was even that distinctive. As he told NPR in 2009, "The first e-mail is completely forgettable. And, therefore, forgotten."[2]

Tomlinson's final clever little hack was to use the @ sign to distinguish emails arriving from remote computers, so the format was "Tomlinson @remotemachine" (the .com and the like would be invented later). The choice was happenstance: as Tomlinson later told the Smithsonian, he'd been looking around for something to use when he noticed the @, poised above "P" on his Model 33 teletype terminal.[3] "I was mostly looking for a symbol that wasn't used much . . . I could have used an equal sign, but that wouldn't have made much sense." That the @ key was even on the computer keyboard was itself rather by happenstance, too. Its origins are obscure (one theory suggests it is an "a" placed within an "e" and an abbreviation for "each at"); it was sometimes used in commerce to designate the price at which each unit was being sold.

Tomlinson's own assessment of his invention was modest: a small but useful hack, hardly something that fulfilled BBN's assignment. But within a year, email had, to use a later vernacular, gone viral and given the Internet arguably its most powerful reason to exist, namely, not just to connect machines, but people. Email endowed the network with a social and human purpose—and in that sense, a soul. By 1973, a survey of network usage revealed that 75 percent of capacity was consumed not by, say, the transfer of important research documents but by email traffic.[4] To use another phrase coined later, email was the Internet's first killer app—the first program that might justify the cost of the entire network.

If email perhaps saved the Internet from a premature death, it also foretold its eventual significance. Its technical achievement would always remain the connection of different networks into one universal net. But its lasting importance to the individual would be the ability it conferred on him to connect with virtually anyone, whether for business, social reasons, or whatever else. As the content of those connections proved to be nothing less than astonishing in its potential variety, the Internet would begin devouring human attention. Together with its eventual portal, the personal computer, it would steadily grow into the greatest collector of human attention since the invention of television. That, however, was decades away, as if in another galaxy.

––––––––––

In the early 1970s, Stephen Lukasik, a physicist, was director of the Pentagon's Defense Advanced Research Projects Agency (DARPA), then the world's main funder of important computer research. But Lukasik was also, in one particular way, more like a twenty-first-century person than anyone we've met so far. Here's why: everywhere Lukasik went in the conduct of his business, he carried with him his "device"—a "portable terminal," manufactured by Texas Instruments. Lukasik's terminal was a massive thirty-pound piece of hardware, a sort of giant typewriter capable of speaking to a telephone. But by lugging it around, he could do something most of us take for granted: check for emails wherever he went (provided he could find a telephone to connect to). As such, Lukasik may have been history's first true email addict.

Stated differently, Lukasik was arguably the first to develop that little habit that consumes the attention of so many of us—the "check-in"— the impulse triggered by the intrusive thought that whatever else one is doing: "I need to check my email." The check-in would eventually become a widespread attentional habit; it would go on to power AOL, Facebook, Twitter, and various other future attention merchants built around various technologies and business models. No other has compelled so many minds with such regularity—regularity that has the feel of a compulsion, of a mental itch constantly in need of being scratched.

Just how the check-in ritual would come to make such a variety of attention merchants viable will become clearer as we see the computer go from Lukasik's thirty-pound terminal to the desktop to the laptop and the smartphone. For now, suffice it to say that among a tiny few, something had been born that would in time be comparable only to prime time in importance among attention rituals.

———————

Just what was it about the check-in experience of email users—or for that matter of chat room visitors, and the later social media variants—that made people keep coming back for more? Each of these activities, it turns out, may effect a form of what is called "operant conditioning."

We have already met John Watson, the psychologist-turned-advertising-executive, who pioneered the idea that humans are essentially like any other animals, reacting predictably to external stimuli. Over the 1930s, a more famous scientist, B. F. Skinner, would take the idea further. He regarded free will to be an illusion and argued that our behavior is a fabric of responses to past stimuli, in particular the rewards or punishments that any behavior attracts. Understood this way, all animal behavior developed through a learning process he called "operant conditioning," whereby some actions are reinforced by positive consequences (rewards), others discouraged by negative ones (punishments). To demonstrate what he meant, he built the so-called Skinner Box or "operant conditioning chamber," wherein he subjected animals to various consequences and observed their conditioning. For instance, by giving a pigeon a food pellet whenever it pecked at a button, Skinner conditioned the pigeon to peck the button so as to be fed. He also showed that pigeons could be conditioned to do things like turn in a circle (by reinforcing left turns), or even play competitive Ping-Pong.*

According to Skinner, we, too, in most aspects of our lives, are like pigeons pecking at a button to receive little snacks. And this, according to the cognitive scientist Tom Stafford, explains the check-in impulse behind email and other online technologies. Unlike a food pellet, email isn't always rewarding; in fact, it is often annoying (though with fewer people and less spam, it was surely more rewarding back in the 1970s). Once upon a time, there could be no new email for days at a time (few of us have that problem now). Much of what we get is uninteresting or indeed difficult to deal with. But every so often we get a message we are very glad to have. That such "rewarding" email comes unpredictably does not dim its allure or keep us from looking for it. On the contrary: as Stafford points out, the most effective way of maintaining a behavior is not with a consistent, predictable reward, but rather with what is termed "variable reinforcement"—that is, rewards that vary in their frequency or magnitude.

In experiments pioneered by Skinner and repeated over the 1970s and 1980s, psychologists demonstrated (again using pigeons in boxes) the somewhat surprising truth that behavior consistently rewarded is in fact more prone to "extinction" than behavior inconsistently rewarded. While they may be initially slower to learn the connection between deed and consequence, pigeons rewarded after an inconsistent number of pecks kept at it. As psychologist David Myers comments, "Hope springs eternal."[5]

Think for a minute about activities that entrance their practitioners, like gambling, shopping, or fishing. They all, in fact, have variable and unknowable reward schedules. A slot machine that rewarded every pull or even every third would offer no thrill; and no one hunts cows for sport. But take away the certainty and the real fun begins. Likewise, Stafford argues, "checking email is a behavior that has variable interval

---

* During World War II, Skinner even designed a missile that relied on a conditioned bird to guide it to its target. The pigeon sat in the very tip of the missile, behind a windshield. The effort was named "Project Pigeon."

reinforcement. . . . Everyone loves to get an email from a friend, or some good news, or even an amusing web link."[6] It is enough to have had such an experience a few times to get you regularly fishing for it; constant checking is thus reinforced, "even if most of the time checking your email turns out to have been pointless. You still check because you never know when the reward will come."

By this understanding, the gradual introduction of email was arguably one of history's greatest feats of mass Skinneresque conditioning. We might imagine those first offices wired in the 1970s and 1980s as so many Skinner Boxes, ourselves as the hungry pigeons. By the 1990s, we would all learned to peck, or check email, in hope of a reward. And once created, that habit would not only open us up to all sorts of commercial possibilities, including various other Internet applications depending on the almighty power of check-in to regularly collect human attention. Of course, in the 1970s, no one imagined the commercial value of email. Well, almost no one.

———————

In May 1978, Gary Thuerk, a marketing manager at the Digital Equipment Corporation (DEC), was thinking of a way to publicize the launch of a new line of advanced computers, the VAX T-series. DEC was based in Massachusetts, but Thuerk wanted to gain the attention of West Coast techies as well. So he decided to stage demonstrations in Los Angeles and Silicon Valley. But how would he get people to come?

"I looked at sending out invitations and calling all of those people," Thuerk would recall, "but it was too hard to reach them by phone and too expensive and slow to print out invitations and send them."[7] So, fully aware that he was "pushing the envelope," he decided to send out the world's first mass, unsolicited email blast. Using a directory of West Coast Internet users, he and his project manager laboriously typed 393 separate email addresses into a giant header that went on for several pages.

In all caps, his email read:

DIGITAL WILL BE GIVING A PRODUCT PRESENTATION OF THE NEWEST MEMBERS OF THE DECSYSTEM-20 FAMILY; THE DECSYSTEM-2020, 2020T, 2060, AND 2060T. . . .

WE INVITE YOU TO COME SEE THE 2020 AND HEAR
ABOUT THE DECSYSTEM-20 FAMILY AT THE TWO PROD-
UCT PRESENTATIONS WE WILL BE GIVING IN CALIFOR-
NIA THIS MONTH. THE LOCATIONS WILL BE:
TUESDAY, MAY 9, 1978—2 PM
HYATT HOUSE (NEAR THE L.A. AIRPORT)
LOS ANGELES, CA
THURSDAY, MAY 11, 1978—2 PM
DUNFEY'S ROYAL COACH
SAN MATEO, CA. . . .[8]

Unfortunately for Thuerk, the response was immediate and negative.
The Pentagon wrote an email describing the blast as a "FLAGRANT
VIOLATION" of federal policy. Thuerk got a call from a testy official
at the Pentagon, who informed him that the Internet was for official government business only. Thuerk said someone "called me up and chewed
me out. He made me promise never to do it again."

The incident also prompted a philosophical discussion among early
Internet designers as to whether advertising should be allowed on the
network at all. The consensus was a clear "no." Yet as Mark Crispin,
another early scientist who detested the DEC message and saw no place
for advertising, wrote: "I shudder to think about it, but I can envision
junk mail being sent to [regular] people . . . and no way it could be prevented or stopped. I guess the ultimate solution is the command in your
mail reading subsystem which deletes an unwanted message."[9]

As for Thuerk, for the rest of his life he seemed to take some pride in
his small moment of notoriety; he told *Computerworld* in 2007 that he
prefers to call himself "the father of e-marketing" and also made himself available for inspirational speeches.[10] At one point, he argued that
he shouldn't be blamed for the plague of spam. "You don't blame the
Wright Brothers for every flying problem."

Thuerk was indeed history's first spammer, and as such also an ancestor to the troll, two consistently recurring characters in the new bottom-
up, people-powered attention industries. The spammer and the troll
have their differences, but they have this in common—they defy social
conventions to harvest attention for their own purposes. Email, until
1978, was strictly noncommercial, limited to social and business functions. Thuerk broke that unwritten rule and gained as much attention

for himself as for DEC, perhaps at some cost to his reputation. But the other characteristic of the troll is not to care.

To give Thuerk his due, he did see, just as clearly as Benjamin Day or other pioneering attention merchants had, that there was value to all those eyeballs focused on the same thing. No one remarked it at the time, but the mind tended to fix on this new screen even more attentively than to television. Such a mind was therefore in the state most naturally primed for being sold something. But it would be another generation before the commercial potential of the computer would be manifest.

On the thirtieth anniversary of his email, for reasons known only to him, maybe just to be annoying, Thuerk would compose a poem:

> I do not eat Green Eggs and SPAM
> The Father of Email-spam I am.
> I do not drink Green Beer with SPAM
> The father of cyber-spam I am.
> I sent the very first e-spam,
> So in the Guinness Book I am.
> It is the Day for Green Eggs & SPAM.
> For it's the Anniversary of the first e-spam.[11]

The text perhaps bears close reading, but as the saying goes, "Do not feed the trolls."

CHAPTER 15

INVADERS

One day in the late 1960s, Ralph Baer was one of countless Americans sitting in front of his television set. But this engineer, who worked for the defense contractor Sanders Associates, wasn't flipping channels. Rather, he was asking: "What can I do with this?"

> There are forty million of them in the U.S., and another forty million of them elsewhere, and all I can watch here is stupid channels 5, 7, and 9—if I have a good antenna. And if I'm lucky, maybe I'll get Public Television channel 2, and if I don't like what I see, all I can do is turn the damn thing off. And after all, it's a pretty complex display. . . . If I could just latch on to plugging something into a set for one percent of them, that's 400,000 sets. . . .
>
> So I thought about it and said, "Maybe we could play games."

By 1972, Baer's idea had become a product, the Magnavox Odyssey, a primitive home video console; it had no sound and ran on C batteries. Most of its graphics, such as they were, were produced by affixing a plastic decal to the television screen connected to it; players controlled a spot of light, and used it to bat around other lighted spots in stylized versions of tennis or hockey. Baer ultimately sold about 350,000 units.[1]

Since its invention at midcentury, the electronic computer had been an object of enduring fascination. But by the 1970s, it remained a machine for serious business, institutional and industrial, not a consumer item, let alone one that might be used to harvest the public's attention in any way comparable to how radio or television did. But when it was shown to have the potential for personal entertainment, the computer's fate—and our story—were irrevocably changed.

The breakthrough game would come in a form largely lost to our times. Over the 1970s, a California company, Atari, built a cabinet with a computer inside. Atari's founder, Norman Bushnell, had seen the Odyssy and, like Baer, was enough of a tech geek to know that computers could, in fact, be great fun. He and other computer scientists with access to the mainframes had already been playing a game named *Space-War!* So Bushnell designed a cabinet, about the height of a man, configured somewhat like a phone booth (another obsolete receptacle); for a quarter, one could play the game inside like a pinball machine. Soon cabinets with various games—beginning with *Pong,* another tennislike challenge—started cropping up in various public places, sometimes collected in amusement arcades, alongside pinball machines. But it wasn't until Japanese developers got involved that computer games really hit the mainstream.

In 1977, Tomohiro Nishikado's boss at the Tokyo firm Taito, a manufacturer of jukeboxes and arcade games, asked him to make a Japanese version of the American video game *Breakout.** Earlier in his career Nishikado had done the same with Atari's *Pong,* resulting in *Ele-pong,* which proved a modest success, making him the natural choice. Nishikado took the assignment, and for some reason decided to carry it out entirely alone. Working long hours, he made substantial changes to the original. The opponents now moved across and down the screen, dropping bombs on the player's paddle, now transformed into a crude artillery unit, capable of firing back laser beams in response.[2]

In an early prototype, the opponents were tanks and soldiers but Nishikado's supervisors rejected it. "You must not create the image of war," he was told, perhaps out of Japanese sensitivity about past imperial

* *Breakout* was written by Apple's cofounders, Steve Wozniak and Steve Jobs, as a side project, as described in the *Master Switch,* chapter 20.

aggression. As it happened, Nishikado had around the same time been reading about the American hit film *Star Wars*. So he decided to name his game *Space Monsters*. In 1978, Taito released it in Japan as *Supēsu Inbōdā*—and everywhere else as *Space Invaders*.

In both markets *Space Invaders* was a sudden and unexpected success—nothing quite like it had ever been seen. "Outer Space Invaders are taking over the U.S.," reported the *Youngstown Vindicator*. The *Washington Post* reporter assigned to try the game described his experience this way: "I dropped in a quarter and saw 55 rectangles waving little arms and dropping laser bombs on earth, which is at the bottom of the screen. I fired back with my three laser bases, which got bombed out in about 30 seconds. . . . I was still pounding on the FIRE button at end of game. End of quarter. Start of addiction."

The themes of addiction and engrossment could be found in writing about video games from their debut. "It's like drugs," a *Space Invaders* distributor told *The Washington Post* in 1980. "They'll tell you: 'I got a $4-a-day habit.'" The first thing everyone noticed about *Space Invaders* was just how captivated its players were. It was a hard game—seemingly hopeless—yet something kept players coming back, trying to conquer it.[3]

"What we are dealing with is a global addiction," the novelist Martin Amis would write in his own meditation on video games in 1982. "I mean, this might all turn out to be a bit of a problem. Let me adduce my own symptoms, withdrawals, dry outs, crack-ups, benders." Psychologists and other experts were perplexed and disturbed by the appeal of the games, especially to children. "Most of the kids who play them are too young for sex and drugs," a Dr. Robert Millman told *The New York Times* in 1981. He proceeded to compare playing video games to sniffing glue. "The games present a seductive world. . . . [Young people want] to be totally absorbed in an activity where they are out on an edge and can't think of anything else. That's why they try everything from gambling to glue sniffing." Others seemed to think *Space Invaders*'s success had to do with America's recently ended war. "It's really Vietnam," wrote Ted Nelson, a magazine editor. "It's a body count war. You do it and you never ask why."

With *Space Invaders,* computers broke through as an indisputable part of the entertainment industry. Indeed, in 1982, the game would be the highest grossing entertainment product in the United States; outperforming even its inspiration, *Star Wars,* it earned more than $2 billion, one quarter at a time. But it was perhaps no surprise: by 1980, in the United States alone, video games were consuming 11.2 billion quarters annually, yielding $2.8 billion in revenue; by the early 1980s, the estimate was $5 billion, exceeding, for a while, the income of the film industry.

Video games also consumed something else, human attention, in a way that was both old and new at the same time. As in any real game—be it tennis, pinball, or blackjack—the fast-flowing stimuli constantly engage the visual cortex, which reacts automatically to movement. No intentional focus is required, which explains why children and adults with Attention Deficit Disorder find the action of video games as engrossing as anyone else. Unlike games in reality, however, video games are not constrained by the laws of physics, making possible a more incremental calibration of the challenges involved, duration, and related factors in the attempt to keep players coming back.[4]

But there were big differences between the new games and other things we have discussed that get us to pay attention, whether it be listening to *Amos 'n' Andy,* watching a sitcom, or reading email. For one, the business model: it was cash for an experience, rather like seeing a play or reading a book. The attention merchant model would not be contemplated until much later. Second, playing a game like *Space Invaders* was, as we've said, challenging—to the point of utter frustration. Most couldn't last longer than a minute. The games, at this stage at least, aimed for something completely different. The early players of *Space Invaders* were captured not by the dazzling graphics and sounds of today's narrative-based games, but by the urge to match their skills against the machine in the hope of finding, if only for a moment, that perfect balance between their abilities and the ghosts or space monsters chasing them. In this way, you might say they effected another form of operant conditioning.

Only a few games seem to have successfully achieved that balance. Some were simply too hard, others too easy, and those aren't really the only variables anyhow. But the best could sustain excitement, or even induce a "flow state," that form of contentment, of "optimal experience," described by the cognitive scientist Mihalyi Csikszentmihalyi, in which people feel "strong, alert, in effortless control, unselfconscious, and at the peak of their abilities." It was more than enough to keep people coming back, in their billions, across the world, and parting with their hard-earned money for a chance at such transcendence.

———————

As *Space Invaders* took off, Japanese and California companies rushed in to replicate its success, producing games like *Asteroids, Galaga, Caterpillar,* and the epic *Donkey Kong.* Genre aficionados would later describe the period between 1978, the release of *Space Invaders,* and 1985 or so as a golden age. Martin Amis described the English arcades of the early 1980s: "Zonked glueys, swearing skinheads with childish faces full of ageless evil, mohican punks sporting scalplocks in violet verticals and a nappy-pin through the nose." The places, meanwhile, were run by "queasy spivs, living out a teen-dream movie with faggot overtones."[5]

As with any business, initial success in the new video game industry stirred thoughts of expansion. Moving beyond male teenagers would be a start.

Namco, another Japanese company, had set its sights on winning over girls and women. "Back then," said Namco designer Toru Iwatani, the arcade "was a playground for boys. It was dirty and smelly. So we wanted to include female players, so it would become cleaner and brighter." Iwatani, then twenty-five, was the creator of *Gee Bee* and its two sequels, *Bomb Bee* and *Cutie Q;* he was tasked with producing something suitable. As he describes it, "My aim was to come up with a game that had an endearing charm, was easy to play, involved lots of light-hearted fun, and that women and couples could enjoy." He originated a concept centered on eating, because he noticed his girlfriend liked desserts. Then, "the idea occurred to me of constructing a maze in which movement was restricted to the four basic directions—up and down, left and right." For the game play, he decided on a "chase" inspired by *Tom & Jerry,* the cat and mouse duo of cartoon fame. He then created, as lead character, the great eater, who was nothing more than a moving mouth named "Pakku Man," based on the onomatopoeia "paku-paku," the sound Japanese speakers would say the mouth makes while it is eating. Visually, the eater was inspired, in part, by a stylized version of the Japanese character for mouth, O, with a part removed, like a pizza missing a slice.

In the United States *Pakku Man* became *Puck Man;* and later, to remove any temptation for vandals, *Pac-Man.* Finally, out of nowhere really, Iwatani had the idea of making the antagonists ghosts with distinct personalities. They were, in the original game, the "Urchin," "Romp," "Stylist," and "Crybaby," and each had a different way of chasing Pac-Man. In English their names were Blinky, Pinky, Inky, and Clyde.

Pac-Man soon became an even more lasting and profitable hit than *Space Invaders,* as its appeal went beyond its demographic target. Some early video game critics were dismissive. *Omni* magazine decried "the latest craze," which it called "a silly 'gooble or be goobled' game." "Those cute little PacMen with their special nicknames, that dinky signature tune, the dot-munching Lemon that goes whackawhackawhackawhacka: the machine has an air of childish whimsicality," wrote Amis. Nonetheless, 400,000 of the arcade cabinets were sold worldwide, grossing billions of quarters, 100-yen coins, and other denominations. Over its entire run, by one estimate, *Pac-Man* earned more than $2.5 billion by the 1990s. To his credit, Amis gave solid advice on how to play the game. "PacMan player, be not proud, nor too macho, and you will prosper on the dotted screen."[6]

Having conquered, and then diversified, the arcade, there was really only one place for gaming to go: back to the future, where Magnavox Odyssey had started. And so the computer would enter the home to resume the contest whose seeds Ralph Baer had planted: that between the second screen as broadcast platform and as gaming peripheral. Atari, still run by its founder Bushnell, thought a home video game system could succeed by allowing people to play the most popular arcade games, like *Space Invaders,* on their televisions. The effort gained heft when Warner Communications (forerunner of Time Warner) bought Atari and started pushing the consoles. But real success wouldn't come until Atari licensed *Space Invaders* in 1979; it would go on to sell a million units that year; then two million units in 1980, and by 1982 it had sold 10 million, making Atari at that point the fastest growing company in U.S. history.

The significance of those little Atari 2600 consoles appearing in homes would only become apparent later. For many people, here were the first computers to come into the home, and the first new screens, after the television, to breach those walls. They made easier the entry into the home of not just more consoles, but also home computers, like the Apple II or the Commodore 64, for it was one thing to buy an expensive machine that supposedly would be used for work or programming; it was another to get all that along with the spoonful of sugar, namely, a machine that also came with even better games than the Atari had. In this way video games were arguably the killer app—the application that justifies the investment—of many computers in the home. As a game machine, sometimes used for other purposes, computers had gained their foothold. There they would lie for some time, a sleeping giant.[7]

CHAPTER 16

AOL PULLS 'EM IN

In 1991, when Steve Case, just thirty-three years old, was promoted to CEO of AOL, there were four companies, all but one lost to history, that shared the goal of trying to get Americans to spend more leisure time within an abstraction known as an "online computer network." Their names were CompuServe, Prodigy, AOL, and GEnie, and merely to state their mission is to make clear why theirs was no easy sell.

Despite a certain whiff of excitement and novelty, neither personal computers nor online networks were seen as particularly entertaining, except to those who used them to play video games. The machines had a devoted cult following, and there was a mystique to them as portals into the mysterious virtual world named "Cyberspace" as depicted in novels like William Gibson's *Neuromancer* or Neal Stephenson's *Snow Crash*. But most who had a computer usually kept it in the den or basement; the machine itself was unwieldy and ugly, consisting of a large, boxy body and a screen smaller than today's laptops. In an age before widespread use of graphical interfaces like Windows, a glowing text, orange or green, was still what one faced; it had been that way since the first fully assembled home computers with dedicated screens, the Apple II and the Commodore PET, were marketed in 1977.* As for a mouse, that was still a creature known to reside in a small hole.

Meanwhile, just as today, the television remained prominent in the living room, with its large attractive screen and dozens of channels; to use it required little expertise, nothing of the sort of arcane knowledge needed to operate a modem. Thus even to speak of the computer as a competitor to television in 1991 would have been a laughable proposition.

So if they were going to get people to sit in front of a computer screen and "dial-in" to networks (the commercial predecessors of the Internet), the online networking companies needed to do *something* to lure Americans away from television (as well as family, magazines, and other lesser draws). Over the 1990s each of our four companies tried something different. The story of what finally worked is in many ways the story of how networking and the Internet—and the third screen—would come to win for itself such an amazing share of the nation's and the world's attention. It's also the story of how a new breed of attention merchants came into being.

Before going further, let's observe that, with one exception, the business model of these "computer information services" as they called themselves, was not that of attention merchant but solely subscription-based. At the time, there was no easy way to reach the Internet, which was still a government-run network devoted mainly to research. The four services offered customers access to proprietary networks, primitive little Internet-like spaces, with attractions such as news, discussion forums, and online games. To go online—connect to a network—also required the purchase of a modem, into which one had to enter a string of somewhat byzantine commands, while also occupying the family phone line.† The firms charged a fixed monthly fee, plus an hourly rate for time spent online and various extras. AOL for instance charged $9.95 for up to five hours a month and $3.50 for every additional hour. That it expected roughly 90 percent of its customers to be satisfied with five hours a month gives some indication of usage levels, and attractions, at the time.

---

* Before this, personal computers had come in the now unrecognizable form of hobbyist kits, assembled and programmed by guys like Steve Wozniak of Apple. For more, see *The Master Switch*, 274–75.

† Example: +++, ATDT (416) 225-9492.

The market leader in 1991 was the oldest of the four firms, the solid and serious CompuServe, owned by H&R Block. Its subscribers, numbering roughly 600,000, were largely male, a mix of computer hobbyists and some businessmen. CompuServe took the way of substance over style, betting that pure data was what mattered to its customers, who seemed to appreciate the no-nonsense, text-only interface. Since it originally used idle time on commercial mainframes, CompuServe gave its users numerical identifications (example: "70014,2316"), and sold them on utility: "When you join CompuServe," its ads promised, "your computer becomes a time-saving, money-making, life-enhancing tool."[1]

Just behind CompuServe—even ahead of it by some measures—was the most ambitious and audacious of the four. Prodigy was a fast-growing operation founded by the odd combination of Sears, CBS, and IBM. It styled itself as the visionary alternative, the kind of place where managers would say things like "The future is here." Aiming for mainstream consumers, Prodigy was betting that, for most users, online would be a world of shopping and entertainment, and that whoever had the most and best of both to offer would win. It also foresaw the importance of being an attention merchant, by betting on online advertising as its business model. That approach certainly put them ahead of GEnie, or the "General Electric Network for Information Exchange"; run by GE on CompuServe principles, GEnie was another text-only service with about 350,000 users.

Lingering in fourth place was the D.C.-based America Online (previously called Quantum Link). With just thirty thousand subscribers and no rich owners, it had an uneven track record, including several flirtations with bankruptcy. Its founder, William von Meister, had once been described as "a cackling Amadeus . . . the ringmaster at the circus."[2] He was long gone, but the zany spirit remained. To the degree it had a strategy, AOL was catering to people who knew nothing about computers, the shopping and entertainment users that Prodigy had more of.

———————

Of the four, it was Prodigy that, in many ways, would prove most interesting, particularly considering the gap between its soaring vision and what it ultimately offered. The big corporate backing bred wild over-confidence. "The issue really isn't success or failure," the chairman of Sears, Edward Brennan, said in 1989. "We're not going to fail. It's really a question of how big the success is going to be."[3]

Prodigy initially spent an enormous sum (about $650 million) to develop and advertise its network, and built a veritable virtual palace, at least by the standards of the early 1990s. Seeing the text-only approach as too dreary or intimidating, they created a primitive graphic user interface, making it as easy to use as possible. Then came more heavy investment, now in branded content from partnerships with CNN, expensive commissions of well-known columnists, paid interviews with movie stars and athletes, and even a full-time newsroom staffed 24/7 with human reporters in its White Plains, New York, headquarters. To draw in new users, it turned to advertising, and in particular to J. Walter Thompson, which developed the slogan "You gotta get this thing!" in magazines, newspapers, and even national broadcast spots.

Prodigy pushed ideas that wouldn't come to real fruition until at least a decade later. From its beginnings in 1989, it saw itself reselling the attention directed to computer screens. "IBM and Sears executives envisioned a new advertising medium," wrote *Wired* in 1993, "that would assemble audiences for marketers much as niche TV channels do." It believed that if its content was good enough and the service were cheap enough to attract a crowd, it would eventually attract enough eyeballs to resell for profit. "Visionaries at IBM and Sears figured they could sell advertising on every screen and tap a potential revenue stream far larger than the sum of the hourly fees charged by existing online services."[4] Like the penny press, Prodigy sought its mass audience by offering a low price—$9.95 a month, a money-loser unless advertising paid off. Unfortunately, unlike the *New York Sun,* revenue didn't meet expenses, and by the early 1990s Prodigy had lost hundreds of millions.

In case advertising didn't work out, Prodigy also envisioned another lucrative revenue stream, this one reflecting Sears's ownership. It saw itself becoming the world's dominant computer-based shopping network, something akin to an early Amazon. "We had a belief that goods will be sold electronically," said the CEO, Ross Glatzer, "so why not establish dominance in the marketplace?"[5] Unfortunately, the entire retail strategy was based on a faulty premise: that online retailers would naturally be able to charge more than brick-and-mortar stores. It didn't help that, given the state of computer graphics in 1992, one only had a rough idea of what one was paying a markup for.

Under its relatively new CEO, Steve Case, AOL was hardly in a position to do what Prodigy did. As the smallest and most poorly funded of the networks, they had no money to spend on content and no relationships with advertisers. Almost by default, then, AOL's approach was to let users entertain themselves, which the firm optimistically described as a bet on the "electronic community." "We recognized that communications—a combination of chat and e-mail—were critical building blocks," Case later told journalist Kara Swisher. "So our bias was on creating tools, empowering people, and letting them use them in any way they thought appropriate—sort of 'Let a thousand flowers bloom.'"[6]

AOL's software did make it easy for users to get in touch with, and in that way effectively entertain, one another. Its designers were dedicated to making AOL a happy, friendly place—and as such perhaps something of a cure for loneliness. As one employee, Randy Dean, later put it, "We wanted [our users] to have these little epiphanies, out there by themselves typing on their computer, that they were part of something bigger, that technology did not have to be a cold place, that there was comfort out there."[7] Just as television had initially presented itself as bringing family together, AOL would allow those living in modernity's increasing isolation to reach out.

Among the sources of such comfort would be AOL's infamous chat rooms. Chat rooms had actually been invented by CompuServe in the 1980s (under that '70s handle "CB simulator"), but AOL allowed the creation of "private rooms," which anyone could open, hosting up to twenty-three total strangers. By 1997, they would claim to have nineteen thousand different rooms. One key to this success: AOL had female users—not many, but enough to create a completely different atmosphere than the average CompuServe chat room, which might be, for example, a group of dudes conversing in medieval English. CompuServe may have had much the same setup, but being distinctly and persistently inhabited by hard-core computer users and other breeds of geek and nerd, they just didn't know how to get the party going, not one the general public would care to join anyway. (A note to puzzled younger readers: in the 1990s, nerd-cool had not yet been invented.)

With its wide-open chat rooms, AOL seemed to tap into the excitement of what people then called "cyberspace," and its tantalizing possibility for a new disembodied kind of human connection. Chat rooms could be used to discuss anything, and since no one had to use a real name, they allowed for a taste of that liberation Marcuse had dreamt of. One of AOL's employees, Joe Schober, called them "frontier towns" and later recalled, "As a gawky kid entering high school, chat rooms were a haven from the awkwardness of real human interaction. I'd use them to discuss punk bands like Operation Ivy with other teenagers, to play the chat room–equivalent of *Dungeons & Dragons,* and talk to what I very much hoped were actual girls."[8] The AOL chat rooms developed a reputation for excitement and transgression. There was "the feeling that this was a new and semi-lawless space, that unexpected things could happen."[9]

Like virtual sex, of course. There's a popular folk theory, apparently of Freudian inspiration, that the driver of any technological advance is either sex or warfare. However exaggerated, like a broken clock, this theory is occasionally right. It was in the case of AOL, where users flocked for, if not sex exactly, then potential titillation, and who knows what might follow—much the same proffer that draws college students to frat parties. In any case, chat rooms catering to seekers of anonymous sexual titillation and flirtation were by far the most numerous and popular, so much so that over the mid-1990s, AOL became fairly synonymous with cybersex, anonymous virtual sexual encounters conducted entirely by typed messages. "The idea that you could play out your kinky fantasies and ideas with these strangers across the country who you'd never met, and have them be excited and responsive and engaged, was incredibly exciting to people," said psychologist Rob Weiss.[10] Here was the harbinger of the sexual future.

Early users of AOL are now grown up and have some tawdry experiences to recount. In 2014, writer EJ Dickson wrote of her virtual relationships when she was a ten-year-old.

His AIM handle was FrankZappy, and I believe he claimed to be a married man from Queens. I was Dana, a name I had lifted from a character on my favorite Purple Moon CD-ROM. Dana was 19, an aspiring veterinarian, and everyone told her she looked like Britney Spears. We met in an AOL chatroom in the "Friends" category, bonding over a shared interest in baseball and the inspiration for his screen name; I'd impressed him by referencing the lyrics to "Don't Eat the Yellow Snow."[11]

Eventually, one thing led to another. "Of course, I had no idea what I was saying; much of what I said was based on what I had seen on *General Hospital* and read in Jackie Collins paperbacks. And to be honest, I don't think he knew what he was saying either. He wasn't particularly imaginative, or even literate." But in defense of the chat room, she writes that "early cybersex allowed young women to explore their early sexual identities and desires without the fear of guilt, judgment, or censure that would usually accompany such efforts at school or elsewhere."

The chat rooms would persist even after the opening of the World Wide Web. Unsurprisingly, having so many sex-charged ones gave the service something of a seedy reputation. In a 1995 headline, the *Philadelphia Inquirer* called the service "A Tawdry Back Alley, Just Off the Information Superhighway." Perhaps just as unsurprising, that reputation hardly slowed AOL's growth and probably enhanced it, especially when the content of some chats was revealed in congressional committee, managing to scandalize members. Senator Herb Kohl, Democrat of Wisconsin, declared in a Senate subcommittee that "most Americans don't know what it is out there on the Internet. If they did, they would be shocked."[12]

In October 1992, Walter Mossberg of *The Wall Street Journal* reviewed Prodigy and AOL (which he referred to as "online database services"). Prodigy, he concluded, was "organized more like a broadcast network than a common carrier of information." While he praised its news service, he ultimately found it "seriously flawed." As he wrote, "its content promises more than it delivers" while splashing "distracting paid advertising across the bottom of many of the information screens." AOL, in contrast, simply ran more smoothly; its "electronic-mail system is sophisticated and easy to use" and, Mossberg concluded, "I see America Online as the sophisticated wave of the future."[13]

For almost all of its history, AOL's most important feature was email; even more subscribers used it than visited the chat rooms. We have already seen how email was able to induce a Skinneresque check-in habit even among the first scientists to use it. Perceiving straightaway email's habit-forming properties, Steve Case and his team applied themselves to encouraging the addiction among subscribers. For one thing, users could send an unlimited number of emails. Prodigy, by contrast, having been slow to offer email, foolishly decided to charge users who sent more than thirty per month. At AOL, email was sent early and often. In fact, the whole user interface centered on the application. Immediately after logging on, one heard a pleasant male voice saying: "You've got mail." With that appeared a whimsical picture of a postbox stuffed with letters, a virtual cornucopia of potential rewards in human connection.

Of course, by the 1990s AOL wasn't alone in providing email to people outside computer science and government. Universities had begun handing out email addresses early in the decade to anyone interested, and to all students by the mid-1990s. In the late 1990s, companies began creating email addresses for their employees. The race was on, and in a classic example of network effects, the more people who had email, the more valuable it became.

It may be hard for some to imagine a moment when receiving email was considered a big deal. At the time, however, it seemed exciting enough for Nora Ephron to base a Warner Bros. romantic comedy on the story of two strangers (played by Tom Hanks and Meg Ryan) meeting through AOL email.* *The Washington Post* wrote that Ephron, herself a subscriber, depicted "the service as smooth, cool, a glamorous tool of glamorous people."[14] To capitalize on that aura, the original title of her film, *You Have Mail,* was changed to echo exactly AOL's "You've Got Mail."

In 1993 AOL had the rather brilliant idea to promote email by using what we now call snail mail. It had been a challenge for all of the services just getting people to try them. While Prodigy relied on retail sales (the "starter kit" cost $50, and was sold at Sears) and national advertising, that summer AOL mailed out several hundred thousand floppy disks,†

---

* The movie also proved an opportunity for the first meetings between AOL and Time Warner executives: Steve Case and Jerry Levin met at a White House screening of the film. See *The Master Switch,* chapter 19.

† The "floppy" disk was a magnetic storage medium used in the 1980s and early 1990s, originally the size of a dinner napkin, that was inserted into a "disk drive" that resembled a toaster. Its name was derived from the fact that, unlike the metal "hard" drives that remain in usage today, the floppy disk was made of a flexible plastic.

offering a free promotional membership. The program was extraordinarily successful, achieving an average response rate of 10 percent (the norm is about 1 percent or less). Thus emboldened, AOL doubled down, and then doubled down again, moving to CDs, as people kept on signing up. By the mid- to late 1990s, "50% of the CD's produced worldwide had an AOL logo on them," according to Jan Brandt, then AOL's chief marketing officer. "We were logging in new subscribers at the rate of one every six seconds."[15]

By mid-decade, in fact, usage of all the networks (except GEnie) had soared; it was just as Prodigy had predicted but not for the reasons they had thought. For one thing, these "private" networks were also a way to get onto the Internet, which was its own sensation and attraction, and a stroke of luck for AOL and company. But the networks had also uncorked something that they did not themselves fully understand—the effect that in later jargon would be called "social." The strategy of using people to gain the attention of other people was in retrospect inspired, even if arrived at more or less by accident.

As the new craze for social hit all the networks, Prodigy, with its fixed business model and regimented corporate culture, reacted more with alarm than excitement. It began to panic at the overuse of its email system, especially when an internal survey revealed that just 5 percent of members were sending over 3.5 million email messages. And so the overlords decided to levy surcharges on "email hogs"—those who sent more than thirty per month.

It would prove part of a pattern of misapprehension. Later, when its chat rooms took off, Prodigy became concerned that the wild, unpoliced forums might discourage advertisers and damage the company's "family friendly" image. They therefore decided to ban profanity and other offensive speech, as well as any chats that reflected negatively on Prodigy's owners or advertisers. Later, it banned flame wars (those extended bouts of troll against troll) among members. Eventually, postings even mentioning another member by name were forbidden. By then, every message was being examined for potential infractions. And so Prodigy wound up creating something more akin to the *Camel News Caravan* of the 1950s or today's Chinese Internet than anything we would recognize as the free and open web.

Prodigy's censorship, as well as its stubborn adherence to the ad-based model, helped AOL gain enough momentum to come from behind and overtake both Prodigy and CompuServe. By 1995, AOL would boast over four million subscribers. Slow and steady CompuServe had ridden the boom to just four million, while Prodigy was at two million and dropping. By 1997, when AOL cemented its dominance by buying CompuServe, which had effectively thrown in the towel, its usership rose to nearly 12 million.

AOL had, over the 1990s, decisively proven that the surest allure of the new computer networks was social—the prospect of interacting with other people. The point is more profound than it may at first appear. The discovery that traditional content was not the only basis for capturing attention, that our friends and acquaintances (or at least representations of them)—to say nothing of the attractive strangers we might hope to meet—that they, too, might have the same potential was nothing less than revolutionary. Of course it seems obvious in retrospect: however much of our attention we may devote to television, most of us pay at least as much, if not more, to friends, family, and co-workers, particularly if all our various means of communicating with them (texts, phone calls, etc.) are taken into account.

Ultimately it also suggests how incomplete the conquest of human attention was from the 1910s through 1960s, even after television had entered the home. For, though it had breached the private sphere, the domain of the interpersonal remained inviolate. In retrospect it was virgin territory for attention merchants, though before the home computer one couldn't conceive how this attention might be commercialized. Certainly no one had ever considered the possibility of advertising messages over the telephone—before one placed a call, for instance—not that the telephone was in need of a business model. And so, as AOL finally turned to the reselling of attention, it brought the commercial model of the attention merchant to one of the last spaces thought sacred—our personal relationships.

While America Online was by the late 1990s pulling past its competitors, it nonetheless faced what its investors and Wall Street analysts perceived to be serious problems with its business model. By 1996 it was charging $19.95 a month for twenty hours, and then $2.95 an hour after that. But it faced price competition from both Microsoft and other "bare-bones" Internet services that were offering "all you can eat" for $19.95 a month or even less. At the end of 1996, AOL switched to unlimited time for $19.95. That brought in millions of new users but also crashes, busy signals, and an investigation by New York State's attorney general accusing AOL of offering a service it could not provide. Its revenue growth trimmed, AOL began a mildly desperate search for alternatives.

That year AOL's board hired its first executive from "old media"—Bob Pittman, cofounder of the cable network MTV who had also worked at Time Warner. With no particular experience in computing or networks he was, nonetheless, the new president. Yet another son of a minister (Methodist), Pittman had described himself while at MTV as "wildly passionate and naturally argumentative *and* incredibly inflexible."[16] By the 1990s he was known as a "brand master," a "marketing genius," and a "synergy guru."

Most important for the board, Pittman brought with him the business mind-set of the New York media industries. At the time, in its search for revenue alternatives, AOL thought it could perhaps sell books, or offer its own brand of telephone services.* But on first look Pittman noticed that AOL had millions of customers staring at screens, and instantly concluded that its financial future was as an attention merchant. No matter that AOL had distinguished itself in the early 1990s as "ad-free" (in contrast to Prodigy). After years of building the AOL brand and attracting millions of customers, it was now time to "leverage the asset," or, in Pittman's alternative terminology, time to "harvest."

To sell the advertising, AOL tapped an experienced New York adman, Myer Berlow, who like Pittman had no experience with anything computer-related. But arriving in the suburban cubicle-land of AOL in black Armani suits and silver ties, with his hair slicked back à la Gordon Gekko, Berlow did bring with him the culture of Madison Avenue in its more lurid manifestations. Already wealthy, he might fly in the off hours to Las Vegas and park himself at a blackjack table to relax.

---

* The AT&T breakup and the 1996 Telecom Act had made reselling long-distance services appear attractive. See *The Master Switch,* chapter 21.

Consequently, his tenure at AOL, amidst the khaki-clad geeks, had the makings of a fish-out-of-water story television writers used to love. And it wasn't long before he began to clash with AOL's programmers, who had the traditional geek's antipathy to advertising (perhaps because they viewed it as a form of darkish Jedi mind control). When they refused to rewrite code to run ads, Berlow asked, "Who do I have to fuck to get you people to do your jobs?" Even CEO Steve Case, while no programmer, was geek enough to dislike the new advertising. When reviewing a healthy deal with Sprint to run a banner ad, he balked. "What really bothers me," he said, "is the ads are in a place where members will see them." Berlow asked his CEO with admirable candor: "Are you out of your fucking mind?"[17]

Nonetheless, despite resistance, over the late 1990s Pittman and Berlow managed to transform AOL's business model; from a standing start, they brought it to nearly $2 billion in annual advertising revenue (one third of AOL's total) by 2000. But if that revenue growth was staggering, it was carefully planned to seem that way, the result of an internal scheme named "Project Confidence" whose principal goal was to validate the theory that the real value of AOL lay in advertising potential. We have noted that the path of the attention merchants is risky, for it can call for compromises in quality and ethics. AOL, over a five-year period, would demonstrate that fact in a manner rarely equaled over such a short span.

On later, closer inspection (some of it performed by federal law enforcement), much of AOL's new advertising money was coming in based on methods that were unorthodox and unsustainable. It didn't begin that way: in the early days, Berlow and Pittman tried the traditional sales approach. As the biggest "interactive" firm they figured they might land the whales of advertising: companies like Coca-Cola, Procter & Gamble, General Motors. But there were no takers. Ad buyers at major brands can be conservative, and tend to favor established channels with well-worn metrics. And to be fair, there was at the time absolutely no empirical evidence that Internet advertising worked. As Michael Wolff wrote in the 1990s, "No products have disappeared off America's supermarket shelves because of the Internet . . . no commercial fads have been created, and no buying habits have shifted." AOL was well known, but it lacked the data that advertisers had grown to crave, and on the basis of which it made buys with the established attention merchants, like television networks and newspapers. Even with access to millions of minds, AOL advertising seemed to most big brands like throwing money into the vortex.

Deciding to try something more "synergistic," Pittman changed tack. With Berlow and another colleague, David Colburn, in the lead, the firm turned to less orthodox approaches to reach its revenue goals, approaches ranging from the merely questionable to the clearly unethical and, ultimately, criminal.

AOL started treating its users as a captive audience, and replaced the limited "content" and "services" that subscribers were ostensibly paying for with sponsored content and services—i.e., companies that paid AOL—in what was later called its "walled garden" strategy. Consequently, in the 1990s CBS was paying AOL to be the primary provider of sports reporting, and ABC paid to be a general news provider; 1-800-FLOWERS was designated the flower delivery service, and so on.* Whether such sponsored content was a form of advertising is an interesting question, and the paid-for news surely blurred the old line between editorial and advertising, but no one seemed to care. Instead, Pittman likened it to renting real estate in AOL's garden—"location, location, location," he liked to say.[18]

The walled garden proved AOL's first good means for booking advertising revenue. It got better when, while selling those rights, Myer Berlow had a brilliant realization. Perhaps his gambler's instinct picked up a tell. When negotiating with a company named Music Boulevard, at the last minute he tore up the price sheet and doubled AOL's asking rate from $8 million to $16 million. Shockingly, Music Boulevard was still prepared to do the deal. So Berlow upped it again, to $18 million plus a cut of profits. No problem.

Berlow had struck gold. It was the IPO-mad late 1990s, and the dot-coms, as it turned out, were willing to do nearly anything to make their deal with AOL, so as to prove to potential investors that they had "made it" in the online space and thereby gain support for the outrageous valu-

---

* In this, its pay-for-play content, AOL was setting up a system that would be the exact opposite of the Net Neutrality that prevailed on the Internet. That, in the long term, set up another reason for AOL's downfall, for the walled garden ultimately was a weaker offering than the full variety offered on the Internet.

ations characteristic of the era. Thus the executives negotiating those deals with AOL had personal stakes in them worth millions in each case. In gambling terms, AOL held "the nut hand"—one that could not lose. And thus began what professor William Forbes would call the "systematic looting of Internet ventures seeking an advertising deal."[19]

As another AOL employee put it, "It was life or death to them if they couldn't cut a deal with AOL. It was ludicrous."[20] Consequently, AOL would sometimes set up auctions between two dot-coms—say, two online grocery services—to extract the most it could. Using that method, it scored an astonishing $60 million from a start-up named HomeGrocer.com. It all followed from a bracingly direct internal mantra—"Kill 'em." The team's goal became taking at least half of the partner's venture funding in any deal.

The problem with this approach is that it depended on the unusual—indeed insane—conditions of that moment in time. It also sometimes left the partner companies so cash-strapped that they quickly began collapsing (though their generally weak business models were surely a contributing factor, too). Music Boulevard, for example, was gone by 1999; HomeGrocer toppled by 2001. With the level of rents being asked, the walled garden turned out to be fairly poisonous for its resident saplings.

Years before Facebook or Google undertook a similar mission, AOL's business team also began coming up with ways to cash in on the "big data" they had collected: that is, the addresses, phone numbers, and credit card numbers of millions of users. The walled garden, by its nature, was already giving companies direct access to users and some of their information; now AOL also began allowing them, for instance, to insert ads into emails (making the service, in effect, a spammer of its own users). But there were more audacious plans still. AOL sold its users' mailing addresses to direct mail companies. It was going to sell the phone numbers to telemarketers as well, shamelessly describing these maneuvers in its terms of service as a membership benefit. Alas, an inadvertent leak of the plan prompted a user revolt and the telemarketing part was abandoned.

Finally, when these methods failed to produce enough revenue to meet the aggressive targets set by Pittman, the business group would resort to "special deals." For example, money owed AOL for other reasons might somehow be accounted as "advertising revenue." Sometimes, pre-booked advertising contracts were recorded twice, even though the revenues would have already been booked. In a pinch, AOL might also take a "barter" deal from a dot-com start-up, counting the barter—usually worthless web services—as revenue. As a last resort, it would just find ways to pay companies to place ads. While the methods of accounting fraud are myriad, AOL seemed to find ways to practice most of them. We know all of this because the Securities and Exchange Commission would eventually charge the firm with knowingly executing a scheme "to artificially and materially inflate the company's reported online advertising revenue."[21] But by then most of the earlier executives had already taken their money and run.

"Project Confidence" was, in short, a type of confidence scheme, undertaken to make AOL seem like the almighty owner of millions of eyeballs that serious advertisers were intent on reaching. It impressed Wall Street sufficiently (albeit, a Wall Street not asking particularly hard questions) that by 2000 the company had a stock price valuation of over $160 billion (General Motors, for comparison, was then at $56 billion). AOL's turn to advertising was widely lauded as an inspired strategy play; and once again Pittman was hailed as a "hard-driving marketing genius" and "synergy master."

Even if it really did have some 30 million subscribers at its height (maybe it lied about that, too), it didn't have particularly good control over its members' attention or interests.* The walled garden made AOL money, some of it real, but also hastened the site's loss of allure to the Internet, whose open design was the opposite of AOL's, and which was by now growing a greater variety of things to see and do. By 2000, many people were just using AOL to connect to the web, finding ways to escape the walled garden and avoid AOL's advertising blight altogether. These were only some of AOL's many hidden weaknesses that contributed to its catastrophic implosion over the early 2000s. It was already, in Steven Levy's memorable description, a "dead man walking"[22] in advance of a meltdown fully chronicled elsewhere. Suffice it to say here:

---

* As detailed in *The Master Switch* on pp. 265–68: "But by 2000 AOL was less a destination in itself . . . than simply the most popular way to reach the Internet. While it could boast 30 million subscribers, it could exercise no meaningful control over them. Once online, a user could go wherever he wished, the Internet being set up to connect any two parties, whoever they might be."

despite a $164 billion merger with Time Warner and its rich troves of content, AOL, as originally conceived, would become irrelevant, ultimately brought down by the rise of the popular, open Internet and its fast-multiplying attractions.

Prodigy did no better. As it continued to shed users and cash, by the late 1990s the original owners had given up and sold out for $200 million to a group of executives funded in part by the Mexican telecom authority, Telmex. The company was later sold to AT&T, where, after a short-lived effort to co-brand it with Yahoo!, it was never to be heard from again. Yet the original management was onto something, for all of the ideas that Prodigy pioneered would eventually come to fruition in other places. Its reliance on advertising was not only copied by AOL but most of the Internet's most successful companies. Paying professionals to make content that was accessed online would look less foolish by the mid-2010s, the age of Netflix. Finally, online shopping also turned out to be a source of decent revenue. Prodigy's masters didn't have the wrong ideas, but they blew it anyway.

In the big picture, by 2000 change had come; the present was one we would now recognize. Millions of people—soon to be hundreds of millions, and then billions—were now spending leisure time logging in, catching up on email, attending to other business, or chatting with strangers. In its totality, online check-in became a daily, or even hourly, attention ritual, one second in importance only to prime time in our story. While still primitive in various ways, and still offering nothing like the draw of television, the computer, the third screen, had arrived. In the end, AOL was no corporate Ozymandias; though a failure, it would have a lasting and monumental legacy. True to its name, it got America online—reaching out to one another, ready for the biggest attention harvest since television.

PART IV

THE IMPORTANCE
OF BEING FAMOUS

AOL's alignment of the new technology entering American homes with a new social interest of individuals was not without cultural context. No adoption of technology ever is. In this case, it might be seen as part of a progression we have been following right along in this book, that of the individual in society. We have seen it as the attention industries shifted their focus from the mass of consumers to a diverse range of identities and variously constituted market segments.

But to understand where the attention industries would wind up, why our present attentional environment looks the way it does, another phenomenon centered on the individual must be addressed: the individual as deity, as object of worshipful attention.

The first great harvester of human attention, it must never be forgotten, was religion. The impulse to idolize has not faded in our secular age, only gone seeking after strange gods. The very expression "celebrity worship" may seem a figurative exaggeration; but insofar as intensity and duration of attention can separate devotion from other motivations, it would be hard to argue that what we have seen in our culture is anything less than an apotheosis. Still, in our predominantly monotheistic sense of religion, the idea of describing our intense regard for people who are famous as being essentially religious may ring false. But if we would remember that the ancient version of celebrity was a hero, and that the line between heroes and deities was never absolute, who could dispute that our attention industries have enabled the creation of a new pantheon? And as we shall see, it was the indefinite expansion of that pantheon that would carry the attention merchants into the twenty-first century.

CHAPTER 17

ESTABLISHMENT OF THE

CELEBRITY-INDUSTRIAL COMPLEX

In 1972, the magazine publisher Time-Life Inc. was facing serious trouble. Its legendary founder, Henry Luce, was dead, and one of its two flagships, *Life* magazine, was in terminal decline, having hemorrhaged some $47 million since 1969. Like nearly anything mainstream or conventional, it had suffered during the 1960s, becoming "irrelevant" to youth; it was now on course toward that form of extinction peculiar to the attention economy, not dying but being forgotten. *Life*'s essential levity, its tendency to gloss over unpleasant details, fit the 1950s perfectly, but by the 1970s it read like propaganda to the furrowed brows concerned with civil rights, the Vietnam War, and the remaking of American culture. "Gone is the almost palpable air of invincibility," declared *New York* magazine in 1971, "that was as much a part of Time-style in palmier days as its fabled expense accounting."[1]

Luce's successor, Andrew Heiskell, shuttered *Life* in 1972. He had been *Life*'s publisher during its golden years, and so the decision was painful. But seeing no alternative, he went ahead and scattered its five million subscribers to the winds and swore to himself that he would invent a replacement: "I kept reaching and scratching for a good, big idea that would restore the company's health." The "if you can't beat 'em, join 'em" logic of television networks and advertising agencies during the 1960s might have argued for launching a magazine to ride the countercultural wave, something serious yet hip, like *Esquire* or *Rolling Stone.* But Heiskell had something else in mind—something closer to the founder's original vision, and a key to Time-Life's earlier success.

Back in 1923, the twenty-four-year-old Luce had founded *Time* relying more on bravado than experience. He was a "with-it" young man, whose idea was that readers wanted their news in a breezy, conversational style, one more in line with the Jazz Age sensibility. He was also willing to bet that American attention spans were shorter than anyone fully appreci- ated. *The New York Times,* with its eight-column format, was, to quote the *New Yorker* writer A. J. Liebling, "colorless, odorless, and especially tasteless."* By contrast, *Time* would be a digest of the weekly news, or as Luce put it in a 1921 letter, "all the news on every sphere of human inter- est, and the news organized. There will be articles on politics, books, sport, scandal, science, society, and no article will be longer than 200 words." During its first years, *Time* ran more than one hundred short articles each week, none longer than four hundred words.

Time was, however, not the only news digest launched in the 1920s, and the key to its eventual success was in all likelihood a different insight of Luce's. The news, he believed, could and should be told through sto- ries about people—the day's most interesting and famous personalities. "People just aren't interesting in the mass," Luce once explained. "It's only individuals who are exciting." And so he launched his new venture based on celebrity, by which he would profit immensely. This is not to say that he had any interest in the merely famous, or what we today might call the "famous for being famous." The important personalities to his mind were men of great power or other significant achievement. (Women would appear only rarely in *Time,* and even more rarely on the cover; another exception was made for a dog once.) As historian Alan Brinkley writes, "Major public figures—statesmen, business lead- ers, generals, and the royalty of the worlds of art, entertainment, and sport—were the staples." To emphasize this philosophy, *Time* would, from the beginning, put a different notable face on the cover every week,

---

* Liebling also complained about the Grey Lady's politics at the time, saying that the *Times* was "a political hermaphrodite capable of intercourse with conservatives of both parties at the same time."

and late in the autumn it would announce a "Man of the Year." The magazine had its favorites: by Brinkley's count, Stalin appeared on the cover twelve times in its first half century; Roosevelt, Churchill, Franco, and Mussolini eight times each;* Hitler seven; and Chiang Kai-shek ten. And for years, *Time* would faithfully detail what the president had done that week, no matter how trivial or insignificant. The relentless focus on personalities was a different way to do news, but Luce played down his innovation: "TIME didn't start this emphasis on stories about people," he insisted. "The Bible did."[2]

Heiskell's idea harked back to these origins, but it would go a step further. The reporting in *Time* and its offspring, though personality driven, had always had a topic of some seriousness, whether in politics, sports, the arts, or business. Heiskell would do away with that limitation. While it may seem obvious now, in the 1970s it was daring to part with even a pretense of newsworthiness and devote a magazine to nothing more than famous people and their lives. He named his idea the "People of the Week." As the new title's managing editor, Richard Stolley, would later explain, "A lot of American magazines had gotten away from the personality story; they'd become more issue-oriented. We intended to reverse that idea with *People*."[3]

Now, in truth, Heiskell's idea was not quite the innovation he would claim. Celebrity magazines long pre-existed *People;* gossip and scandal rags about Broadway stars and society swells had been around since before Luce established *Time.* More recently the *National Enquirer* had occupied the niche once filled by publications with names like *Confidential* or *Hush-Hush* and cover lines like "We tell the facts and name the names" or "Uncensored and off the record." But these had been coarse, down-market operations, devoted to exposing salacious stories with little regard for the truth. *People*'s real innovation was as an upgrade of this format for a mainstream audience.

To run the new magazine with a measure of respectability, Time-Life chose Stolley, an in-house editor and established journalist. He'd made his reputation covering the civil rights movement for *Life* in the 1950s,

---

* In its first decade, *Time* hastily declared Mussolini a "virile, vigorous" man of "remarkable self control, rare judgement, and an efficient application of his ideas to the solving of existing problems."

and was also famous for having persuaded Abraham Zapruder, who'd inadvertently filmed the assassination of John F. Kennedy, to sell his film to Time-Life for $150,000. But all that was now ancient history, and if Stolley had any qualms about the new venture he never showed them. In fact he apparently took to it with relish. "*People* never sounded downscale when he talked about it," said a colleague. "If they thought *People* was garbage, Stolley would just say, 'Well, that's your opinion.'"

The test issue, developed before Stolley's appointment, tended to confirm an intention to copy the *Enquirer.* On the cover was perennial gossip fodder: the marriage of Elizabeth Taylor and Richard Burton, both best known in the 1970s for their notoriously stormy relationship. To focus groups, as well as Time-Life's board, the effort seemed to be aiming rather low. It "exuded a sleazy, tabloid quality, with its rough photographs and its typewriter type . . . there was even a picture of the Chiquita banana girl, with her breasts bared." At a managing editor's lunch, the words most frequently used were "sleazy" and "cheap." Stolley would later allow that it "looked like a whorehouse magazine."[4]

Nearly a year later, on March 4, 1974, *People* finally arrived on news-stands. From the press release: "This week Time Inc. takes its co-founder's [Henry Luce's] thought a large step forward by bringing out PEOPLE, a new magazine based on the old journalistic precept that names make news." Indeed, under Stolley's influence, the new *People* looked like *Time,* with its glossy paper, conventional fonts, and modest-sized headlines. The first cover was graced with a strikingly beautiful photograph of Mia Farrow, holding a string of pearls in her mouth; that year she would star as Daisy Buchanan in the film version of *The Great Gatsby.* As to what was inside, however, that was little different from the old gossip rags. There was a story about Marina Oswald (widow of Lee Harvey), who professed to being "finally at peace with herself"; another featuring Stephen Burrows, "fashion king of the sexy cling," and yet another in which heiress-turned-denim-designer Gloria Vanderbilt told of "a fourth marriage that finally works."

With $40 million sunk into it by Time-Life, the new *People* was one of the largest investments in magazine history. Stolley was unabashed explaining the concept, "There is nothing abstract about the name. People is what we are all about." The critical class, however, did not appreciate the beauty of that simplicity. William Safire, for instance, then a new columnist for *The New York Times,* wrote an essay entitled "Who Needs

People?," describing the magazine as an "insult to the American mass audience."[5]

> When the world's most powerful publishing empire launched "the first national weekly magazine to be started in twenty years," its executives must have asked themselves: What will compel magazine buyers to snatch our new magazine off the newsstands? What subjects are sure-fire audience-grabbers at this point?
>
> By their choice of topics the Time people have given us a stop action view of what they think most interests wealthy young people, their prime target audience. By their handling of these topics, the editors give us their frank assessment of that audience: a collection of frantic, tasteless fadcats deeply concerned with social climbing and intellectual pretension, panting for a look at celebrities in poses that press agents staged back in the thirties. . . . People fails on the tawdry terms it has chosen: the sex is not sexy, the gossip is not current, the exploitation not with-it. Great effort is needed to lift it up to superficiality.

Safire was not alone. There were even voices within Time-Life expressing dismay. A senior editor at *Time* was anonymously quoted as calling *People* the product of "no richness of genius, but rather a poverty of ideas" and one edited to "exploit the baseness of the market." Donald M. Wilson, Time's vice president of publicity, would write in his memoirs that "of all the new developments in the company, [*People*] was the only one I secretly deplored. I disliked *People* from the beginning. Like many other journalists, I too thought it was unworthy of Time Inc. But in my capacity as head of public affairs for the company, I did my very best to support it in its success." The conscience of an attention merchant![6]

Of course *People* was an outrageous success. The very first issue sold almost a million copies, a debut matched only by *Playboy*'s launch in 1953, with Marilyn Monroe on the cover, waving to the reader and promising more. Heiskell, like Luce, had not erred by betting low, for *People* was hardly a passing fad. If the late 1960s and early 1970s had managed to achieve a measure of liberation without renouncing seriousness, by now the seriousness had begun to wane, and liberation was yielding to license, in a climate of easy indulgences. It was reflected in broadcast, where *60 Minutes* was now keeping company at CBS with *Charlie's Angels* and other examples of "jiggle television." It is no surprise, then, that from 1976 to 1980, *People*'s income more than quadrupled, with the largest paid audience of any American magazine. By 1991, it was the most profitable magazine in the world, and thus the most valuable. So it has remained ever since. (By the 2010s, a full-page advertisement in *People* was running about $350,000, as compared to a mere $12,000 for an advertisement in *Harper's,* or about $160,000 for a full-page advertisement in *The New York Times* newspaper.)[7]

His life as a hard-hitting reporter behind him, Stolley would now focus his journalistic acumen on deciding each week's cover, a crucial part of the magazine's appeal and the chief determinant of newsstand sales. In time he would devise a few rules. First, to appear on the cover, "the face had to be recognizable to 80% of the American people." Second, "there had to be something about the person you wanted to know." After that it was a matter of hierarchy, one of almost Darwinian brutality:

> Young is better than old.
> Pretty is better than ugly.
> Rich is better than poor.
> TV is better than music.
> Music is better than movies.
> Movies are better than sports.
> And anything is better than politics.

————————

No one at *People* or Time-Life really understood exactly why stories about celebrities captured so many readers; it was enough that they did. And despite decades of academic and quasi-academic writing on the topic, there isn't a completely satisfying answer as to what gives celebrities such a powerful grip on human attention—why so many of us seem to care about the lives of men and women we have seen only in films or on television, "people who make no material impact on our lives and are, in many respects, just like ourselves."[8]

Even if you don't consider yourself particularly interested in famous people, it is nonetheless likely, through some informational form of osmosis, that you can recognize a few hundred strangers who are celebrities, and probably can even recite some basic facts about them. How they found their way into your mind you may not really know; it can sometimes feel as if you've been the victim of an involuntary mental implantation. You don't have to be a fan to identify Matt Damon, Angelina Jolie, or Leonardo DiCaprio as famous actors, known to you the same way you might know the names of major cities you've never visited. And that would be to describe an ordinary participant in our attention economy. There are many who take a more active interest, who know by name and sight many thousands of strangers, and hold in their minds veritable memory palaces of personal facts and relationship histories, enough synaptic investment to put a medieval Jesuit to shame.

Nor can the physical sensation caused by meeting celebrities—feeling "starstruck"—be denied, except by the most jaded. You might think back to a moment when you saw or met a very famous person, and remember that you began to feel your heart beat faster, that urge to take a picture, the sense that this moment was somehow important. Time can seem to stand still; it can feel like breaking through, momentarily, to what seems a slightly different realm. When you meet Scarlett Johansson, Barack Obama, or someone known to you and many others from afar, when that face, familiar from your screen yet usually somehow transformed in the translation to three dimensions, is suddenly before you, an icon manifest in real flesh and blood, at that moment it is hard to deny that something happens in the typical nervous system.

The strength of these feelings is one reason why our celebrity culture is so frequently linked with older traditions of worship. For that ecstatic possibility of transcending the ordinary and glimpsing the infinite hardly originates in the twentieth century, but is a universal longing reflected in almost every spiritual tradition. The historian Karen Armstrong describes it as an "essential craving" of all humanity to be connected with the "extraordinary": "It touches us within, lifts us momentarily beyond ourselves, so that we seem to inhabit our humanity more fully than usual and feel in touch with the deeper currents of life." Such transcendence of the mundane condition has since ancient times been identified with heroes, demigods, and saints, humans who occupy a somewhat exalted position yet also remain accessible, allowing us some taste of another realm. At one time, this was also true of royalty (and in a few places it still is).[9]

What is particular to modernity, then, is not the existence of such individuals but rather the idea of constructing an industry based on the demand for feeling some communion with them, on our willingness to idolize them (literally)—an industry that monetizes their capacity to capture our rapt attention.

Perhaps, as the sociologist Chris Rojek theorizes, this is "secular society's rejoinder to the decline of religion and magic," for in the "absence of saints or a God to look up to, for many people in western societies the void is being filled by celebrity culture." Of course, this is hardly to suggest that celebrity culture actually *is* a religion. *People* and other celebrity pantheons do not aim to provide cosmogonies, or ethical teachings, even if celebrity manners do have a depressing tendency to become normative. The point is simply that whatever the neurological basis of religious experiences, something of the same mechanism seems to be activated by the existence, and particularly the proximity, of the most illustrious. That perhaps explains why, for some, celebrity culture is so abominable; it is the ancient disgust with idol worship, triggering an atavistic emotional reaction, like the rage felt by Moses when he burned the golden calf, ground it into a powder, and, scattering it on the water, forced his people to drink it.[10]

In the age of mass culture, industry always sought to harness the power of celebrity. With the rise of the studio system, stars were cultivated for their power to draw audiences to otherwise mediocre productions, as they still even are in our day of their free agency. From their initial appearance on what we have called the first screen (the silver one), it was clear that realistic visual representations of famous figures had a stirring effect. In his essay "The Face of Garbo," critic Roland Barthes describes the awe inspired by Greta Garbo's iconic image; he also mentions how previously that of Valentino, following his death, was driving fans to suicide. But the reaction needn't be so ecstatic or traumatic. Indeed, the sensation would later become one more of familiarity than reverence.

In 1956, two psychologists, Donald Horton and Richard Wohl, would conclude that television's representation of celebrities was carefully constructed to create an "illusion of intimacy"—to make viewers believe that they actually were developing a relationship with the famous people on TV. Certain techniques particular to variety but also the chat shows produced this effect: recourse to small talk, the use of first names, and close-ups, among others, acted to close the gap between the audience and the guests, engendering the sense in the viewer of being "part of a circle of friends." The two coined the term "para-social interaction" to describe this "intimacy at a distance."[11]

So it is that, for many people, celebrities have become part of their built attentional environment, allowing them regular glimpses into that other world inhabited by magical creatures who look something like us, yet are beyond us. Our deities are of course nothing like the God of Abraham, or even His saints. They are, rather, more like the pagan gods of old, prone to fits of anger and vindictiveness, petty jealousies, and embarrassing bouts of drunkenness. But this only lends to their illusion of accessibility, and at least for commercial purposes makes them more compelling to follow.

Over the 1970s, as *People* took off, its editors made a crucial observation, not about their audiences but about the figures they were covering. It had once been understood as the goal of the rich and powerful to keep their personal lives as private as possible. There were exceptions, like Elizabeth Taylor, an actress whose spectacular string of marriages and divorces were far more public than most stars', but many famous people either did not care to be in the public eye, or could afford not to be. In the era of *People,* that was changing.

Richard Stolley could not fail to notice: "We found out that people in the news were quite willing to talk to us about themselves. They'd talk about lots of personal things—their sex lives, their families, their religion. They'd talk about things that a few years earlier wouldn't even be brought up." Perhaps it was the glossy paper or the fact that Time-Life, not the *National Enquirer,* was the publisher. Whatever the case, *People* found that celebrities were now increasingly willing to discuss the very sorts of things about themselves and their families that all people, the famous most of all, had once jealously guarded. All you really had to do was ask.

What was becoming evident was something that now seems virtually axiomatic: celebrities were becoming attention merchants in their own right. Fame, they were discovering, was not merely the by-product of what they did; it was their professional capital. And while endorsements were in vogue during the 1920s, during the 1970s celebrities began leveraging their drawing power as never before. Now was the time of Polaroid's pathbreaking campaign engineered by the daring firm of Doyle Dale Bernbach. The camera maker, then a cutting-edge tech company, did a series of spots with stars including James Garner, Candice Bergen, Alan Alda, the Muppets, and perhaps most famously, the great Shakespearean actor Sir Laurence Olivier. Two years later, ad agency Ted Bates would open the door for athlete endorsements when it tapped Buffalo Bills star running back O. J. Simpson for Hertz Rent-a-Car.

Eventually, the most successful actors would be the ones who transcended acting and began reselling the audiences they could attract. In this, however, they would find themselves in fierce competition with other celebrities, resulting in a veritable arms race of exposure. Of course, some are so famous that gaining more attention is unnecessary. But among those less secure in their prospects, revealing embarrassments or personal failings, appearing less than fully clothed on red carpets, and sometimes engaging in even more extreme exhibitionism would be the secret to besting their rivals in a zero-sum game. What *People* ultimately created was a platform for attracting attention through self-revelation that remained something short of tawdry, a kind of self-flaunting for the polite mainstream. Both *People* and the celebrity attention merchants have continued to gain from the new confessional culture, since the fans can never get enough. Once the race to the bottom had begun, it was nigh impossible to return to the old status quo—being a celebrity in the new sense now meant telling all, or facing the consequences.

People was important in and of itself, but also for what it spawned, directly and indirectly. Profits drew imitators, as they inevitably do; in 1977, even the New York Times Company could not resist launching *Us Weekly,* a close copy of *People.* Other media, like television, followed naturally, yielding shows like *Entertainment Tonight.* But the greater influence was more subtle and less measurable: on whatever platform was to be invented, celebrity would become the attention merchant's go-to bait, offering a lure infinitely more dependable than any more artfully developed content. While not the beginning of celebrity or celebrity culture, *People* was nevertheless a turning point in both, the start of the "celebrification" of the entire mainstream, including, as we shall see, the lives of many with no reasonable basis for expecting to become famous. Some would experience this as fulfilling the promise of a better life through technology, others as the logical extreme of a race to the bottom begun by the penny papers in the nineteenth century.

CHAPTER 18

THE OPRAH MODEL

In 1982 the then well-known film reviewer and television personality Roger Ebert was a guest on a local morning television show in Baltimore, hosted by a young and unknown host named Oprah Winfrey. As he later recalled, she seemed talented but suffered from poor bookings. "The other guests on the show included a vegetarian chef and four dwarfs dressed as chipmunks" who, as he recalled, sang the Chipmunks' Christmas song while Hula-Hooping.[1]

Ebert, rather smitten, asked Winfrey on a date after she moved back to her hometown to host a program named *AM Chicago*. Airing weekdays at 9 a.m., the show faced tough competition in *The Phil Donahue Show,* airing at the same time. Phil Donahue was serious—for a talk show host at least—and popular. But Winfrey would rely on the age-old tactic of stealing attention by being more outrageous. She booked a group of nudists (who, naturally, did the show in the nude) and the Ku Klux Klan (who appeared in full regalia). On one episode exploring the question "Does sexual size matter?," Oprah memorably pronounced, "If you had your choice, you'd like to have a big one if you could. Bring a big one home to Mama!" Scandalous it may have been, but hers was soon the leading talk show in Chicago.[2]

On their date Ebert took Winfrey to a place called Hamburger Hamlet and gave her some unsolicited advice. Having begun to do so himself, he suggested she leave the networks and take charge of her media destiny. Winfrey wouldn't continue to date Ebert but she did take his advice, achieving a degree of independence that defied nearly all the existing strictures of the attention industries. She decided to take ownership of her show and sell it directly to television stations, becoming, in effect, a competitor to NBC, CBS, and other networks. She was the beneficiary of a federal rule enacted in 1972—part of a progressive backlash against broadcasters that President Richard Nixon found agreeable—designed to weaken their control over television.[3] The bet was that her proven capacity to attract attention was sufficient to sell advertisers on her, and in turn, to sell her show to others.

The bet would pay off. Debuting in 1986, her show relied on an emotional, confessional style that was now what viewers wanted, combined with the lure of her own irresistible persona. She tacked toward respectability, shrewdly toning down the most lurid and shocking elements of *AM Chicago,* and thereby gained an even larger audience, rather as CBS made radio respectable in the 1930s, and as *People* had gentrified gossip journalism. Spectacle was now couched in principle, too. As one critic observed, she "cast her professional choices, persona, and style as *moral* ones" and "practiced a form of public 'moral accountability' with her audience."[4] Like *People,* too, she recognized that everyone loved to unburden herself, given the right conditions. Yet her winning wager was obvious only to her. As *Time* wrote in 1988,

> Few would have bet on Oprah Winfrey's swift rise to host of the most popular talk show on TV. In a field dominated by white males, she is a black female of ample bulk. . . . What she lacks in journalistic toughness, however, she makes up for in plainspoken curiosity, robust humor and, above all, empathy. Guests with sad stories to tell are apt to rouse a tear in Oprah's eye. . . . They, in turn, often find themselves revealing things they would not imagine telling anyone, much less a national TV audience. It is the talk show as a group therapy session.[5]

Even now the scale of Winfrey's ambitions was clear. She told *Spy* magazine, "I knew I'd be a millionaire by the time I turned 32."[6] The *Spy* reporter could not believe his luck: "She told me this in the first hour

I spent with her. By the second hour she had added, puffing up with purpose, 'I certainly intend to be the richest black woman in America. I intend to be a mogul.'" Her evident ambition invited some fairly sharp jabs in the early days. A *New York Times Magazine* cover piece entitled "The Importance of Being Oprah" took a dim view of her program, suggesting it was popular because it made white viewers feel better about themselves. It further derided her viewers as, in effect, losers, those "lonely and uninstructed" who "draw sustenance from her, from the flickering presence in their living rooms they call a friend."[7]

It didn't prevent Winfrey from winning wild adulation—particularly in her core demographic, white and black women over the age of fifty. What made her audiences love her so? She is a clear and fluent interlocutor with a talent for connecting with her guests, but it goes beyond that. Fans say they "trust her," find her "sincere" and "open," and respect her overcoming a challenging childhood (she freely revealed a past scarred by episodes of drug use and other behavior). "Oprah is a sweetheart, a good person, who treats people with love and respect, despite her wealth and power," wrote one fan.

Winfrey's success as a one-woman celebrity-attention merchant was distinct enough to draw imitators over the late 1980s and 1990s, who usually relied on a distinctive personality to draw audiences (usually niche) to their independent businesses. In 1987, a former ABC host named Geraldo Rivera launched his competitor to Winfrey's show that tacked downmarket with the kind of topics that the early Winfrey had used to take attention from Donahue (example: "Men in Lace Panties and the Women Who Love Them"). He successfully garnered national attention during his second season after a brawl erupted on his show between a volatile mix of white supremacists, antiracist skinheads, black activists, and Jewish activists. Rivera joined the melee himself, throwing punches and suffering a broken nose, which he displayed prominently for weeks afterward.[8]

Howard Stern, originally a radio personality, began his own television show in the 1990s and gained a national audience with a show centered on offensive and taboo topics. With radio, television, and bestselling books as platforms, he described himself as "The King of All Media." Meanwhile, the tabloid format (described by some as "freak shows") was popular enough to sustain not just Rivera but also a former politician named Jerry Springer, whose show centered on topics like incest and whose specialty was creating dramatic on-show confrontations between his guests. Others, like the Ricki Lake show, the Jenny Jones show, and Sally Jessy Raphael, all, in the words of one critic, relied on "the low risk strategy of class voyeurism."[9]

But even with new, more lurid competition, Winfrey's show retained its audience, and academics and journalists have churned out untold pages explaining just what makes Winfrey's audiences feel such a connection to her. Laurie Haag puts it down to her communication style, which she calls "girl talk," and includes careful, supportive listening, accompanied by truly spontaneous reactions to what she's told: "hooting, howling, laughing, or crying as the situation dictates, allowing the viewer at home to do the same." Others credit her "courageous" candor about her own life. "It is her fearless ability to self-disclose," writes Linda Kay, "that most distinguishes Winfrey from her peers."[10]

But apart from all her undeniable talents and abilities and charms, Winfrey also offered something unique in daytime television: food for the hungers traditionally fed by organized religion and spirituality. Her shows were a daily dose of redemptive confession or suffering, a vision of justice, and the promise of salvation in this life.

The promotion of the Oprah Winfrey show didn't shy away from describing its spiritual objectives: it was created "to transform people's lives, to make viewers see themselves differently, and to bring happiness and a sense of fulfillment into every home."[11] At times Winfrey described her work as a religious mission: "I am the instrument of God. I am his messenger. My show is my ministry."[12]

If we take Winfrey at her word and consider her work a ministry, it would have been one virtually unrivaled in size and influence in the late twentieth century. Oprah's teachings, as a rule, hewed to a generally Christian view of existence, emphasizing love for the distressed, human weakness, life as a struggle, the value of confessing sin, and an ongoing effort to achieve redemption. She also emphasized ideas with twentieth-century origins, like the importance of self-esteem and self-respect, of positive thinking, and of treating oneself well. "Live your best life" was one of the show's mottos.

But in one major respect Winfrey's teaching tended to differ considerably from both Christianity and other traditional religions, which steadfastly warn of the spiritual dangers of materialism.* The show's pre-scriptions for personal growth always included consumption as a means of self-actualization and self-reward. "For her, transformation is about self-esteem and about buying stuff," says Susan Mackey-Kallis.[13] View-ers were encouraged to treat themselves well with their purchases ("show yourself love"). And by the program's very design, commerce was always unashamedly at the center, not only because Winfrey was running a business but also because spiritual growth and consumption were theo-logically linked, not in tension. Oprah's great innovation was to amal-gamate the ancient attention-capturing potential of a great faith with the programming function of a broadcaster, and the mass drawing power of her own celebrity. It was by the standards of any attention merchant a potent proffer for advertisers.

Advertising was indeed Winfrey's main revenue source, and when she sold her audiences she was delivering not mere eyeballs but minds whose buying decisions had been conditioned by her unusually strong influ-ence, which eventually "exceed[ed] that of any other celebrity—perhaps in history," according to Craig Garthwaite of Northwestern's Kellogg School of Management.[14] It did not happen overnight, however. As one biographer writes, Winfrey was an enthusiastic shopper, and "for years she had shared her spending orgies with her viewers—her towels, her pajamas, her cashmere sweaters, her diamond earrings."[15] As time went on, her enthusiasm would morph into quasi-endorsements of particular products, her magical touch performing little miracles for small com-panies. To take one minor example, there was the firm named Light-Wedge, maker of a reading light; when Oprah said on air, "I need to get one of those," the little company booked $90,000 in sales in a single afternoon.[16]

This, the "Oprah effect," would always have its most dramatic influ-ence in markets with relatively little advertising and marketing, like book publishing. In 1996, Winfrey launched what she called "the big-gest book club in the world." She would announce her selection and then give her viewers a month to read it. In the meanwhile, her producers would film the author at home and produce other B-roll footage for the

---

* Consider Matthew 16:9: "Do not store up for yourselves treasures on earth, where moths and vermin destroy, and where thieves break in and steal."

eventual show about the book, featuring discussion, sometimes with an expert. Her first choice was *The Deep End of the Ocean,* by Jacquelyn Mitchard. Far from a dud, it had previously sold 68,000 copies; after its selection, however, it would sell four million. Within its first year, her book club had accounted for nearly 12 million volumes sold, making Oprah beloved of the publishing industry for her magic ability to turn modestly successful novels into bestsellers.[17]

Given such power, a less sophisticated attention merchant might have simply sought to sell endorsements outright (as subsequent corporatized personalities like the 2010s reality TV star Kim Kardashian have done). But whether out of ethical considerations, or an astute sense of preserving her credibility capital, or both, Winfrey never accepted payment for on-air endorsements. By never selling out explicitly as another flogger of products, she remained unpredictable, her power only growing as a result.

Scattershot at first, by the late 1990s her endorsements had become systematized in several ways. First, she produced a program called "Oprah's Favorite Things"; for this annual event, the entire show was devoted to promotion of the products she liked most, some of which were given out to the excited studio audience. Combining the ecstasy of a religious revival meeting with the acquisitive intensity of Black Friday, the episode featured screaming, often crying men and women from the audience receiving their swag. As on a 1950s game show, ordinary people were suddenly showered with prizes. It typically started with pairs of boots, books, popcorn, digital cameras, and the like, before leading up to big-ticket items. Oprah, like a beneficent goddess of abundance, presided over it all, blessing her flock with one deliverance of riches after another. Her biographer Kitty Kelley describes the climax: "Nearly spent with orgasmic delight over what they had already received, her studio audience trembled as the drums rolled and the velvet curtains opened to reveal an LG refrigerator with a high-definition TV built into the door, a DVD hookup, and a radio . . . 'it [retails for] $3,789,' Oprah screamed."[18]

Winfrey also began to turn parts of her episodes into de facto infomercials. For example, on one episode, Winfrey abruptly gave her audience 276 brand-new Pontiac G6s, worth $28,000 each. When asked about it in a rare moment of press access, she said, "It was not a stunt, and I resent the word *stunt.*"[19] Just as astonished as the audience were the pundits of advertising and marketing. Thirty-second spots on the show retailed for about $70,000, yet Oprah had spent about half an entire show on Pontiac, including a taped visit to their factory.

In 2000, Oprah widened her brand and attention harvest with the launch of *O, The Oprah Magazine,* named for her, of course, and with a flattering photo of her on the cover of every issue. The magazine, which surged to a circulation of over two million, had roughly the same demographic target as the show, women over fifty. Here was more attentional real estate, carefully balancing free endorsements with paid advertisements. It showed what an elixir first-order celebrity had become; clearly it had the power to reanimate even fading media sectors like consumer magazines.

It never fully escaped notice that Winfrey's advertisers were those whose products often, if not invariably, enjoyed her on-air or in-print blessing as well. Over the mid-2000s, for example, Dove soap was the subject of major segments featuring its various products and their merits. True, the ostensible topic was the brand's new advertising campaign, which promoted "real beauty" by featuring ordinary women as models. The messaging was a good fit with Winfrey's goal of encouraging self-esteem. It's also true, however, that Dove spent $16.4 million for commercial spots on the syndicated TV show and another $32.8 million on print ads in *O.* The company had even been kind enough to award one of Oprah's friends and *O, The Oprah Magazine*'s editor at large, Gayle King, their very first Dove Real Beauty award.

A reporter for *Advertising Age* who asked whether ad buys were helpful for gaining endorsements, described Oprah's answers as "a tad vague."[20] Indeed they were: "Editorial and creative decisions drive mentions and product inclusions on the show. If a brand gets mentioned, it is as often serendipity as it is business. When we do partner with brands, it is usually because we have an editorial direction we're pursuing."[21] In other words, advertising usually didn't matter, but it didn't not matter either.

By the 2000s, Oprah Winfrey was one of the richest women in the United States, and the first African American billionaire in American history. Though hugely successful, she was not interested in being a dispassionate attention merchant in the manner of a William Paley. Rather, she remained convinced of the possibility of doing well by doing good, according to her vision. She would bring attention to many under-attended issues, like the abuse of children or dearth of opportunities for women or blacks. These were worthy pursuits by any measure. The difficulty arose when she pursued more controversial aspects of her vision of the good.

As mentioned, Winfrey's self-described ministry had been intended as a source of uplift and moral guidance. It had been clear from the beginning that she was offering an alternative to organized religion, but to the extent that her values seemed in sync with Christian ones, there was little objection either by churchmen or Christians in her audience. American Christian devotion is fairly polymorphous by the standards of most Western societies; even Joel Osteen, the TV evangelist who preaches the Gospel of Wealth ("God wants you to be rich!"), seems to pass. But when Winfrey began espousing heterodox or explicitly un-scriptural teachings, one could see the beginning of a backlash.

In the early 2000s, Winfrey became an advocate in a spiritual doctrine called "the Law of Attraction," an idea actually dating from nineteenth-century mind cure practice and with roots in other traditions. The law posits that one's thoughts have the power to shape reality, and by the right sort of rumination, one can draw desired things, like money or love, into one's life. Here is how Oprah explained it on her website: "The energy you put into the world—both good and bad—is exactly what comes back to you. This means you create the circumstances of your life with the choices you make every day."[22] In 2006, Winfrey repeatedly featured a book called *The Secret,* together with its author and associated gurus, on her show. The book describes the law and its applications, for instance, in financial matters: "The only reason any person does not have enough money," it explains, "is because they are blocking money from coming to them with their thoughts."[23] It may be hard to see how this is any less Christian than Joel Osteen's preaching, but the critics did not see it that way.

Winfrey's endorsement of *The Secret* and other spiritual practices drew criticism from the religious mainstream. Albert Mohler, president of the Southern Baptist Theological Seminary, wrote that "Oprah has become a high priestess and icon of the psychologization of American society. . . . Her substitution of spirituality for biblical Christianity, her promotion of forgiveness without atonement, and her references to a god 'without labels' puts her at the epicenter of a seismic cultural earthquake."[24] Perhaps not an earthquake: Oprah was not so far from the therapeutic deism that had long been the American religion. But her attentional reach made her a substantial danger to traditional faith—even perhaps to the nonreligious as well. From the rationalist side, Michael Shermer found it necessary to write in *Scientific American,* "Oprah, please, withdraw your support of this risible twaddle [*The Secret*] . . . and tell your vast following that prosperity comes from a good dollop of hard work and creative thinking, the way you did it."[25]

Perhaps Winfrey's most consequential endorsement would be the one she made during the Democratic primaries in 2007, when she backed first-term senator Barack Obama against the presumptive nominee, Hillary Clinton. Campaigning with Obama in Iowa, New Hampshire, and other important states, Winfrey may have been responsible, according to one analysis, for between 420,000 and 1.6 million votes.[26] If so, it is possible that Winfrey's support won Obama the nomination, and consequently, the presidency.

There were those who had objected to Winfrey's political activities on a smaller scale. "Oprah is far more than a cultural force," argued political commentator Ben Shapiro. "She's a dangerous political force as well, a woman with unpredictable and mercurial attitudes toward the major issues of the day."[27] Now, however, there was pushback from within the ranks of her viewers, some of whom had backed Hillary Clinton and took to the show's message boards to complain.[28]

In 2009, with ratings in decline, Winfrey announced that her show would end after its twenty-fifth season, in 2011. In the first of the last episodes, she abruptly flew three hundred audience members to Australia on a plane piloted by John Travolta. The last season brought back some of her largest audiences, and might have been thought of as a fitting retirement; but in fact the ever-ambitious Winfrey was simultaneously launching her own cable network, OWN, the Oprah Winfrey Network.

But even Winfrey was not immune to larger industry trends, and launching into an era of cable's decline would not prove easy. Many could either not find the network amidst the hundreds of channels on offering, or did not care to bother; in its first year, the network lost as much as $330 million. Winfrey used various means to try to recapture the lightning she once held in a bottle—most successfully, an interview of Lance Armstrong, the cyclist, who confessed to using performance-enhancing drugs. But these were one-off events and the audiences did not stay. She also made a go of her old show's religious aspiration with an ecumenical series named *Belief,* a program that would have qualified as public interest programming by the old metrics. While never quite losing her celebrity or strong reputation, she could no longer quite be considered the nation's Attention Merchant-in-Chief.

By 2015, OWN had reverted to the basic logic of cable programming, which has always demanded catering to a niche audience. It repositioned itself primarily as a competitor to BET, Black Entertainment Television, finding success with soap operas like *The Haves and Have Nots* and *If Loving You Is Wrong.*[29] But in any event, Winfrey's own fade as a celebrity attention merchant might be taken as irrelevant given the spiritual survival of the model she created. For her one-woman show gave rise to successors like Ellen DeGeneres, Dr. Phil, Rachael Ray, and other celebrity-attention-product-endorsers faithfully following the Winfrey path.

CHAPTER 19

THE PANOPTICON

Since the day Tom Freston took over as CEO of MTV in 1987, he was determined to broaden what the network did. "What if MTV wasn't just about music?" he liked to ask. It was a somewhat surprising question from the former advertising man and music lover who had been present at the creation and thus understood better than anyone the hidden genius of MTV's founding business model. To outsiders, MTV's concept was captured by the first video it had run, the Buggles' "Video Killed the Radio Star"; this was rock music for television, a network targeting teenagers and twenty-somethings. That it was, but there was more going on; for it was also one of those businesses—the best kind—with a secret that makes it much more lucrative than anyone would imagine.[1]

Bob Pittman had been MTV's first CEO, and he drove its unorthodox business model. Unlike nearly any other channel, MTV got nearly all of its content for free, nominal amounts, or even better than free. Pittman understood that the music labels wanted MTV to play their videos for a simple reason: it had become clear that a great video—say, Michael Jackson's *Thriller*, or anything by Duran Duran—could create an indelible association for that artist and ultimately drive record sales through the roof. But the deal was even better than that. Not only was MTV getting its content for free, but the labels gave MTV exclusive rights to the most important videos, protecting the network from competition.* MTV was thus relieved even of the burden of devising its own programming.

In short, over the 1980s MTV was in the enviable position of selling advertisements off the attention captured from what were, essentially, advertisements in another form. Its costs were therefore limited to things like rent, paying its executives, and the young people, the "VJs," who introduced the videos. The latter were cheap, too—salary was less than $30,000 a year, but there were perks like doing cocaine with rock stars during the MTV New Year's special and other experiences beyond price.[2] The combined effect of these favorable conditions meant that MTV defied the usual laws of gravity operative in most media businesses. By the mid-1980s, it was easily the most profitable of all the new cable networks.[3]

But Freston, when he took over from Pittman, was concerned that the network had an Achilles' heel, the ultimate doom of all media businesses, really: it was what we have called the disenchantment effect. Flush though it was, MTV was utterly dependent on the popularity of music videos, which in the early 1980s had seemed so exciting and novel, as the decade wore on were starting to show their age. By 1987, there were troubling signs that the era defined by *Thriller* was coming to an end. "Problem was," Freston said, "people started to feel they'd seen it all with regard to music videos."[4] It was also true that the labels, worried about piracy, were tightening their controls over new music arriving by video. All this implied that the music labels, from which so much revenue derived, might themselves be on borrowed time (as indeed they were). Like any prudent businessman, he wanted a hedge—something else, some other format, to prop up the business. But what else could MTV do?

MTV's executive programmers thought hard into the 1990s about what they could try without incurring the sort of brutal content overhead that had made life so precarious for other media and which stockholders

---

* An antitrust challenge to this arrangement brought by the start-up Discovery Music Network floundered and was settled for a nominal fee.

would not abide anyway. They tried scheduling reruns of the 1960s hit *The Monkees,* with mixed results. One enterprising programmer was fixated on the idea of MTV running NFL games, wisely foreseeing that the real money would eventually be in sports; but it was not the best fit for the brand. Another idea was to rerun *Saturday Night Live* cut into pieces with music videos sprinkled in. Eventually the network began running a low-budget game show named *Remote Control;* with questions based on MTV trivia, it was "an excuse to do jokes."[5]

One day, looking at their audience data, a young executive named Van Toffler had a different idea. He had noticed something striking: an overlap between MTV's core audiences and viewers of daytime soap operas. Maybe MTV should start running soap operas. Serial dramas, if not traditionally the hippest kind of show, had since the 1930s been solid bets; and they tended to build long-term audience loyalties. It so happened that a new, teen-oriented prime-time soap called *Beverly Hills 90210* was just then pulling viewers to the new Fox Network. And so MTV "decided to do a teen soap opera, with a rock n' roll attitude."[6]

Freston consulted Fred Silverman (whose programming had revived CBS in the early 1970s), and he suggested hiring Mary-Ellis Bunim. Over the previous decade, she had run one of the great legacy soaps, *As the World Turns,* a never-ending story of family drama and romance that had been running for some thirty years. Since its 1956 debut on CBS, it had been sponsored by the same soap company, Procter & Gamble, for which it had been created by Irna Phillips herself, the inventor of the genre.[7]

When MTV called, Bunim teamed up with another producer, Jonathan Murray, and began to work up a teen soap opera tentatively entitled *St. Mark's Place.* It was planned as a serial drama about young people living in the East Village, hoping to make it as performers or artists or whatever—a kind of forerunner to the musical *Rent.* But when Bunim and Murray presented their budget, MTV's executives balked. As Murray recalled, they said, "We get our music videos for free, and now we're going to spend $300,000 for half an hour of television?"[8] Apparently Freston and MTV had not completely thought through the idea of new formats; virtually any of them would require actually spending money on content.

Undaunted, Bunim and Murray regrouped. Looking for new inspiration, they got their heads out of the 1930s and found what they were looking for in perhaps an even unlikelier place: early 1970s public television, and more specifically, the documentary format. They starting thinking hard about a PBS show from the period called *An American Family*.

An American Family, filmed in 1971, was an innovative, twelve-part documentary created when PBS was at the height of its countercultural ambitions. For seven months, the producers followed the fairly typical upper-middle-class family of Pat and Bill Loud, who lived in Santa Barbara, California, with their five children. Intending to capture the intergenerational friction of the time, the creator Craig Gilbert opened the show with these words: "The Louds are neither average nor typical, no family is. They are not *the* American Family, they are simply *an* American Family."[9]

Over those seven months, the Louds saw considerable turmoil. There were, for instance, the continuing tensions between Pat, the mother, and her eldest son, Lance, a long-haired twenty-year-old obsessed with the Velvet Underground. During the course of filming, Lance moved to New York, took up residence at the Chelsea Hotel, and made it clear to the audience that he was gay—making him perhaps the first openly gay person to appear on nonscripted television, certainly the first to out himself. Later in the season, deciding that she was dissatisfied with her life, Pat asked Bill for a divorce; by the end of the program, Bill had moved out of the house. The end was decidedly melancholy—yes, it was still an American Family, but now a broken one.

When it ran in 1973, *An American Family* had attracted large audiences—gigantic by public television standards—and also provoked a national discussion. Gilbert's frame was essentially critical; he portrayed the Louds, particularly the father, Bill, as being obsessed with material success at the cost of family itself. They became "a symbol of disintegration and purposelessness in American life." As such, the show was generally regarded as a serious documentary achievement, with one critic allowing that "never was there greater realism on television except in the murders of Oswald and Robert Kennedy." It is difficult to describe the extent of its resonance; as *Esquire* contended, "I doubt if in the history of the tube there has been so much talk about anything."[10] Many wondered about what social scientists call the Hawthorne effect, the extent the very act of observation and filming had influenced what happened; and thus, there were those who thought the show exploitative and misleading—including, eventually, the family themselves. Among the documentary's most prominent defenders was the anthropologist Margaret Mead. "It may be as important for our time," she said on public television, "as were the invention of drama and the novel for earlier generations: a new way to help people understand themselves."[11]

By the 1990s, the Louds and *An American Family* were but a distant memory for most, and unknown to the young. Bunim and Murray seized on the idea of adapting the documentary format and its use of ordinary people to the dramatic purposes of soap opera; the aim was to produce a new kind of program, a "documentary soap." Unlike the original, which had relied on an actual family, their show would feature a less traditional kind of group—a "new nuclear family." Still evidently musing about their pricey idea for a proto-*Rent,* Murray and Bunim decided to assemble a group of twenty-year-old aspiring artists to live together in a group house. They would film all that transpired there.[12]

For MTV the price was right. Each of the cast members was paid a mere $1,400 for living several months of their lives on camera and creating enough raw footage for thirteen episodes.[13] While it was never expressed this way, it became clear, over time, that the "talent" was actually being paid in attention, as opposed to cash; and so in this way a new format, not yet known as reality television, managed to preserve MTV's existing business model.

Bunim and Murray interviewed some five hundred applicants, finally narrowing the pool down to seven "ordinary people" ranging in age from nineteen to twenty-five. They wanted a diverse mix and they got one: there was a Southern girl, Julie, who would be the "fish out of water"; a male model from the Midwest, named Eric; Heather, a hip-hop performer; Kevin the poet; and so on. The next step was finding the show's "stage." After an exhaustive search, the producers found a four-thousand-square-foot loft in New York's SoHo, which in the early

1990s was still considered an artistic neighborhood. The place was converted into a four-bedroom residence and outfitted with hidden cameras, microphones, and spaces from which the producers could watch the residents. With that setup in place, Bunim and Murray let the cameras roll (albeit with plenty of close-ups, a soap opera standby) and waited for the hoped-for soap opera to play out.[14]

In May 1992, the show debuted with this voice-over:

> This is the true story of seven strangers picked to live in a loft and have their lives taped to find out what happens when people stop being polite and start getting real—*The Real World.*

The new show gained immediate attention for its courageous and unusual format, but also met with some fairly rough initial reviews. "Watching *The Real World,* which fails as documentary (too phony) and as entertainment (too dull), it's hard to tell who's using who more," wrote a critic for *USA Today.*[15] By the end of the first season, however, the critical tide had begun to turn. John J. O'Connor of *The New York Times:* "Billed as a reality-based soap opera, MTV's 'Real World' is real largely by accident, and its seven principal players are far too independent to be stuffed into a tidy little soap opera. Yet this force-fed documentary series . . . has been steadily evolving into the year's most riveting television, a compelling portrait of twentysomethings grappling with the 90's."[16]

O'Connor argued that it would probably be best if *The Real World* were to end after one season. But Freston had other ideas. As the ratings came in, he began to realize that he might have found his dreamed-of hedge against a coming video crash; and so MTV commissioned a second season, set in Los Angeles. It attracted much larger audiences than its predecessor, and so there naturally followed a third season and a fourth. Over time the show and its format became the cornerstone of the new MTV, freeing it from its parlous dependence on music videos.

As early as season two, there were subtle changes made to the format of *The Real World,* carrying it further in spirit from *An American Family.* The first season had put more faith in the concept of simply filming young people struggling for a break; the characters, if callow, are likable and thoughtful. At times the show plays like an edited college seminar, albeit with some romance thrown in. But by contemporary standards it is very talky and somewhat short on action. As a retrospective written in 2011 by *The A.V. Club* put it, the show seemed "incredibly, achingly earnest, bracingly raw, and sweetly idealistic."[17]

Fairly early on, Bunim and Murray learned how hard it was to conjure up drama among reasonable, thoughtful people, even those in their twenties. So as the show went on, it came to depend on casting more inherently ridiculous or difficult people who could be guaranteed to stir up trouble in the house. In the second season, for example, David Edwards, a twenty-one-year-old aspiring comedian, is led by his comic instincts to pull the blanket off a female housemate clad in only her underwear, and in the aftermath, to expose himself to his housemates. After a lengthy debate, David was eventually expelled from the house—creating the "kicked off the island" narrative that would soon drive many shows.[18]

The success of *The Real World* drew forth imitators, including several from within MTV itself, hoping to re-create the same formula of low costs and good ratings. Bunim and Murray, having discovered the potential of naturally ridiculous people, would go on to produce *The Simple Life,* centered on a dim-witted heiress named Paris Hilton making her way on a farm, a revival of the "rural" motif that Fred Silverman had thrown overboard in the 1970s.

But each iteration of the formula faced that same question: What could create enough friction and drama to make the show interesting, but still supposedly real, without the power of the pen? *The Real World*'s unpredictability was good enough for a comparatively low-rent MTV slot, but if the new format was to be grafted on the more expensive evening schedule of network television, consistent dramatic effect was a prime imperative. Answering the problem would once again mean drawing inspiration from the past, in this case the 1950s.

While many people were probably drawn to the same idea, in 1994 a British producer named Charlie Parsons pitched the idea of mixing *The Real World*'s documentary format with a 1950s game show structure and dramatic competition. The idea was called, fittingly, a "documentary game show." As part of a production team, including Bob Geldof, onetime lead singer of the Boomtown Rats and later the founder of Live Aid, Parsons pitched the new format to Swedish public television. Originally named *Castaway* and later *Expedition Robinson,* the show, set on a remote desert island, staged an ongoing physical competition under constant surveillance. The sixteen contestants were divided into two "tribes," who would live on the island for about a month; at the end of each episode, one player would be voted off the island by the others.[19]

The show was a hit in Sweden, and when Parsons sold it elsewhere it was renamed *Survivor*. In the United States, its viewership grew and grew, just as the hit game shows of the 1950s had. When the first season's final episode in 2000 managed to attract 50 million viewers, matching some of the larger audiences in television history, it was clear that the new mode of content—by this time widely described as "reality television"—was literally ready for prime time.

What was the draw? In some ways the appeal of the new reality shows was no mystery. Like soap operas and other serial dramas, they had had story lines and plots that only seemed spontaneous. These largely involved interpersonal relationships and conflict, as well as memorable (if broadly drawn) characters, like "Snooki" and "The Situation" from *Jersey Shore* or any of the "housewives" from *The Real Housewives*. All those elements were arguably as old as *Amos 'n' Andy*. At the same time, game-show-inspired reality programs like *Survivor* depended on the classic drama of a sports match: the game had rules, the outcome was uncertain, there would be winners and losers, and meanwhile there was plenty of suspense and elbows thrown. There isn't much mystery to that formula at all.

––––––––––––––

Since *An American Family,* it had been a consistent and predictable consequence of reality television that cast members became famous, if only fleetingly. It was not star power of the sort one could pack up and sell elsewhere; it was the sort of celebrity Charles Van Doren had enjoyed before he was disgraced. But it was enough to pull viewers in and also to compensate the players. Indeed, as we've said, performers in these low-budget affairs were largely paid in attention. That carried the hope of a more lasting celebrity and the opportunities that come with it. It certainly felt like actual celebrity while it lasted. As Kevin Powell, an original *Real World* cast member, described attending the Video Music Awards in 1992, "You're talking Red Hot Chili Peppers, Nirvana, Howard Stern—and then the cast of *The Real World.* And I swear, bro, the fans screamed for us as if we were the Beatles. That's when I really knew the show was a game-changer."[20]

In this effect, too, *An American Family* was the prototype. "This series," Lance Loud later said, "was the fulfillment of the middle-class dream that you can become famous for being just who you are."[21] It wasn't Gilbert's intent, but the unexpected effect was to make the Louds famous for a brief time. Pat Loud would publish her autobiography, and the five children would perform as a rock band on *The Dick Cavett Show,* à la the Partridge Family. Bill Loud would pose in his bathrobe for *Esquire,* and Lance in his birthday suit for *Screw* magazine. And yet by the 1980s, the Louds' name would scarcely ring a bell; the exception was Lance, who would achieve immortality as a gay icon.

In a limited way, "ordinary Joe" species of celebrity had existed before—game show champions of the 1950s being the clearest antecedent. But the emergence of an entire program genre "celebrifying" ordinary people, and soon to dominate television, was something new. As such, it marked the beginning of a subtle but significant change in the very nature of celebrity. If once it comprised heroes, demigods, kings, and saints, and then later icons of the screen or sports, by the 1990s celebrity was becoming something that could happen to anyone. Thus it became a worthwhile, reasonable goal for the great generality. This, ultimately, may account for the genre's lasting appeal.

The reality format took a category that had always existed, the god-like among us, and democratizing it, brought the realm of the formerly unreachable ever closer. It had always been a paradox that celebrities were the Other, beyond us, yet at the same time like us (perhaps this was modernity's version of the ancient duality of God transcendent and God immanent). The paradox, we might say, resulted from their celebrity having been constructed by our collective attention, producing an incomprehensibility that managed to be comprehensible. But the attention that celebrities had previously captured had some more or less objective basis in their attainment, appearance, wealth, or talent. Reality television inverted the process, industrializing the manufacture of celebrity for the pure sake of attention capture. Having devised a way to harvest attention by presenting the ordinary, it fairly revolutionized the attention merchant's business model. For the attention gathered this way could, like any other, be sold to advertisers; but it also served to compensate talent.* With so many new celebrities minted every year, the attention economy would come close to validating the suggestion, sometimes credited to Andy Warhol, that television was building a system to ensure that everyone would be famous, or have a chance to be. This would sustain the system, rather in the way that everyone in post-industrialized nations is given to believe they have some chance of being rich.

For ordinary people, reality TV came to seem almost like a lottery. The winning ticket of stardom might remain a statistical rarity, but the chances hadn't seemed so good since the days when a girl might frequent the soda counter at Schwab's hoping to be "discovered." The difference was that, unlike traditionally constituted celebrities—a president, an actor, or a musician—once the show was over, the star had no means to sustain the attention that had become a way of life. Acting fast, some might convert their fame into a new, usually less glamorous gig. Most would suffer the usual vicissitudes of the entertainment industry, in which breaking out is against the odds. Eventually, they would go back to normal life, the subject of an occasional Internet joke.

Consider the tail-off of one of the more successful early stars, Eric Nies, the male model from *The Real World;* he was the show's biggest star, thanks to his good looks and penchant for taking off his shirt to reveal a finely muscled torso. Nies did enjoy some success after the program's run: he became co-host of another MTV show, *The Grind,* dancing on its stage for a few years. After being replaced in 1995, he produced a series of dance exercise videos, in which he slowly disrobed while the other dancers stayed dressed. He next showed up in an infomercial for the "Abaratus," a long elastic band used for abdominal exercises. And that is where his public career would have ended, but for one final appearance on a short-lived reality show entitled *Confessions of a Teen Idol.*

Whatever the consequences for the individuals exposed, reality television was like manna from heaven for the attention merchants. It came down to simple economics, or as one television executive observed: "A reality show can grab a primetime audience just as effectively as a good

---

* At least initially. When a reality show becomes a huge hit, its performers bargain for pay raises like any other talent. But most attention merchants don't mind drifting back toward the older model if by then the ad revenues are strong enough.

drama or comedy, but sometimes at half the price."[22] For this reason, and with little remark, over the early 2000s the business of television was fundamentally reset, as the reality model, by almost any measure, became the dominant form of programming, capturing by the 2002–2003 season 63.1 percent of prime time, or 124 million or so regular viewers. It would remain at that level for the better part of the decade.[23]

The key demographic for reality television had always been young viewers. Perhaps this was because of the genre's origins on MTV, or simply youth's relative willingness to believe in their own chance of achieving fame in their lifetime (outside of the political class, the middle-aged are under fewer such delusions). Nevertheless, over time, programmers found that the reality moss could overgrow other demographics, too: there would be offerings for middle-aged men, like *The Deadliest Catch* (a show featuring fishermen); ones for women with children, like *Wife Swap*, focused on keeping house; and for unreconstructed materialists of all ages, *Real Housewives*, an unscripted soap set in the McMansions of the affluent but never satisfied. Indeed, over the next decade, there would be almost three hundred new reality shows trying almost every conceivable permutation of attention capture tricks, including talent shows (*American Idol*), launching your successful start-up (*Shark Tank*); pathology voyeurism, formerly known as freak shows (*Hoarders*); variations on a theme of *The Real World* (*Jersey Shore*, group living featuring the Italian American "Guido" subculture), celebrity family life (*The Osbournes*, showing the ordinary domesticity of former Black Sabbath front man Ozzy Osbourne); women marrying for money, men for trophy (*Million Dollar Matchmaker*); making it yourself—a better life through real estate (*The Million Dollar Listing*). And then there were the truly bizarre experiments, for instance, a match-making game show on which the contestant chooses a husband from among twenty men wearing masks—the kicker: it's called *Mr. Personality* and hosted by the former White House intern Monica Lewinsky. The shows were so cheap to produce, no idea was deemed too ridiculous to try.

Perhaps the greatest of all, at least with respect to encapsulating the quintessence of the genre and the alteration it effected in the attention industries, would be *Keeping Up with the Kardashians*. Kim Kardashian was the friend, and then frenemy, of former reality star heiress Paris Hilton, later to become a successful DJ. Kardashian was an heiress of a different kind. Daughter of the late Robert Kardashian, O. J. Simpson defense attorney, she lived with her two sisters (Khloé and Kourtney) and their disaffected brother Rob. Her mother, Kris, had married Olympic legend Bruce Jenner (now named Caitlyn), and so Kim's household also included half-siblings Kylie and Kendall. Kim, once a stylist for Lindsay Lohan and others, always had a flare for the dramatic, having at a tender age married and divorced, the latter not accomplished before producing an infamous sex tape with her then lover, which somehow leaked, as Paris's had too, after all. Mother Kris, always looking out for her brood, thought they would be naturals as the subject of a television show. This fact came to the attention of Ryan Seacrest, producer and host of *American Idol*, who, joining with the venerable team of Bunim and Murray, launched *KUWTK*, as it is known, in 2007. The rest, as they say, is history.

It is a requirement for successful reality television that it be critically panned. *The New York Times* called the new show a "a window into a family . . . that seems to understand itself only in terms of its collective opportunism" and commented that "the Kardashian show is not about an eccentric family living conventionally; it is purely about some desperate women climbing to the margins of fame, and that feels a lot creepier."[24] *PopMatters* opined that "there is something disturbing about the Kardashians' intense hunger for fame. But even worse—it is downright boring to watch this family live out their tedious lives."[25] Yet what the Kardashians must be given credit for is breaking the curse of ephemeral reality fame; for close to a decade they have sustained a multimillion-dollar empire. The family demonstrated a reality TV version of synergy—should audiences grow tired of the tedious antics of one family member, another quickly jumped in to provide a new hot mess, like lipstick-wearing tag-team wrestlers. Meanwhile, over the 2010s the Kardashians' earnings increased at a pace to make a banker jealous. The family made $65 million collectively in 2010, while Kim's individual earnings had reached $28 million by 2014 and $52.5 million by 2015.

With the show as primary attention platform, virtually every known subsidiary revenue stream has been tapped or developed by them. There have been product endorsements; paid appearances, tweets, and sponsored birthday parties; eponymous apparel lines, fragrances, books (like *Selfish,* composed entirely of selfies), show spinoffs; and an impressively lucrative and popular iPhone game—all of it kept aloft by *KUWTK,* whose dramatic potential never seems to wane, no matter how many sister-on-sister or mother-daughter catfights, no matter how many romances, divorces, pregnancies, unmentioned facial alterations, or rides on private jets the audience is shown. Professor Elizabeth Currid-Halkett writes: "It's clear that the Kardashians have turned generating publicity, and possibly profit from that attention, into an artform."[26]

The urge for what's next seems to be insatiable, and for that reason the Kardashians and the world of television in all likelihood have cause to worry. It is simply not conceivable that the future of commercial television, whatever it may turn out to be, can indefinitely sustain attention for any particular format, particularly one with as much market share and overdevelopment as reality TV. No matter how desirable the financial calculus, no attention capture strategy has been able to stay ahead of the disenchantment effect indefinitely. Eventually, even the goose that lays the golden egg gets old and dies. Tom Freston knew this and with a bit of foresight saved his network from irrelevancy.

Nevertheless, reality had been a momentous discovery, even if something of a misnomer. For what viewers were flocking to was both real and not real, a distortion for the sake of spectacle, calibrated to harvest the most attention at the lowest price possible. It was, however, real enough to be believed—not literally perhaps, but in the way scripted drama is believed—and, by the new millennium, to have a whole nation of viewers content, in effect, to watch versions of themselves with vicarious delight. Thus would television enter the new millennium, perilously dependent on someone else's idea of real life yet still the reigning champion of the twentieth century's breathless contest for attention.

WON'T BE FOOLED AGAIN

It was promoted as "the most elaborate, complex and ambitious television program produced." On December 31, 1999, the new millennium was welcomed by a grand coalition of the world's television broadcasters, who put together a twenty-three-hour-long live program to cover New Year's as it occurred around the globe. Correspondents reported live from festivities at each meridian, and in the United States, the ageless Dick Clark, a fixture of television since the 1950s, hosted a countdown program featuring an all-star musical lineup that included the Bee Gees, Christina Aguilera, Barry Manilow, NSYNC, and Aerosmith.

The networks would claim audiences of more than 800 million worldwide, but who could blame one for thinking it television's last hurrah? For in that epochal year, there was no denying that mass attention seemed to have migrated irresistibly to a new medium that had lately evolved into a form we would now recognize and yet was plainly still only in the infancy of its possibilities. The BBC had declared 1999 "the year of the Net," and CNN.com invited users to "uncork the bubbly, boot up the computer, and usher in the new era in an appropriately futuristic way."[1] A site named the Earth-Cam offered "the Webcast of the century," with cameras sending pictures from New Year's celebrations around the world, just as broadcast was doing with such expensive fanfare.[2] CNN.com further allowed that "by staying home this New Year's Eve with your computer, you really aren't missing a thing."

By 2000, the consensus was that the "old media"—the industries that had captured the preponderance of human attention over the last century—were basically doomed. They could try as they might to delay the future, but ultimately the new would replace the old as it always had. The legacy attention merchants and their collaborators in advertising were, by this understanding, on a path to extinction. "It's our country. It's our media now. It's our time and attention," wrote Jeff Jarvis, prominent booster of the new media. "Sorry if we, the people, disappoint you. But does it occur to you that you disappointed us?"[3]

Television, for its part, seemed to confirm its own desperation as it churned out increasingly bizarre reality shows (like *The Swan*, centered on extreme plastic surgery), refitted game shows, like *Who Wants to Be a Millionaire?*, a retread of *The $64,000 Question*, and ever stranger hybrids of celebrity and reality, like *Vanilla Ice Goes Amish*.[4] Whether it was the passive, suppliant state it induced in audiences, the abhorrent executives who plotted it, or the shameless catering to the lowest common denominator, this unprecedented destitution of the second screen, the previous century's mightiest attention harvester, had those not yet ready to despair asking when something better would appear.

That's what made the 2000s different. Perhaps it was a kind of millenarianism, but there was a widespread expectation of a great transformation, a belief in the liberating influence of something new and fundamentally different. In 2001, Lawrence Lessig published *The Future of Ideas,* prophesying that the web would serve as a new commons, liberating the ordinary individual from the "electronic bondage" of television, and recasting him as a contributor and creator.[5] The 2000s would create a different kind of citizen: a nation of creators, as interested in one another as they had been in the mass-marketed offerings of the dominant attention merchants. But how this might work in practice remained vague, and even mysterious, in a manner befitting any prophecy. It would take a decade to see what it all meant.

CHAPTER 20

THE KINGDOM OF CONTENT:

THIS IS HOW YOU DO IT

In 1996, Microsoft was at the height of its powers, the technology sector's most intimidating behemoth, brutally efficient and plainly bent on the conquest of all that surrounded it. Its billions in profits based on sales of its ubiquitous, if unloved, Windows and Office, the graphical operating system of most computers on earth, had made it the most valuable company in the world. If anyone had made a fortune by cornering the market for nuts and bolts and sticking to it, it was Microsoft.[1] It was a surprise, therefore, when on January 3, 1996, its chief executive, Bill Gates, wearing his large, dark-framed glasses that were not yet a hipster affectation but still the sign of the true nerd, posted an essay on Microsoft's website, with a counterintuitive title: "Content Is King."[2]

At the time of that coronation, Internet "content" consisted mainly of homemade web pages with flashing words and the text forums where geeks discussed the pluses and minuses of object-oriented programming languages. Nevertheless, Gates prophesied an explosion of new creativity that would dominate the Internet's future. "Content is where I expect much of the real money will be made on the Internet, just as it was in broadcasting," he wrote, adding, "The television revolution that began half a century ago spawned a number of industries . . . but the long-term winners were those who used the medium to deliver information and entertainment." But his prediction also came with a warning that to succeed, Internet content would have to be good:

> If people are to be expected to put up with turning on a computer to read a screen, they must be rewarded with deep and extremely up-to-date information that they can explore at will. They need to have audio, and possibly video. They need an opportunity for personal involvement that goes far beyond that offered through the letters-to-the-editor pages of print magazines.[3]

And so, at the command of its great leader, the world's most profitable company would spring to action, beginning a massive, multibillion-dollar effort to seize the emerging market being created by "convergence," a world called "Internet-television." A new breed of attention merchant was being born, and Microsoft planned to rule them all. Unfortunately, as Gates had warned, anyone who would rule the Internet had better make his content good. For Microsoft, that turned out to be the sticking point.

It was not for want of effort or resources. Microsoft opened an entire new complex in Redmond, California, at some distance from its main offices, which it staffed with "content people" specially imported from New York and Los Angeles. The team was comprised of "black-clad creative types," reported *The New York Times,* tasked with "building a new, chic kind of media business." In reality, the new hires were given an impossible task: that of inventing both a new platform and an entirely new form of content—one that was not television, film, or a computer game but instead "interactive" and that capitalized on "convergence" via a new portal named "MSN 2.0." That was the name of the interface being preinstalled on every new Windows machine and designed to make the Internet feel more like a television.[4]

Reviews of MSN 2.0—which had launched with the slogan "Every new universe begins with a big bang"—were unkind. The *Times* complained of complicated instructions that began "with a pushy multimedia commercial whose irritating 20-something host declares, 'I see you have good taste!' He also says, 'I promise you, this won't hurt a bit.' Dentists say that, too." The effort left the user with a feeble browser that could download and play a series of interactive shows that somewhat resembled video games but were much slower to load, and lacking any action to speak of. Microsoft later admitted the shows were "spectacularly unsuccessful."[5]

If the Internet was still too new to achieve its content potential, perhaps Microsoft could for now hasten the convergence by making television more like the Internet. Following this logic they sank hundreds of millions into a new cable news network named Microsoft-NBC, or MSNBC for short. They had the vague notion that the network would eventually populate the Internet in some way. As Microsoft explained in a press release, "From now on, the promise of the Internet and the power of television become one." Commentators weren't entirely sure what to make of it. "Some very interesting and powerful creature will be created," said media critic Steve Rosenbaum, "but I don't know what it is." If he didn't know, it turned out that no one at Microsoft or NBC quite did either. When it finally launched, MSNBC elected to make itself a copy of CNN, with one exception: it featured a show named *The Site,* devoted to the Internet revolution.[6]

The synergy, whatever it was supposed to be, failed to materialize, and facing low ratings MSNBC executives turned to old-school cable thinking. Mining demographics, they noticed that left-leaning viewers lacked their own cable news network. MSNBC would therefore become the mirror image of Fox News; the "MS" in MSNBC would linger there, like an old store sign that the new owner forgot to take down. Microsoft's only successful investments in this period were *Slate,* which billed itself as the very first online magazine and ultimately proved the viability of the concept, and the Xbox gaming console, which was the kind of nuts-and-bolts market entry that Microsoft had always done well. Most of the rest was a fiasco of the first order.[7]

In short, Microsoft couldn't quite crack the nut; the idea of merging television and the Internet was just too simplistic. In effect, Microsoft treated the Internet as if it were merely a new channel on which it could broadcast content, as if what had been invented was an extension of cable television. But the impulse was not altogether misguided, for someone was going to make money selling all of the attention the Internet was capturing. It just wasn't going to be Microsoft. The most successful contestant would be the one that truly understood the new platform and how it would be used.

By the late 1990s, as Microsoft's content initiative faded, word was spreading about a new company named Google, whose specialty was search. Search became a major application as the Internet got more populated, fast becoming wild and woolly, too vast to tune in to like a TV channel. There were a number of search engines running—Lycos, Magellan, AltaVista, Excite, Yahoo!, which originally launched as an Internet directory, to name a few. But it was soon clear that Google did search better than anyone else; its inventors were smart, its algorithm was wicked, and its code was tight. With a simple search box placed on a white page, it was both elegant and technically a quantum leap over what was then available. But all who followed the company knew it had one massive and potentially fatal problem. Google was more like an academic project than a firm, and as it gained in popularity, it was burning through cash at a terrifying rate, with nary a business model in sight. As cofounder Sergey Brin reflected later, "I felt like a schmuck. I had an Internet start-up—so did everyone else. It was unprofitable, like everyone else's and how hard is that?"[8]

It is a fascinating moment to contemplate. Tech's hottest firm stood at a fork in the road, pondering its future and, being an unusually deliberative company, tried to think through the consequences of each choice. Thanks to the growth of search, Google was capturing bushels of attention, but how to capitalize on that? As we've seen, there have always been two ways of converting attention into cash. The older is to charge admission, as to the spectacle, on the model of the opera or HBO or a book; for Google this would mean licensing or selling access to a premium product. The second is to resell the attention gained, that being the model of the attention merchant.*

It didn't take a genius to see that the safest and most immediate revenue stream for a firm with Google's potential to harvest attention was in advertising. And that way it went. "Every day, millions upon mil-

---

* Actually, there were two other ways to go, neither of them seriously considered. One would have been to rely on donations or patronage, a course later pursued by other publicly spirited projects like Wikipedia. The other was even more radical, and might have been contemplated by men like Google's founders in an earlier time before the heady seductions of the dot-com boom. They might have made Google a truly public project, like email or the Internet itself.

lions of people lean forward into their computer screens," John Battelle, cofounder of *Wired,* would write in 2005, "and pour their wants, fears, and intentions into the simple colors and brilliant white background of Google.com."[9] If radio had promised a "relaxed" audience, here was something better: people who really wanted something and ready to tell exactly what—"intentional traffic," in the jargon. Google could serve up minds to advertisers in this particularly valuable mental state—open, desirous, and impressionable. Thanks to the attention merchant's proprietary alchemy, advertising would make Google feel "free" to its users— as if it were just doing them a big favor.

It retrospect, it was a no-brainer. But the firm's principal founder, Larry Page, was unusually sensitive to the corrupting potential of advertising. Before Google had come to its fork in the road, he had strenuously insisted in a piece coauthored with Brin that "advertising funded search engines will be inherently biased towards the advertisers and away from the needs of the consumers."[10] As an engineer and scientist, Page had wanted to build a clean, pure tool, free of commerce's distortions. His aversion, moreover, was not purely academic: he had seen what an advertising-driven search engine looked like, peddled by a man whom both Brin and Page found distasteful—a character, now mainly forgotten, who was for a while Google's greatest rival. His name was Bill Gross.

Two years earlier, in 1998, Bill Gross was at the then newish "Technology, Entertainment, Design" conference in Monterey, California, peddling his ideas for an advertising-driven search engine. Launched in the early 1990s, the TED conference staged short speeches by innovators and visionaries, with the intention of inspiring audiences; the flogging of products was strongly discouraged. Gross, who made a career out of ignoring such admonitions, went to TED to hawk his latest product. He proposed a new concept for Internet search: instead of some fancy algorithm, he said, why not just sell places in search results to the highest bidder?

While Gross's presentation was engaging, the response was not friendly. TED is famous for its easy and adoring audiences, yet on this occasion hisses were heard. Afterward, in the hallway, the buzz was downright negative; as John Battelle wrote, the model "was in clear violation of every ethical boundary known to media."[11]

But Bill Gross was not the type to be deterred. Issuing from a rough-and-tumble 1990s dot-com culture, he was famous for turning one idea (supposedly inspired by Steven Spielberg) into a company nearly overnight at his start-up incubator Idealab. He was given to saying things like "The old rules don't apply when you're an Internet company."[12] In retrospect what Gross meant by the "old rules" was often what others might call "ethics" or "valuation" or "generally accepted accounting practices."

Many of Gross's innovations took the attention merchant's model to new extremes. eToys, an online toy retailer, spent a huge portion of its venture capital on advertising during its short life, on the assumption that nothing more was needed to succeed. Gross also founded FreePC, which, while it lasted, gave people low-end Compaq computers in exchange for detailed personal information and the right to monitor their Internet surfing and buying habits. His NetZero was a "free" Internet service that depended on ads and similar tracking practices, at least until its collapse.

Gross would turn his "highest bidder" search idea into a company named GoTo.com, which got its start seven months before Google and was, for a while, its main competitor. Unlike Google, GoTo took payment from advertisers in return for higher search rankings in the search results; "relevance" depended on dollars spent in this scheme of search payola. Or, as Gross spun it, "We're not letting a blind algorithm decide." GoTo's approach was a relative of AOL's paid-for walled garden, and its trick of baiting users with search and delivering ads was branded misleading and unethical by critics; one complained, "If a middle school student does a search for 'nutrition' on GoTo, the first 221 sites listed are bidders" (mainly sites selling diets). When asked by *The New York Times* whether his search systematically favored commercial results, Gross answered that anyone could pony up for the same privilege. "Mr. Gross insists that nonprofit groups, universities and even medical organizations will find it in their interests to pay for placement," the *Times* reported. As Gross said, "Even if it's philanthropic, it wants your attention."[13]

Among Gross's most exercised critics were Brin and Page, who found his methods repulsive. In their seminal 1998 paper describing Google's search algorithm, the two graduate students blasted the paid search model for creating a problem not easy to detect. "Search engine bias is particularly insidious," they wrote. "It is very difficult even for experts to evaluate search engines."[14] Mixed incentives were the enemy, and that is precisely what being in the pay of advertisers produced. For this reason, search, the men believed, should be transparent and dispassionate.

More than anything, these sentiments reflected the personality of Larry Page, the main driving force behind Google. Page does not ooze charisma; he has a famously flat and unassuming manner; if you saw him in a meeting, at which he'd likely be eating lunch from a cafeteria tray, you might easily mistake him for some insufferably opinionated middle manager. Yet he's a man of unusually bold brilliance and almost preternaturally instinctive—once he's made up his mind. He is in his heart of hearts a purist, devoted to an engineering aesthetic whose beauty is hard to deny once you've understood it.

Google's unspoken motto has always been "We do it better"; its founding culture a radical meritocracy, where brilliant code and ingenious system design count above all. The early Page had no patience for less technical sides of the business, including things like marketing, administration, even raising or making money. Not that he thought he was above all that; rather, he believed, with some reason, that companies often wasted most of their time and energy on such mundane matters, at the expense of the true goal.* That, of course, was inventing and building beautiful, perfect tools that were outrageously better than those that came before.

Two features distinguish Brin and Page's favorite creations. First, they were always courageous new solutions to seemingly intractable old problems; ideally they were counterintuitive, even crazy seeming, yet once executed, utterly magical. Second, they were fast. Google demanded that its things work faster and better than anyone else's, and without the

---

* As Google's first CEO, Page once fired all of Google's managers, reasoning that they were not only useless, but interfered with engineering, what with all their meetings, planning sessions, and so on. He genuinely believed that engineers, like a flock of birds, were self-organizing creatures without need of oversight, and that, left to their own, they would produce miracles. See Nicholas Carlson, "The Untold Story of Larry Page's Incredible Comeback," *Business Insider*, April 24, 2014.

compromises so many other products put up with. Combined, these two qualities came close to defining "Googley," an adjective used on campus for things that reflected the firm's idea of the good.[15]

However they could express this ideal they did. Why *not* have a campus where the food is both delicious and free, so you didn't waste time in line at the cash register? Why *not* give away gigabits of free storage to users? Scan the world's books? Drive trucks mounted with cameras through the streets everywhere and create a pictorial map? But nothing should be Googley-er than the flagship itself: and so Google search had to be not merely better than the rest but a thousand times better than those ugly and slow stepsisters, like Yahoo! and GoTo. The terms of Google's self-styled triumph were indeed aesthetic. Where Google was fast, unadorned, and untouchable—Shining! Incorruptible!—it saw its rivals as essentially "sucky"—slow, festooned with advertising, and, ultimately, venal.

All of this made the prospect of advertising very difficult for Google and for Page in particular. To the purist, few things are smellier than advertising, and once you step in it, there is no easy way to fully wipe it off. Yet the time had come when Google had to show it could make money somehow. As pure as they were, Page and Brin also admired efficacy. Neither much respected idealists who never got anything done, the high-minded academics and programmers whose eyes and ideas never saw daylight. Google had come too far to founder on its own ideals.

And so, with the optimism of Silicon Valley engineers, Page and the other technical minds started to consider how they might invent their way out of their revenue problem. The question they would ask was whether there was some way of accepting ads that didn't compromise their product. Could they come up with a "Diet Coke" solution—all of the taste, none of the calories? It went without saying that those "sucky" competitors freely taking ads weren't as inventive. If Google took a crack at it, the company might create a form of ad that actually improved the product, instead of degrading it.

The idea of advertising that actually *adds* value is something of a Holy Grail in both tech and the advertising industry. Engineers knew exactly what ads were doing to web pages—slowing them down, taking up screen space, and diverting the user's attention from what she really wanted to do; in some cases they were doing truly horrible things, like deliberately inserting bugs. But there had always been the theory that advertising, if not deceptive, could serve the useful purpose of informing the consumer—what marketers call "discovery." Outside of the web, not all advertising was or is despised by customers. Print advertisements can be as beautiful as editorial content—for instance, the lavishly produced ads in *Vogue;* some can usefully connect a unique buyer and seller—as with classified listings in the newspaper. And some viewers of the Super Bowl tune in mainly for the commercial spots, which are famously the industry's most innovative and witty. Could Google invent some web version of desirable advertising?

With a primitive advertising system devised by 2000, Page tapped a top engineer to make it better. Eric Veach was a brilliant Canadian mathematician, who, among his other qualifications, absolutely detested advertising. They got to work (long hours being another Google tradition) and by mid-2001 Veach and his team were convinced they'd solved the riddle. Borrowing some of Gross's ideas (like auctions), they had invented an advertising system that turned prevailing wisdom about reselling attention on its head.

The attention merchant had always tried to reach as broad an audience as possible, bombarding them with as many ads as they'd stand before going into total revolt. Such had been the strategy in television since Pat Weaver first introduced the commercial break: cram fourteen to sixteen minutes of ad time into every hour, along with a further three to seven minutes of other forms of branding, eating up roughly one third of the broadcast; the content was devised essentially to cue up the ads, with a little cliffhanger before each one. It was in some ways little different from a mass mailing. It was worth the cost just to catch a tiny percentage at the optimal moment, when the viewers were receptive or in need of what was being sold, and also for the sake of building "brand awareness" among others who might turn into consumers. Everyone else was, as it were, collateral damage.

An annoying ad today might make you try Anacin tomorrow. But Google had something different: access to people who were plainly expressing a commercial intent: when someone types in "drug rehab," "male pattern baldness," or "find a mortgage," there's little doubt what's on their mind. The new system would therefore show relevant advertisements *only* at those moments, and—quite radically—stay out of your way otherwise. In short, Google took the decision to leave a lot of attention on the table; the theory was that advertisers would value surgical strikes at least as much as carpet bombing. Imagine a television channel that read your mind and showed you just one commercial an hour, keyed to your interests, reasoning that it would make you like that channel better: that was the early Google's idea.

The technological implementation was called "AdWords," and it would create auctions for text-only advertisements that would run alongside the search results when a specific search term (say, "plaintiff's lawyer" or "mortgage") was entered. A further brilliant stroke was to assign each ad a "quality score," based on how often it was actually clicked on. Google insisted on running only ads that, in addition to being relevant, people had actually liked. And so, if you were searching for "Dead Sea scrolls," you wouldn't end up with advertisements for "mortgages" or "diet aids"—most likely, you wouldn't see any ads at all.[16]

As soon as AdWords launched, it "accelerated past the outer moons of Jupiter on its way to some distant galaxy made entirely of money," to quote Douglas Edwards, Employee Number 59.[17] That happened for two reasons. First, Google, even while running ads, remained better than Yahoo!, Lycos, GoTo, and the rest, thus eating into their market share. Second, more importantly, Google's advertising system finally delivered on metrics that satisfied advertisers and might even have elicited a nod from Arthur Nielsen in his grave. Among the various reasons for the dot-com crash was the fact that, over the late 1990s, AOL and everyone else had trouble proving that online ads necessarily did anything at all (hence AOL's need to fabricate revenue). But with Google's direct proof of clicks and tracking of customers, advertisers could finally see a direct link between their ads and eventual purchases. The beauty, once again, was that Google users were advertised to at a moment often very close to purchase. There was no need to prove the search engine could build brands—instead, it found users who were like travelers coming out of an airport, in a hurry, looking for a taxi, and there was the advertisement—"click." With these innovations, the money started pouring in, first by the millions, then by the hundreds of millions, and finally billions upon billions. Google would soon become the most profitable attention merchant in the history of the world.*

---

* Meanwhile, GoTo's founder began to spiral downward as the dot-com market crashed. Battelle writes that "like so many leaders of the early Internet era, Bill Gross was smoking a little too much of his own stuff, and the party came to an abrupt and unhappy end." An "unhappy end" may be an unusual description for a man who would sell his GoTo search

. . . .

Ironically, it was contempt for advertising (on the part of the founders and the chief engineers) that would ultimately pave the way to the company's unrivaled success as an attention merchant. The key was in renegotiating the terms under which the public was asked to tolerate ads. For as Google became a part of everyday life over the 2000s—its name becoming a synonym for search—it presented what seemed by the standards of the day a very reasonable tradeoff, which few would ever question, and which caused no degradation, to judge by earnings growth. So unintrusive was AdWords that some people didn't even realize that Google was ad-supported: it just seemed to be there for the taking like manna from the heavens. Google had, in fact, laid bare what had originally been so miraculous about the attention merchant model—getting something truly desirable at no apparent cost. For what really seemed like nothing, the public got the best search ever designed and, in time, other goodies as well, like free email with unlimited storage, peerless maps, the world's libraries, and even research devoted to exciting innovations like self-driving cars. Of course, there was, as there always is, a quid pro quo: in its ripest state, the buying public was exposed to sales pitches; which might prove useful but then again might not. Google also began to collect a lot of information about a lot of people. Nevertheless, Page, who had the most qualms about advertising, told *Wired*'s Steven Levy that he'd begun to feel that AdWords was a good and just innovation. "From that point on," writes Levy, "Brin and Page saw nothing but glory in the bottom line."[18]

Page may have felt he'd outwitted the Devil, but so do all Faustian characters. While the safeguards in AdWords would keep Google's core product uncompromised for the time being, corporate life is long, and shareholder demand for growth unremitting. In Wall Street's view, even

---

engine to Yahoo! for over a billion dollars. Nonetheless, according to Battelle, "A Tone of regret and a tinge of pain shade his recollections." Gross would later put a brave face on his role. "I'm wildly proud," he said to *Slate* in 2013, "of coming up with the paid-search model." See Will Oremus, "Google's Big Break," *Slate,* October 13, 2013. GoTo would also create regulatory problems for Yahoo! with the Federal Trade Commission. Like Brin and Page, the FTC looked at the practice of mixing advertised and organic results and did not like it. But where the engineers saw a corrupted process, the lawyers saw a form of consumer deception. In the FTC's view, the paid-for search results were a form of advertisement that was not clearly labeled as such, and therefore illegally deceptive.

the most robust advertising revenues always have room for improvement. In time, this reality would put pressure on the original bargain
that Google struck with the public. Even if AdWords was a paradigm
shift, it was still advertising, and Google, however ingenious, was still an
attention merchant. It would, henceforth, always be serving two masters,
beauty and the beast.

CHAPTER 21

HERE COMES EVERYONE

Google and a few other West Coast companies had demonstrated that web advertising wasn't just hype: there was real money to be made reselling attention captured by the Internet. But Google had effectively put AdWords on the remote control; there remained a lot more attention to be harvested the old-fashioned way. That much was clear from the simple fact that by the early 2000s, the average white-collar worker had a screen on his desk with a fairly high-speed connection to the Internet. Designed, theoretically, to create a more productive work environment, this setup, by the law of unintended consequences, also created ripe new opportunities to harvest attention. As observer Jonah Peretti had noticed:

> Hundreds of millions of bored office workers sit in front of computers forwarding emails, blogging, IMing, and playing. . . . These distracted corporate employees have accidentally created the Bored at Work Network (BWN)—a huge people-powered network with even greater reach than traditional networks like CNN, ABC, or the BBC.

Whose harvest would it be? The race was on.

In November 2000, *The New Yorker* ran a piece introducing the world to something new. It went like this:

> Meg Hourihan was in a bad mood. She had nothing major to worry about, but she was afflicted by the triple malaise of a woman in her late twenties: (a) the weather was lousy; (b) she was working too hard; and (c) she didn't have a boyfriend. Nothing, not even eating, seemed very interesting to her. The only thing that did sound appealing was moving to France and finding a hot new French boyfriend, but even when she talked about that idea she struck a sardonic, yeah-right-like-I'm-really-going-to-do-that kind of tone.
>
> I know this about Meg because I read it a few months ago on her personal Web site, which is called Megnut.com. I've been reading Megnut for a while now, and so I know all kinds of things about its author. I know that she's a little dreamy and idealistic; that she fervently believes there is a distinction between "dot-com people," who are involved in the Internet for its I.P.O. opportunities, and "web people," who are in love with the imaginative possibilities presented by the medium, and that she counts herself among the latter.[1]

What was this new form of confessional? It was, the author Rebecca Mead explained, "a new kind of Web site that is known as a 'weblog,' or 'blog.'" As she explained, "Having a blog is rather like publishing your own, on-line version of Reader's Digest, with daily updates"; yet with a conversational element: "other people who have blogs—they are known as bloggers—read your blog, and if they like it they blog your blog on their own blog." Of course, one didn't have to blog about your problems, the way Meg did. You could blog about anything. Here was an attention-capturing format that was truly different, even if the force drawing attention to it was not quite clear.

One would have thought that the traditional news media—newspapers and magazines—were in the best natural position to capture the attention lavished on all those connected screens at work and at home. After all, such media were originally designed for such slivers of attention, the little breaks that people take during their day. But newspapers were particularly slow and resentful about adapting their content to the web; they fretted about unreliable Internet reporting, erosion of revenues from print, and other typical concerns of an incumbent business being disrupted. Their hidebound attitude did not excite new users of the web.

And so the opportunity was seized from them by a wide and disparate group who came effectively out of nowhere, or at least no place previously recognized as a precinct of the attention industries. "Here comes everybody" is how Clay Shirky described it.[2] It was the arrival of an unsuspected creative class, fulfilling Lawrence Lessig's prophecy that putting the new tools in the hands of anyone who wanted to try publishing or any creativity for a broader audience would yield a boon to society. Shirky again: "Social tools remove older obstacles to public expression, and thus remove the bottlenecks that characterized mass media. The result is the mass amateurization of efforts previously reserved for media professionals."[3]

On the web, the early 2000s belonged to the bloggers and their fellow travelers, a surprising cohort different from most of what had come before.[4] Their cultural roots lay in the Internet's noncommercial prehistory of the 1980s. In 1999, a book titled *The Cluetrain Manifesto* described these years on the web. "It was technically obscure, impenetrable, populated by geeks and wizards, loners, misfits"; but it "became a place where people could talk to other people without constraint. Without filters or censorship or official sanction—and perhaps most significantly, without advertising. . . . The attraction was in speech, however mediated. In people talking, however slowly. And mostly, the attraction lay in the kinds of things they were saying. Never in history had so many had the chance to know what so many others were thinking on such a wide range of subjects."[5]

David Weinberger, an early online marketing guru and a blogger since, explains what the early webloggers were getting at. "When blogs came along, they became the way we could have a Web presence that enabled us to react, respond, and provoke."[6] Already by that period, the web offered a way to create and project a public version of the self, a path toward Marcuse's liberation and the transcendence of hierarchy that the old media world imposed. As Weinberger writes, "My blog was me. My blog was the Web equivalent of my body. Being-on-the-Web was turning out to be even more important and more fun than we'd thought it would be. . . . We thought we were participating in a revolution. And we were somewhat right."

By their nature the new creators varied but were unified by a pioneering spirit and a bracingly amateur affect. Among them were: a site named the *Drudge Report,* launched in the 1990s, which gained much attention with its timely leaks related to a scandal surrounding President Bill Clinton's affair with an intern; Slashdot.org, launched in 1997, to bring "news for nerds"; the Robot Wisdom, with links to news stories and aiming to establish a link between artificial intelligence and the work of James Joyce; Megnut.com and Kottke.org, the personal blogs of two Internet entrepreneurs who would eventually marry; "The Instapundit" Glenn Reynolds, a libertarian expert on the law of outer space, who gained an audience coupling his pithy one-liners with news of the day. Boing-Boing, originally a printed zine published by Mark Frauenfelder, added author Cory Doctorow and other writers to become a wildly popular blog, presenting a daily "directory of mostly wonderful things."

Those are only a few of the better known. In this golden age of "conversational content" or "user-generated media," a following of some kind suddenly seemed within reach of just about anyone with something to say. It was as if some vault in which the public's attention was kept had been blown open and the looters were taking what they could. A blog about ex-boyfriends; reflections on *Brideshead Revisited,* vintage Honda motorcycles—all had their constituency. And thanks to search, it wasn't that hard to match one's interests with a new world of content. Some of the more prominent new bloggers were current or former journalists, trained to write freely and quickly. Technologists started their own blogs, too, unreadable to the general public. Philosophers, economists, scientists, and other experts emerged from their ivory towers to address one another and motivated laymen in a manner far more recondite than might ever be found in the mainstream media. Some would blog essentially for themselves and those nearest to them, to keep track of their travels, or as a kind of family journal. They sometimes called themselves "escribitionists" before "blogger" became the word.[7] Like an army of miniature Oprah Winfreys, each successful blog created a following and its own little community. Zephyr Teachout, the director of Internet organizing for the 2004 Howard Dean campaign, likened successful bloggers to pastors, each leading their loyal flocks.

Consequently, audiences were fragmented to a degree that made cable television look like the days of *The Ed Sullivan Show.* The regular follower of, say, the blogger Andrew Sullivan would have to be interested in a pro-war gay conservative viewpoint that also advocated for Catholicism, marijuana, beards, beagles, and same-sex marriage. Readers of Boing Boing or Slashdot were people whose truest affiliation was to a neo-geek mentality that celebrated eccentricity and arcane obsessions. Such groups were nothing like the clear demographic categories of old, or even the relatively precise PRIZM clusters. In fact, bloggers sometimes claimed they were creating a-geographical communities, aggregations purely by common interest and passion. And since bloggers had, at least initially, no expectation of making money, there was no temptation to compromise their standards or temper their opinions.

That anyone could start one was not the only radical feature of the blog. The form also popularized the idea of "sharing" as a means of drawing attention to things. This represented a real break with earlier models of attention harvesting, whose ideal of centralized authority was somewhere between the Third Reich's enforced listening and the nationwide audiences of *I Love Lucy*: everyone gathering to listen to a single voice reaching the entire nation. Sharing was still primitive, amounting mostly to the trading of links, but it was already proving a powerful alternative means for information to spread, more in the manner of gossip or a conversation than a broadcast. It was another step toward what we now experience as the "social" proliferation of information and opinion.*

The eventual dichotomy would be between "packaged media" (what

---

* The micro-fragmentation represented by blogging audiences caused panic to some thinkers like Noam Chomsky and Cass Sunstein. Chomsky argued that blogs lacked the power to constrain powerful actors. "There's plenty to criticize about the mass media, but they are the source of regular information about a wide range of topics. You can't duplicate that on blogs." Natasha Lennard, "Noam Chomsky, the Salon Interview: Governments Are Power Systems, Trying to Sustain Power," *Salon,* December 29, 2013. Sunstein, at the height of blogging's popularity, wrote a rare academic attack on the choices made possible by technologies like cable or the Internet. He argued that blogs and other technologies were dividing the country into informational factions who pay attention only to what they care to hear. "In a Democracy," wrote Sunstein, "people do not live in echo chambers or information cocoons. They see and hear a wide range of topics and ideas." This vision of democracy, says Sunstein, "raise[s] serious doubts about certain uses of new technologies, above all the Internet, about the astonishing growth in the power to choose—to screen in and to screen out." Cass Sunstein, *Republic .com 2.0* (Princeton: Princeton University Press, 2007). Both he and Chomsky preferred an environment where the nation regularly tuned in, together, to something like NBC or CBS or perhaps a public broadcaster.

the attention merchant traditionally offered) and the new "user-generated content" or "social media" created by the public at large, and of which the blog was but one element. The wave of noncommercial content creation produced would spread across formats and media with varying degrees of success. Wikipedia, the user-created encyclopedia with no central editor, became a surprising triumph over the early 2000s, drawing on the labor mainly of obsessive young men interested in making relatively anonymous contributions to a larger project. But unlike Google and others, when Wikipedia came to its own fork in the road, gaining enough traffic to rival or exceed that of nearly any other site, save the search engines, it chose the other path; deciding to remain free of advertising, it effectively forsook billions in potential revenue. The founder, Jimmy Wales, officially explained the decision as follows: "I think of Wikipedia as I do a library or a school—and commercial advertising is not right in that space. . . . Maximizing revenue is not our goal."[8]

Subscribing to the same basic philosophy as the bloggers and Wikipedia was a new company named YouTube, which launched in 2005; based on user-generated video along with a fair number of clips borrowed from other sources, its purpose was to facilitate the sharing of such content. With consumer digital video technology now cheaper and better than ever, YouTube proved an instant and enormous hit; and it was particularly attractive in its early days, when there was no advertising, and no enforcement of the copyright laws. Within a year, the company reported that it was serving 100 million daily video views and accepting uploads of some 65,000 new videos. Thus YouTube became the Internet's first successful challenge to what television offered. But unlike Microsoft's blinkered efforts to seize that turf, YouTube was, for better or for worse, actually creating a new genre; the site attracted snippets of commercial content, along with performances of amateur and professional musicians, raconteurs, anyone who imagined they might become a star in their pajamas.

In a new blog for *The New York Times,* still creeping web-ward, Virginia Heffernan argued in 2006 that the long-anticipated "convergence" of television and the Internet—what Microsoft had trumpeted in the 1990s—seemed finally to be happening. And it was taking a bewildering number of forms: "web video, viral video, user-driven video, custom interactive video, consumer-generated video, embedded video ads, web-based VOD, broadband television, diavlogs, vcasts, vlogs, video pod-casts, mobisodes, webisodes and mashups."[9]

Whether highbrow or low, the bloggers and their fellow travel-ers reveled in the sense that they were upending the entire attentional dynamic—democratizing speech and attention to the point that "every-one" could now potentially be both a speaker and an audience, repli-cating, in some ways, the naïveté of the world before the rise of a mass media. There was some sense that bloggers were essentially entertaining one another, as people did before radio or the record player. But there is no doubt that a platform anyone could use jostled the media hierarchy and its authority.

The statistics bore out a sense that there were countless voices speak-ing (if sometimes only to themselves, but never mind). In 2005 Nielsen estimated that at least 35 million people were reading blogs; yet that same year, another organization estimated there were 50 million blogs in existence, suggesting more blogs than readers.[10] Collectively, the blogs exerted the influence of a kind of ongoing national conversation. In his somewhat obscure way, Jeffrey Jarvis declared that "in our post-scarcity world, distribution is not king and neither is content. Conversation is the kingdom, and trust is king."[11]

In 2006, *Time* magazine, struggling to stay hip to it all, named "YOU" as its person of the year. "Yes you. You control the information age. Welcome to your world."[12] The journalist Jon Pareles wrote that " 'user-generated content' [is] the paramount cultural buzz phrase of 2006. . . . I prefer something a little more old-fashioned: self-expression. Terminol-ogy aside, this will be remembered as the year that the old-line media mogul, the online media titan and millions of individual Web users agreed: It demands attention."[13]

No one quite knew how much or what it all meant, but user-generated content had clearly seized its beachhead. The erasure of barriers to entry in markets for speech had, as predicted, released an outpouring. The quality was perhaps uneven (one critic called it "the cult of the Amateur"),[14] but that wasn't the point—it attracted millions, perhaps billions, of hours of attention anyhow, attention no one had the chance to resell.

Let us now take account of what was happening economically. The attention merchants had developed a business model based on directing the public mind toward commercial, well-packaged media products on television. But as the web grew in popularity, people started to pay more attention to one another instead, with no money changing hands. Bloggers did not, at first anyway, advertise, just as friends in the course of conversation do not usually plan to resell the attention they've gained by shilling for a product. Not that commerce had ground to a halt: everyone was using Google to find things they needed, and perhaps a few they didn't. The ones suffering for this happy state of affairs were those industries that had spent the past century devising how best to get people to look at them and listen, to enjoy their diversion and tolerate a word from their sponsors.

In that way the early web was exactly like the 1960s counterculture: it encouraged both a Great Refusal of what had always been handed down from on high, and asked people to spend more time with each other. It asserted that money need not be involved in attentional barter, and that everyone had an inherent potential to be a creator. In the early days at some companies, like Google, the link was more explicit, with much of the company retreating to the Burning Man festival every year and management espousing the value of putting in place a practical, pragmatic implementation of the counterculture's ideas. Perhaps that's why in the early 1990s, Timothy Leary advised people to "turn on, boot up, jack in"; he even wrote a computer game.[15]

As in the 1960s, this great turning away was the cause of no little consternation, if not degrees of panic, in the old attention industries. As the columnist-writer Dave Barry put it, "We can no longer compel people to pay attention. We used to be able to say, there's this really important story in Poland. You should read this. Now people say, I just look up what I'm interested in on the Internet."[16] Also as before, the change was so strong and apparent that seriously questioning it became mainly the province of cynics, naysayers, and Luddites. The reasonable pundit's challenge was to capture in adequately epic terms what was happening. Yochai Benkler explained that "the removal of the physical constraints on effective information production has made human creativity and the economics of information itself the core structuring facts in the new networked information economy."[17] Clay Shirky, for his part, compared the "radical spread of expressive capabilities" to "the one that gave birth to the modern world: the spread of the printing press five centuries ago."[18] But few could compete with Jeff Jarvis's penchant for proclamation. "We are undergoing a millennial transformation from the industrial, mass economy to what comes next" is how he once put it. "Disruption and destruction are inevitable."[19]

Lawrence Lessig, the darkest of the bunch, would turn out to be the one asking the most pertinent question: how long can this last? For even in the golden age of the user-driven web, there was reason to wonder whether the noncommercial model could persist. Bloggers and other creators of content were not Renaissance aristocrats; they faced the material constraints of most individuals or small-scale enterprises—most still needed to make a living, and as things progressed and improved, and expectations rose, it took ever more work to keep a blog up to date and engaging. A few would make a decent living, some through advertisings, others through newspaper acquisition. But for most, the effort would remain a hobby, and a time-consuming one at that. Burnout and attrition were perhaps inevitable.

As so often, as in the 1960s, the triumphalism would prove premature. Far from being unstoppable, both the blogosphere and the amateur were in fact quite vulnerable, but not, as Lessig predicted, to the established powers, devouring their upstart progeny to prevent the inevitable future, as the Titan Kronos did. Instead, the commercial forces that would overgrow this paradise came from the web itself. Indeed, we can now see that there was nothing about the web's code that would keep it open, free, and noncommercial, as its architects intended. Where attention is paid, the attention merchant lurks patiently to reap his due. *Et in Arcadia ego.* The fall of the web to this force was virtually preordained.

In retrospect, the first wave of bloggers and their fellow travelers can be likened to a first wave of visitors to some desert island, who erect crude, charming hostels and serve whatever customers come their way, and marvel at the paradise they've discovered. As in nature, so, too, on the web: the tourist traps high and low are soon to follow; commercial exploitation is on its way. Such, unfortunately, is the nature of things.

CHAPTER 22

THE RISE OF CLICKBAIT

Back in 2001, at MIT's media laboratory in Cambridge, Massachusetts, a former schoolteacher named Jonah Peretti was sitting at his desk and, like so many graduate students, not doing his work. Peretti was meant to be plugging away at his master's thesis; instead he was playing around with what was already the greatest procrastination aide ever devised, the World Wide Web.

Born in California to a Jewish mother and Italian American father, Peretti was a pretty ordinary and sober-looking young guy. But there was always a slight smile on his lips, a clue to the inveterate prankster beneath the facade of the typical grad student. In fact, he was fascinated by the line between the serious and the absurd, which in his mind also often delineated art from commerce, if not always respectively. Most of his ventures, even those that would prove important, seem to have been conceived as a kind of inside joke, and a test of the limits of possibility.

While goofing off—"surfing the web" in the vernacular of the time—Peretti went to Nike's website and noticed a feature allowing customers to order shoes personalized with any word they might like. On a whim, he placed an order for Nike Zoom XC USA running shoes with the following embroidered on them:

SWEATSHOP

He thought nothing more of it until the next day, when he received the following email:

From: Personalize, NIKE iD
To: Jonah H. Peretti
Subject: RE: Your NIKE iD order 016468000

Your NIKE iD order was cancelled for one or more of the following reasons.
1) Your Personal iD contains another party's trademark or other intellectual property.
2) Your Personal iD contains the name of an athlete or team we do not have the legal right to use.
3) Your Personal iD was left blank. Did you not want any personalization?
4) Your Personal iD contains profanity or inappropriate slang. If you wish to reorder your NIKE iD product with a new personalization please visit us again at www.nike.com

Thank you, NIKE iD

Seeing comic potential, Peretti wrote back asking just which rule he had broken. A Nike customer service representative replied: "Your NIKE iD order was cancelled because the iD you have chosen contains, as stated in the previous e-mail correspondence, 'inappropriate slang.'"

Peretti, just warming up, wrote back:

Dear NIKE iD,

Thank you for your quick response to my inquiry about my custom ZOOM XC USA running shoes. Although I commend you for your prompt customer service, I disagree with the claim that my personal iD was inappropriate slang. After consulting Webster's Dictionary, I discovered that "sweatshop" is in fact part of standard English, and not slang. The word means: "a shop or factory in which workers are employed for long hours at low wages and under unhealthy conditions" and its origin dates from 1892. So my personal iD does meet the criteria detailed in your first email. Your web site advertises that the NIKE iD program is "about freedom to choose and freedom to express who you are." I share Nike's love of freedom and personal expression. The site also says that "If you want it done right . . . build it yourself." I was thrilled to be able to build my own shoes, and my personal iD was offered as a small token of appreciation for the sweatshop workers poised to help me realize my vision. I hope that you will value my freedom of expression and reconsider your decision to reject my order.

Thank you,

Jonah Peretti

In response, Nike simply canceled the order. Peretti wrote one last one email:

From: Jonah H. Peretti
To: Personalize, NIKE iD
Subject: RE: Your NIKE iD order 016468000

Dear NIKE iD,
Thank you for the time and energy you have spent on my request. I have decided to order the shoes with a different iD, but I would like to make one small request. Could you please send me a color snapshot of the ten-year-old Vietnamese girl who makes my shoes? Thanks, Jonah Peretti

[no response][1]

Amused, Peretti sent a copy of the email chain to twelve or so friends, including one who posted it on his personal website. Within a week, Peretti's exchange had been shared by people far and wide; first thousands and within a few weeks, millions. Along the way, it was picked up by mainstream media outlets around the world. To use a phrase that did not exist in 2001, the email "went viral."

"So then I found myself on the *Today* show talking with Katie Couric about sweatshop labor," says Peretti. "It was, like, what do I know about sweatshops?" Here was that mind-warping rush of unexpected renown, of reaching an audience way beyond your wildest expectations. Peretti would later remember it simply: "Something very small became something very big." Unbeknownst to him at the time, the experience would end up changing his career and his life.

Popular email chains have been around nearly as long as email itself, but back in 2001 words like "viral," "Internet meme," and "clickbait" were as yet unknown. What Peretti naively experienced was an early version of what would become a pervasive means of harvesting attention in the early twenty-first century. Peretti, who has a curious, scientific mind, started to consider the phenomenon carefully and systematically. "I looked at stories like the Nike shoe story, and there were actually plenty of other ones. Someone did something, it went big for a while, but then that's where the story ends." Having done it once, by accident, he wanted to see if he could make it happen at will. He wanted to see if he could understand what it took to make something "go viral." For he realized that his weird experience had a deeper significance; it marked a change, made possible by the Internet, in how attention might be captured, and from whom.[2]

———————

A few months later, Peretti left MIT to take a job at the Eyebeam art and technology center, a giant space in New York's West Chelsea neighborhood; from the outside it looked like many of the art galleries that surrounded it. Here, in his "contagious media laboratory," he tried to figure out if he could make lightning in a bottle.

Peretti started throwing stuff against the web to see if anything might stick. It turned out he was not alone; there were others who shared his fascination with creating zany stuff that might, almost magically, erupt across the Internet. He got to know a man who called himself "Ze Frank," a sort of self-styled web-jester. Ze Frank's own road to Damascus had involved a web-based birthday invitation in which he featured, performing funny dance moves; it had earned millions of hits and won him a Webby Award. Peretti also met Cory Arcangel, a conceptual artist who, among other things, had made art that required him to hack Nintendo's *Super Mario Brothers*. Then there was a social scientist, Duncan Watts, who tried to understand media contagion with mathematical models. In these guys, Peretti found a posse.

His sister, Chelsea Peretti, also got in on the act. Together, they launched www.blackpeopleloveus.com, a fake website featuring a white couple inordinately proud of having made black friends; it attracted 600,000 hits. There was also the "Rejection Line," a service for those who found it too inconvenient to reject people themselves. As the site said:

> Someone won't leave you alone?
> Give them "your" number: 212-479-7990
> The official New York Rejection Line!
> (operators are standing by!)

It was as if stories from *The Onion* had actually been put into production.[3]

Peretti and his pals definitely had some fun at Eyebeam. They held how-to workshops for the public with titles like "The Mass Hoax." In 2005 they hosted something called the "Contagious Media Showdown," giving contestants three weeks to get as much traffic as they could. Entries included "hire-a-killer.com," "Crying While Eating," "email god," and "change your race"; the winner (possibly as a result of cheating) was "Forget-me-not-panties.com," a prank site purporting to sell women's underwear that broadcasts the wearer's location to possessive fathers and husbands. "Unlike the cumbersome and uncomfortable chastity belts of the past, these panties are 100% cotton, and use cutting-edge technology to help you protect what matters most." The site suckered both bloggers and mainstream press, remaining operational for quite some time, albeit with a notice that stock was currently sold out.[4]

Peretti may not have been able to create anything while at Eyebeam on the scale of his Nike experience, but he would author a twenty-three-point manifesto that he called "Notes on Contagious Media," expounding just what distinguished that variety from others. Some of it was obvious: "Contagious media is the kind of media you immediately want to share with all your friends. This requires that you take pleasure in consuming the media but also pleasure in the social process of passing it on." Some more theoretical: "Contagious media is a form of pop conceptual art" in which "the idea is the machine that makes the art (LeWitt, 1967) and the idea is interesting to ordinary people." For that reason, "a contagious media project should represent the simplest form of an idea. Fancy design or extraneous content made media less contagious. Anything inessential constituted a 'payload' that the contagion must drag along as it spreads. The bigger the payload, the more slowly the entire project spreads." Peretti had more or less made himself the world's expert on contagious media, but the recognition of peers was not enough; the measure of his success would be the ability to generate traffic. "For the artist, a work can be celebrated even if the only people who like it are a small group of curators and collectors," he wrote. "For the contagious media designer, all that matters is how other people see the work. If people don't share the work with their friends, it is a failure regardless of the opinion of the creator, critics, or other elites."

In 2004, Peretti was still puttering around at Eyebeam, teaching and throwing stuff on the web, when he was approached by Ken Lerer, a former communications executive at AOL and a committed political activist. A journalist by training and adept at raising money, Lerer presented what he considered an urgent project. Despite every kind of blunder in office, President George W. Bush seemed likely to be reelected. This was incomprehensible to Lerer and other Democrats, who considered Bush an obvious incompetent; in their view, the Internet was in part to blame. The right-wing blogs—above all, the *Drudge Report,* the most widely read aggregator of news links—just captured more attention than all the left-wing ones. "You know the Internet, let's build something," Lerer cajoled Peretti, who would later explain, "I'm the son of a public defender and a public school teacher" and "it seemed pretty important."[5]

"Something" was at first quite vague. As it evolved, the idea seemed to be this: leverage the left's superior hold on Hollywood celebrities, as well as Peretti's knack for driving traffic and Lerer's touch for fundraising, to create a counterweight to conservative online media. The celebrity part, they decided, was best handled by the third partner, and by far the best connected, Arianna Huffington.

On May 10, 2005, just two days after the contagious media contest, *The Huffington Post,* an online aggregator of news, blogs, and other content, debuted to widespread mainstream coverage. The first issue featured blog posts by Huffington herself and, as planned, various famous people: the renowned historian and Kennedy confidant Arthur M. Schlesinger Jr.; the actor John Cusack; Larry David, producer of *Seinfeld;* the husband-and-wife acting pair Julia Louis-Dreyfus (also of *Seinfeld*) and Brad Hall, jointly posting on the issue of gun violence.

Some credited the idea, but in media it's not the thought that counts; critics were harsher and louder. And no one came in for more abuse than the partner who'd lent her name. "Celebs to the Slaughter," wrote *LA Weekly:* "Judging from Monday's horrific debut of the humongously pre-hyped celebrity blog the *Huffington Post,* the Madonna of the mediapolitic world has undergone one reinvention too many. She has now made an online ass of herself. . . . Her blog is such a bomb that it's the movie equivalent of *Gigli, Ishtar* and *Heaven's Gate* rolled into one."

In retrospect, critics like the *LA Weekly*'s were only proving how little they understood the Internet. Peretti, Lerer, and Huffington were each masters of attention capture, and their collaboration proved more than the sum of its parts. Over time, the political mission was dialed back somewhat—Huffington herself had, after all, previously been a conservative pundit who'd called for the resignation of President Clinton. Soon the *Huffington Post* was inviting not just celebrities to contribute but students, politicos, activists, book authors—just about anyone except the professional reporter or normal freelancer who expected to be paid. It was a degree of openness more akin to the early days of the web and blogosphere than any older model of media. Minimal costs, maximum traffic, and irresistible content above all—that was the formula.[6]

In pursuit of the third element of its triad, the *HuffPo* pioneered what would become known as clickbait: sensationally headlined articles, paired with provocative pictures—a bikini-clad celebrity was always good. ("Watch Naked Heidi Klum in Seal's New Video").* When properly calibrated, such content seemed to take control of the mind, causing the hand almost involuntarily to click on whatever was there. The *HuffPo*'s "news" was more provocative, more enticing—more clickable—than its competitors'; even for serious topics it managed to channel lurid fascination. To the chagrin of its critics, it quickly outpaced sites like *LA Weekly* and by the fall of 2007 was capturing more attention than other

---

* The phrase clickbait is related to earlier slang like "draft bait" or "jail bait" and was first recorded in 1999, though it came to widespread usage in the early 2010s.

web magazines like *Slate* and *Salon,* despite their paid writers. By 2010 it was beating most of the newspapers as well. With 24 million monthly readers, it was slightly behind *The New York Times,* but ahead of *The Washington Post,* the *Los Angeles Times,* and the rest of what was then called the mainstream media. As the *Columbia Journalism Review* put it, "The Huffington Post has mastered and fine-tuned not just aggregation, but also social media, comments from readers, and most of all, a sense of what its public wants."[7]

And yet *The Huffington Post* never actually made much money. While its financials have never been fully public, there is good reason to believe it has never turned a solid profit. For one thing, advertisers categorized *The Huffington Post* as political commentary, and generally, the big-brand advertisers, the Fortune 500, despite the numbers weren't willing to put their names on *HuffPo*'s pages. Others tended to credit Google for its traffic. All of this combined to make the site able to sell its impressions for only the lowest rates to bottom-tier advertisers (e.g., "This weird trick can take an inch off your waistline"). *The Huffington Post* wasn't making money, but it was nonetheless sucking attention from everything else— especially journalists—on the web. That's probably why *The Washington Post*'s executive editor slammed it and similar sites as "parasites living off journalism produced by others."

The Huffington Post wasn't alone. Over the 2000s, none of the pure, content-driven attention merchants were lucrative. This was, in part, because advertisers realized with so many attention merchants in competition, they didn't necessarily need to "underwrite" the media industry in the manner that they had for newspapers, radio, or television. As advertising executive Rishad Tobaccowala put it in 2010, advertisers long since had grown tired and resentful of any project other than reaching consumers with ads. Fundamentally they "don't want to pay for creation of content."

So while *The Huffington Post* certainly succeeded in its original goal of driving more web traffic toward the political left, in most other ways it ended up pleasing no one. Established, traditional newspapers, with their crushing overhead, hated it most. Bill Keller, the executive editor of *The New York Times,* was indignant. "Too often it amounts to taking words written by other people, packaging them on your own Web site and harvesting revenue that might otherwise be directed to the originators of the material. In Somalia this would be called piracy. In the mediasphere, it is a respected business model." Meanwhile, for the dreamers and idealists who always wanted the web to be not just different but loftier and better, the *HuffPo*'s relentless dependence on celebrity and clickbait was something of a bitter pill.

If they weren't good at making money, no one could deny that those running the site knew how to harvest attention, and for that reason it changed the rules of the game. Like the *New York Sun* in the 1830s or *People* magazine in the 1970s, *HuffPo* forced the competition to become more like it. Relatively sober sites like *Slate* and *Salon* grew more gossipy, superficial, and click-driven; in time, even traditional newspaper websites were also forced to adapt themselves to the standard set by a site with unpaid writers and features on celebrity sideboob. To varying degrees, the style of everything seemed to drift toward tabloid and away from broadsheet, to borrow the parlance of print.[8]

AOL, seeking its own resurrection,* and having noticed the gap between *The Huffington Post*'s traffic and its advertising rates, bought the site in 2011 for $315 million and began throwing money at it in an effort to make the site more respectable. This bearing upwind, a variant on CBS's "Tiffany" strategy from the 1930s, would, it was hoped, attract a higher class of advertiser. With more money, *The Huffington Post* was now able to hire seasoned reporters who were given full freedom and resources to write on what they wanted. The strategy yielded a Pulitzer Prize for *The Huffington Post*'s David Wood, a war correspondent who'd cut his teeth at *Time* in the 1970s and had also worked at the *Los Angeles Times, Baltimore Sun,* and other papers. So the *HuffPost* gained some dignity, but because it was expensive still failed to create large profits. Yet by 2015, it was attracting more attention than ever, and management was still saying things like "We could make it profitable right now if we wanted it to be." Perhaps the site was by its nature never really meant to be a business exactly, but instead just a giant vacuum sucking up human attention.[9]

---

* Despite its advertising-related accounting fraud and other problems in the early 2000s, AOL nonetheless stayed in business based on its large if declining base of subscribers who continued to pay a monthly fee for their email accounts or dial-up access.

Looking for work and blogging in his spare time, in late 2004, Mario Armando Lavandeira Jr., a young Cuban American actor in Miami, was one of many doing the same thing. He'd scored one appearance on *The Sopranos,* as "Male Student," as well as a role in the low-budget horror film *Campfire Stories,* which received an audience rating of 2.9 out of 10 on the *Internet Movie Database.* Blogging was something he started, he would later confess, "because it seemed easy." Whether or not it turned out to be so, Lavandeira was inspired to blog at almost the very moment Lerer approached Peretti about *The Huffington Post.* But rather than use famous people to bring attention to a political point of view, Lavandeira would put them to the purest use an attention merchant can have. He devoted his blog to celebrity gossip, purposefully making it snarkier and more malicious than anything ever seen before.

He named it "Pagesixsixsix.com" a mash-up of the *New York Post*'s gossipy Page Six and, presumably, the Antichrist; riffing on *The New York Times*'s motto that his blog was "All the news, gossip and satire that's unfit to print (anywhere else)." Lavandeira described himself as the "Raconteur, Iconoclast, Proselytizer and the Maniacal Mastermind behind Page SixSixSix." A sample headline from his early work: "Hilary Duff Is a Lying Bitch!! In a recent interview, Hilary not only had the fucking audacity to defend Ashlee Simpson's lip-synching fracas on *Saturday Night Live,* but she went so far as to actually claim that she doesn't lip-synch herself. Puhhhleeeaze biyatch!'"

The blog might have gone unnoticed and, like most, expired, but something about Lavandeira's particular blend of venom and star adulation made it take off. It didn't hurt that it was named "Hollywood's Most Hated Website" by one TV show, leading to a traffic boom, or that it received a legal complaint from the *New York Post,* which noticed that its trademark "Page Six" had been appropriated. Lavandeira gave up on Pagesixsixsix.com (which was anyhow hard to type) and took as his nom de blog Perez Hilton. Who, exactly, was Perez Hilton supposed to be? Lavandeira posed as the "trashtastic Cuban cousin of Paris and Nicky [Hilton]," the socialite sister heiresses famous in the early 2000s. Over the latter part of the decade, Perez Hilton, and commercial imitators, like TMZ, presented a new face of blogging. Far from the highbrow musing of citizen journalists of the digital commons, the sort imagined at the turn of the millennium, the gossip blogs were full-fledged attention merchants in the most conventional sense. By 2007, Perez Hilton was claiming some four million unique visitors a day and selling advertisements for $9,000 a week.[10]

Perez Hilton was not the only wildly popular fictive persona made possible by the anonymity of the web. In 2006 the best-known face on YouTube was Lonelygirl15, a cute but awkward teenage girl whose first video was entitled "First Blog / Dorkiness Prevails." Speaking to the camera, her chin on one raised knee, she plaintively intones, "Hi guys . . . this is my video blog . . . um. . . . I'm such a dork . . ." It was only later revealed that Lonelygirl15 was in fact a paid actress. Her show was scripted, based on her producers' guess of what an amateur video blogger might look like. Their success in getting the right effect would lead to more business for the production company EQAL, which, having proved it could aggregate a boatload of attention, would be commissioned to produce more content, including an original web series for CBS. As for Jessica Rose, the actress hired for the hoax, she would be cast in a web TV series called *Sorority Forever,* as well as the cable series *Greek.* An Anaheim Ducks fan, she would also begin blogging for the National Hockey League. Every bit of attention helps.[11]

The success of *The Huffington Post* and of Lonelygirl15 and the celebrity gossip sites was something of an early sign that even by the end of its first decade, the amateur phase of the web was already coming to an end. Wikipedia reached its peak of 51,000 active editors in 2007, and from that point onward began to shed contributors; by 2013 it would lose more than 20,000, never having expanded beyond its committed core of young men with time on their hands. Across the web, one sensed a general waning of enthusiasm, as if the air were escaping from the balloon.

It was no different among the original amateur bloggers, whose creative energy once seemed inexhaustible. A common story line emerged: after posting away for some time, many began to notice that their pronouncements were reaching far fewer souls than they'd thought, perhaps based on an imperfect understanding of the web itself. Even trying to get more seemed hopeless: "If you do everything people tell you to do," one blogger lamented, "you can get up to about 100 visitors a day, but then it's like you hit an invisible wall." David Weinberger recalls the moment that, for him, "rang the tocsin":

[Clay Shirky's] analysis showed that the blogosphere wasn't a smooth ball where everyone had an equal voice. Rather, it was dominated by a handful of sites that pulled enormous numbers, followed by a loooooooooong tail of sites with a few followers. The old pernicious topology had reasserted itself. We should have known that it would, and it took a while for the miserable fact to sink in.

Not that it was all wine and roses for the bloggers who did persist and claw their way up to being full-blooded attention merchants. Like the New York newspapers of the 1830s, they would find themselves in ever more intense competition, in which the lurid and titillating and exaggerated typically prevailed. For every serious and earnest political blog, there was always an alternative prepared to throw red meat before fire-breathing partisans, or else go the full tabloid route. *Wonkette,* for instance, became the Perez Hilton of Beltway gossip, gaining enormous attention by showcasing Jessica Cutler, a congressional staffer who blogged about steamy details of her affairs with various government officials. Likewise, serious blogs by esteemed law professors found themselves vying with "Article III Groupie," an anonymous poster who covered the federal judiciary in tell-all style.[12]

As if tabloid journalism weren't challenge enough, the amateur bloggers also now faced professional competition of several kinds. A British journalist living in New York named Nick Denton launched a carefully curated blog named *Gizmodo,* covering gadgets and technology, and another named *Gawker,* co-launched with Elizabeth Spiers, which disseminated media gossip (*Wonkette* was also part of what would become the *Gawker* group). The political blogs also professionalized: the *Daily Kos,* a one-man left-leaning *Talking Points Memo,* hired staff to run more ambitious coverage. Major newspapers, including *The New York Times* and *The Washington Post,* assigned experienced journalists to blog full-time, leveraging all of the authority and prestige of the old media to go after the new audience. Whatever power lay in what Yochai Benkler had called the "wealth of networks," the old media's trick of paying people still had some power as well. More work for the journalists, perhaps, but it did stem the flow of attention away from legacy media.

In 2008, *Wired* magazine offered the following advice to those interested in launching a blog:

Don't. And if you've already got one, pull the plug. . . . The blogo-sphere, once a freshwater oasis of folksy self-expression and clever thought, has been flooded by a tsunami of paid bilge. Cut-rate jour-nalists and underground marketing campaigns now drown out the authentic voices of amateur wordsmiths. . . . Scroll down Technorati's list of the top 100 blogs and you'll find personal sites have been shoved aside by professional ones. Most are essentially online magazines: The Huffington Post. Engadget. TreeHugger. A stand-alone commentator can't keep up with a team of pro writers cranking out up to 30 posts a day.

By the end of the decade, the truly amateur blogger or videographer was something of a rarity, an eccentric hanging on from a different age. Most everyone else was either blogging as part of his job, writing for some professional blog, or had long since hung up his guns. Even Law-rence Lessig, the prophet of a free culture, retired his blog, claiming a degree of exhaustion.

But the public remained online, and in ever greater numbers. Just where were all those creative energies so recently unleashed going now? As the decade ended, a new set of companies were learning how they could effectively feed off that energy themselves, in some sense co-opting all the yearning for conversation and user-generated content. The new sites called themselves "social networks," and keeping up on one was much easier than maintaining a blog. As that *Wired* magazine piece further advised: "The time it takes to craft sharp, witty blog prose is [now] better spent expressing yourself on Flickr, Facebook, or Twitter." Old wine in new bottles? Not quite. In the guise of bringing people together, these networks would wire the most invasive attention cap-ture apparatus yet invented into millions upon millions of lives. What were the terms for that arrangement? As with any user agreement, it was in the provider's interest that one click "accept" quickly, and not wade into the fine print.[13]

CHAPTER 23

THE PLACE TO BE

In 2004, with the Internet revolution already in its adolescence, Harvard University's computer services began work on what it described as an "electronic facebook." The term "facebook" traditionally referred to a physical booklet produced at American universities to promote socialization in the way that "Hi, My Name Is" stickers do at events; the pages consisted of rows upon rows of head shots with the corresponding name, and perhaps the class and residence underneath. How else were total strangers thrown together in dormitories to find friends and maybe romantic or sexual partners? "We've been in touch with the Undergraduate Council, and this is a very high priority for the College," said Harvard's residential computing director in mid-2004. "We have every intention of completing the facebook by the end of the spring semester."[1]

So Harvard computer services had an idea and they were running with it. But a nineteen-year-old undergraduate named Mark Zuckerberg—a gifted programmer in full possession of all the arrogance of youth, who loved nothing more than to hack out code overnight—felt compelled to show he could do the job better and faster. Zuckerberg had already accomplished a number of complicated computer projects with his friends. "We were just building stuff," he said later, " 'cause we thought it was cool." Unfortunately, his last little effort, hacking the student picture database while under the influence, had landed him on academic probation. He recounted the mischief in real time on his blog:

> I'm a little intoxicated, not gonna lie. So what if it's not even 10 pm and it's a Tuesday night? What? The Kirkland dormitory facebook is open on my desktop and some of these people have pretty horrendous facebook pics. I almost want to put some of these faces next to pictures of some farm animals and have people vote on which is more attractive. . . . Let the hacking begin.[2]

With that he created Facemash, a Harvard-only version of the rating site "Hot or Not." In Zuckerberg's adaptation, two undergraduate women's photos appeared, and the user selected the more attractive. Zuckerberg showed a certain flair for gaining attention, but after complaints, he went before the school's Administration Board charged with breaching security, infringing the photograph copyrights, and violating individual privacy. He was let off with a warning.*

So it took some nerve when Zuckerberg, now calling himself the "Founder, Master and Commander, Enemy of the State," gathered his code posse to throw together a site named "Thefacebook." He announced the undertaking with his usual confidence or presumption, depending on your view. "Everyone's been talking a lot about a universal face book within Harvard," Zuckerberg said. "I think it's kind of silly that it would take the University a couple of years to get around to it. I can do it better than they can, and I can do it in a week."

A callow determination to prove himself better than everyone else, combined with a notable whiff of amoral heedlessness: in these traits the young Zuckerberg bore more than a passing similarity to the man he would follow in the race to become Harvard's most successful dropout, Bill Gates. "He is not a bad guy," would say a future employee eventually fired by an older Zuckerberg. "Maybe he's not a good guy, but he's not a bad guy." In one respect, however, young Zuckerberg was quite different from the young Gates, who while on a first date at Harvard asked the woman her SAT score.† Though hardly a charmer himself, Zuckerberg

---

* Zuckerberg was fortunate; a superficially similar stunt pulled off on the MIT network by a hacker named Aaron Swartz led to a federal indictment on multiple felony counts.

† Gates, incidentally, scored a 1590/1600 on his SAT, while Zuckerberg scored a perfect 1600.

had a subtle social sense, and was a particularly astute judge of other people's vulnerabilities and needs. He did a dual concentration in psychology and computer science, later claiming, "I was always interested in how those two things combined." When people asked if psychology had been a waste of time, Zuckerberg would answer, "Understanding people is not a waste of time." He had, above all, an intuition, surely refined at Harvard, for what makes something seem socially desirable; and how the dynamics of acceptance and rejection work to create a sense of the cool crowd. Not that Zuckerberg was himself ever cool, exactly, but he understood what makes things seem to be.[3]

In business, invention is often said to be overrated as compared with execution. Perhaps the best proof of this idea yet to be offered by the twenty-first century is the success of Facebook, a business with an exceedingly low ratio of invention to success. There is no lightbulb, or telephone, let alone a truly ingenious algorithm in the company's history. And yet no firm, save Google, has harvested as much attention from the Internet, or commercialized it as effectively. As with Google, that attention would be a by-product of the needs, desires, and efforts of its users. But where Google prevailed by offering the best search, Facebook reached the top thanks to stable code and "network effect": the phenomenon by which a system of connections grows in value with the number of its users. Zuckerberg understood this from the start.

In its primitive way, AOL had proven decisively that the surest means of getting people to spend more time with their computers was to promise some kind of social experience. Since the 1980s, the geeks and nerds had embraced the online world as a safe space in which to socialize; AOL's signal achievement was proving that with a much wider range of social milieus, a great many other types could be lured online as well to visit "cyberspace."

As that name suggests, over most of the 1990s, going online still had an element of science fiction or fantasy to it. Unlike our day of always-on Internet, back then one "jacked in" or perhaps passed through the back of the family wardrobe, and under a made-up name entered an entirely different kind of world populated by strangers, one where none of the usual rules applied. "Imagine," said the cyber-pioneer John Perry Barlow, "discovering a continent so vast that it may have no end to its dimensions . . . where only children feel completely at home, where the physics is that of thought rather than things, and where everyone is as virtual as the shadows in Plato's cave."[4]

It was pretty cool stuff for the 1990s, intriguing enough to get AOL and the early web its first user base. In retrospect, however, the concept had its limitations. For one thing, once the novelty wore off, online content was circumscribed by the imagination of its users; that makes it sound unlimited, but in practice that wasn't the case. Anyway, the more serious problem was the trolls. From the early days, they (and their commercial cousins, the spammers) were a persistent and predictable feature of nearly every online environment. And they ruined not a few of them, including AOL.

The troll abuses the terms of the attention agreement, by violating the decorum of what is meant to be quasi-conversation with outrageous and intemperate comments—expressing opinions not necessarily sincerely held but said for the purpose of provoking an emotional response. Most people aren't trolls, but it doesn't take many. One academic study found that trolling "correlated positively with sadism, psychopathy, and Machiavellianism. . . . [of] all personality measures, sadism showed the most robust associations with trolling and, importantly, the relationship was specific to trolling behavior."[5]

AOL was an environment guaranteed to attract trolls, given its anonymity and sizable audience. In chat rooms and forums, mischief makers polluted perfectly pleasant interactions with impunity, eventually rendering the whole site noxious in one way or another to all other visitors. This only compounded media reports that AOL was a haven for pedophiles; the charge was mostly, though not entirely, untrue, but it's not one easy to spin or brush off. (That great scourge of modern reputation, Internet rumor, a force often in league with the trolls, was already showing its speed and puissance.) It was as if the entire thing were designed to vindicate Freud's view that repression of violent or sexual impulses was necessary to a functioning society. There was far more to the decline than just the trolls, but as AOL shed users to the point of collapse, it left in its wake enormous opportunities for anyone who could offer some kind of online place to express social desires and needs without the troll menace. The fall of online's once mighty oak gave a series of Internet acorns their chance to grow into something quite different in the same niche. A big, proven horde of online attention was up for grabs.

When Facebook launched in 2004, it was a hit at Harvard, registering thousands of users immediately; within the first month, half of the campus had joined. But in the bigger picture, Zuckerberg's brainchild was a late entrant in the "social networking" stakes race. Since as early as 2000, others had been in the running; by 2004 there were platforms focused specifically on finding romance, like SocialNet and Match.com. All of these dating sites, as well as interest connectors and career sites, like Meetup.com and LinkedIn, required real names and real personal information, flushing out the usual hiding places and dark corners of cyberspace.

Facebook's clearest antecedent was Friendster, which in 2002 was the first company to crack the social networking nut. Jonathan Abrams, a Canadian living in San Francisco, was founder and designer of the company whose concept Facebook essentially copied. Like the dating sites, Abrams's idea was inspired by the dissatisfactions with an anonymous cyberspace; his network designed to be "real," and a troll-free zone: "No fakesters" was the policy. "I wanted to bring that real-life context that you had offline online—so instead of Cyberdude307, I would be Jonathan," he explained.[6]

Rather than drop you in a Hobbesian world of antisocial maniacs, Friendster made you a profile and sought to re-create online your actual social world—the people you really knew, friends, co-workers, family, and the like—while providing one place to deal with all of them. Like so many successful tech companies, it was marketing a form of human augmentation, in this case of social capacities. As *Fortune* magazine put it in 2003, if rather oddly: "There may be a new kind of Internet emerging—one more about connecting people to people than people to websites."[7]

By 2004, the field was nearly full of Friendster copies, of which Facebook was just one more. Google's version, for instance, was Orkut, named after the employee who wrote the code in his spare time, Orkut

Büyükkökten. There was a flamboyant Southern California–based clone named MySpace, which was somewhat looser, saving a bit of the "anything goes" ethos of AOL. It soon became a popular promotional site for bands and had a million users by the time Facebook launched.

Facebook's rise in the face of this existing competition was something remarkable to behold. Over the course of 2004, it leapfrogged from campus to campus, landing everywhere with a splash. It arrived with better, more stable software, but that wasn't the key to its success. Still enrolled at Harvard, Zuckerberg and his team had an on-the-ground feel for the college social environment and its vectors, and thus a deep intuition of what could make his site seem rewarding and essential to his target audience. It didn't hurt that it was based at Harvard, an object of some fascination on other campuses. The student newspapers welcoming Thefacebook give the best sense of how well it managed to encapsulate what users were looking for—namely, an affirmation of their social significance. As *The Stanford Daily* exclaimed:

> Classes are being skipped. Work is being ignored. Students are spending hours in front of their computers in utter fascination. Thefacebook .com craze has swept through campus. . . . Modeled after social networking Web sites like Friendster.com, this site provides Stanford students with a network of their peers. . . . A student with just over 100 friends can have a network of over 1,500 people. "I signed up on Tuesday morning and I was immediately addicted," [a student] said. "Nothing validates your social existence like the knowledge that someone else has approved you or is asking for your permission to list them as a friend. It's bonding and flattering at the same time."[8]

"This is absolutely ridiculous," Duke's student newspaper quoted a freshman named Tyler Green, gleeful to find himself with so many friends. "I just logged on and approved a bunch of people as my friends, and apparently I'm connected to 170 people. I've spent maybe 20 minutes on this in the past 24 hours." From the beginning, there were critics. "It's a system designed for people who feel insecure and need to numerically quantify their friends," huffed one Stanford senior. It would indeed make the accumulation of "friends" another species of competition on already competitive campuses.[9]

These early reports touch upon the effect that would always represent Facebook's *apologia pro vita sua:* it was bringing people together. In truth, however, what Facebook was offering users was not a fuller and more ordered "social" life but something even more alluring: an augmented representation of themselves. Not as they were, exactly, but at their contrived best, with hundreds of friends (before success became equated with thousands) and others still in queue awaiting "approval." It is useful to recall what limited functionality the site had when it started tempting thousands of students to spend hours playing with it. There were no messages, no pokes—no forms of social interaction but the invitation to be friends. Apart from stalking others on the network, there was nothing to do there except refine one's own profile, reconsider one's photograph, and marvel at one's own numerically and geographically determined social cachet. The profile was really the attentional bait, the pool into which untold undergraduate Narcissi were staring while they ditched class.

Of course, all of the networking sites had profiles and friends. What was Facebook doing that Friendster, Google, and MySpace were not? Nothing technical, to be sure; rather, it unmistakably defined itself as the place to be. The key to this was its campus origins. While the others obliged users to find their cohort in the great mass of undifferentiated humanity, Facebook re-created an existing and relatively bounded social reality of colleges, within and among which actual connections already existed. Everyone at Harvard knew at least someone on several of the campuses across which Facebook's network was proliferating. The original university facebook goal of facilitating socialization was thus served by this thing that was student made, a fact that only lent it more social credibility. So Facebook was actually providing not something new but an enhanced representation of an existing social reality. The networks, so-called, were there already: Facebook simply made them visible, graphically manifest, and easier to keep track of.

Many have theorized that this difference was only significant insofar as it pertained to the potential for hooking up; that Facebook's success came from revealing the universe of people it might be practical to sleep with. Was that the case? It's complicated. There can be no doubt that

Facebook gained in its early days owing to potential for erotic encounter, particularly at a moment when volume was prized over quality of connection by many users. No student newspaper failed to mention dates arranged on the site; yet Facebook was always coy on this point, maintaining a plausible deniability, and never marketed itself as a dating site. Rather, it replicated the ambiguity of college life itself, with its collisions more like Brownian motion than traditional romantic pursuit. Everyone knew that joining a certain club or even attending college would eventually lead to opportunities; making it too explicit would only ruin the effect.

In the long run Facebook's indeterminacy would prove strategically shrewd, as other sites demonstrated the limitations of being defined by sex or romance. With its paying customers looking for love, Match .com would make some money but never approach Facebook financially, despite a head start. The social bonds created by dating are inherently more fragile, and of course only some fraction of the population is actively seeking a lover at any time. The older and more enduring links of friendships, family, classmates, and co-workers would turn out to be pretty important as well, without excluding the possibility of friendship with benefits, of course. A decade later, in fact, Facebook's lure would be more sentimental than sexual, its necessity having less to do with hooking up than keeping up: the need to see what old friends or family were up to without the burden of talking to them. And in this way, the image of a social reality would more and more become the reality itself, with less connection "in real life" and more online.

The danger of being cast as a dating site wasn't the only bullet Facebook dodged in its early history. Original Facebook was also attractive by dint of its lack of advertisements—there were almost none, or so few that no one noticed them. From Google, Zuckerberg and company had learned both the promise and peril of ads, as well as the existential importance of doing them right. On the one hand, Facebook knew perfectly well from the outset that in advertising lay its eventual big payday—for the founders the ultimate point of aggregating so much attention in the first place. The earliest pitches to advertisers in 2004 touted the platform's "addicted" users and the potential of nanotargeting consumers at a level of specificity only dreamed of by PRIZM's designers, using age, gender, stated interests, and—when the "like" button was first activated in 2009—all manner of preferences. Amazingly, it was information that users were all handing over for free, because, well, everyone else was, too. The power of networks. The madness of crowds.

Zuckerberg, like Google's founders, understood advertising's potential to degrade his product; he had the technologist's wariness of advertising and its tendency to ruin websites. As with Larry Page, so with Mark Zuckerberg, the Holy Grail was advertising that people actually wanted to see; Facebook figured that nanotargeting could make that happen. Until then, Zuckerberg would remain manifestly averse to anything that might interrupt the experience of his users. When, early on, Sprite offered $1 million to turn the site green for a day, he didn't even consider it. As he once put it: "I don't hate all advertising. I just hate advertising that stinks."[10]

Such an attitude was another competitive advantage, for MySpace, Facebook's main competitor, had no such scruples. Its managers or its owners, the News Corporation, jammed the site with paid content. In its desperate desire to gain as many users as fast as possible—doubtless seeing this as the key to the social chase—MySpace was very casual about verifying user identities—the fatal flaw of AOL. MySpace also let users customize their pages using their own HTML code, while Facebook kept everyone on the same basic blue and forced them to come up with better content. Consequently the MySpace site was a mess of flashing ads and pseudonymous members, who were invariably scantily clad women (or at least claiming to be). It all began to look and feel a lot like Times Square circa 1977: squalid and a little dangerous.

Friendster, in a way, had the potential to be the more formidable competitor. It had buzz, many of the right ideas, and had even begun making inroads into college campuses, but it was technically unprepared for its own success. Zuckerberg and his friends had hired better programmers than Friendster could ever find. As Friendster gained millions of users, its software collapsed under their weight, and was rarely if ever working again. As the founder Abrams admitted in a 2014 interview, "Fundamentally, people could barely log into the website for two years."[11]

In what was at the time a shocking collapse, MySpace and Friendster emptied like a bar at last call, and it was as if the Internet migrated en masse to Facebook. The social media critic danah boyd described it as a form of "White Flight."[12]* As *The Huffington Post* wrote, by 2008 "MySpace lost over forty million unique visitors per month, lost both co-founders, laid off the vast majority of its staff and more generally, has diminished to a cluttered afterthought of the power it once was."[13]

The credible claim to being a social necessity was, in retrospect, the most important thing that Facebook achieved; its rivals would never come close to matching it. As Zuckerberg said in 2009, "Think about what people are doing on Facebook today. They're keeping up with their friends and family, but they're also building an image and identity for themselves, which in a sense is their brand. They're connecting with the audience that they want to connect to. It's almost a disadvantage if you're not on it now." It was not merely a matter of utility but a different way of being in the world that Facebook was able to offer and also to cultivate. The idea of the self as brand did not originate with Zuckerberg, but would certainly gain currency with the Facebook generation, who would be known for not remaining in one job too long and for thinking of themselves and their experience unironically as products to be marketed, professionally and even socially. As celebrities had become, the ordinary individual was now more of a business proposition.[14]

Meanwhile, life goes on. It eventually became not only acceptable but proper etiquette to use Facebook for announcing important developments in one's life, like new relationships, the birth of a child, even someone's death. It became widely used for the most primitive varieties of social display, whether of one's children or things. It also supplanted the holiday card as the means for cultivating the perimeter of one's acquaintance. The sociologist Zeynep Tufekci argued that Facebook and other social media had formed a substitute for "gossip, people-curiosity and small talk," which, she wrote, were "the human version of social grooming in primates: an activity that is essential to forging bonds, affirming relationships, displaying bonds, and asserting and learning about hierarchies and alliances." Significantly, she wrote, "Social grooming should be seen as both a bonding activity and a *competitive* activity: it is a means

---

* In her study, boyd quoted a white teenager who explained why she'd made the switch. "I'm not really into racism," she said, "but I think that MySpace now is more like ghetto or whatever." The many spammers, in Boyd's view, were like gangs, the excessive, eyesore advertising not unlike urban blight.

to improve one's reputation and status as well as access to resources and social and practical solidarity."[15]

In February 2012, having accumulated 845 million active monthly users, Facebook announced its long-anticipated initial public offering. It had not, however, conquered all doubts surrounding its business model, for as compared with Google—its most obvious predecessor—Facebook faced additional challenges. On the positive side, it did know more about everyone in the world than anyone else ("big data" in the vernacular of the 2010s), allowing advertisers to nanotarget at an unprecedented level. Facebook ran side ads that allowed an advertiser to home in on his quarry with criteria like location, gender, age, schools attended, stated interests, and more. Thus, the advertiser of vintage 1970s speakers could target men between fifty and sixty-five living in suburban New Jersey who listed an interest in the Kinks and Led Zeppelin. That was the good part.

The bad part for Facebook was that it didn't quite have the metrics Google did. On Google one knew people were looking for something, and also what they were looking for. People went to Facebook for a different reason the "social grooming" just described. In advertising jargon, if Google's users were very close to the final stage before making a sale, Facebook users were, at best, at an initial, awareness stage.* Translated, that means people didn't click on Facebook ads very often. As blogger and venture capitalist Chris Dixon wrote in 2012, "Facebook makes about ⅒th of Google's revenues even though they have twice the pageviews. Some estimates put Google's search revenues per pageviews at 100–200x Facebook's."[16]

During the 2010s, Facebook found a few answers to this problem. First, it invested heavily in developing metrics to convince advertisers that its advertisements were valuable even though people weren't clicking on them. A well-funded "Measurement and Insights" Department endeavored to prove that Facebook was creating brand awareness, even

---

* In sales and advertising jargon, the "purchase funnel" refers to the steps consumers go through before making a purchase. Typical stages are "awareness," "consideration," and "conversion"—versions of the funnel have different steps.

without conscious notice of ads, let alone clicks. Its head, Brad Small-wood, would tell advertisers that "99 percent of sales generated from online branding ad campaigns were from people that saw but did not interact with ads," claiming to prove "that it is the delivery of the marketing message to the right consumer, not the click, that creates real value for brand advertisers." In this way, Facebook left much of the hard selling to Google, or *The Huffington Post,* while itself posing as heir to the MacManus tradition of branding. And over time, advertisers would agree that Facebook had game.[17]*

Facebook also began letting commercial entities and even products create their own pages, and then, effectively, pay to gain lots of friends. This dovetailed with the site's invention of the "like" button—a particularly brilliant idea that could be put to noncommercial use (like approving of a friend's engagement, or weirdly an announcement in memoriam) while also allowing companies to know precisely those in whom they'd instilled brand loyalty. Facebook allowed people to buy advertisements in one's news feeds, giving its advertisements more contextual relevance. Finally, those "like" buttons also justified Facebook's heavy investments in tracking technologies. Scattered around the web, they allowed Facebook to follow users wherever they wandered online, sending messages back to the mother ship ("She's looking for cruises"). That would allow, for example, the Carnival Cruise Line to hit the user with cruise ads the moment they returned to Facebook, perhaps by throwing a sponsored "cruise" message into her "news feed." Facebook relied on those tracking, or spying, technologies to improve the data it held on each and every user—a group rapidly approximating the size of the entire world's buying public.†

Ultimately, the public had struck a grand bargain with Facebook—not exactly unknowingly, but not with full cognizance either. Having

---

* Especially after 2012 on mobile platforms, where, by good fortune, Facebook was one of the few companies putting large ads in front of consumers' faces on iPhones and even Google's Android phones.

† The foregoing is just an incomplete summary of the advertising technologies that Facebook devised over the 2010s. Others included inventions such as creating a "Lookalike Audience"—that is, allowing a company to use their existing customers to target those who are very similar, or look-alikes, based on everything that Facebook knows about them. It also, on mobile, began selling "install" and "engagement" ads that encouraged the installation or usage of apps.

been originally drawn to Facebook with the lure of finding friends, no one seemed to notice that this new attention merchant had inverted the industry's usual terms of agreement. Its billions of users worldwide were simply handing over a treasure trove of detailed demographic data and exposing themselves to highly targeted advertising in return for what, exactly? The newspapers had offered reporting, CBS had offered *I Love Lucy,* Google helped you find your way on the information superhighway. But Facebook?

Well, Facebook gave you access to your "friends." And now, much of the energy formerly devoted to blogs or other online projects was now channeled into upgrading one's Facebook profile and, with it, the value of Facebook itself. In this way, the public became like renters willingly making extensive improvements to their landlord's property, even as they were made to look at advertisements. Facebook's ultimate success lay in this deeply ingenious scheme of attention arbitrage, by which it created a virtual attention plantation.

If they noticed, most seemed not to mind being used this way, especially since everyone was now on Facebook, not just the college crowd, but kids of all ages, their parents and grandparents—even some pets had their own page. At the same time, more and more people began to complain that being on the site made them unhappy. It should have been no surprise, given what we know about human nature and the way Facebook was first conceived to play on the social dynamics of anxious adolescents, but watching the highlight reels of other people's lives was bound to make you feel inadequate. Others found Facebook (like email) a compulsion in that same Skinneresque manner—usually disappointing, but rewarding occasionally enough to keep you hooked. A variety of studies—none entirely conclusive, to be sure—associated depressive symptoms with Facebook usage, one finding that "compared to browsing the Internet, Facebook is judged as less meaningful, less useful, and more of a waste of time, which then leads to a decrease in mood." One is reminded of Marcuse's observation that people in the industrialized West had "made their mutilation into their own liberty and satisfaction."[18]

Facebook had supposedly replaced cyberspace with something more "real," but what it created in fact was just another realm of unreality, one that, on account of looking real, was more misleading. Here was a place where friends always congratulated and celebrated; where couples did lit-tle but eat at nice restaurants, go on vacation, or announce engagements or newborns; and where children never cried or needed diaper changes or hit each other. On Facebook, all happy families were alike; the others may have each been unhappy in their own way, but they were not on Facebook. Of course, all human communication is slightly inauthentic, but in person or even on the telephone there are limits to our dissimula-tions. The sugared-cookie-cutter self-styling enabled by Facebook made America seem a Lake Wobegon online. In retrospect, the 1950s looked dark and angst-ridden by comparison.

CHAPTER 24

THE IMPORTANCE

OF BEING MICROFAMOUS

In 2008 a young man named Rex Sorgatz moved from Seattle to New York City to seek his fortune in the New York tech business. "That was a weird time," he later reflected, for "media and tech were clashing for the first time." Perhaps not exactly sure what line of work he'd end up in, he printed a business card that listed everything he could do. "Rex Sorgatz," it read, "creative technologist, strategist, entrepreneur, writer, designer, advisor, consultant." Being recently from the West Coast, he was slightly ahead of the New Yorkers in some ways. He remembers telling people to try Twitter, but "they would just laugh, laugh, laugh at me."[1]

With an odd manner, spiky hair, and a good sense of humor, Sorgatz turned out to be a pretty good fit in the New York scene, proving particularly popular with the ladies. But not long after his arrival, he noticed something weird about New York web entrepreneurs, bloggers, and associated hangers-on: most of them were trying to become famous. Well, not traditionally famous, in the manner of a Hollywood celebrity or the Queen of England. They were studiously seeking something else, which Sorgatz called "microfame" and others called "Internet famous." Through their blogs, start-ups, cultivation of journalists, and endless rounds of parties, New York's tech people pursued this goal with a kind of grim determination. In this, the scene was just different from the one back West, where glory belonged solely to those who wrote the best algorithm. There, people wanted to be rich. Here, everyone wanted to be Internet famous.

"When we say 'microfamous,' our inclination is to imagine a smaller form of celebrity, a lower life-form striving to become a mammal—the macrofamous or suprafamous, perhaps," Sorgatz wrote with his accustomed wit. "But microfame is its own distinct species of celebrity, one in which both the subject and the 'fans' participate directly in the celebrity's creation. Microfame extends beyond a creator's body of work to include a community that leaves comments, publishes reaction videos, sends e-mails, and builds Internet reputations with links."

That definition appeared in his 2008 article for *New York* magazine entitled "The Microfame Game," which was ostensibly a guide to becoming microfamous. As Sorgatz explained, "Microfame is practically a science. It is attainable like running a marathon or acing the LSAT. All you need is a road map." He recommended, among other things, "oversharing," "self-publishing," and one tip that Sorgatz may himself have followed: "separat[ing] yourself from the cacophony by being a little weird. Scratch that—really weird."[2]

Meanwhile, Sorgatz himself says that he was most certainly not seeking microfame ("Oh dear God no."). Yet having become the apparent expert on the subject, he did gain a measure of it. As he recounts, "When social media started to embed itself into people's lives, I somehow appeared sage, so people associated it with me—for better and worse." He had his blog readers, his Twitter followers, consulting deals aplenty, and profiles in the *New York Observer* and *New York Times* (the latter calling him a "Social Networking Butterfly"). In retrospect, he writes, "I definitely got caught up in some of the personal drama of that era, but the only thing I ever 'wanted' was to hang out with people who had unique ideas about the world."

The oxymoron "microfame" is among those terms from the early 2000s, which include "blogging," "hashtag," and "selfie," that would have made absolutely no sense to people from the last century. There was, once upon a time, a relatively clear line distinguishing the famous from normal people. Crossovers were extremely rare, like the rise of a star, or ephemeral, as in the case of Charles Van Doren or participants of the 1950s and 1960s show *Queen for a Day.* As *People*'s editor defined it, to be "famous," and therefore worthy of a cover, meant having a face known to 80 percent of the public. Hence, Princess Diana was famous; Robert Redford was famous; but tech entrepreneurs, video bloggers, and those who took daily pictures of themselves were not, even if a surprising number of people recognized them.

Even the *ancien régime* did recognize gradations, however, and these found expression in the Ulmer Scale, created in the 1980s by a reporter named James Ulmer; he named it after himself, perhaps in his own small bid at microimmortality. The scale was designed to measure the celebrity status of actors, for the express purpose of estimating their "bankability" (i.e., how much value they added to a production just by appearing in it). In practice the scale divided famous actors into an A-list, B-list, and C-list, not unlike a bond-rating service on Wall Street. Ulmer called it a movie star "racing form."[3]

In the early 2000s, the D-list entered common parlance as a loose category meant to cover a new kind of figure who was somehow famous but not in a way understood by existing metrics. As Gareth Palmer writes, those on the D-list occupied the "space between the unknown mass of ordinary people and the celebrity."[4] The D-listers had no bankability; their achievement, instead, was, as one writer put it, having "triumphed over obscurity."[5] The archetype was, of course, the reality television star, though it could include others like models, romantic partners of celebrities, or faded pop stars. To be D-listed was not necessarily flattering, for it seemed also to refer to those who didn't know their place; whose efforts to become or remain famous were embarrassing and therefore worthy of broadcast for general amusement. Nonetheless, the very establishment of a D-list undeniably suggested that the line between famous and not was beginning to blur.

But as information technology grew more sophisticated, the D-list began to seem far too crude a measure; new tools, like powerful telescopes, could recognize faint glimmers of fame previously invisible. By the early 2000s, a Google search of someone's name represented a significant metric of fame. Consider, say, Fred Savage, a former child star, with his 494,000 hits, versus Scarlett Johansson, actress, at 18.2 million, or the highly bankable George Clooney, 29.7 million.

But it was Twitter that would provide the first finely calibrated measurement of microfame, nanofame, and smaller trace levels. Not that this had been its founding vision exactly. Instead, its four quarreling founders, Jack Dorsey, Evan Williams, Biz Stone, and Noah Glass, had repackaged a fairly mundane idea, AOL's "status update," and made it easy to broadcast on the web. The first tweets were true status updates, nuggets of TMI, like "I am eating eggs for breakfast." If it had launched later, Twitter might still be announcing breakfasts. But fortunately it arrived just when the enthusiasm for full-form blogging was beginning to wane, even though the taste for public self-expression persisted. Tweeting thus evolved to become blogging lite, a far less taxing form. With Twitter, one could post interesting links, thoughts, denouncements, cheers, and so on, just as on a blog, but with the 140-character limit it was never as much bother. At the time, much was made of the character limit as a quasi-poetical form. But in truth it was just easier. Where blogging demanded something close to professional dedication, on Twitter a sentence a day was good enough to keep a following engaged, and the famous could rely on a staffer to craft that sentence anyhow.

If there was an ingenious innovation, it was Twitter's system of "followers"—anyone could "follow" anyone else and thereby receive their tweets, or posts, automatically. Unlike blogs, one did not need to go looking for new tweets; they just arrived. And by indicating interest, even though roughly, the follower system became the new measure of fame. Those of established celebrity amassed millions of followers, like the singer Katy Perry (83.2 million followers) or President Barack Obama (70.3 million). But Twitter was sufficiently sensitive to detect and indicate the smallest quantities. Rex Sorgatz, new in town, had his 10,000 followers. A fairly obscure tech founder whose companies never quite took off nonetheless had 80,000 Twitter followers and therefore a measure of fame within his world. And it might turn out that a given blogger was read widely enough to have roughly three times the followers of Fred Savage. But following was not genetically determined or written in stone. With ably managed utterances, one could grow one's following, and with it one's general sense of influence and currency in the new sector of the attention economy. Everyone felt compelled to tweet, and everyone thus submitted to being weighed in the balance: microlevels of fame could now be ascribed to print journalists, some scientists and professors, cable television pundits, minor politicians, outspoken venture capitalists—essentially anyone willing to shoot their mouth off to their micropublic. In this way, figures could remain unknown to 99 percent, 99.9 percent, or even 99.99 percent of the population and nonetheless be "famous" in the highly granular sense. Twitter thus sparked microfame, measured it, and threw fuel on the fire.

Of course, by the numbers, even the achievement of microfame was a rarity. But perhaps the odds were beside the point. As Mark Zuckerberg said of Facebook users, "They're also building an image and identity for themselves, which in a sense is their brand." Indeed, with Facebook and Twitter, everyone could now have a brand, and derive a little of the excitement and attention that went with traditional celebrity—perhaps even find a way to resell a bit of that attention. It portended a future a bit different than Andy Warhol had predicted, for in this future "everyone will be famous to fifteen people," as the technologist David Weinberger quipped.[6] Nonetheless, as Rex Sorgatz argued, "It feels like a step toward equality. You can become Facebook friends with the microfamous; you can start IM sessions with them. You can love them and hate them at much closer proximity." And so just as American democracy promised that any child could grow up to become president, and American capitalism promised that through hard work anyone could become rich, the attention economy threw up its own mirage for the discontented masses: fame for everyone.

That was the utopian version. In actuality, fame, or the hunger for it, would become something of a pandemic, swallowing up more and more people and leaving them with the scars of chronic attention-whoredom. Ironically, though few of the traditional rewards of fame were forthcoming, more of the costs were. And that was in the relative age of innocence: the dominion of Twitter and Facebook alone, when they were tethered to the home. A still rougher beast was slouching toward the Bay Area waiting to be born. But before its coming, when social networks could take their present form, something else had to happen, something even more momentous in the history of attention capture—the arrival of a new and ultimate gathering point for all our longings as well as commerce's designs upon them: the fourth screen.

CHAPTER 25

THE FOURTH SCREEN

AND THE MIRROR OF NARCISSUS

A s the first decade of the new century rolled on, something was happening in major cities around the world. More and more men and women, most in suits, could be seen compulsively pulling out a device with a tiny screen and craning their necks to stare at it. At that point, there would begin the familiar exercise of rolling a little dial before urgently typing away with both thumbs. In those years, this distinctive habit marked one as either of the corporate class or of government employment. To everyone else, it looked self-important and faintly ridiculous. Few realized they were beholding an image of their future selves.

This new attentional habit—actually an extension of the check-in—originated in the late 1990s, when, with no particularly grand vision, two young Canadians, Mihalis (Mike) Lazaridis and Doug Fregin, developed what they styled as an improvement on the pager.* Their device, a clamshell of sorts, allowed both the sending and receiving of pages, but also, in a very primitive way, the capacity to read and write emails while on the go. They named it "The 900 Inter@ctive Pager." The @ sign was meant to position it toward the future, and at the same time to reflect the

---

* The pager was a portable device used in the 1980s and 1990s that allowed the bearer to receive notifications that a return call was desired.

engineering aesthetic at the heart of the company, Research in Motion, located in Waterloo, Ontario.

The RIM 900 was primitive; its monochrome screen was the size of a piece of bacon on its side, a cooked piece at that. But it was a modest success, leading Lazaridis and Fregin to develop a more advanced version, which they boldly called the "Research in Motion 950 Inter@active Pager." This one was smaller overall, but with a bigger screen, a well-designed keyboard, and the capacity to retrieve emails automatically (at the time, this was heralded as "push" technology). It also ran for weeks on a single AA battery, a feature even current smartphone users can envy.

While no marketing expert—indeed, he had an engineer's hostility to marketing's influence—Lazaridis nonetheless sensed that his product's name lacked pizzazz. He considered, for a while, calling it the "Pocket-Link" but at the last moment decided to consult some branding experts from California. After some analysis, in a way that might have done Ernest Dichter proud, the experts opined that the letter B conveyed reliability, and the device's little keyboard looked like a strawberry. Out of that came the "BlackBerry." Thus rechristened, the device finally began to feel some wind in its sails.

Slowly the new fruit began cropping up across North America and then the world, but while it was ultimately a great success, it was not a mass-market product like the television or radio; it remained the instrument of a certain elite. Indeed, so it was marketed not to the general public but rather to corporations keen on keeping their employees in reach, or on call, at all times. Thus it was those corporate types, and also federal government types (most famously Barack Obama), who pioneered an attentional habit that would define the coming century. In comparison, television's momentous conquest of time and space in the twentieth would seem woefully incomplete.

As we've repeatedly seen in chronicling the past hundred years, it is such habits that make and break great attention merchants. The attending public were first captured reading daily newspapers, then listening to evening broadcasts, before they were entranced into sitting glued to the television at key intervals, and finally, over the 1990s, into surrendering some more of their waking time, opening their eyes and minds to computers—the third screen—in dens and offices around the world. Now a new device appeared capable of harvesting the attention that had been, as it were, left on the table, rather in the way fracking would later recover great reserves of oil once considered wholly inaccessible. Of course, the terms of this surrender seemed favorable, as they usually do: email on the go meant you could take your work with you and weren't stuck at home or the office. By 2015, the fourth screen would be in the hands of virtually everyone, seizing nearly three of the average person's waking hours. And so it would become the undisputed new frontier of attention harvesting in the twenty-first century, the attention merchants' manifest destiny. From now on, whither thou goest, your smartphone goes, too, and of course the ads.

As so often happens in tech industries, Research in Motion started the game but did not master it. That job would be left to the world's two mightiest computing empires, which by the 2010s had clued in to the potential for far broader adoption of what the BlackBerry represented. With their nearly unlimited reserves of engineering and design talent, Apple and Google would go on to create iPhones and Androids, respectively, and thoroughly clobber the Canadians at their own game, offering a much more appealing user interface. BlackBerry seemed to many invincible even with a mere 9 million subscribers in 2007, when the iPhone was first launched. By 2011, there would be 472 million smartphones sold worldwide in one year. There would soon follow not just an attentional habit but a new social norm, that of never parting from one's device; of standing and staring at it, as if paralyzed, as the world goes by; of not looking up in the presence of others, except when the urge to take a picture erupts at the strangest moment—*autre tech, autre moeurs:* it is probably the thing a visitor from a previous century would find the weirdest.

Where the human gaze goes, business soon follows, and by the 2010s virtually everyone in the attention industries was trying to figure out what might be the best way to get a piece of all that attention now directed downward at billions of palms. Google and Apple had the proverbial head start, but there was not a company that did not have at least someone trying to devise what was called at the time "a strategy for mobile," now that the web was following millions of people everywhere.

Some of the adaption would be obvious from the start: clickbait, for instance, could certainly travel, if one imagined the bored commuter. Yet these were still early efforts, transplants from other platforms, the way radio shows had been adapted to TV. More specific to mobile were games like *Angry Birds, Candy Crush,* or *Flappy Bird.* Designed for passing the time on a little screen, these tended, in their simplicity, to resemble the earliest video games, like *Space Invaders, Pac-Man,* or *Tetris.* Facebook earned billions by selling advertisements that encouraged and made easy the installation of other apps. But the first attention-harvesting applications to make full use of the smartphone's distinctive capabilities were, as usual, unpredictable, yet once they'd arrived, utterly obvious.

Instagram was begun by a soft-spoken, fairly square serial tech entrepreneur named Kevin Systrom, whose inspiration came, in part, from his tenure as president of his high school photography club. He and his coding partner and cofounder, Mike Krieger, were rather typical San Francisco entrepreneurs of the 2010s, if there was such a thing: young, restless, looking for an idea, having already failed at one effort to create a saleable social media app—there was no shame in that; most of them went nowhere. They lacked the chutzpah of a Zuckerberg. Their invention was not at the level of an Edison or Bell; but as we've seen, in the attention industries, if the right chord is struck, it does not take much. Their new iPhone app did two things. First, it enhanced the device's camera with a series of attractive filters that could be applied to photos, creating some immediate utility. Its second innovation, ultimately more influential, was to create a photo-centered social network—a sort of Twitter built on images. On Twitter, one shared a message; a photo was optional. Instagram made the photo mandatory and the message optional. Yep, that was it.

The simplicity of Instagram's concept was its calling card—people got it—and it gained users quickly: by the spring of 2012, just eighteen months after its launch, it had 30 million. The thing was fun and easy to use, but it was also well timed, for it was the first popular social networking app that truly made full use of the smartphone's functionality, tying its integrated camera to its Internet connection and app functionality. Moreover, it connected those devices with what, for want of a better name, can be called the market for aspiring celebrity. Like Twitter, Instagram users had followers—and the followers had the option with the click of a ♥ to "like" photos they enjoyed or otherwise approved. That "like" feature was the heart of Instagram, even more than of Facebook. Every photograph was, in a sense, rated by peers, thus providing a kind of instantaneous feedback.

Some would use Instagram to showcase their photographic skills or the luscious dishes they were tucking into. But far and away Instagram's best known feature—its killer app—was the self-portrait, or as the Australians called it, "the selfie," the term that became the *Oxford Dictionary's* Word of the Year in 2013. Early on, Instagram reported that it had 53 million photos so designated (with #selfie). The selfie was so important that the form and the platform rose in tandem.

While Facebook was also a place for posting photos, and at some level presenting oneself as one would like to be seen, Instagram allowed for a seamless and more continuous visual narrative. In this way, active Instagrammers "created an Instagram life," telling their own stories, or at least a stylized and idealized version of it, in images. If the average Facebook post showed a group of friends or a family in good times (perhaps posing with the dog, or holding up drinks at a party), Instagram's photos would generally be more dramatic, glamorous, and often edgier, for the simple reason that they were posted with the calculated intent to seize attention and to elicit a reaction. This was particularly true for the app's many younger users, who flocked to it as their grandparents started joining Facebook. A number of them would cultivate multiple narratives with different accounts: the "real" one (Rinstagram), which was the more contrived to impress; and the "fake" one (Finstagram), on which, for a smaller circle, they were content to be more themselves. Instagram thus occupied the territory on which Zuckerberg had originally positioned Facebook: *the* place to be. And the real-time fix of "likes" and comments would become for untold numbers an addictive form of self-affirmation.

Typically Instagram feeds looked as much like Facebook as *Vice* magazine spreads resemble a high school yearbook. The photos were not candid but posed, retouched, art directed. Some users adapted the form to more explicitly imaginative expression, creating themed accounts. For instance, a teenager called Liam Martin posted low-budget re-creations of celebrity glamour shots, usually with himself in drag; and @socality barbie artfully chronicled the life of "Hipster Barbie" in a way meant to mock Instagram culture. "Hipster Barbie is so much better at Instagram than you."[1]

Like the early blogs, a good Instagram feed was labor-intensive. When she quit, Socality Barbie noted "the insane lengths many of us go to create the perfect Instagram life."[2] A "fashion" Instagrammer named Amanda Miller who offered an online guide to gaining followers confesses that "getting to 18.5k followers was A LOT of work."[3] In addition to composing and shooting photos, the feed demands interacting with strangers to make them feel engaged or heard, the way a politician or other public figure might—the way a real celebrity doesn't have to do. As Miller writes, "Engagement: This is the hardest part because it takes something money can't buy, and that is TIME. It takes A LOT OF TIME."

Occasionally, the effort was monetized. Some of the more popular users of Instagram (typically young, attractive, and female) managed to become attention merchants, selling product placements in their photographs. "Companies have realized that one photo on the Instagram account of someone with over 100,000 followers is reaching more people directly than any traditional ad campaign," explained a new social media ad agency; a popular, microfamous Instagrammer might charge brands $1 per "like" earned by a sponsored photo.[4]

For the better known—those already in the business of capturing and reselling attention, the utility of Instagram as an additional platform and revenue stream was obvious; of course their publicists or other staff could be expected to do most of the work for these incorporated personalities. In a major attention-capture stunt, Kim Kardashian famously used Instagram in 2014 to send out a picture of her nearly naked backside in an attempt to "break the Internet." It may not quite have done that, but it paid off in attention earned; it must have, because Kardashian's management, normally so efficient about getting paid, negotiated no other compensation. It was further evidence of attention's having become an accepted form of currency. James Franco, a C-list actor under the old metrics, and himself a self-confessed "Instagram addict," would speak to its broad acceptance: "It's what the movie studios want for their products, it's what professional writers want for their work, it's what newspapers want—hell, it's what everyone wants: attention. Attention is power."[5]

In Franco's case, tending his image has become a career in itself, more or less, and so he is driven to self-market to maintain his audience. Calling it a business model as opposed to mere narcissism at least provides an excuse, insofar as many careers excuse what would otherwise be considered unhealthy or insane behavior.

But the resale remains the main opportunity. For a sense of the range of possibilities, a tale of two backsides may suffice: one, as just mentioned, was that of Kim Kardashian. Upon her attempt to "break the Internet," she was in possession of some 55 million Instagram followers. Such is the power of multi-platform, *People*-cover-worthy celebrity. Now consider Jen Selter, a twenty-two-year-old fitness advocate. Selter's renown came about almost exclusively from social media, based on photographs revealing her own assiduously developed posterior. As of this writing, Selter has some 8.5 million Instagram followers, more than enough to attract all kinds of business opportunities, including sponsorships, appearances, and others enjoyed by Kardashian, if on a more modest scale. Unknown to most, she is nevertheless enough of an Instagram star to be a perfectly successful attention merchant.

But what of all those many among us busily keeping up an Instagram feed with no hope of ever reselling the attention? For most, the effort is an end in itself, and the ultimate audience is the very subject of the camera's interest. Understood this way, Instagram is the crowning achievement of that decades-long development that we have called the "celebrification" of everyday life and ordinary people, a strategy developed by attention merchants for the sake of creating cheap content.

Let us review our story in brief, as it might relate to Instagram: For most of human history, the proliferation of the individual likeness was the sole prerogative of the illustrious, whether it was the face of the emperor on a Roman coin or the face of Garbo on the silver screen. The commercialization of photography may have broadened access to portraiture somewhat, but apart from wanted posters, the image of most common people would never be widely propagated. In the twentieth century, Hollywood created a cohort of demigods, whose image everyone recognized and many, in effect, worshipped. With the arrival of the smartphone and Instagram, however, much of the power of a great film studio was now in every hand attached to a heart yearning for fame; not only could one create an image to rival those of the old icons of glamour, but one could put it on a platform where millions might potentially see it.

Perhaps a century of the ascendant self, of the self's progressive liberation from any trammels not explicitly conceived to protect other selves, perhaps this progression, when wedded to the magic of technology serving not the state or even the corporation but the individual ego, perhaps it could reach no other logical endpoint, but the self as its own object of worship.

Of course, it is easy to denigrate as vanity even harmless forms of self-expression. Indulging in a bit of self-centeredness from time to time, playing with the trappings of fame, can be a form of entertainment for oneself and one's friends, especially when undertaken with a sense of irony. Certainly, too, the self-portrait, and the even more patently ludicrous invention, the selfie stick, has become too easy a target for charges of self-involvement. Humans, after all, have sought the admiration of others in various ways since the dawn of time; it is a feature of our social and sexual natures. The desire of men and women to dress up and parade may be as deeply rooted as the peacock's impulse to strut. Like all attention harvesters, Instagram has not stirred any new yearning within us, merely acted upon one already there, and facilitated its gratification to an unimaginable extent. Therein lies the real problem.

Technology doesn't follow culture so much as culture follows technology. New forms of expression naturally arise from new media, but so do new sensibilities and new behaviors. All desire, the philosopher and critic René Girard wrote, is essentially mimetic; beyond our elemental needs, we are led to seek after things by the example of others, those whom we may know personally or through their fame. When our desires go beyond the elemental, they enter into their metaphysical dimension, in which, as Girard wrote, "All desire is a desire to be," to enjoy an image of fulfillment such as we have observed in others. This is the essential problem with the preening self unbound by social media, and the democratization of fame. By presenting us with example upon example, it legitimates self-aggrandizement as an objective for ever more of us. By encouraging anyone to capture the attention of others with the spectacle of one's self—in some cases, even to the point of earning a living by it—it warps our understanding of our own existence and its relation to others. That this should become the manner of being for us all is surely the definitive dystopic vision of late modernity. But perhaps it was foretold by the metastatic proliferation of the attention merchants' model throughout our culture.

In the fall of 2015, an Australian teenager, Essena O'Neill, quit Instagram in utter despair. A natural beauty and part-time model, she had become an Instagram celebrity, thanks to her pictures, which had drawn half a million followers. But her Instagram career, she explained, had made her life a torment.

"I had the dream life. I had half a million people interested in me on Instagram. I had over a hundred thousand views on most of my videos on YouTube. To a lot of people, I made it," she confessed in a video. But suddenly it had all become too much.

> Everything I was doing was edited and contrived and to get more views. . . . Everything I did was for views, for likes, for followers. . . . Social media, especially how I used it, isn't real. It's contrived images and edited clips ranked against each other. It's a system based on social approval, likes, validation in views, success in followers. It's perfectly orchestrated self-absorbed judgement. . . . I met people that are far more successful online than I am, and they are just as miserable and lonely and scared and lost. We all are.[6]

A survey of Instagram and other social media users by the London *Guardian* yielded similar responses, suggesting that even among those with relatively few followers the commitment is grim. "I feel anxiety over how many likes I get after I post a picture. If I get two likes, I feel like, what's wrong with me?" wrote one woman.[7] "I do feel insecure if I see girls who look prettier than me," wrote another, "or if they post really pretty pictures, and I know I won't look as good in any that I post. I do feel pressure to look good in the photos I put up. I don't feel anxious about not getting enough likes on a photo but if it doesn't get enough likes, I will take it down."

––––––––––

In April 2012, a mere eighteen months after its debut, Instagram was purchased by Facebook for $1 billion. The high-flying start-up's founders had cashed out without ever having devised a business model. No matter: by November the following year, the first ad feed would run in Instagram, following Facebook principles of limited targeting. The acquisition would prove astute. In April 2012 Instagram had 30 million users, but by the fall of 2015 it had 400 million, more than Twitter. And so Facebook would join the ranks of hoary behemoths with a war chest. A transfusion of young blood would preserve their status in the uppermost echelon of attention merchants.

As for Instagram, its upward glide portended a future in which the line between the watcher and the watched, the buyer and the seller, was more blurred than ever. The once highly ordered attention economy had seemingly devolved into a chaotic mutual admiration society, full of enterprising Narcissi, surely an arrangement of affairs without real precedent in human history.

CHAPTER 26

THE WEB HITS BOTTOM

"Which Ousted Arab Spring Ruler Are You?" "You Might Be Cleaning Your Penis Wrong," "37 Things Conservatives Would Rather Do Than Watch Obama's State of the Union Speech," "29 Cats Who Failed So Hard They Won."

Here was BuzzFeed, at its height in the 2010s, undisputed king of clickbait, and the grandmaster of virality. As a cofounder of *The Huffington Post,* Jonah Peretti had gained a measure of success, recognition, and personal wealth. But it wouldn't be long before he lost interest in the operation, which had begun to run itself, and felt compelled to return to his original passion: the pure art and science of harvesting attention with "contagious" or "viral" media. He was still at *The Huffington Post* when he began to conceive the endpoint, or perhaps the punch line, to his long obsession: a site whose mission would be nothing but to build pure contagion and launch it into the ether.

BuzzFeed billed itself as the "first true social news organization," which meant it was designed for a post-Facebook and post-Twitter world, where news gained currency by being shared on social networks, through newsfeeds, Twitter feeds, and the like. It was also designed to be read on the now ubiquitous mobile platforms; by 2015, 60 percent of its traffic was via phones and other wireless devices (including 21 percent from Snapchat)—the key to success was now getting people to share stuff socially from mobile.

By the time Peretti built BuzzFeed, viral media were not an occasional phenomenon, but reaching the public like successive waves crashing on a metaphorical shore, they thus both rivaled and complemented (depending on the context) existing means of capturing attention. It was a time when a random picture of a grumpy-looking cat (Grumpy Cat) posted on the online bulletin board Reddit made a viable career for its owners; when a ridiculous dance video like "Gangnam Style" amassed more than 2.4 billion online views (while the 2014 World Cup, the most watched event in human history, reached about 1 billion).

As nothing but a pure embodiment of Peretti's techniques, BuzzFeed did without even the pretense of a public mission, the only goal being to amuse viewers enough to trigger their sharing. With content often nearly devoid of any meaningful communication, the medium truly was the message. And while this might sound like unprecedented cynicism vis-à-vis the audience, the idea was to transfer creative intention to them; they alone would "decide if the project reaches 10 people or 10 million people."[1] To help them decide, BuzzFeed pioneered techniques like "headline optimization," which was meant to make the piece irresistible and clicking on it virtually involuntary. In the hands of the headline doctors, a video like "Zach Wahls Speaks About Family" became "Two Lesbians Raised a Baby and This Is What They Got"—and earned 18 million views. BuzzFeed's lead data scientist, Ky Harlin, once crisply explained the paradoxical logic of headlining: "You can usually get somebody to click on something just based on their own curiosity or something like that, but it doesn't mean that they're actually going to end up liking the content."

BuzzFeed also developed the statistical analysis of sharing, keeping detailed information on various metrics, especially the one they called "viral lift." Let's take, for example, a story entitled "48 Pictures That Capture the 1990s," which garnered over 1.2 million views. BuzzFeed would measure how many people read it (views), and of those, how many went on to share it, whether on Twitter, Facebook, or other sites. If, say, twenty-two people with whom the link was shared were moved to click on it, the story would be said to have a viral lift of 22x. Such data would help BuzzFeed's experts refine their understanding of what gets shared, and what doesn't.

Collectively BuzzFeed and its rivals—Mashable, Upworthy, and in time parts of the mainstream media—began to crack the code; eventually they could consistently make content go viral. Much of what they discovered validated Peretti's original theories—particularly about the necessity of stimulating "pleasure in the social process of passing" something along and of ensuring that the contagion "represent[s] the simplest form of an idea."[2] But the "pleasure" of sharing did not necessarily mean that viewing the content had been pleasurable. The urge to share was activated by a spectrum of "high-arousal" emotions, like awe, outrage, and anxiety. A story with a headline like "When All Else Fails, Blaming the Patient Often Comes Next," or "What Red Ink? Wall Street Paid Hefty Bonuses," or "Rare Treatment Is Reported to Cure AIDS Patient" would trigger one of these emotions—or even better, several at once.

Naked plays for attention always draw scorn, and as BuzzFeed's fortunes rose in the 2010s, it was no exception. As Ben Cohen, founder of the journalism site *The Daily Banter,* wrote: "I loathe BuzzFeed and pretty much everything they do. . . . It could well trump Fox News as the single biggest threat to journalism ever created."[3] When BuzzFeed presented the Egyptian democratic revolution as a series of GIFs from the film *Jurassic Park,* Cohen fulminated: "To say this is childish, puerile bullshit would be a massive understatement. . . . Doing funny GIF posts about cats and hangovers is one thing, but reducing a highly complex political crisis into 2 second moving screen shots of a children's dinosaur movie is something completely different. If BuzzFeed really is the future of journalism, we're completely and utterly fucked."[4] Indeed, by 2012, the scramble for eyeballs against forces like BuzzFeed seemed to bring news media to a new low. When Fox News broadcast a video of a man committing suicide and BuzzFeed reposted the link, the *Columbia Journalism Review* was compelled to ask, "Who's worse? @FoxNews for airing the suicide, or @BuzzFeed for re-posting the video just in case you missed it the first time?"[5]

BuzzFeed was indeed proving the envy of all other online attention merchants, in traffic at least. By 2015, its 200+ million monthly unique viewers exceeded most of its competitors, and 75 percent of its traffic was coming from social media. Ultimately its techniques were widely copied, not just by its direct competitors like the *Daily Mail* or Cracked.com but by *The Huffington Post*, Peretti's previous venture, and more obliquely, by magazines like *Slate* as well as newspapers like *The Washington Post*. Even literary magazines like *The Atlantic* and *The New Yorker* got in on the act. BuzzFeed thus became the reference point, the gold standard, for attention capture on the web.

Not that BuzzFeed was terribly profitable. It lost money for most of its early years, only began to turn a profit in 2013, and never exceeded $10 million (while hardly a fair comparison, Apple's iTunes store alone, also in the content business, and not considered highly profitable, has been estimated to clear $1 billion in profit per year). Its fortunes reflected the still-low price of digital ads; BuzzFeed's annual ad revenues of roughly $100 million were still far less than, say, *People* magazine (about $1 billion). Nonetheless, BuzzFeed was still growing, and as the decade reached its midpoint, was pegged at $850 million in value; then, over the summer of 2015, the cable giant Comcast bought a stake that valued the company at $1.5 billion.

Comcast's investment in BuzzFeed was at last a consummation of the union between the old and the new media such as Microsoft and AOL–Time Warner had once contemplated, though now involving far less money than in those headier days. For comparison's sake, though, it is worth remarking that *The Washington Post*, with its forty-seven Pulitzer Prizes, was purchased by Amazon for $250 million in 2013—old media valuations clearly weren't what they used to be, either. And yet even if BuzzFeed had attracted real dollars, the deal with Comcast nonetheless seemed to diminish the new media in some way. Blogging and other forces that Jeff Jarvis and others had predicted were going to demolish the establishment had eventually yielded to BuzzFeed. BuzzFeed was then bought by old media for what amounted to chump change. So much for all of that.

Peretti had never been less than forthright and consistent about the objectives of his work: it was attention capture for its own sake. But the entry of contagions and clickbait and even social networks in the ecosystem of the content-driven media inevitably had its degrading influence on the latter. Mark Manson well described the state of the web in the 2010s:

> Last week, I logged onto Facebook to see a story about a man who got drunk, cut off his friend's penis and then fed it to a dog. This was followed by a story of a 100-year-old woman who had never seen the ocean before. Then eight ways I can totally know I'm a 90's kid. Then 11 steps to make me a "smarter Black Friday shopper," an oxymoron if I ever saw one. This is life now: one constant, never-ending stream of non sequiturs and self-referential garbage that passes in through our eyes and out of our brains at the speed of a touchscreen.[6]

Within twenty years of having been declared king, content seemed to be on the road to serfdom.

Once a commons that fostered the amateur eccentric in every area of interest, the web, by 2015, was thoroughly overrun by commercial junk, much of it directed at the very basest human impulses of voyeurism and titillation. To be sure, there were exceptions, like Wikipedia, a healthy nonprofit; Reddit, still a haven for some of the spirit of the old Internet; small magazines like *Verge, Vox, Quartz,* and the *Awl;* even some efforts to reboot blogging, like the *Medium.* Likewise, faced with an existential crisis of relevancy, traditional news media, so long allergic to the Internet, dramatically improved their online content over the decade. But these bright spots were engulfed by the vast areas of darkness, the lands of the cajoling listicles and the celebrity nonstories, engineered for no purpose but to keep a public mindlessly clicking and sharing away, spreading the accompanying ads like a bad cold. As the clicks added up, what was most depressing perhaps was that all this was for the sake of amassing no great fortune, but in fact relatively paltry commercial gains, rounding errors in the larger scheme of commerce. The idealists had hoped the web would be different, and it certainly was for a time, but over the long term it would become something of a 99-cent store, if not an outright cesspool. As with the demolition of Penn Station, a great architectural feat had been defaced for little in return. But as so often in the history of attention merchants, when competition mounts, the unseemliness soars and the stakes plummet.

And that was just the content; the advertising, meanwhile, was epically worse. By the mid-2010s the average reader on news sites like the *Boston Globe*'s boston.com would be subjected to extraordinary surveillance methods, with only the barest degree of consent. Such operations would be invisible to the user, except for the delays and solicitations they triggered. Online tracking technologies evolved to a point that would have made a Soviet-era spy blush. Arrival at NYPost.com would trigger up to twenty or more urgent "tracking" messages to online ad agencies, or "ad networks," advising them of any available intelligence on the user, in addition to specifying what stories they were reading. Attention merchants had always been ravenous for attention, but now they were gobbling up personal data as well. Perhaps the oversharing on social media had simply lowered the standard of privacy. Perhaps the Internet, with its potential to capture every turn of our attention, made this inevitable. Whatever the case, several commercial entities were now compiling ever more detailed dossiers on every man, woman, and child. It is a more thoroughly invasive effort than any NSA data collection ever disclosed—and one of even more dubious utility.

The automation of customized advertising was intended, in theory, to present you with things more likely to seize your attention and make you click. It must be seen as a continuation of the search we have described for advertising's Holy Grail: pitches so aptly keyed to one's interests that they would be as welcome as morning sunshine. The idealists foresaw a day when ad platforms would be like a loyal valet who detected his master's needs before he was aware of them, who suggested a new pair of shoes as a reasonably priced replacement for those you hadn't noticed were wearing out. Perhaps he would remind you of your mother-in-law's birthday while offering to send an appropriate gift at a one-day discount.

But the gap between this theory and its execution was wide enough to march Kitchener's Army through it. Google's CEO Eric Schmidt had once said that the ideal was to "get right up to the creepy line and not cross it."[7] Unfortunately, by the mid-2010s, that line was being crossed constantly. While promising to be "helpful" or "thoughtful," what was delivered was often experienced as "intrusive" and worse. Some ads seemed more like stalkers than valets: if, say, you'd been looking at a pair of shoes on Amazon, an ad for just those shoes would begin following you around the web, prodding you to take another look at them. What was meant to be "relevant" to your wishes and interests turned out to be more of a studied exploitation of one's weaknesses. The overweight were presented with diet aids; the gadget-obsessed plied with the latest doo-dads; gamblers encouraged to bet; and so on. One man, after receiving a diagnosis of pancreatic cancer, found himself followed everywhere with "insensitive and tasteless" ads for funeral services. The theoretical idea that customers might welcome or enjoy such solicitations increasingly seemed like a bad joke.

To make matters worse, the technology of behavioral advertising added layers of complexity to the code of any website, causing the sys-tem to slow or freeze, and sometimes preventing the page from loading altogether. According to a *New York Times* study in 2015, despite the fact that every other technology had improved, some websites were now taking five seconds or more to load; and the situation was even worse on mobile phones, with their slower connections.[8] Videos had a way of pop-ping up and starting to play unbidden; and the user looking for the stop button would find it was the tiniest of all, and often oddly located. And something of a ruse as well: if you missed hitting it directly, yet another website would open, with yet more ads.

In nearly every possible way, ad tech was terrible for consumers and, to compound the pity of it all, not particularly lucrative for advertis-ers either. As the programmer Marco Arment lamented in 2015, "In the last few years . . . web ad quality and tolerability have plummeted, and annoyance, abuse, misdirection, and tracking have skyrocketed. Pub-lishers don't have an easy job trying to stay in business today, but that simply doesn't justify the rampant abuse, privacy invasion, sleaziness, and creepiness that many of them are forcing upon their readers."[9] Even the tech people managed to draw a short straw, for all of this mischief took a surprising amount of programming talent to accomplish. "The best minds of my generation are thinking about how to make people click ads," commented scientist Jeff Hammerbacher. "That sucks."[10]

Ultimately, the problem was as old as the original proposition of seizing our attention and putting it to uses not our own. It is a scheme that has been revised and renewed with every new technology, which always gains admittance into our lives under the expectation it will improve them— and improve them it does until it acquires motivations of its own, which can only grow and grow. As Oxford ethicist James Williams put it,

Your goals are things like "spend more time with the kids," "learn to play the zither," "lose twenty pounds by summer," "finish my degree," etc. Your time is scarce, and you know it. Your technologies, on the other hand, are trying to maximize goals like "Time on Site," "Number of Video Views," "Number of Pageviews," and so on. Hence clickbait, hence auto-playing videos, hence avalanches of notifications. Your time is scarce, and your technologies know it.[11]

In this game of trackers and profile builders, as in so many others, Google and Facebook, de facto diarchs of the online attention merchants, reigned supreme. By design, both firms had acquired the best data on just about every consumer on earth, as well as possessing the best tools for collecting more of it, which by the 2010s both were prepared to exploit as far as possible. Never mind that each had originally been hesitant even to allow advertising to pollute its pages or interfere with the user experience. That was then. Since those years of initial hand-wringing, as investors and Wall Street demanded their quarterly increases in revenue, there was little choice but to turn up the heat, intensifying the reach of ads while hoping that their respective market positions were secure enough to prevent too many users from bolting. The essential bind of the attention merchant began tightening even on those Faustian geniuses who thought they had beaten the Devil.

YouTube, now a Google subsidiary, offers perhaps the starkest example of the change. Once entirely ad-free, by the mid-2010s many of its videos required users to watch a fifteen or thirty-second commercial to see a few minutes of content, making television's terms look almost respectful by comparison. That priceless impression of getting great stuff for free, the attention merchant's most essential magic trick, was losing its charm. As with any bit of legerdemain, once the actual workings are revealed, the strings made visible, it becomes ugly and obvious, drained of its power to enchant.

Targeting and tracking were not the only innovations in web advertising over the 2010s. Trying to stay ahead of the growing disenchantment, sites like BuzzFeed brought forth their own inventions, if such ideas could merit the term. One was known as the "advertorial," or "native advertising," ads designed to look like content native to the site, aping its form and functionality. The idea was that if it didn't look like an ad it might get past more users' defenses. "We work with brands to help them speak the language of the web," said Peretti in the 2010s of this Trojan horse approach, uncharacteristically compromising the integrity of his shameless love of contagion. "I think there's an opportunity to create a golden age of advertising, like another Mad Men age of advertising, where people are really creative and take it seriously."[12]

In practice this supposedly new *Mad Men* age consisted of BuzzFeed-style stories written at the behest and expense of corporations. Consider "The 14 Coolest Hybrid Animals," a series for Toyota's Prius, or "11 Things You Didn't Know About [the Sony] PlayStation" joined with "10 Awesome Downloadable Games You May Have Missed." Since BuzzFeed also wrote "real" news stories about the Hybrid Sony PlaySta-tion, it was sometimes awfully hard to distinguish the content that was sponsored, not that it mattered much in BuzzFeed's case.

"Maybe I'm old-fashioned but one core ethical rule I thought we had to follow in journalism was the church-state divide between editorial and advertising," wrote Andrew Sullivan, the prominent blogger and former journalist, about this approach.[13] Nonetheless, by mid-decade native advertising had become a commonplace and even heralded as a potential solution to journalism's woes. It would be embraced by media companies as reputable as *The New York Times* and Condé Nast, which now, like BuzzFeed, had on-site units aping their own in-house style for their advertisers. "The 'sponsored content' model is designed," Sullivan observed, "to obscure the old line as much as possible."

The world was slow to turn on the web, still after all the fountain of the new. Whether for reasons of politics or politesse, the web would suffer a lot of ruin before many critics, who'd fallen in love with its openness, would admit that things had gone awry. Even so, by the mid-2010s, more and more ordinary users had their own impression of the emperor's new clothes. Perhaps the first sign of elite revolt was the idea best articulated by Nicholas Carr that the web was making us stupider. Maybe it was the growing talk of an "information glut," or Jaron Lanier's argument, in his manifesto *You Are Not a Gadget,* that the culture of the web had resulted in a suppression of individual creativity and innovation. Even the incredibly powerful tools of sharing and communication—email,

Twitter, YouTube, Facebook, Instagram—once employed by entities like BuzzFeed, didn't seem so magical, having collaborated in building an attentional environment with so little to admire. For in its totality the web seemed to be bobbing in the crosscurrents of an aggressive egotism and neurasthenic passivity. Thus trapped, it was suddenly vulnerable to capture by anyone with a promise of something different or better.

CHAPTER 27

A RETREAT AND A REVOLT

In 2011, the independent studio Media Rights Capital was shopping an American remake of a modestly successful British political drama named *House of Cards*. Among other advantages, the producers boasted of having attached to the show David Fincher, the Oscar-winning director of *The Social Network*. They hoped, ideally, to sell the idea to HBO, or maybe a cable channel like A&E interested in buttressing its reputation for serious drama since the success of *Mad Men*.

Unexpectedly, while in Los Angeles, Fincher received a call from Ted Sarandos, a senior executive at Netflix. Netflix was, at the time, a company that had made its name shipping DVDs by mail; more recently it had begun streaming content over the Internet, with variable success. Sarandos was already known to Hollywood for buying its leftovers—the rights to old films that had already seen theatrical release, DVD sales and rentals, in-flight screening, and every other channel of distribution. Netflix was thus something of a town scrap dealer, at the bottom of the content food chain.

"We want the series," Sarandos told Fincher, "and I'm going to pitch you on why you should sell it to us."[1] Convincing a famous auteur to bring his talents to a medium—the Internet—then best known for cat videos was not going to be easy. But Netflix promised a lot. Though he'd never directed a TV series before, Fincher would be given enormous creative control. Rather than putting it through the pilot process, the usual way to test a TV show's prospects, Netflix was willing to pay for two thirteen-episode seasons up front. Last but not least, Sarandos offered a pile of money: a reported $100 million, or as much as would be ordinarily invested in an expensive feature blockbuster.

The risk for Netflix was that in exchange for its millions it would wind up stuck with a bomb that exploded in slow motion. At that moment, moreover, the company, while valued at hundreds of millions, had just $17 million in profit to show for 2012. The risk for Fincher, of course, was that no one would watch the series or that Netflix would go bankrupt. But that $100 million was an offer he couldn't refuse, and so *House of Cards,* arguably the first serious feature drama to debut on the Internet, began looking for its cast.

This of course was no lark for Netflix. With the purchase of *House of Cards,* the rising firm was aiming to cause a definitive shake-up in both the television and Internet content markets. Consider that in 2011, all commercial Internet content was driven by advertising. Sure, there were different types: programmatic advertising, native advertising, Google AdWords, YouTube prerolls, Facebook ads, and Twitter's sponsored tweets. But behind everything was the same old model: that of the attention merchant. Not since television in the 1950s had any medium become so quickly dominated by it.

Netflix, then, was virtually alone, as an Internet company, in blazing a different path. From the beginning of its streaming venture, the firm had taken the bold and seemingly foolhardy decision to forgo advertising altogether. It rejected the attention merchant model, despite the obvious revenue potential. There was, perhaps, something natural to that decision, given that its DVD service was not ad-driven but by subscription. Still, the call was not inevitable. When asked to explain the company's aversion to advertising, Reed Hastings, Netflix's CEO, described it as part of a strategy of putting the viewer "in control of the experience."[2] Therefore, he said, "It's fundamental to that control orientation that we don't cram advertisements down people's throats."

The intuition was, in retrospect, informed by a deeper insight than most anyone knew at the time. In business, there is always potential to gain something by zigging while everyone else is zagging. With everyone else—including its closest rival, Hulu, a joint venture of other media companies—reliant on advertising, Netflix could distinguish itself by offering a different kind of experience. But there was something more; in a sense, Netflix rediscovered a lost trove of human attention; not the splintered and fleeting kind being plundered by the web and cable TV, but deeper, sustained attention. It was a rich vein indeed, filled with an evident hunger for more engaging, immersive content. Netflix wasn't the only one providing it, but it was the only Internet company.

In 2013, when *House of Cards* premiered, Netflix made a splash by releasing all thirteen episodes of *House of Cards* at once. What it didn't necessarily predict was the binging. The logical opposite of web or channel surfing, binging does not involve idly flipping through stuff, but engaging so deeply with a program that one can watch hours and hours in one sitting; the experience goes far beyond that of watching a feature-length film, instead competing with experiences like attending a performance of Wagner's Ring Cycle. *House of Cards* was thirteen hours long, yet Netflix reported that thousands of viewers consumed it in one gulp over the weekend of its release.*

A Netflix poll of TV streamers found that 61 percent defined their viewing style as binge watching, which meant two to six episodes at a sitting. Grant McCracken, a cultural anthropologist paid by Netflix to investigate (and promote) the habit, reported that "TV viewers are no longer zoning out as a way to forget about their day, they are tuning in, on their own schedule, to a different world. Getting immersed in multiple episodes or even multiple seasons of a show over a few weeks is a new kind of escapism that is especially welcomed today."[3] By that, he meant in the context of everything else having become crazy-making.

---

* The first uses of "binge watching," "binge viewing," and other variants date to the late 1990s on online user forums, perhaps for the *X-Files*. In 1996, a fan looking for VHS tapes of the show wrote: "There are three of us who all got hooked at the same time, so I'd predict that there'd be some MASSIVE binge watching right away! :-)." The phrase, however, only began to show up in mainstream sources in 2003; Emily Nussbaum, of *The New York Times,* wrote an article on the growing popularity of TV show DVDs. "DVD's are perfect for fast-paced arc shows like '24,' increasing the intensity of the action and introducing the sickly pleasures of binge-viewing." But the word became widely used in 2013 after Netflix began releasing the full seasons at once, prompting the *Oxford Dictionary* to add it to the language and also short-list it as "Word of the Year" (the ultimate winner was "selfie").

Netflix's success was a token of something unexpected despite having roots in the early 2000s. Television, the idiot box, the dreaded "unity machine," the reviled "boob tube," was declared by the smart money to be dead meat in the twenty-first century, destined perhaps to survive out of sheer inertia serving the poor and elderly shut-ins but eventually to go the way of the typewriter or horse and buggy. Always ahead of everyone in being wrong, the futurist George Gilder had published a book in 1990 entitled *Life After Television.* By 2007, even Damon Lindelof, co-creator of the hit series *Lost,* was boldly ready to wrongly proclaim that "television is dying."[4]

Many of the cable networks suffered from disenchantment caused by the slow surrender to pointless spectacle and inane personality. At the same time, however, the purveyors of high-quality, commercial-free programs—not only Netflix but HBO even earlier, as well as other networks like A&E and Showtime—began suddenly to prosper and attract audiences that approached the size of those attending prime time at its peak. HBO's wildly popular show *The Sopranos* had more than 18 million viewers per episode over the early 2000s; a decade on, the network's *Game of Thrones* would begin to reach 20 million per episode.

Of course, certain segments of the population had never really left television at all. As faithful, regular, and predictable as the prime-time audiences of the 1950s were lovers of baseball, American football, soccer, and other sports; in the United States and abroad, such broadcasts demonstrated an almost uncanny immunity to the laws governing other kinds of programming. Remember, *Amos 'n' Andy,* with 40 million listeners in 1932, would lose its entire audience not long after. *I Love Lucy,* among the most successful sitcoms in history, petered out after six seasons. Yet no such fading away has been detected among sports viewers, who renew themselves in every generation. Perhaps it is because in sports there is no abuse of one's attention, no jumping the shark. There may be long-term rises and declines in audiences, but overall, as ESPN's John Skipper put it, they are "shockingly reliable." In all other formats, however, attention and audiences were declining for free TV.

The diminuendo had even forced the traditional advertising industry to up its game over the decade's first century. In the long years of prime time's uncontested sovereignty, and before the remote control, viewers could be expected to sit through commercials or, at worst, go off to get a snack of something they were being shown. The remote had done some damage to that fixity, but now a veritable revolution was relocating real control and choice in the hand of the viewer—at first through DVRs and the effectively unbounded selection of digital channels, and then streaming. Faced with unprecedented competition, advertising, as in the 1980s, was forced to become more intrinsically entertaining in order to have any chance of being effective. Once again, a thousand and one experts trumpeted the necessity of creating ads that viewers actually wanted to watch.

But with so many ways of not watching advertisements, it was not enough to suppress increasing doubts as to whether anyone was actually watching the commercials. The industry also started returning to older strategies. Product placements became more common; late-night comedians incorporated products into their monologues. A show like *Portlandia,* a satire about earnest Oregonians, would begin incorporating Subaru into its skits, pursuant to a sponsorship contract. Shows also began to incorporate "live commercials," in which characters suddenly stop what they are doing and begin finding reason to speak on the merits of a product. It still wouldn't be enough to deter the hard-core ad-avoiders, but it cannot be denied that advertising, from the early 2000s onward, was trying much harder to be unavoidable and also likable.

But by far the most important innovation was the immersive, commercial-free television to which addled audiences bombarded from all sides were now flocking. A few clever producers like Tom Fontana, creator of HBO's *Oz,* and later David Chase, who conceived *The Sopranos,* were not only themselves attracted to the idea of making more filmic television, with psychological texture, but intuited that some viewers would be looking for a fully formed alternative reality they might enter for a time, a natural response when the built attentional environment becomes inhospitably chaotic. Indeed, what we witness in the disenchanted TV viewer is a return of something older—the deep, high-quality attention of motion picture viewers, those engrossed in a good book, or early television audiences, completely lost in the presentation. This is and always was the durable advantage of film and television, before the former was carved up by chase scenes and the latter by commercial breaks.

To pay this kind of attention can be rewarding. Here is the journalist Andrew Romano on his favorite viewing fare:

After watching *Game of Thrones* for a mere 30 seconds, my brain begins to produce the alpha waves typically associated with hazy, receptive states of consciousness, which are also generated during the "light hypnotic" stage of suggestion therapy. At the same time, my neurological activity switches from the left hemisphere to the right— that is, from the seat of logical thought to the seat of emotion. Whenever this shift takes place, my body is flooded with the natural opiates known as endorphins, which explains why viewers have repeatedly told scientists that they feel relaxed as soon as they switch on the television, and also why this same sense of relaxation tends to dissolve immediately after the set is turned off.[5]

If that sounds like an experience worth more than all the mindless diversions of free TV, it probably is. Buffeted by websites designed to distract, who-wants-to-be-a-celebrity, and the rest, streamed television—the convergence Microsoft could not quite foresee—was suddenly and unexpectedly emerging as a haven in the digital pandemonium. Television— which once had shown such promise to improve the human condition, but which had been kidnapped by commercial interests virtually at birth and raised to be the greatest attention harvester of the twentieth century and still the attention merchant's favorite servant—was now repaying the attention it attracts in a way that put the viewer's experience first.

To make things not for grazing but for deep engagement required a new set of narrative strategies, though it was possible to make such television at various levels of quality and sophistication, depending on what the viewer sought. So it had been, too, with the new idiom's progenitors, feature film and even the Victorian novel. While *House of Cards* might have made binging mainstream, in the decade before, writers of shows were inventing what Vince Gilligan (of *Breaking Bad*) termed the "hyperserial." Unlike the dramatic series of old, this kind made sense only to those who committed to every episode and indeed multiple seasons of viewing.

For television, this change was radical. Let us remember that back in the 1950s, early programs—variety shows mainly—lacked plots altogether. The first plotted shows were, in the language of programming, "episodic." And so a viewer could tune in to any episode of *I Love Lucy,* or *Gilligan's Island,* knowing that only the plot was (in the first case) breaking into show business or (in the second case) getting off the island; any particular episode was merely a freestanding enactment of that story line, the principal aim being to showcase the characters, who, oddly, never learned. At the end of every episode (or, in an exceptional case, every few) the show would reset to its eternal starting point, like a video game returning to its starting screen for a new player.

In a hyperserial, the plot, like that of a long film or novel, has more of the flow of life. Each installment has its consequences; characters might disappear or reappear; a larger story is actually told. The press of characters and incident can vary; some hyperserials, like some lives, are easier to drop in to than others. But like any good story they are nearly impossible to understand from the middle.

That good storytelling should have emerged as a priority is perhaps the most dramatic statement one could make about what was happening to television, although its appearance attests a potential that the medium always possessed. That expression of this potential was first undertaken by shows that had eliminated commercials gives some indication of what the attention merchants have to answer for. That it took so long made one wonder why we had put up with anything else for so many years.

CHAPTER 28

WHO'S BOSS HERE?

On June 1, 2015, Tim Cook, CEO of Apple, the world's most valuable company, gave a speech at the annual dinner of a small Washington nonprofit named EPIC, the Electronic Privacy Information Center. Apple's leaders almost never give speeches in Washington, making Cook's appearance something of a surprise; though to be fair, he didn't actually show up at the dinner, but rather videoconferenced his way in. All the same, even more surprising was what he had to say. "I'm speaking to you from Silicon Valley, where some of the most prominent and successful companies have built their businesses by lulling their customers into complacency about their personal information," said Cook. "They're gobbling up everything they can learn about you and trying to monetize it. We think that's wrong."[1]

Cook proceeded to lay into the very foundation of the attention merchant's model, which, since the early 2000s, had become dominant on the web. "You might like these so-called free services, but we don't think they're worth having your email, your search history and now even your family photos data mined and sold off for god knows what advertising purpose. And we think someday, customers will see this for what it is."[2] There was reason to suppose so, since "[a] few years ago, users of Internet services began to realize that when an online service is free, you're not the customer. You're the product."[3]

That phrase was, nearly verbatim, what critics had been saying about all advertising-supported media for decades. "In selling commercial time to advertisers to sell products," wrote Robin Anderson in the 1990s, "broadcasters are also selling a product—their audiences."[4] Richard Serra, the artist and cultural critic, put it this way in 1973: "Television delivers people to an advertiser. . . . It is the consumer who is consumed. . . . You are delivered to the advertiser who is the customer. He consumes you."[5]

At the dinner, Cook's remarks were roundly applauded by the privacy advocates in attendance. They elicited less positive responses elsewhere. *The New York Times* accused Cook of ignoring "the substantial benefits that free, ad-supported services have brought to consumers worldwide."[6] Mark Zuckerberg, CEO of Facebook, shot back, too. "What, you think because you're paying Apple that you're somehow in alignment with them? If you were in alignment with them, then they'd make their products a lot cheaper!"[7] Cook was not claiming that Apple maximized value for what it charged, but then he had not appeared there to praise his own business model, only to bury someone else's. It didn't take an MBA to notice that Apple's defense of individual privacy was also an assault on the principal revenue scheme of its competitors.

Although it was a hardly subtle indictment of Facebook and Google, Cook's speech was also aimed at the entire web and what it had become. For behind the scenes, Apple had grown impatient with the practices of those publishing content on the web; they were loading up their sites with bloated advertisements, complex tracking technology, and other junk that was making the mobile web an unattractive and unpleasant experience. Sites froze, or were so crowded with come-ons that one could hardly find what one came to them for. None of it enhanced the use of Apple's devices.

The web, in theory, belongs to everyone, so no one likes an 800-pound gorilla telling them what to do there. But while Apple could be constitutionally controlling to a fault, in this case the wish to control the experience of its iPhone and iPad was a popular one. For as Apple had noticed, thanks to out-of-control advertising the mobile web was burning through the data plans, the battery life, not to mention the attention that all rightly belonged to its users, and violating their privacy for good measure. As the owner of the platform, and a company with no qualms about throwing its weight around, Apple was in a position to do something about the mobile web. Few who weren't attention merchants had cause to complain.

Just a few days after Cook's speech, the company, quietly and wholly without ceremony, released what one analyst called its "atomic bomb." Buried in the documentation of its upcoming release of iOS 9, its latest operating system for the iPhone and iPad, Apple had included the following:

> The new Safari release brings Content Blocking Safari Extensions to iOS. Content Blocking gives your extensions a fast and efficient way to block cookies, images, resources, pop-ups, and other content.[8]

The nonprofit Nieman Lab was the first to realize what this really meant: "Adblocking is coming to the iPhone."[9] An adblocker is a program that detects that a web page carries advertisements—say, pop-ups, embedded audio and video, etc.—and prevents them from loading; it also usually blocks "tracking," that is, the sending of information to attention merchants like Google or Facebook, who build profiles of you based on where you go online. An iPhone that blocks ads works better and faster, consuming less power and bandwidth. It also chokes off the business model that has dominated the web ever since the year 2000 or so.

When September arrived, and with it, Apple's new operating system, it was worse than the web publishers and advertisers could have imagined. Adblockers, overnight, became far and away the most popular of apps. Millions of copies were downloaded, turning what had been a trend into a torrent. By the end of the year, an estimated 100 to 200 million Americans were now using some kind of adblocker some of the time. Apple's plot, if such it was, had paid off masterfully.

Attention merchants, advertisers, every company that hoped to make money reselling attention on the mobile web reacted to Apple's move with a mixture of anger, fear, and moral indignation. "Ad blocking is robbery, plain and simple," opined *Ad Age*.[10] "Ad-blocking threatens democracy," pronounced the president of the Newspaper Association of America; the industry also released a study estimating that $22 billion of revenue was being destroyed and warned of far worse.[11] "Every time you block an ad," wrote another editor, "what you're really blocking is food from entering a child's mouth."[12]

Mostly, the developers and users of adblockers were unfazed. One developer wrote that "web advertising and behavioral tracking are out of control. They're unacceptably creepy, bloated, annoying, and insecure, and they're getting worse at an alarming pace."[13] Others called it the last chance to fight what the web had become. James Williams, the Oxford ethicist, wrote that "ad blockers are one of the few tools that we as users have if we want to push back against the perverse design logic that has cannibalized the soul of the Web."[14]

The problem for the attention merchants is that once people get used to avoiding advertisements, it's hard to accept the terms of the old arrangement. The scales fall from one's eyes, and sitting there staring at product pitches doesn't make sense any longer. As Michael Wolff put it, "If people can avoid advertising, they do. And further: as soon as they do figure out how to circumvent advertising, they don't go back to it."[15]

Apple's maneuvers can be understood as a policing of its platform, which depends on payment. Hence, it could be seen taking the moral high ground on behalf of users, while also damaging its greatest rival, Google, at its point of greatest vulnerability. The adblocking campaign was, in the lingo, a twofer.

As for Google, it was left fighting with one hand tied behind its back; for it was now being haunted by the choice it had made at that fork in the road in 2000, when it went the way of the attention merchant. Android is, of course, a competitor of the iPhone, and thus Google's prime channel for accessing the minds of mobile users, a must-win cohort. But being wedded to an advertising model, Google was in no position to follow Apple and make Android the best experience it possibly could be. For the company was in a bind of its own making, stuck serving two masters, trying to enact the attention merchant's eternal balancing act between advertisers and users, at a time when the latter were losing patience.

In 1998, Larry Page and Sergey Brin had written that reliance on advertising would inevitably make it difficult to create the best possible product; in the late 2010s, in competition with Apple, they faced their own prophecy. Since the death of its founder, Steve Jobs, Apple had softened somewhat in its opposition to open platforms, and was able to use its enormous profits to build better products. Google had bested rivals like Yahoo!, who were hamstrung by their own excessive reliance on advertising, but over the late 2010s, in competition with Apple, Google got a taste of its own medicine.

Whether Apple was truly serving its users and business model and only incidentally exploiting Google's Achilles' heel is a matter of debate. But there is no doubt that the sentiment of revolt against the shabbiness of the mobile web was coming from an even deeper and broader place. Writing in the 1960s, Marshall McLuhan described the media as "technological extensions of man"; in the 2010s it had become more obvious than ever that technologies like the smartphone are not merely extensions but technological prosthetics, enhancements of our own capacities, which, by virtue of being constantly attached to us or present on our bodies, become a part of us. Whether called a "phone" or a "watch," the fact remains that "wearables" take the check-in habit begun with email and turn it into something akin to a bodily function, even as they measure the bodily functions that naturally occur. The ambitious efforts over the mid-2010s to cover the eyes, and create virtual realities, only served as a further example; a well-known photo of Mark Zuckerberg grinning as he strolled past hundreds of begoggled users caused no little alarm. It seems only natural that the closer a technology feels to being part of us, the more important that we trust it; the same goes for someone who is creating a virtual reality for you to inhabit. And so, in the coming decade, the attention merchants will need to tread very lightly as they come as close as one can to the human body. Nonetheless, adaptation is a remarkable thing, and if our history has shown anything, it is that what seems shocking to one generation is soon taken for granted by the next.

THE TEMENOS

Was it, maybe, all a dream? By the late 2010s, for the rich or tech-savvy cord-cutters, it could feel that way, as they watched commercial-free television on Netflix or Amazon, read eBooks or browsed the web on an ad-blocked phone or computer. It was quite possible to think that the reign of the attention merchants had been an aberration, a sordid interval on the way to a better world, albeit a spell that lasted a century. Perhaps the long, dark night of attention arbitrage, even advertising itself—by which our very awareness was bought cheap and sold at a markup—was finally coming to an end. Certainly among its most desired target demographics, the young and the affluent, advertising seemed to become one more avoidable toxin in the healthy lifestyle, another twentieth-century invention mistakenly assumed to be harmless, like sugary soft drinks, processed foods, and tanning beds.

An overstatement, perhaps. Still, the new millennium's growing distaste for advertising and unprecedented willingness to pay for peace and quiet were hardly good news for the attention merchants or their brokers in the advertising industry. As Michael Wolff points out, television, as a whole, was now reliant on subscription charges for 50 percent of its revenue, an unheard-of portion; meanwhile, the mobile web was under siege, and the tethered web was being forgotten. These trends, coinciding with a growing sense that media had overtaxed our attentions to the point of crisis, certainly made it look as if the attention merchant had nowhere left to go.

But taking the long view, as our story does, such revolts against advertising must be seen as part of a larger dynamic. We are speaking, after all, of an industry left for dead at least four separate times over the past hundred years. Again and again, it has seemed as if the party was over, that consumers had fled once and for all, and yet the attention merchants have always found a way to overgrow the bright new machines that seemed to be hacking through the old-growth foliage. The 1960s, the very zenith of anticommercialism, remarkably left the attention merchants stronger than they'd ever been. The World Wide Web, designed by research scientists, was supposed to strike a fatal blow against commercialism in communications, but these things have a logic of their own: Advertising always becomes less annoying and intrusive, and people rediscover their taste for "free" stuff. In this long view, it is hard to imagine that a business with such a marvelously simple premise— capture people's attention in exchange for a little fun and then resell it to firms sponsoring the amusement—might simply wither away.

What the cord-cutters and ad-avoiders of the 2010s were doing was important but not new; rather, it was part of the general and continuous effort to police our deal with the attention merchants, whether the content is the CBS Evening News or hamster videos on YouTube. Since the attention industry, like any other, demands constant growth, the terms of the deal are constantly evolving, usually to our disadvantage, with more attention seized for less diversion in return. Periodic revolts against the arrangement are therefore not just predictable but necessary. For if the attention economy is to work to our benefit (and not merely exploit us), we need to be vigilant about its operation and active in expressing our displeasure at its degrading tendencies. In some cases, as we've seen, its worst excesses may have no remedy but law.

The most urgent question raised by this book does not, however, relate to the eternal debate over whether advertising is good, bad, or a necessary evil. The most pressing question in our times is not *how* the attention merchant should conduct business, but *where* and *when*. Our society has been woefully negligent about what in other contexts we would call the rules of zoning, the regulation of commercial activity where we live, figuratively and literally. It is a question that goes to the heart of how we value what used to be called our private lives.

This book begins with a story about the growth of advertising in public schools, a new phenomenon based on the unstated premise that every sliver of our attention is fair game for commercial exploitation. That norm, as we've seen, has spread slowly but inexorably over the past century, until it has become a default position respecting virtually every bit of time and space we occupy. It is shocking how little it has been necessary to defend the sheer reach of the attention merchant into the entirety of our lived experience. Formerly the state of technology imposed its own limits, but at a time when these limits have been effectively eliminated, it is for us to ask some fundamental questions: Do we draw any lines between the private and the commercial? If so, what times and spaces should we consider as too valuable, personal, or sacrosanct for the usual onslaught?

Custom answered these questions in previous times, but just as technology has transcended its former limitations, we seem less moved by the imperatives of tradition. At one time, tradition set limits on where people could be intruded upon and when. Even with the necessary technology, it was not always so easy to reach people in their homes, let alone while walking or in a taxi. For the majority, religious practice used to define certain inviolable spaces and moments. Less formal norms, like the time reserved for family meals, exerted considerable force as well. In this world, privacy was the default, commercial intrusions the exception. And while there was much about the old reality that could be inconvenient or frustrating, it had the advantage of automatically creating protected spaces, with their salutary effects.

The past half century has been an age of unprecedented individualism, allowing us to live in all sorts of ways that were not possible before. The power we have been given to construct our attentional lives is an underappreciated example. Even while waiting for the dentist, we have the world at our finger tips: we can check mail, browse our favorite sites, play games, and watch movies, where once we had to content ourselves with a stack of old magazines. But with the new horizon of possibilities has also come the erosion of private life's perimeter. And so it is a bit of a paradox that in having so thoroughly individualized our attentional lives we should wind up being less ourselves and more in thrall to our various media and devices. Without express consent, most of us have passively opened ourselves up to the commercial exploitation of our attention just about anywhere and anytime. If there is to be some scheme of zoning to stem this sprawl, it will need to be mostly an act of will on the part of the individual.

What is called for might be termed a human reclamation project. For comparison, consider the sort of effort undertaken to reclaim some (other) natural resource, as when returning the land under an abandoned parking lot to wilderness. Over the coming century, the most vital human resource in need of conservation and protection is likely to be our own consciousness and mental space. In practice, a movement might begin with individuals making incremental changes, ones as simple as setting aside blocks of time, like the weekend, to be spent beyond the reach of the attention merchants. The first stirrings can be seen in the existing practices of "unplugging" or taking "digital Sabbaths." The same impulse can lead also to reclaiming more physical sanctuaries, not only the writer's backyard shed, but the classroom, the office, and the home, as well—any place where we mean to interact with one another or achieve something we know requires a serious level of concentration. In this way, the practice starts paying communal dividends as well as profiting the individual.

While the goals of reclaiming our time and attention are easy to praise, they can prove surprisingly difficult to achieve. Even for a weekend, it can be painful to resist deeply ingrained habits like checking email, Facebook, and other social media; browsing random news stories, let alone more titillating clickbait; or flopping onto the couch to channel surf for a few hours. The difficulty reflects years of conditioning and the attention merchants' determination to maximize, by any means possible, the time spent with them. When engrossed in work, reading a book, or playing with children, we may as well be stealing by the attention merchants' lights. They want—need—us to be constantly poking around for dibs and dabs of their entertainment, to be tuned to commercial breaks in their programming, or to be catching up with friends in a manner that can also serve some branding effort.

If any practical motivation were needed to work through the discomfort of reclaiming the attention that is one's own, it is useful to consider the accruing costs of our failure to do so. Whatever our personal goals, the things we'd like to achieve, the goals of the attention merchants are generally at odds with ours. How often have you sat down with a plan, say, to write an email or buy one thing online, only to find yourself, hours later, wondering what happened? And what are the costs to a society of an entire population conditioned to spend so much of their waking lives not in concentration and focus but rather in fragmentary awareness and subject to constant interruption? In this respect our lives have become the very opposite of those cultivated by the monastics, whether in the East or the West, whose aim was precisely to reap the fruits of deep and concentrated attention. What an irony it is that the lamentably scattered state of mind arises not from our own lack of drive but rather from the imperatives of one peculiar kind of commercial enterprise that is not even particularly profitable much of the time. The rest of the private sector may well have as much cause for complaint as the individual and society. It would no doubt be shocking to reckon the macroeconomic price of all our time spent with the attention merchants, if only to alert us to the drag on our own productivity quotient, the economist's measure of all our efforts.

At bottom, whether we acknowledge it or not, the attention merchants have come to play an important part in setting the course of our lives and consequently the future of the human race, insofar as that future will be nothing more than the running total of our individual mental states. Does that sound like exaggeration? It was William James, the great pragmatist philosopher, who, having lived and died before the flowering of the attention industry, held that our life experience would ultimately amount to whatever we had paid attention to. At stake, then, is something akin to how one's life is lived. That, if nothing else, ought to compel a greater scrutiny of the countless bargains to which we routinely submit, and, even more important, lead us to consider the necessity, at times, of not dealing at all. If we desire a future that avoids the enslavement of the propaganda state as well as the narcosis of the consumer and celebrity culture, we must first acknowledge the preciousness of our attention and resolve not to part with it as cheaply or unthinkingly as we so often have. And then we must act, individually and collectively, to make our attention our own again, and so reclaim ownership of the very experience of living.

ACKNOWLEDGMENTS

I wish to thank my editor, George Andreou, who brought focus and style to a scattered and awkward draft, and my agent, Tina Bennett, who does her job better than anyone I've met, and who intervened at important moments. Columbia Law School deans David Schizer and Gillian Lester provided enormous support for this work, as did my Columbia colleagues. Many of the ideas for this book were worked out in writings for *The New Yorker,* under Nick Thompson's editing, and at *The New Republic,* where James Burnett was my editor. Scott Hemphill and Kathryn Tucker were generous early readers, Philip Bobbitt helped set a tone, and Onil Bhattacharyya provided guidance at the end. Other helpful readers were Derek Slater, Jonathan Knee, Michael Wolff, and James Williams. My extended family also helped steer the book, especially Barbara Burton and Charles Judge, and my mother who helpfully panned the (original) introduction. I also thank audiences at Oxford Internet Institute, Yale Law School, Cleveland-Marshall Law School, the New American foundation, and Columbia Law School, where I presented early drafts. I thank the Columbia Journalism School and Dean Steve Coll as well. Early work also benefited from the Derek Brewer fellowship at Emmanuel College, Cambridge University.

I am grateful for help researching this book provided by Rebecca Shafer of the New America foundation, Chloe Nevitt of McGill, and at Columbia, Kathleen Farley, Tim Grey, Morgan Petkovich, Janice Lee, Erin Patricia Walsh, Greg Wolfe, Zoe Carpou, Patricia Haynes, Scott Yakaitis, Julia E. Murray, and Stephanie Wu. I am enormously grateful to the research librarians at Columbia Law School who hunted down some particularly obscure materials, especially related to Zenith and telepathy. Thanks also to Brenna McDuffie, Helen Tobin, Dani Toth, and other members of the Knopf publicity team. I am grateful to Jacqueline Gottlieb of the Kavli Institute for Brain Science who along with some of her students helped me better understand the science of attention.

I am most grateful to my loving wife and partner, Kate—an unfailingly enthusiastic supporter of this book who also put up with an awful lot along the way, including not just the usual obsessions but also a run for public office. And finally, to my dear daughter, Sierra, "without whose never-failing sympathy and encouragement this book might have been finished in half the time."

NOTES

CHAPTER 1: THE FIRST ATTENTION MERCHANTS

1. Sources for the rise of the *New York Sun* and its rivals include Frank O'Brien, *The Story of the Sun, New York, 1833–1918* (New York: George H. Doran, 1918); Matthew Goodman, *The Sun and the Moon: The Remarkable True Account of Hoaxers, Showmen, Dueling Journalists, and Lunar Man-Bats in Nineteenth Century New York* (New York: Basic Books, 2010). Other sources on the New York press of the 1830s include John D. Stevens, *Sensationalism and the New York Press* (New York: Columbia University Press, 1991); Lorman A. Ratner and Dwight L. Teeter Jr., *Fanatics and Fire-eaters: Newspapers and the Coming of the Civil War* (Urbana: University of Illinois Press, 2003).

2. Blair Converse. "The Beginnings of the Penny Press in New York" (MA thesis, University of Wisconsin, 1918); Leo Bogart, "The Business of Newspapers," in *Press and Public: Who Reads What, When, Where, and Why in American Newspapers* (Hillsdale, NJ: Lawrence Erlbaum Associates, 1989).

3. Day imported one more trick from Britain: hiring boys, some as young as five, as well as poor immigrants to hawk his papers in the street, shouting out the headlines, a preindustrial way of gathering attention. Supplied with 100 papers for 67 cents cash (or 75 cents credit), the boys were guaranteed a nice profit if they could sell out their supply.

4. The theory of a growing "public sphere" in the eighteenth and nineteenth centuries belongs to Jürgen Habermas, who premised it on the rise of newspaper reading, coffeehouse discussions, and other places for communications among members of the public. See also Jürgen Habermas, *The Structural Transformation of the Public Sphere*, trans. Thomas Burger (Cambridge, MA: MIT Press, 1991); and Robert E.

Park, "Sociology and the Social Sciences: The Social Organism and the Collective Mind," *American Journal of Sociology* 27 (1921).

5. For more on cognitive models on attention, see Michael I. Posner and Charles R. R. Snyder, "Attention and Cognitive Control," in *Information Processing and Cognition: The Loyola Symposium*, ed. R. L. Solso (Hillsdale, NJ: Lawrence Erlbaum Associates, 1975).

6. The original text of the story has since been reprinted. See Richard Adams Locke and Joseph Nicolas Nicollet, *The Moon Hoax; or, A Discovery That the Moon Has a Vast Population of Human Beings* (New York: William Gowens, 1859), 8.

7. H. Hazel Hahn, *Scenes of Parisian Modernity: Culture and Consumption in the Nineteenth Century*, 189 (New York: Palgrave Macmillan, 2009); and Alexander Cowan and Jill Steward, eds., *The City and the Senses: Urban Culture Since 1500* (Burlington, VT: Ashgate Publishing, 2007), 167–70.

8. The great William James understood how important is the ability to ignore, when in 1890, he wrote that attention "is the taking possession by the mind, in clear and vivid form, of one out of what seem several simultaneously possible objects or trains of thought" and that it "implies withdrawal from some things in order to deal effectively with others." William James, *The Principles of Psychology*, vol. 1 (New York: Henry Holt and Co., 1890), 403–4.

9. Guus Pijpers, "Brain Matters," in *Information Overload: A System for Better Managing Everyday Data* (Hoboken, NJ: John Wiley & Sons, 2010); E. Bruce Goldstein, *Cognitive Psychology: Connecting Mind, Research and Everyday Experience*, 4th ed. (Boston: Cengage Learning, 2015).

10. H. Hazel Hahn, "Street Picturesque: Advertising in Paris, 1830–1914" (PhD diss., University of California, Berkeley, 1997). See also "A Brief History of the Poster," International Poster Gallery, accessed November 25, 2015, http://www.internationalposter.com/about-poster-art/a-brief-history-of.aspx.

11. Karl Marx and Friedrich Engels, *The Communist Manifesto* (Minneapolis: Filiquarian Publishing, 2005), 10.

12. Terry E. O'Reilly and Mike Tennant, *The Age of Persuasion: How Marketing Ate Our Culture* (Toronto: Random House of Canada, 2009), 35–40.

CHAPTER 2: THE ALCHEMIST

1. Claude C. Hopkins, *My Life in Advertising* (New York: Harper & Brothers, 1917), 202. Though an autobiography, and therefore anecdotal in nature, Hopkins claims that his book was primarily intended to serve not "as a personal history, but as a business story" to coach others in the art of advertising.

2. For more detailed information about Hopkins, see Stephen R. Fox, *The Mirror Makers: A History of American Advertising and Its Creators* (New York: William Morrow, 1984), 52.

3. Drayton Bird, *Commonsense Direct and Digital Marketing* (London: Kogan Page, 2007), 336.

4. Hopkins had first been hired as assistant bookkeeper, eventually becoming head bookkeeper for the Bissell Carpet Sweeper Company. Later, he had come across an inadequate advertising pamphlet for carpet sweepers and requested to re-create it. The company eventually adopted Hopkins's advertising pamphlet. Subsequently, he focused on ways to increase product demand and recognized that Christmas was fast approaching. For this reason, Hopkins designed a campaign that would advertise the

carpet sweepers as "the Queen of Christmas Presents." For more information, see Jeffrey L. Cruikshank and Arthur W. Schultz, *The Man Who Sold America: The Amazing (but True!) Story of Albert D. Lasker and the Creation of the Advertising Century* (Boston: Harvard Business Review Press, 2010); and Robert Schorman, "Claude Hopkins, Earnest Calkins, Bissell Carpet Sweepers and the Birth of Modern Advertising," *Journal of the Gilded Age and Progressive Era* (2008).

5. See Philip M. Taylor, *The Projection of Britain: British Overseas Publicity and Propaganda, 1919–1939* (Cambridge, UK: Cambridge University Press, 1981), 78, for more information on perspectives of publicity and propaganda during the era.

6. Phillip Schaff, ed., *The Ante-Nicene Fathers* (Peabody, MA: Hendrickson Publishers, 2004).

7. Paul F. Bradshaw, *Early Christian Worship: A Basic Introduction to Ideas and Practice* (Collegeville, MN: Liturgical Press, 1996), 73.

8. According to a recent Pew study, one fifth of the U.S. public do not affiliate with religion, increasing just over 15 percent from five years prior. The growth of these religiously unaffiliated Americans, known as the "nones," likely results from generational displacement. For more information, as well as leading theories that attempt to explain the rise of the "nones," see " 'Nones' on the Rise," Pew Research Center, last modified October 9, 2012, http://www.pewforum.org/2012/10/09/nones-on-the-rise/; and "A Closer Look at America's Rapidly Growing Religious 'Nones,' " Pew Research Center, last modified May 13, 2015, http://www.pewresearch.org/fact-tank/2015/05/13/a-closer-look-at-americas-rapidly-growing-religious-nones/.

9. At Dr. Shoop's he met and likely worked with a Canadian copywriter named John C. Kennedy. Kennedy would later be remembered as the inventor of something called "reason-why" advertising, though early advertising lore, like early advertising itself, is full of spurious claims. (For his part, Kennedy claimed to be a former Royal Canadian Mountie, though doubts have been raised about the truth of that as well.)

10. For images of the described advertisements Kickapoo Indian Medicine Co.'s Sagwa and Clark Stanley's Snake Oil, among other similar medical remedy advertisements from the late 1800s and early 1900s, see "Here Today, Here Tomorrow: Medical Show," U.S. National Library of Medicine, last modified September 21, 2011, https://www.nlm.nih.gov/exhibition/ephemera/medshow.html.

11. The full advertisement can be found in the *Farmers' Review,* published on January 1, 1902. See "Farmers' Review, 1 January 1902," Illinois Digital Newspaper Collections, accessed January 26, 2016, http://idnc.library.illinois.edu/cgi-bin/illinois?a=d&d=FFR19020101.2.37.

12. Dan Hurley, *Natural Causes: Death, Lies, and Policies in America's Herbal Supplement Industry* (New York: Broadway Books, 2006), 24. It appears, however, that the original fascination with snake oil followed from the arrival of the Chinese railroad workers in the 1800s, who had brought with them snake oil. The remedy was made from the oil of the Chinese water snake, which was rich in omega-3 acids and reduced inflammation of the joints. Eventually, the remedy would be shared with Americans, but with the lack of Chinese water snakes in the U.S., many wondered how they would be able to create their own version. Ultimately, Clark Stanley touted the healing power of the rattlesnake, without reference to the original Chinese snake oil. For more information on the history of snake oil, see Lakshmi Gandhi, "A History of 'Snake Oil Salesman,' " NPR, August 26, 2013, http://www.npr.org/sections/codeswitch/2013/08/26/215761377/a-history-of-snake-oil-salesmen.

13. This Liquozone ad, including a coupon for a free bottle, appeared in many newspapers. For an example, see *T.P.'s Weekly* 6 (December 1, 1905).

14. Within a year of running the first ad for Liquozone, the company received over 1.5 million requests for a free bottle. While the average cost per request was only 18 cents, the average sale per request was 91 cents.

15. This claim by Liquozone was later featured in Samuel Hopkins Adams's article "Liquozone," part of a series exposing the fraudulent patent medicine industry. Samuel Hopkins Adams, *The Great American Fraud* (New York: P. F. Collier & Son, 1906).

16. Samuel V. Kennedy, *Samuel Hopkins Adams and the Business of Writing* (Syracuse: Syracuse University Press, 1999).

17. Samuel Hopkins Adams, "Medical Support of Nostrums," *Maryland Medical Journal* 49 (1906). Hopkins urged those investigating patent medicine to make sure that their attacks on the industry were careful and supported by the truth, or else they would lose public confidence.

18. Samuel Hopkins Adams, *The Great American Fraud, supra.*

19. In fact, the six guinea pigs inoculated with diphtheria bacilli and treated with Liquozone died within seventy-two hours, whereas two out of three untreated guinea pigs remained alive after receiving the same amount of diphtheria culture.

20. Theodore Roosevelt, "Applied Ethics in Journalism," *The Outlook,* April 15, 1911, 807.

21. U.S. Food and Drug Administration, "Notices of Judgment Under the Food and Drugs Act," N.J. 4944 (1918).

22. Hopkins gave a speech before the Sphinx Club of New York on January 14, 1909, confessing, "Perhaps you, as I, have longed to be a Jack London. It is a happy position where one may contribute to the amusement of mankind. Such men are known and applauded. They are welcomed and wanted, for they lift the clouds of care. But those who know us, know us only as searchers after others' dollars." Stephen R. Fox, *The Mirror Makers: A History of American Advertising and Its Creators* (Chicago: University of Illinois Press, 1997).

CHAPTER 3: FOR KING AND COUNTRY

1. John Oakes, *Kitchener's Lost Boys: From the Playing Fields to the Killing Fields* (Stroud, UK: History Press, 2009).

2. Henry D. Davray, *Lord Kitchener: His Work and His Prestige* (London: T. F. Unwin Limited, 1917), 96; Edmund Burke, *The Annual Register,* Vol. 158 (London: Longmans, Green, 1917).

3. Niall Ferguson, *Empire: The Rise and Demise of the British World Order and the Lessons for Global Power* (New York: Basic Books, 2004), 242. See also John Oakes, *Kitchener's Lost Boys: From the Playing Fields to the Killing Fields* (Stroud, UK: History Press, 2009).

4. Bernard Lewis, *Swansea in the Great War* (Barnsley, UK: Pen & Sword Books, 2014); "Talk: Otto von Bismarck," last modified July 27, 2015, www.wikiquote.org/wiki/Talk:Otto_von_Bismarck. For more facts about the German army, see Spencer C. Tucker and Priscilla Roberts, eds., *The Encyclopedia of World War I* (Santa Barbara: ABC-CLIO, 2005).

5. This quote is from Geraldine M. Boylan, "Wilfred Owen's Response to Propaganda, Patriotism and the Language of War," *Revista Canaria de Estudios Ingleses* 38 (1999). See also Sir George Arthur, *Life of Lord Kitchener,* Vol. 3 (New York: Macmillan, 1920); and Robert K. Johns, *Battle Beneath the Trenches: The Cornish Miners of 251 Tunnelling Company RE* (Barnsley, UK: Pen & Sword Books, 2015).

6. Philip M. Taylor, *The Projection of Britain* (New York: Cambridge University Press, 1981), 11.

7. Mark C. Miller, "Introduction," in *Propaganda* (New York: Ig Publishing, 2005).

8. An image of the recruiting poster and the statistics on the campaign's success can be found at Peter Simkins, *Kitchener's Army: The Raising of the New Armies, 1914–1916* (Barnsley: Pen & Sword Books, 2007), 32. For more general discussion on Kitchener's call to arms, see Sir George Arthur, *Life of Lord Kitchener*, Vol. 3 (New York: Macmillan, 1920). For statistics on the size of the active American army in 2015, see Jim Tice, "Active Army Drops Below 500,000 Soldiers," ArmyTimes, February 5, 2015, www.armytimes.com/story/military/careers/army/2015/02/05/active-army-drops-below-500000-soldiers/22922649/.

9. These statistics were drawn from Dr. Spencer C. Tucker, ed., *World War I: The Definitive Encyclopedia and Document Collection*, Vol. 1: A–C (Santa Barbara: ABC-CLIO, 2014); and Alan G. V. Simmonds, *Britain and World War One* (New York: Routledge, 2012). For descriptions and images of several posters created for the campaign, see John Christopher, *British Posters of the First World War* (Stroud, UK: Amberley Publishing, 2014).

10. This quote, by Private Thomas McIndoe of 12th Battalion, Middlesex Regiment, can be found in Max Arthur, *Forgotten Voice of the Great War* (London: Random House, 2003), 9. The poster can be found at *Britons. Join Your Country's Army,* Imperial War Museum, Art.IWM PST 2734, www.iwm.org.uk/collections/item/object/16577.

11. John Allison, *World War I and the Origins of Nazi Propaganda,* 39 Southern Academic Report (Birmingham, AL: Birmingham-Southern College, 1993).

12. *The New York Times Current History of the European War,* Vol. 1: August–December 1914 (New York: New York Times Co., 1917), 106.

13. Catriona Pennell, *A Kingdom United: Popular Responses to the Outbreak of the First World War in Britain and Ireland* (New York: Oxford University Press, 2012), 60.

14. John R. Currie and Alexander G. Mearns, *Manual of Public Health: Hygiene* (Baltimore: Williams & Wilkins, 1948). These statistics were drawn from Alan Simmonds, *Britain and World War One.*

15. It should be noted that the effort had some private actors as well. A group known as the "Order of the White Feather," for instance, organized women to shame unenlisted men by presenting "slackers" with a white feather as a sign of cowardice.

16. Jacques Ellul, *Propaganda: The Formation of Men's Attitudes* (New York: Alfred A. Knopf, 1968).

17. The total number of volunteers enlisted in the army between August 1914 and the end of 1915 was higher than the total number of men enlisted by conscription in 1916 and 1917 combined. Simkins, *Kitchener's Army*; Jeff Hatwell, *No Ordinary Determination: Percy Black and Harry Murray of the First AIF* (Fremantle, Australia: Fremantle Press, 2014); Michael Sanders and Philip M. Taylor, *British Propaganda During the First World War, 1914–18* (Basingstoke, UK: Macmillan, 1982), 1.

18. Simkins, *Kitchener's Army*. For further discussion on the theories behind Lord Kitchener's death, see Colin Wilson, "The Mystery of Lord Kitchener's Death: Accident or Murder?," in *The Encyclopedia of Unsolved Mysteries* (New York: Diversion Publishing, 2015). More of Sir Arthur Conan Doyle's inscription can be found at Henry D. Davray, *Lord Kitchener: His Work and His Prestige* (London: T. F. Unwin Limited, 1917), 96–97.

19. Creel later went on to chronicle the domestic and overseas activities of the Committee on Public Information in *How We Advertised America* (New York: Harper & Brothers, 1920), 4.

20. Creel defended President Wilson's initial stance on the impending war during the 1916 presidential reelection as consistent with prior administrations that "had the courage to hold to the orderly diplomatic procedure of Washington and Adams, eventually winning justice without resort to war." In *Wilson and the Issues* (New York: Century Company, 1916).

21. Benito Mussolini, "Fascism," in *Princeton Readings in Political Thought*, Mitchell Cohen and Nicole Fermon, eds. (Princeton, NJ: Princeton University Press, 1996), 572.

22. George Creel, *Rebel at Large: Recollections of Fifty Crowded Years* (New York: G. P. Putnam's Sons, 1947), 158. In fact, Creel portrayed the purpose of the Committee on Public Information as one of information distribution, and rejected the notion of propaganda as used by the Germans, which "had come to be associated with lies and corruptions. Our effort was educational and informative only, for we had such confidence in our case as to feel that only fair presentation of its facts was necessary." *Complete Report of the Chairman of the Committee on Public Information* (Washington, DC: Government Printing Office, 1920).

23. Alan Axelrod, *Selling the Great War: The Making of American Propaganda* (New York: Palgrave Macmillan, 2009), 1.

24. Creel estimated the total audience members to whom the 505,190 speeches were made in the *Complete Report of the Chairman of the Committee on Public Information*. Creel calculated a total of 755,190 speeches made from the 505,190 speeches made during the regular campaign, 70,000 speeches made during the early campaigns, and 180,000 speeches in the concluding periods of the campaign. Approximately 202,454,514 audience members attended the regular campaign, with an additional 40,000,000 audience members in the early campaigns and 72,000,000 audience members in the concluding periods of the campaigns, totaling 134,454,514 audience members throughout the campaigns. Creel believed, however, that the numbers were far greater than the total 314,454,514 audience attendance calculated because he assumed that there were a considerable number of communities who did not report audience totals. As a result, Creel claimed that the incomplete or lack of reports "received justifies an estimate of final totals of a million speeches heard by four hundred million individuals." Though Creel's estimates were based on incomplete figures, they would not be completely unreasonable given that there had been a total of thirty-six distinct national campaigns and a growing attendance of moviegoers at the time.

25. James R. Mock and Cedric Larson, *Words That Won the War: The Story of the Committee on Public Information, 1917–1919* (New York: Russell & Russell, 1968), 152.

26. When creator James Montgomery Flagg later presented a copy of the poster to President Franklin D. Roosevelt, Flagg revealed that he had used himself as a model for the image of Uncle Sam to avoid paying a modeling fee. The real-life inspiration for Uncle Sam, however, is somewhat more ambiguous and still in dispute. One popular theory links the inspiration for the national symbol to Samuel Wilson, a meatpacker from Troy, New York, who during the War of 1812 supplied meat to the American troops. Complying with labeling requirements, Wilson marked each package with "E.A.-U.S.," which likely stood for Elbert Anderson Jr., Wilson's contractor, and United States. But local soldiers attributed the U.S. stamp as standing for "Uncle Sam" Wilson.

27. The case, *Debs v. U.S.,* was one of three cases where the Court had upheld the Espionage Act convictions during the war that restricted free speech. In preparing his speech at Canton, Ohio, Debs had been careful to comply with the act and claimed to deliver a speech predominantly for the purpose of "Socialism, its growth, and a proph-

ecy of its ultimate success." Nonetheless, the Court identified parts of the speech, which sympathized and praised individuals convicted for obstructing the enlistment service, and concluded that one could construe such parts as encouragement to those present to act similarly. As such, the Court found that "one purpose of the speech, whether incidental or not . . . was to oppose not only war in general but this war, and that the opposition was so expressed that its natural and intended effect would be to obstruct recruiting."

28. Walter Lippmann, *Public Opinion* (New York: Harcourt, Brace, 1922), 249.

29. The district court decision in the case, *Masses Publishing Co. v. Pattern,* rested on principles of the First Amendment, which the court reasoned, under certain circumstances, could protect certain seditious speech from government prosecution. The decision was subsequently reversed by the Court of Appeals.

30. In fact, the case, *Whitney v. California,* would later be explicitly overruled in *Brandenburg v. Ohio.*

31. Edward Bernays, *Propaganda* (New York: Ig Publishing, 1928), 37.

32. *Printers' Ink* 105 (New York: Decker Communications, 1918), 44.

CHAPTER 4: DEMAND ENGINEERING, SCIENTIFIC ADVERTISING,

AND WHAT WOMEN WANT

1. S. N. Behrman, "The Advertising Man," *The New Republic,* August 20, 1919.

2. Cynthia Clark Northrup, *The American Economy: A Historical Encyclopedia, Volume 1* (Santa Barbara: ABC-CLIO,2011).

3. Claude C. Hopkins, *Scientific Advertising* (Minneapolis: Filiquarian Publishing, 2007), 3.

4. For more information on C. C. Hopkins, see David Ogilvy, *Ogilvy on Advertising* (New York: Vintage, 1985).

5. Charles F. McGovern, *Sold American: Consumption and Citizenship, 1890–1945* (Chapel Hill: University of North Carolina Press, 2006), 25.

6. For more information on Albert Lasker and Claude Hopkins, see Edd Applegate, *The Rise of Advertising in the United States: A History of Innovation to 1960* (Lanham, MD: Scarecrow Press, 2012).

7. Advertising history is full of the reinvention of things, and some of these approaches and techniques had technically been invented in the late nineteenth century, at least in some form. However, they reached full institutionalization in the 1920s.

8. Cynthia B. Meyers, *A Word from Our Sponsor: Admen, Advertising, and the Golden Age of Radio* (New York: Fordham University Press, 2014).

9. Cruikshank and Schultz, *The Man who Sold America.*

10. American Academy of Pediatrics Committee on Nutrition, "The Use and Misuse of Fruit Juice in Pediatrics," *Pediatrics* 107, no. 5 (May 2001), 1211–12.

11. Linda S. Watts, Alice L. George, and Scott Beekman, *Social History of the United States: The 1920s* (Santa Barbara: ABC-CLIO, 2009).

12. James B. Twitchell, *Twenty Ads That Shook the World: The Century's Most Groundbreaking Advertising and How It Changed Us All* (New York: Three Rivers Press, 2000).

13. For an example of advertisements for Pepsodent, see "The Film Danger," advertisement, 1926, *Boys' Life.*

14. "Business: Coalition," *Time,* June 14, 1926.

15. Stephen R. Fox, *The Mirror Makers: A History of American Advertising and Its Creators*

(Urbana: University of Illinois Press, 1984), 100; Claude Hopkins, *My Life in Advertising and Scientific Advertising* (McGraw Hill Professional, 1966).

16. The phrase comes from a speech by John Watson in 1935: "Since the time of the serpent in the Garden of Eden influenced Eve and Eve in turn persuaded Adam, the world has tried to find out ways and means of controlling human behavior." Tom Farley and Deborah A. Cohen, *Prescription for a Healthy Nation: A New Approach to Improving Our Lives by Fixing Our Everyday World* (Boston: Beacon Press, 2005), 110.

17. Martin Kornberger, *Brand Society: How Brands Transform Management and Lifestyle* (Cambridge, UK: Cambridge University Press, 2010), 53; John B. Watson, "Psychology as the Behaviorist Views It," 20 *Psychological Review* 158-177 (1913), 249.

18. C. James Goodwin, *Research in Psychology: Methods and Design* (Hoboken, NJ: John Wiley & Sons, 2010).

19. Joel Spring, *Educating the Consumer-Citizen: A History of the Marriage of Schools, Advertising, and Media* (Mahwah, NJ: Lawrence Erlbaum Associates, 2008), 51; Farley and Cohen, *Prescription for a Healthy Nation*, 110.

20. John McDonough and Karen Egolf, *The Advertising Age Encyclopedia of Advertising* (Chicago: Fitzroy Dearborn Publishers, 2002); Fox, *The Mirror Makers*, 73.

21. Theodore F. MacManus, "The Underlying Principles of Good Copy," in *Masters of Advertising Copy* (New York: IPL, 2007).

22. Robert E. Ramsay, *Effective Direct Advertising: The Principles and Practice of Producing Direct Advertising for Distribution by Mail or Otherwise* (New York: D. Appleton, 1921); Lisa Rado, *Modernism, Gender, and Culture: A Cultural Studies Approach* (New York: Routledge, 2009).

23. Linda M. Scott, *Fresh Lipstick: Redressing Fashion and Feminism* (New York: Palgrave Macmillan, 2005).

24. Harry Tipper, *Advertising, Its Principles and Practice* (New York: The Ronald Press Co., 1919); Ramsay, *Effective Direct Advertising*, 554.

25. Denise Sutton, *Globalizing Ideal Beauty: How Female Copywriters of the J. Walter Thompson Advertising Agency Redefined Beauty for the Twentieth Century* (New York: Palgrave Macmillan, 2009), 27.

26. Christine Seifert, *Whoppers: History's Most Outrageous Lies and Liars* (New York: Houghton Mifflin Harcourt, 2015).

27. Kerry Segrave, *Endorsements in Advertising: A Social History* (Jefferson, NC: McFarland, 2005).

28. Alan Brinkley, *The Publisher* (New York: Alfred A. Knopf, 2010).

29. *Motion Picture*, Vol. 27, 1924, 67. For more information about Alva Belmont, see Sylvia D. Hoffert, *Alva Vanderbilt Belmont: Unlikely Champion of Women's Rights* (Indianapolis: Indiana University Press, 2012).

30. *Ladies' Home Journal*, Vol. 43, Part 2, 1926, 53.

31. Inger L. Stole, *Advertising on Trial: Consumer Activism and Corporate Public Relations in the 1930s* (Urbana: University of Illinois Press, 2005), 31.

CHAPTER 5: A LONG LUCKY RUN

1. Stephen R. Fox, *The Mirror Makers: A History of American Advertising and Its Creators* (Urbana: University of Illinois Press, 1997), 115.

2. John Gunther, *Taken at the Flood: The Story of Albert D. Lasker* (New York: Harper, 1960). While Gunther cites the advertising budget to have been $19 million in 1931,

various publications, ranging from *Life* and *Billboard,* reporting on George Washington Hill's death, claimed that Hill had spent as much as $20 million for advertising in 1931.

3. There is some historical dispute about the origin of the "It's toasted" tagline. A *Fortune* article seems to suggest that the slogan was first developed by Hopkins when working as a copywriter for Lord & Thomas. "How the Real Don Draper Sold Lucky Strikes," *Fortune,* September 19, 2010, http://archive.fortune.com/2010/09/17/news/companies/Mad-Men_Lucky-Strike_Lasker_excerpt.fortune/index.htm. However, the Stanford Research into Tobacco Advertising has an advertisement with the phrase "It's toasted" dating from 1917, which was long before Lord & Thomas signed on to the Lucky Strike account in 1925. The Stanford Collection of Tobacco advertisements can be found at http://tobacco.stanford.edu/tobacco_main/images.php?token2=fm_st319.php&token1=fm_img13529.php&theme_file=fm_mt010.php&theme_name=Fresh,%20Pure,%20Natural%20&%20Toasted&subtheme_name=It%27s%20Toasted. Moreover, George Washington Hill recounted in a 1938 issue of *Time* that his father had created the "It's toasted" phrase one day when discussing the tobacco cooking process. "ADVERTISING, It's Toasted," *Time,* December 5, 1938, http://content.time.com/time/magazine/article/0,9171,760432,00.html.

4. The copy is from a February 1931 advertisement in *Popular Science.*

5. The advertisement featured Helen Jepson, who was the lead soprano with the Metropolitan Opera from 1935 to 1941. She is quoted as saying that a "season of opera and concert means my voice and throat must be consistently in perfect condition. Therefore . . . it is all important to me that I be careful in choosing my cigarettes. I smoke Luckies . . . because I feel it is wise for me to choose a light smoke for my voice." The advertisement goes on to claim that Helen Jepson is one of a wide range of "leading artists of the radio, stage, screen and opera" in which "their voices are their fortunes" and the "throat protection of Luckies—a light smoke, free of certain harsh irritants removed by the exclusive process 'It's Toasted' . . . are gentle on the throat."

6. Lord & Thomas would send along the cartons to various physicians in the mid-1920s, requesting a response to whether "Lucky Strike Cigarettes . . . are less irritating to sensitive and tender throat than other cigarettes." The survey responses were then used to verify their claim that the "toasting process" made Luckies "less irritating." However there was no substantive proof of the claim. For more information on the relationship between the tobacco industry generally and the medical profession, see Martha N. Gardner and Allan M. Brandt, *The Doctors' Choice Is America's Choice* (*American Journal of Public Health,* 2006), http://www.ncbi.nlm.nih.gov/pmc/articles/PMC1470496/.

7. To further strengthen the credibility of the claim that the "toasting process" made Luckies "less irritating," as verified by the surveyed physicians, the advertisement claimed that "the figures quoted have been checked and certified to by LYBRAND, ROSS BROS AND MONTGOMERY. Accountants and Auditors." The advertisement, originally published in the *Magazine of Wall Street* on July 26, 1930, can be viewed at http://www.ncbi.nlm.nih.gov/pmc/articles/PMC1470496/figure/f1/.

8. Larry Tye, *The Father of Spin: Edward L. Bernays and the Birth of Public Relations* (New York: Henry Holt, 1998), 28.

9. The Sullivan Ordinance, which prohibited any manager or proprietor of a public space from permitting women to smoke therein, was conceived by "Little Tim" Sullivan, who believed that "the public sentiment [was] with him and that he [could] get away with his ordinance, even if it [did] infringe slightly upon woman's inherent and

constitutional rights." "Bars Woman Smokers," *Washington Post,* January 7, 1908. The ordinance was passed on January 21, 1908. "No Public Smoking by Women Now," *New York Times,* January 21, 1908.

The only reported incident in which a woman was arrested under the Sullivan Ordinance was Katie Mulcahey (twenty years old). She claimed that she's "got as much right to smoke as you have. . . . No man shall dictate to me." Nonetheless, Mulcahey was fined $5. "Arrested for Smoking," *New York Times,* January 23, 1908. Interestingly, the law was incorrectly applied, as the ordinance was to be applied against managers or proprietors of public spaces, not the women themselves, should they allow women to smoke.

While the ordinance was in effect for only a short period, there were continued efforts to prohibit women from smoking. For example, New York alderman Peter McGuinness attempted to renew the city ordinance that would prohibit women from smoking in public spaces to protect female morals. This sentiment was mirrored in a *Washington Post* editorial in 1914. "Women and Smoking Share Checkered History," *Wall Street Journal,* March 12, 2008. As one historian notes, public opinion was still against women smoking: "Between the lips of a woman, a cigarette was regarded as a badge of the stage adventuress, or certainly one inclined 'to the Bohemian persuasion.'" Gerard Petron, *The Great Seduction* (Atglen, PA: Schiffer, 1996), 22.

10. Among those present at the New York Easter Parade on April 1, 1929, were a list of debutantes. Bernays procured these names from the editor of *Vogue* magazine and convinced the women that their participation in publicly smoking on Fifth Avenue would lead to the expansion of women's rights. To learn more about Bernays's use of psychoanalysis and Freudian ideas in advertising and shaping consumer culture, see Edward L. Bernays, *Crystallizing Public Opinion* (New York: Boni & Liveright, 1923); and Lisa Held, "Psychoanalysis Shapes Consumer Culture," *American Psychological Association* 40 (2009).

11. For further detail about how Bernays prepared for the event, see Allan M. Brandt, *The Cigarette Century: The Rise, Fall, and Deadly Persistence of the Product That Defined America* (New York: Basic Books, 2007), 85.

12. One article in the *New York Evening World* reported that a woman, who had lit a Lucky Strike, "first got the idea for this campaign when a man on the street asked her to extinguish her cigarette because it embarrassed him. 'I talked it over with my friends, and we decided it was high time something was done about the situation.'" However, according to Larry Tye, biographer of Bernays, this woman, Bertha Hunt, was the secretary of Bernays and likely was speaking on his behalf. Larry Tye, *The Father of Spin: Edward L. Bernays and the Birth of Public Relations* (New York: Crown, 1998).

13. Noam Chomsky, "What Makes Mainstream Media Mainstream," *Z Magazine,* October 1997. Chomsky cites Bernays's *Propaganda* and overall work as "the main manual of the public relations industry."

14. "Easter Sun Finds the Past in Shadow at Modern Parade," *New York Times,* April 1, 1929.

15. Another popular variation of the slogan reads "When tempted—Reach for a Lucky Instead." It's possible that this slogan was a variation on a late 1800s advertisement in which Lydia Pinkham urged women to "reach for a vegetable instead of a sweet."

16. Claude C. Hopkins, *Scientific Advertising* (Minneapolis: Filiquarian Publishing, 2007).

17. Advertising for Lucky Strike cigarettes increased from $12 million in 1926 to $40 million in 1930. Bob Batchelor, *American Pop: Popular Culture Decade by Decade* (Westport, CT: Greenwood Press, 2009). Comparable percentages of GDP in 1929 include

42 percent personal consumption of goods, 32 percent of personal consumption of services, .05 percent gross private domestic investment of structures, .05 percent gross private domestic investment of equipment and software, .04 percent of residential investment, .1 percent of federal and state government expenditures and gross investments. See *Gross Domestic Product—Bureau of Economic Analysis*, https://www.bea.gov/scb/pdf/2012/08%20August/0812%20gdp-other%20nipa_series.pdf.

18. By itself, it went from $10.7 million in billings in 1920 to $37.5 million by the end of the decade, of which more than half was billed by the Women's Editorial Department. The apparent key to its giant billings was this department—as Landsdowne pointed out herself, "The success of the J. Walter Thompson Company had been in large measure due to the fact that we have concentrated and specialized upon products sold to women." Mark Pendergrast, *Uncommon Grounds: The History of Coffee and How It Transformed Our World* (New York: Basic Books, 2010).

19. The Ranch, despite its use as a vacation home for the Resors, was a full-time, self-sustaining operation. The Ranch included "sophisticated electrical generating facility, dairy barns, chicken and turkey coops, machine shops, and cattle and horse-related structures." See "The Snake River Ranch Historic District at the National Register of Historic Places," http://wyoshpo.state.wy.us/NationalRegister/Site.aspx?ID=453.

20. Lasker was Jewish and was therefore unable to attend the local golf club. It is possible for this reason that he created the golf club, among the many other structures, after purchasing the 380 acres of farmland in 1921.

21. Calvin Coolidge, "Address Before the American Association of Advertising Agencies," Washington, DC, October 27, 1926, http://memory.loc.gov/cgi-bin/query/r?ammem/cool:@field(DOCID+@lit(ms221)).

22. Claude Hopkins, *My Life in Advertising* (New York: Harper & Publishers, 1917).

CHAPTER 6: NOT WITH A BANG BUT WITH A WHIMPER

1. For more details about Schlink's work in the National Laboratories, see Rexmond C. Cochrane, *Measures for Progress: A History of the National Bureau of Standards* (Washington, DC: U.S. Department of Commerce, 1974).

2. Stuart Chase and Frederick J. Schlink, *Your Money's Worth: A Study in the Waste of the Consumer's Dollar* (New York: Macmillan, 1936), 258.

3. Ibid., 260. Chase and Schlink agreed that "Chase would do the writing while Schlink would provide the factual information" for the book, later described as "a blistering attack on U.S. business practices." Inger L. Stole, *Advertising on Trial: Consumer Activism and Corporate Public Relations in the 1930s* (Chicago: University of Illinois Press, 2006).

4. Chase and Schlink, *Your Money's Worth.* Sammy R. Danna, ed., *Advertising and Popular Culture: Studies in Variety and Versatility* (Bowling Green, OH: Bowling Green State University Popular Press, 1992), 26. Sociologist Robert S. Lynd first characterized Chase and Schlink's book as "the *Uncle Tom's Cabin* of the abuses of the consumer" in "Democracy's Third Estate: The Consumer," *Political Science Quarterly* 51, no. 4 (December 1936), 497–98. For more about Consumers' Research Inc., see John McDonough and Karen Egolf, eds., "Consumers' Research," in *The Advertising Age Encyclopedia of Advertising* (Chicago: Fitzroy Dearborn Publishers, 2002).

5. "Consumers Union Puts on Muscle," *BusinessWeek* December 23, 1967. See Lawrence B. Glickman, *Buying Power: A History of Consumer Activism in America* (Chicago: University of Chicago Press, 2009), 196; Stole, *Advertising on Trial.*

6. Theodore F. MacManus, "The Nadir of Nothingness," *The Atlantic Monthly* (May 1928), 594–608, https://www.unz.org/Pub/AtlanticMonthly-1928may-00594. For further discussion on each of the critics, see Stephen R. Fox, *The Mirror Makers: A History of American Advertising and Its Creators* (Chicago: University of Chicago Press, 1997).

7. Helen Woodward, *Through Many Windows* (New York: Harper & Brothers, 1926); James Rorty, *Our Master's Voice: Advertising* (New York: John Day, 1934), 18, 66–68.

8. Lawrence B. Glickman, *Buying Power: A History of Consumer Activism in America* (Chicago: The University of Chicago Press, 2009), 196–97. The International Advertising Association hired Charles E. Carpenter to defend the advertising industry. Charles E. Carpenter did so in his book, *Dollars and Sense* (New York: Doubleday, Doran, 1928). See Sammy R. Danna, ed., *Advertising and Popular Culture: Studies in Variety and Versatility* (Bowling Green, OH: Bowling Green State University Popular Press, 1992); *The Tide of Advertising and Marketing* (New York: Tide Publishing, 1943); Fred DeArmond, "Consumer Clans Are Gathering," *Nation's Business* (January 1938), https://archive.org/stream/Nations-Business-1938-01/Nations-Business-1938-01_djvu .txt.

9. "The total annual volume of advertising dropped from $3.4 billion in 1929 to $2.6 billion in 1930 and then to $2.3 billion a year later." Advertising expenditures bottomed out "at $1.3 billion in 1933, only 38% of the pre-Depression level." Fox, *The Mirror Makers*.

10. For more discussion on the Depression's effects on the advertising industry, see Stephen R. Fox, "Depression and Reform," *The Mirror Makers*. See also Eric W. Boyle, *Quack Medicine: A History of Combating Health Fraud in Twentieth-Century America* (Santa Barbara: ABC-CLIO, 2013). To access the listed books, see Arthur Kallet and Frederick J. Schlink, *100,000,000 Guinea Pigs: Dangers in Everyday Foods, Drugs, and Cosmetics* (New York: Grosset & Dunlap, 1935); M. C. Phillips, *Skin Deep: The Truth About Beauty Aids* (New York: Garden City Publishing, 1937); Frederick J. Schlink, *Eat, Drink and Be Wary* (New York: Arno Press, 1935); J. B. Matthews, *Guinea Pigs No More* (New York: Covinci, Friede, 1936); T. Swann Harding, *The Popular Practice of Fraud* (New York: Longmans, Green, 1935).

11. For more discussion, see generally Kathleen Franz and Susan Smulyan, eds., *Major Problems in American Popular Culture* (Boston: Wadsworth, Cengage Learning, 2012).

12. Edward Chamberlin, *The Theory of Monopolistic Competition* (Cambridge, MA: Harvard University Press, 1933); Joan Robinson, *The Economics of Imperfect Competition* (London: Macmillan, 1933). See Roland Marchand, *Advertising the American Dream: Making Way for Modernity, 1920–1940* (Los Angeles: University of California Press, 1986).

13. These facts were drawn from Richard Kluger, *Ashes to Ashes: America's Hundred-Year Cigarette War, the Public Health, and the Unabashed Triumph of Philip Morris* (New York: Alfred A. Knopf, 1996). See also Allan M. Brandt, *The Cigarette Century: The Rise, Fall, and Deadly Persistence of the Product That Defined America* (New York: Basic Books, 2007). For a discussion about the interrelationship between the confectionery industry and the cigarette industry, see Wendy A Woloson, *Refined Tastes: Sugar, Confectionery, and Consumers in Nineteenth-Century America* (Baltimore: Johns Hopkins University Press, 2003).

14. U.S. Supreme Court, *FTC v. Raladam Co.*, 283 U.S. 643 (1931). For more discussion on the Hill-Lasker response, see Kluger, *Ashes to Ashes*. To view the advertisement as originally published, see *The Milwaukee Journal*, July 8, 1930, 3. https://news.google .com/newspapers?nid=1499&dat=19300708&id=wYZRAAAAIBAJ&sjid=qiEEAA AAIBAJ&pg=5016,4850281&hl=en.

15. Wallace F. Janssen, "The Story of the Laws Behind the Labels," *FDA Consumer,* June 1981, http://www.fda.gov/AboutFDA/WhatWeDo/History/Overviews/ucm056044. htm; John E. Lesch, *The First Miracle Drugs: How the Sulfa Drugs Transformed Medicine* (New York: Oxford University Press, 2007).

16. See Stole, *Advertising on Trial.*

17. Eric W. Boyle, *Quack Medicine: A History of Combating Health Fraud in Twentieth-Century America* (Santa Barbara: ABC-CLIO, 2013); Laurence V. Burton, "What the Food Manufacturer Thinks of S. 1944," *Law and Contemporary Problems* 1 (December 1933), 121; Stole, *Advertising on Trial;* Richard Maxwell, ed., *Culture Works: The Political Economy of Culture* (Minneapolis: University of Minnesota Press, 2001). For a newspaper's critique of the Tugwell Bill, see "The Tugwell Bill," *Chicago Tribune,* February 16, 1934, http://archives.chicagotribune.com/1934/02/16/page/12/article /the-tugwell-bill.

18. President Franklin D. Roosevelt signed the Federal Food, Drug, and Cosmetic Act on June 25, 1938. Janssen, "The Story of the Laws Behind the Labels." The Wheeler-Lea Amendment "extended the FTC's jurisdiction to protect consumers as well as competitors against injuries resulting from deceptive acts and practices in interstate (but not in local) commerce." Stole, *Advertising on Trial,* 157. To read more of Milton Handler's critique, see Handler, "The Control of False Advertising Under the Wheeler-Lea Act," *Law and Contemporary Problems* 6 (Winter 1939), 110.

19. For a discussion on the effects the Depression had on the advertising industry, see Ronald Marchand, "Depression Advertising as a Shift in Style," *Advertising the American Dream.*

CHAPTER 7: THE INVENTION OF PRIME TIME

1. Dr. William J. Gies of Columbia University's Department of Biologic Chemistry began studying the composition of tooth powders in 1909, and undertook an extensive inquiry into the validity of Pepsodent's advertising claims. James Wynbrandt, *The Excruciating History of Dentistry: Toothsome Tales and Oral Oddities from Babylon to Braces* (New York: St. Martin's Griffin, 1998), 191.

2. William J. Gies, "Pepsodent," *The Journal of the American Medical Association* 68 (April 28, 1917), 1387.

3. Kerry Segrave, *America Brushes Up: The Use and Marketing of Toothpaste and Toothbrushes in the Twentieth Century* (Jefferson, NC: McFarland, 2010), 65.

4. Colgate's ads were featured in many magazines and newspapers in the 1920s. See *The National Geographic Magazine* 40 (1921) and *The Saturday Evening Post* 191, nos. 40–43 (1919) for examples.

5. John Irving Romer, ed., "Radio as an Advertising Medium," *Printer's Ink* 119 (April 27, 1922), 201.

6. Herbert Hoover, Speech to First Washington Radio Conference, February, 27 1922, in Herbert Hoover, "Reminiscences," Radio Unit of the Oral History Project, 1950, Columbia University, New York, NY.

7. Samuel Lionel Rothafel and Raymond Francis Yates, *Broadcasting: It's a New Day* (New York: Century, 1925), 156.

8. Elizabeth McLeod, *The Original Amos 'n' Andy: Freeman Gosden, Charles Correll and the 1928–1943 Radio Serial* (Jefferson, NC: McFarland, 2005), 40.

9. Charles J. Correll and Freeman F. Gosden, *All About Amos and Andy and Their Creators* (New York: Rand McNally, 1929), 43.

10. Hong Kong–based Hawley & Hazel Chemical Company manufactured Darkie toothpaste and sold the product widely in Hong Kong, Malaysia, Taiwan, and other countries in East Asia. Hawley & Hazel was acquired in 1985 by the U.S corporation Colgate-Palmolive, who announced that it would rename Darkie as Darlie and redesign its logo.

11. "Originality Over the Air Pays Pepsodent," *Broadcasting,* April 15, 1933, 9.

12. Jim Cox, *American Radio Networks: A History* (Jefferson, NC: McFarland, 2009), 48.

13. "Niles Trammell," *Broadcasting,* January 1, 1939, 40.

14. Ultimately, the constant repetition of the slogan has been credited for creating the American habit of twice-yearly dental examinations. Templin also insisted that Hay exclusively read the Pepsodent pitch, ultimately resulting in the public's association of Hay "as a conservative, sincere, honest representative of the Pepsodent Company, not of NBC." See Jeffrey L. Cruikshank and Arthur Schultz, *The Man Who Sold America: The Amazing (but True!) Story of Albert D. Lasker* (Cambridge: Harvard Business Review Press, 2010).

15. Arthur H. Samuels, "On the Air," *The New Yorker,* March 22, 1930, 96.

16. See Cynthia B. Meyers, *A Word from Our Sponsor* (New York: Fordham University Press, 2014), 68–69. Meyers notes the elements in the advertisement that are typical of "reason-why" advertising "in the repetition of key points ('cleaning and policing'), the claim of scientific progress ('Pepsodent laboratories'), use of superlatives ('new and different,' 'new discovery'), and multiple 'reasons why' to buy the product."

17. Kay Trenholm, "Last Night on WJZ," *New York Sun,* August 20, 1929.

18. Erik Barnouw, *A Tower in Babel: A History of Broadcasting in the United States to 1933,* Vol. 1 (New York: Oxford University Press, 1966), 230.

19. For example, in 1920 Westinghouse, a leading manufacturer and seller of radio hardware, established KDKA in order to sell radio through programming. Westinghouse would later have shared ownership with General Electric (GE), another manufacturer and seller of radio hardware, and with the Radio Corporation of America (RCA), a jointly owned subsidiary of Westinghouse and GE of NBC. It therefore is no surprise that Merlin H. Aylesworth, NBC's first president, believed that "the main purpose of broadcasting . . . [was] not to make money" but instead "to give the public such increasingly better programs that people will continue to buy and use radio sets and tubes. And that works to the advantage not only of the manufacturing companies whose money is invested in the National Broadcasting Company, but to all makers of radio equipment, and the general public as well." Frank P. Stockbridge, "Feeding 13,000,000 Radio Sets," *Popular Science Monthly,* October 1929. For more general information about the early history of radio broadcasting, see Thomas H. White, "The Development of Radio Networks (1916–1941)," accessed January 30, 2016, http://earlyradiohistory.us/sec019.htm.

20. Robert C. Allen, *Speaking of Soap Operas* (Chapel Hill: University of North Carolina Press, 1985), 119. Allen quotes Irna Phillips, who created and scripted various soap operas including *Painted Dreams, Today's Children,* and *Guiding Light,* which contained many still popular literary devices, such as the "cliff-hanger" ending. Ultimately, a study in 1932 concluded that "the program sponsor should realize that the housewife in a majority of cases is the member of the family who has the most influence upon family purchases and is the one who spends the greatest amount of time in the home. She is, therefore, the member of the family most easily reached by radio broadcasts." Allen, *Speaking of Soap Operas,* 106–7.

21. George Creel, *How We Advertised America* (New York: Harper & Brothers, 1920).

CHAPTER 8: THE PRINCE

1. Sources for the life and times of William Paley include Sally Bedell Smith, *In All His Glory: The Life of William S. Paley* (New York: Simon & Schuster, 1990); Jim Cox, *American Radio Networks: A History* (Jefferson, NC: McFarland, 2009); Jim Cox, *Goodnight Gracie: The Last Years of Network Radio* (Jefferson, NC: McFarland, 2002). Other sources on radio broadcast industry and the rise of CBS include Michael J. Socolow, "Always in Friendly Competition: NBC and CBS in the First Decade of National Broadcasting," in *NBC: America's Network*, ed. Michele Hilmes (Berkeley: University of California Press, 2007); Erik Barnouw, *The Golden Web: A History of Broadcasting in the United States, Volume 2* (New York: Oxford University Press, 1968); Cynthia B. Meyers, *A Word from Our Sponsor: Admen, Advertising, and the Golden Age of Radio* (New York: Fordham University Press, 2014); Michele Hilmes, *Network Nations: A Transnational History of British and American Broadcasting* (New York: Routledge, 2012); David Halberstam, *The Powers That Be* (New York: Knopf, 1979).

2. The Radio Act of 1927 codified the understanding that broadcasters were to serve "the public interest" and also established the Federal Radio Commission (FRC), which would regulate radio according to "the public interest, convenience, or necessity."

3. For a fuller discussion of Sarnoff's enormously consequential career, see Tim Wu, *The Master Switch* (New York: Vintage, 2011); Kenneth Bilby, *The General: David Sarnoff and the Rise of the Communications Industry* (New York: Harper & Row, 1986).

4. Bernays urged Paley to include "superior educational, cultural, and news programs" in CBS's lineup and "publicize them aggressively—even deceptively," although these programs only constituted a small portion of CBS's total offerings. For more on the theory of the "Tiffany Network," see Smith, *In All His Glory*.

5. Halberstam, *The Powers That Be*, 27.

6. David Halberstam, "The Power and the Profits," *Media* 237, no. 1 (1976).

7. David Patrick Columbia, *Quest Magazine*, 1993.

8. For more on the Elder-Woodruff Audimeter's development, see Hugh Malcolm Beville Jr., *Audience Ratings: Radio, Television, and Cable* (Hillsdale, NJ: Lawrence Erlbaum Associates, 1988); Beville, *Audience Ratings*, 219.

9. Robert Elder letter of February 8, 1978.

10. The Edward R. Murrow Papers, a collection of books, memorabilia, and audiovisual material, can be found at Tufts University, the world's largest collection of Edward R. Murrow material.

11. From an account of a British bombing raid in Berlin on December 3, 1945. See Bob Edwards, *Edward R. Murrow and the Birth of Broadcast Journalism* (Hoboken, NJ: John Wiley & Sons, 2004).

CHAPTER 9: TOTAL ATTENTION CONTROL, OR THE MADNESS OF CROWDS

1. David Welch, *The Third Reich: Politics and Propaganda* (London: Routledge, 1993), 42; Thomas Crosby, "Volksgemeinschaft: Nazi Radio and Its Destruction of Hitler's Utopian Vision," *Valley Humanities Review* (Spring 2014); David Nicholls, *Adolf Hitler: A Biographical Companion* (Santa Barbara: ABC-CLIO, 2000).

2. Roger Manvell and Heinrich Fraenkel, *Doctor Goebbels: His Life and Death* (New York: Skyhorse Publishing, 2013); Marcel Cornis-Pope, *New Literary Hybrids in the*

Age of Multimedia Expression: Crossing Borders, Crossing Genres (Amsterdam: John Benjamins Publishing Company, 2014), 102.

3. See Gustave Le Bon, *The Crowd: A Study of the Popular Mind* (New York: Macmillan, 1896).

4. Richard F. Bensel, *Passion and Preferences: William Jennings Bryan and the 1896 Democratic Convention* (New York: Cambridge University Press, 2008), 231–33.

5. See Margaret Harris and George Butterworth, *Developmental Psychology: A Student's Handbook* (New York: Psychology Press, 2002); and Naomi Eilan et al., eds., *Joint Attention: Communication and Other Minds* (Oxford: Oxford University Press, 2005).

6. "Putzi Hanfstaengl," *Helytimes,* October 18, 2013, http://stevehely.com/2013/10/18/putzi-hanfstaengl/. To read more about Albert Speer's experience hearing Hitler speak, see Robert J. Lifton, *The Nazi Doctors: Medical Killing and the Psychology of Genocide* (New York: Basic Books, 1986), 474. John G. Stoessinger, *Why Nations Go to War* (Boston: Cengage Learning, 2010), 56. For Alfons Heck's account of the Nazi rally, see Alfons Heck, *A Child of Hitler: Germany in the Days when God Wore a Swastika* (Phoenix: Renaissance House, 2001), 21–23. Brian E. Fogarty, *Fascism: Why Not Here?* (Washington, DC: Potomac Books, 2011), 28–29. For more about Leni Riefenstahl's experience, see Leni Riefenstahl, *Leni Riefenstahl* (New York: Macmillan, 1995).

7. Terry Rowan, *World War II Goes to the Movies and Television Guide* (Lulu.com, 2012); John Malam, *Hitler Invades Poland* (London: Cherrytree Books, 2008).

8. This translated quote from *Triumph of the Will* can be found in Al Gore, *The Assault on Reason* (New York: Bloomsbury Publishing, 2007), 93; Anson Rabinbach and Sander L. Gilman, *The Third Reich Sourcebook* (Los Angeles: University of California Press, 2013). For the original German, see *Feuilletons für Triumph des Willens.* For Goebbels's entire speech, given on August 18, 1933, see Joseph Goebbels, "Der Rundfunk als achte Großmacht," *Signale der neuen Zeit. 25 ausgewählte Reden von Dr. Joseph Goebbels* (Munich: Zentralverlag der NSDAP, 1938), http://research.calvin.edu/german-propaganda-archive/goeb56.htm.

9. Nicholas J. Cull et al., *Propaganda and Mass Persuasion: A Historical Encyclopedia, 1500 to the Present* (Santa Barbara: ABC-CLIO, 2003); Thomas Hajkowski, *The BBC and National Identity in Britain, 1922–53* (Manchester: Manchester University Press, 2010). For more on the development and use of radio in Nazi Germany, see Corey Ross, *Media and the Making of Modern Germany: Mass Communications, Society, and Politics from the Empire to the Third Reich* (New York: Oxford University Press, 2008). Daria Frezza, *The Leader and the Crowd: Democracy in American Public Discourse, 1880–1941* (Athens: University of Georgia Press, 2007).

10. The statistics relating to radio in Germany were drawn from Martin Collier and Philip Pedley, *Hitler and the Nazi State* (London: Heinemann Educational Publishers, 2005). Eugen Hadamovsky, "Die lebende Brücke: Vom Wesen der Funkwartarbeit," in *Dein Rundfunk* (Munich: Zentralverlag der NSDAP, 1934), http://research.calvin.edu/german-propaganda-archive/hada3.htm. Michael Burleigh, *The Third Reich: A New History* (London: Macmillan, 2000).

11. For a discussion about legal paternalism, see A. P. Simester and Andreas von Hirsch, *Crimes, Harms, and Wrongs: On the Principles of Criminalisation* (Oxford, UK: Hart Publishing, 2011).

12. Joseph S. Tuman, *Communicating Terror: The Rhetorical Dimensions of Terrorism* (Los Angeles: SAGE Publications, 2010). For more discussion on the influence and psychology of advertising, see Leslie E. Gill, *Advertising and Psychology* (New York: Routledge, 2013). Adolf Hitler, *Mein Kampf* (1939), 236–37. Jacques Ellul, *Propaganda: The*

Formation of Men's Attitudes (New York: Alfred A. Knopf, 1968). Hans Fritzsche, "Dr. Goebbels und sein Ministerium," in Hans Heinz Mantau-Sadlia, *Deutsche Führer Deutsches Schicksal. Das Buch der Künder und Führer des dritten Reiches* (Munich: Verlag Max Steinebach, 1934) 330–42, http://research.calvin.edu/german-propaganda -archive/goeb62.htm.

13. Andrew Defty, *Britain, America and Anti-Communist Propaganda 1945–53: The Information Research Department* (New York: Routledge, 2004); Joseph D. Douglass Jr., *Soviet Military Strategy in Europe* (New York: Pergamon Press, 1981). For a discussion on First Amendment jurisprudence and its effects, see Tamara R. Piety, *Brandishing the First Amendment: Commercial Expression in America* (Ann Arbor: University of Michigan Press, 2012).

CHAPTER 10: PEAK ATTENTION, AMERICAN STYLE

1. Gary Edgerton, *The Columbia History of American Television* (New York: Columbia University Press, 2007), 113.

2. Hugo Münsterberg, *The Photoplay: A Psychological Study* (New York: Appleton, 1916) 153.

3. See Vittorio Gallese and Michele Guerra, *Lo schermo empatico: Cinema e neuroscienze* (Milan: Raffaello Cortina Editore, 2015).

4. Bianca Bradbury, "Is Television Mama's Friend or Foe?," *Good Housekeeping,* November 1950, 263–64.

5. Calder Willingham, "Television: Giant in the Living Room," *American Mercury,* February 1952.

6. Erik Barnouw, *Tube of Plenty: The Evolution of American Television* (New York: Oxford University Press, 1990), 103.

7. Reuven Frank, *Out of Thin Air: The Brief Wonderful Life of Network News* (New York: Simon & Schuster, 1991), 33.

8. Jack Gould, "Radio and Television: Edward R. Murrow's News Review 'See It Now' Demonstrates Journalistic Power of Video," *New York Times,* November 19, 1951, 26.

9. For more information on Murrow's and Friendly's coverage of McCarthy and the Red Scare, see Ralph Engelman, *Friendlyvision: Fred Friendly and the Rise and Fall of Television Journalism* (New York: Columbia University Press, 2009).

10. For more on the rise of CBS and the intense competition it faced in the programming industry, see David Halberstam, *The Powers That Be* (New York: Knopf, 1979), 417.

11. Jacques Ellul, "The Characteristics of Propaganda," in *Readings in Propaganda and Persuasion*, ed. Garth S. Jowett and Victoria O'Donnell (Thousand Oaks, CA: SAGE Publications, 2006). Ellul discusses how individual spectators of mass media, though "diffused and not assembled at one point," become a mass that may be subject to propaganda.

12. Jerry Mander, *Four Arguments for the Elimination of Television* (New York: William Morrow, 1978), 26. Mander, a former advertising executive, was critical of the many problems of television that were inherent to the medium itself.

13. The remark likely first made in 1955 and later appeared in *Confessions of an Advertising Man,* in which Ogilvy wrote a "how-to-succeed" in advertising guide for future generations. See David Ogilvy, *Confessions of an Advertising Man* (New York: Atheneum, 1963), 96.

14. For more information on the Anacin campaign, see "Anacin," *Advertising Age,* last modi-

fied September 15, 2003, http://adage.com/article/adage-encyclopedia/anacin/98501/.
For more information on the M&M's campaign, see "Mars, Inc.," *Advertising Age,*
last modified September 15, 2003, http://adage.com/article/adage-encyclopedia/mars
/98761/.

15. Mark Tungate, *Adland: A Global History of Advertising* (Philadelphia: KoganPage, 2013), 68.

16. For more information about the Marlboro Man and its development as an American icon, see "The Man of Make-Believe," *The Economist,* January 24, 2015, http://www .economist.com/news/obituary/21640293-darrell-winfield-real-marlboro-man-died -january-12th-aged-85-man-make-believe. For more about the Jolly Green Giant, see "The Green Giant," *Advertising Age,* last modified March 29, 1999, http://adage.com /article/special-report-the-advertising-century/green-giant/140172/. For more about Tony the Tiger, see E. J. Schultz, "A Tiger at 60: How Kellogg's Tony Is Changing for a New Age," *Advertising Age,* last modified August 29, 2011, http://adage.com/article /news/kellogg-s-tony-tiger-60-changing-a-age/229493/.

17. Tungate, *Adland,* 65.

18. Edith Witt, "The Personal Adman," *Reporter,* May 14, 1959, 36–37.

19. Ronald Fullerton, "Ernest Dichter: The Motivational Researcher," in *Ernest Dichter and Motivation Research: New Perspectives on the Making of Post-War Consumer Culture,* ed. Stefan Schwarzkopf and Rainer Gries (London: Palgrave Macmillan, 2010), 58, 143, 147.

20. Dichter's theory of "food genders" became especially sought out by advertisers; Dichter claimed that consumers had a subconscious, psychological response to foods, which influenced how they made their purchasing decisions. For this reason, Dichter believed it was important for advertisers to classify various food products along gender lines to gain insight into why consumers prefer one product over another. For more on Dichter's theory of "food genders," see Ernest Dichter, "Creative Research Memo on the Psychology of Food," submitted to the Fitzgerald Advertising Agency (July 1955); Ernest Dichter, "Creative Research Memo on the Sex of Rice," submitted to Leo Burnett Co. (October 1955); Ernest Dichter, "A Motivational Research Study of Luncheon Meats and Wieners," submitted to Bonsib, Inc. (November 1968), 16; and Katherine Parkin, "The 'Sex of Food': Ernest Dichter, Libido and American Food Advertising," in *Ernest Dichter and Motivation Research,* ed. Schwarzkopf and Gries, 140–54.

21. Ernest Dichter, *Handbook of Consumer Motivations: The Psychology of the World of Objects* (New York: McGraw-Hill, 1964), 419.

22. Ernest Dichter, *Handbook of Consumer Motivations: The Psychology of the World of Objects* (New York: McGraw-Hill, 1964), 66; Lawrence R. Samuel, *Brought to You By: Postwar Television Advertising and the American Dream* (Austin: University of Texas Press, 2001), 97.

23. For more on Dichter and his research, see Ernest Dichter, *The Strategy of Desire* (New Brunswick, NJ: Doubleday, 1960), 290, 297; Ernest Dichter, *Getting Motivated by Ernest Dichter: The Secret Behind Individual Motivations by the Man Who Was Not Afraid to Ask "Why?"* (New York: Pergamon, 1979); Vance Packard, *The Hidden Persuaders* (New York: D. McKay, 1957); Fullerton, *Ernest Dichter and Motivation Research,* 47.

24. David Sarnoff hired the "remarkable" Sylvester ("Pat") Weaver in 1949 as head of new television operations. Weaver has been described as "an articulate visionary, viewed by many who worked with him as a brilliant mind." Gerard Jones, *Honey, I'm Home: Sitcoms: Selling the American Dream* (New York: St. Martin's Press, 1993). For more

discussion on NBC's history and success, see Jim Bell, "Introduction," in *From Yesterday to Today: Six Decades of America's Favorite Morning Show* (Philadelphia: Running Press, 2012), xi.

25. Tino Balio, *Hollywood in the Age of Television* (New York: Routledge, 2013); James L. Baughman, *Same Time, Same Station: Creating American Television, 1948–1961* (Baltimore: Johns Hopkins University Press, 2007). Erik Barnouw, *Tube of Plenty: The Evolution of American Television* (New York: Oxford University Press, 1990), 190.

26. John McDonough and Karen Egolf, *The Advertising Age Encyclopedia of Advertising* (Chicago: Routledge, 2015). CBS during the Paley-Murrow years might be first in prestige and quality, but it was nonetheless number two to NBC in programming, advertising revenues, and profit, and always had been. Bill Paley had never really accepted that status." David Halberstam, *The Powers That Be* (New York: Knopf, 1979).

27. These details about *The $64,000 Question* were drawn from "The 64,000 Question," PBS, http://www.pbs.org/wgbh/amex/quizshow/peopleevents/pande06.html; Kent Anderson, *Television Fraud: The History and Implications of the Quiz Show Scandals* (Santa Barbara: ABC-CLIO, 1978); Lawrence Grobel, *The Hustons: The Life and Times of a Hollywood Dynasty* (New York: Scribner, 1989); Su Holmes, *The Quiz Show* (Edinburgh: Edinburgh University Press, 2008). Kent Anderson, *Television Fraud: The History and Implications of the Quiz Show Scandals* (Westport, CT: Greenwood Publishing Group, 1978), 3.

28. "Herbert Stempel," PBS, http://www.pbs.org/wgbh/amex/quizshow/peopleevents/pande01.html; Holmes, *The Quiz Show*, 47; Patricia Mellencamp, ed., *Logics of Television: Essays in Cultural Criticism* (Indianapolis: Indiana University Press, 1990).

29. For more information on quiz shows in the 1950s, see Anderson, *Television Fraud;* and Holmes, *The Quiz Show.*

30. In 1976, CBS fell to third in prime-time ratings for the first time in two decades as ABC took the lead. For more information, see Sally Bedell Smith, *In All His Glory: The Life of William S. Paley, the Legendary Tycoon and His Brilliant Circle* (New York: Random House, 1990); Harold L. Vogel, 9th ed. of *Entertainment Industry Economics: A Guide for Financial Analysis* (New York: Cambridge University Press, 2014).

31. Halberstam, *The Powers That Be* (New York: Knopf, 1979).

32. Fred W. Friendly, *Due to Circumstances Beyond Our Control* (New York: Random House, 1967).

33. Halberstam, *The Powers That Be.* Ken Auletta, "The 64,000 Question," *The New Yorker,* September 14, 1994.

34. Erik Barnouw, *Tube of Plenty: The Evolution of American Television* (New York: Oxford University Press, 1990), 187. Jack Gould, "'See It Now' Finale: Program Unexpectedly Ends Run of Seven Distinguished Years on CBS," *New York Times,* July 8, 1958.

35. John Crosby, "The Demise of 'See It Now,'" *New York Herald Tribune,* July 11, 1958.

36. The fullest description of this point is Erik Barnouw, *The Sponsor, Notes on a Modern Potentate* (London: Oxford University Press, 1978).

37. Edward R. Murrow, "Wires and Lights in a Box," in *Documents of American Broadcasting,* ed. Frank J. Kahn (Englewood Cliffs, NJ: Prentice Hall, 1978). Originally presented as a speech to the Radio and Television News Directors Association, Chicago, Illinois, October 15, 1958.

CHAPTER 11: PRELUDE TO AN ATTENTIONAL REVOLT

1. McDonald was a genuine longtime believer in "thought transference." Thus when Duke University's Dr. Joseph Banks Rhine published his research on telepathy, including one research project that seemed to demonstrate certain individuals were able to guess cards better than if they had by chance, McDonald sought to sponsor network radio experiments in Rhine's technique, conducted by Northwestern University's psychologists Dr. Louis Deal Goodfellow and Dr. Robert Harvey Gault. Each Sunday, the series *The Zenith Foundation* would broadcast on NBC, during which certain individuals would concentrate on cards. Radio listeners would then try to "pick up the senders' thought waves." Ultimately, Dr. Goodfellow concluded "no evidence of extrasensory perception in these experiments." For more information, see Larry Wolters, "News of Radio," *Chicago Tribune,* September 7, 1937; and "Patterns and Peephole," *Time,* September 5, 1938, 16.

2. "McDonald v. the Adenoidal," *Time,* February 4, 1946, 66.

3. In fact, McDonald disliked commercials even during the radio era. He believed that radio commercials had too many "roars, grunts, squawks, yaps, burps, and a mixture of adenoidal and . . . honey-chile voices." "McDonald v. the Adenoidal," 66. For this reason, starting in 1940 McDonald and Zenith spent $75,000 a year, approximately $900,000 in today's terms, to support WWZR, a radio station that only broadcast music, without any commercials.

4. Caetlin Benson-Allott, *Remote Control* (New York: Bloomsbury Academic, 2015), 49. For an image of the cited advertisement in full, as well as various images of the device in use, see "Remembering Eugene Polley and his Flash-Matic Remote (photos)," CNet .com, accessed February 5, 2016, http://www.cnet.com/pictures/remembering-eugene -polley-and-his-flash-matic-remote-photos/.

5. Margalit Fox, "Eugene Polley, Conjuror of a Device That Changed TV Habits, Dies at 96," *New York Times,* May 22, 2012, http://www.nytimes.com/2012/05/23/business /eugene-t-polley-inventor-of-the-wireless-tv-remote-dies-at-96.html.

6. As quoted in the *New York Herald Tribune,* October 12, 1956, and reproduced in Robert Andrews, *The Columbia Dictionary of Quotations* (New York: Columbia University Press, 1993), 900.

7. Jacques Ellul, *Propaganda: The Formation of Men's Attitudes,* trans. Konrad Kellen and Jean Leaner (New York: Vintage, 1973), 103.

8. Vance Packard, *The Hidden Persuaders* (New York: D. McKay, 1957).

9. "The Hidden Persuaders," *The New Yorker,* May 18, 1957, 167.

10. Ellul, *Propaganda.*

11. Packard, *The Hidden Persuaders,* 266.

12. For more on *Dotto,* see David Baber, *Television Game Show Hosts: Biographies of 32 Stars* (Jefferson, NC: McFarland, 2008).

13. House Committee on Interstate and Foreign Commerce, Investigation of Television Quiz Shows: Hearings Before a Subcommittee of the Committee of Interstate and Foreign Commerce, United States House of Representatives, 86th Congress (1960), 624.

14. Walter Lippmann, *The Essential Lippmann: A Political Philosophy for Liberal Democracy,* eds. Clinton Rossiter and James Lare (Cambridge, MA: Harvard University Press, 1982), 411–12.

15. Larry Ingram, "Network TV Faces Day of Reckoning," *Sunday Denver Post,* November 20, 1960, AA1.

16. House Committee on Interstate and Foreign Commerce, Report Pursuant to Section 136 of the Legislative Reorganization Act of 1946, United States House of Representatives, 88th Congress (1963), 372.

CHAPTER 12: THE GREAT REFUSAL

1. Martin Lee and Bruce Shlain, *Acid Dreams: The Complete Social History of LSD: The CIA, the Sixties, and Beyond* (New York: Grove, 2007).
2. Timothy Leary, *Flashbacks: A Personal and Cultural History of an Era: An Autobiography* (New York: Putnam, 1990), 252.
3. Martin Torgoff, *Can't Find My Way Home: America in the Great Stoned Age, 1945–2000* (New York: Simon and Schuster, 2004), 209.
4. Russell Jacoby, *The End of Utopia* (New York: Basic Books, 1999), 152.
5. Herbert Marcuse, *One-Dimensional Man: Studies in the Ideology of Advanced Industrial Society* (London: Routledge Classics, 1964), 6; Herbert Marcuse, *An Essay on Liberation* (Boston: Beacon Press, 1969), ix.
6. Timothy Leary, *High Priest* (Oakland, CA: Ronin Publishing, 1995), 320; Timothy Leary, *Leary to Canada: Wake Up!*, Recorded Speech (1967, Millbrook, New York).
7. Timothy Leary, *Start Your Own Religion* (Berkeley, CA: Ronin Publishing, 2009), 128.
8. Thomas Frank, *The Conquest of Cool: Business Culture, Counterculture, and the Rise of Hip Consumerism* (Chicago: University of Chicago Press, 1997), 24.
9. As described in Stephanie Capparell, *The Real Pepsi Challenge: How One Pioneering Company Broke Color Barriers in the 1940s* (New York: Free Press, 2008).
10. Peter D. Bennett, Robert P. Lamm, and Robert A. Fry, *Marketing*, Volume 1 (New York: McGraw-Hill, 1988), 178.
11. Tristan Donovan, *Fizz: How Soda Shook Up the World* (Chicago: Chicago Review Press, 2013), 182.
12. Frank V. Cespedes, *Managing Marketing Linkages: Text, Cases, and Readings* (Upper Saddle River, NJ: Prentice Hall, 1996), 140.
13. Timothy D. Taylor, *The Sounds of Capitalism: Advertising, Music, and the Conquest of Culture* (Chicago: University of Chicago Press, 2012), 155.
14. Frank, *Conquest of Cool*, 122.
15. Marcuse, *One-Dimensional Man*, 9.
16. Marcuse, *One-Dimensional Man*, 10.
17. To read more on why Jerry Mander thought television should be eliminated, see Jerry Mander, *Four Arguments for the Elimination of Television* (New York: HarperCollins, 1978). For a detailed discussion on both the positive and negative effects of television and its success, see Elihu Katz and Paddy Scannell, eds., *The End of Television? Its Impact on the World (So Far)*, Vol. 625 of *The Annals of The American Academy of Political and Social Science*, ed. Phyllis Kaniss (Los Angeles: SAGE Publications, 2009).
18. To listen to or read Murrow's entire speech, see Edward Murrow, "Wires and Lights in a Box," RTDNA convention, Philadelphia, October 15, 1958, http://www.rtdna.org/content/edward_r_murrow_s_1958_wires_lights_in_a_box_speech. For more on the development and history of noncommercial television, see Ralph Engelman, *Public Radio and Television in America: A Political History* (Los Angeles: SAGE Publications, 1996). The details about Fred Rogers and his various television shows were

drawn from Tim Hollis, *Hi There, Boys and Girls!: America's Local Children's TV Programs* (Jackson: University Press of Mississippi, 2001); Mark Collins and Margaret M. Kimmel, eds., *Mister Rogers' Neighborhood: Children, Television, and Fred Rogers* (Pittsburgh: University of Pittsburgh Press, 1997); and M. Carole Macklin and Les Carlson, eds., *Advertising to Children: Concepts and Controversies* (Thousand Oaks, CA: SAGE Publications, 1999). The details about *Sesame Street* were drawn from Malcolm Gladwell, *The Tipping Point: How Little Things Can Make a Big Difference* (Boston: Little, Brown, 2006); and Michael Davis, *Street Gang: The Complete History of Sesame Street* (New York: Penguin, 2008).

19. Eileen R. Meehan, *Why TV Is Not Our Fault: Television Programming, Viewers, and Who's Really in Control* (New York: Rowman & Littlefield, 2005); Michele Hilmes, *The Television History Book* (London: British Film Institute, 2003). Laurie Oullette, *Viewers Like You: How Public TV Failed the People* (New York: Columbia University Press, 2012), 196.

20. Interview with author, May 12, 2008. For more about Bill Siemering's vision for NPR and about the implementation of that mission, see William H. Siemering, "National Public Radio Purposes, 1970," *Current,* May 17, 2012, http://current.org/2012/05 /national-public-radio-purposes/.

21. Larry Brody, *Turning Points in Television* (New York: Kensington Publishing, 2005). The fact is that 15 million homes tuned in to watch *A Charlie Brown Christmas* and that *Peanuts*-generated high merchandise sales made "Charlie Brown's complaint about Christmas commercialism seem somewhat paradoxical." Joey Green, *Weird and Wonderful Christmas: Curious and Crazy Customs and Coincidences from Around the World* (New York: Black Dog & Leventhal Publishers, 2005).

22. Mander, *Four Arguments for the Elimination of Television*, 31.

23. Laurie Ouellette, *Viewers Like You: How Public TV Failed the People* (New York: Columbia University Press, 2012); Janet Staiger, *Blockbuster TV: Must-See Sitcoms in the Network Era* (New York: NYU Press, 2000); Robert W. Morrow, *Sesame Street and the Reform of Children's Television* (Baltimore: Johns Hopkins University Press, 2011); Thomas Thompson, "In the Life-or-Death Ratings Game," *Life,* September 10, 1971; Kevin M. Kelleghan, "Image Battle Shapes in Mexico as Firms Gear for 'Tomorrow,'" *Billboard,* July 22, 1967.

24. Thomas C. O'Guinn et al., *Advertising and Integrated Brand Promotion* (Stamford, CT: Cengage Learning, 2014); Edward J. Rielly, *The 1960s* (Westport, CT: Greenwood, 2003); Frank, *The Conquest of Cool, 124–25.* For an interesting summary of the ad revolution, see "History: 1960s," *Advertising Age,* last modified September 15, 2003, http://adage.com/article/adage-encyclopedia/history-1960s/98702/; "History: 1970s," *Advertising Age,* last modified September 15, 2003, http://adage.com/article/ adage-encyclopedia/history-1970s/98703/.

25. Fox, *The Mirror Makers*, 270–71.

26. For the full cosmetics ad, see "This Is the Way Love Is in 1969," *Life,* March 7, 1969. To view a Benson & Hedges ad, see "Benson & Hedges 100's Pick-Your-Favorite-Disadvantage Sweepstakes," *Life,* April 3, 1970. Stephen R. Fox, *The Mirror Makers: A History of American Advertising and Its Creators* (Chicago: University of Illinois Press, 1984).

27. Frank, *The Conquest of Cool*. To watch the full Virginia Slims commercial, see "Virginia Slims Commercials," September 1969, https://industrydocuments.library.ucsf .edu/tobacco/docs/#id=yhyd0111.

28. These statistics were drawn from "TV Basics: A Report on the Growth and Scope of

Television," *TVB Local Media Marketing Solutions,* last modified June 2012, http://www.tvb.org/media/file/TV_Basics.pdf.
29. Taylor, *The Sounds of Capitalism,* 157.

CHAPTER 13: CODA TO AN ATTENTIONAL REVOLUTION

1. Wallace Stegner, *Angle of Repose* (New York: Doubleday, 1971), 18.
2. David Burnham, *The Rise of the Computer State: The Threat to Our Freedoms, Our Ethics, and Our Democratic Process* (New York: Random House, 1983), 90.
3. Michael J. Weiss and Kelly Nelson, "ZIP: How Marketers See Portland . . . and Why They Look," *Casco Bay Weekly,* March 2, 1989, 10.
4. Throughout the 1960s, Robbin developed programs for the Office of Economic Development. One such program includes "The Index of Susceptibility of Civil Disorder," which predicted cities that would likely experience riots. Ultimately, the model achieved 87 percent accuracy.
5. The concept of this socio-spatial segmentation first appeared in Charles Booth's *Descriptive Map of London Poverty,* in which Booth developed a descriptive map that categorized neighborhoods and provided insight into patterns of poverty in London. Booth's study ultimately influenced sociologists Robert E. Park and Ernest W. Burgess, who developed a theory of urban ecology. Park and Burgess proposed that competition for land in urban environments cause social groups to naturally divide themselves into geographic "niches." For more on the historical background of geodemographic segmentation, see Austin Troy, "Geodemographic Segmentation," in *Encyclopedia of GIS,* eds. Shashi Shekar and Hui Xiong (New York: Springer, 2008), 347–55
6. Charles Taylor, *Multiculturalism,* ed. Amy Gutmann (Princeton, NJ: Princeton University Press, 1994).
7. Troy, "Geodemographic Segmentation," 347.
8. While Robbin was interested in using his program to help companies tailor their products and their marketing to the forty lifestyle clusters, Michael Weiss, who elaborated on sociological characteristics of the clusters in *The Clustering of America,* hoped to explore the cultural implications and form "a composite understanding of American lifestyles" and "explore the diversity of the way Americans really live." For additional information about the PRIZM cluster system and the detailed description of the cluster lifestyles, see Michael J. Weiss, *The Clustering of America* (New York: Harper & Row, 1988); Michael J. Weiss, *The Clustered World: How We Live, What We Buy, and What It All Means About Who We Are* (Boston: Little, Brown, 2000).
9. Weiss, *The Clustering of America,* 290.
10. Weiss, *The Clustering of America,* 300.
11. For additional information on the history and development of Diet Coke, see Jay Moye, " 'We Needed a Big Idea': The Extraordinary Story of How Diet Coke Came to Be," Coca-Cola, last modified February 4, 2013, http://www.coca-colacompany.com/stories/we-needed-a-big-idea-the-extraordinary-story-of-how-diet-coke-came-to-be/.
12. Kenneth N. Gilpin, "Prospects," *New York Times,* July 26, 1981, http://www.nytimes.com/1981/07/26/business/prospects.html.
13. Red Smith, "Cable TV for Sports Junkies," *New York Times,* December 3, 1979.
14. With "dualcasting," Bravo used gay content in order to cater to both women and gays as two distinct audiences. The show that sparked this trend was *Queer Eye for the Straight Guy,* in which five gay men would make over a heterosexual male in order

to transform him into a "better straight man." See Katherine Sender, "Dualcasting: Bravo's Gay Programming and the Quest for Women Audiences," in *Cable Visions: Television Beyond Broadcasting,* eds. Sarah Banet-Weiser, Cynthia Chris, and Anthony Freitas (New York: NYU Press, 2007).

15. Sandra Salmans, "Playboy's Hopes in Cable TV," *New York Times,* March 15, 1983, http://www.nytimes.com/1983/03/15/business/playboy-s-hopes-in-cable-tv.html.

16. Murdoch held conservative political opinions, leading to speculation that the news broadcast would offer a "conservative alternative to what he views as liberal bias among traditional news." However, Murdoch, at the time, claimed that he would not champion a conservative agenda because he believed "it's more important to be fair." See Lawrie Mifflin, "At the New Fox News Channel, the Buzzword Is Fairness, Separating News from Bias," *New York Times,* October 7, 1996, http://www.nytimes .com/1996/10/07/business/at-the-new-fox-news-channel-the-buzzword-is-fairness -separating-news-from-bias.html.

17. Fred W. Friendly, "Asleep at the Switch of the Wired City," *The Saturday Review,* October 10, 1970, 3.

18. See Peter Ainslie, "Confronting a Nation of Grazers," *Channels,* September 1988, 54–62; and Jib Fowles, *Why Viewers Watch: A Reappraisal of Television's Effects* (Newbury Park, CA: SAGE Publications, 1992), 37.

19. Bernice Kanner, "The Newest Ploy: Bait-and-Wait," *New York,* June 17, 1985, 41.

20. Rena Bartos, "Ads That Irritate May Erode Trust in Advertised Brands," *Harvard Business Review* 59 (1981), 137.

21. Kanner, "The Newest Ploy," 41.

22. Those responsible for the Coca-Cola advertisement believed that juxtaposing an intimidating man to a young, vulnerable boy would naturally build tension and warm hearts when the Coke would be handed over. In fact, Greene recalls how the advertisement drastically changed his image: "I was suddenly approachable . . . kids were no longer afraid of me, and older people . . . would come up and offer me a Coke." Jay Moye, "Commercial Appeal: 'Mean' Joe Greene Reflections on Iconic Coca-Cola Ad That Changed His Life," Coca-Cola, last modified January 16, 2014, http://www .coca-colacompany.com/stories/commercial-appeal-mean-joe-greene-reflects-on -iconic-coca-cola-ad-that-changed-his-life/.

23. David Burnham, "The Computer, The Consumer and Privacy," *New York Times,* March 4, 1984, http://www.nytimes.com/1984/03/04/weekinreview/the-computer -the-consumer-and-privacy.html.

CHAPTER 14: EMAIL AND THE POWER OF THE CHECK-IN

1. Ray Tomlinson, "The First Network Email," http://openmap.bbn.com/~tomlinso /ray/firstemailframe.html.

2. "The Man Who Made You Put Away Your Pen," *All Things Considered,* NPR, November 15, 2009, http://www.npr.org/templates/story/story.php?storyId=120364591.

3. William F. Allman, "The Accidental History of the @ Symbol," *Smithsonian Magazine,* September 2012, http://www.smithsonianmag.com/science-nature/the -accidental-history-of-the-symbol-18054936/?no-ist.

4. Katie Hafner and Matthew Lyon, *Where Wizards Stay Up Late: The Origins of the Internet* (New York: Simon & Schuster, 1998).

5. David G. Myers, *Exploring Psychology,* 8th ed. (New York: Worth Publishers, 2009), 253.

6. Tom Stafford, "Why Email Is Addictive (and What to Do About It)," *Mindhacks,* September 19, 2006, http://mindhacks.com/2006/09/19/why-email-is-addictive-and -what-to-do-about-it/.

7. Kate Stoodley, "Father of Spam Speaks Out on His Legacy," *Datamation,* November 19, 2004, http://www.datamation.com/article.php/3438651.

8. Jonathan A. Zdziarski, *Ending Spam: Bayesian Content Filtering and the Art of Statistical Language Classification* (San Francisco: No Starch Press, 2005), 5

9. Finn Brunton, *Spam: A Shadow History of the Internet* (Cambridge: MIT Press, 2013), 33.

10. Gina Smith, "Unsung Innovators: Gary Thuerk, the Father of Spam," *Computerworld,* December 3, 2007, http://www.computerworld.com/article/2539767/cybercrime-hacking /unsung-innovators—gary-thuerk—the-father-of-spam.html.

11. Gary Thuerk, "Anniversary," *LinkedIn* (blog), May 2014, https://www.linkedin.com /in/fatherespam.

CHAPTER 15: INVADERS

1. Ralph H. Baer, *Videogames: In the Beginning* (Springfield: Rolenta Press, 2005). For more of Baer's own words on his inspirations and influences, see his interview in Benj Edwards, *The Right to Baer Games—An Interview with Ralph Baer, the Father of Video Games,* http://www.gamasutra.com/view/feature/1690/the_right_to_baer_games_ _an_.php?print=1.

2. Just a few months after Baer invented the Magnavox Odyssey, Bushnell founded Atari with Ted Dabney "with an initial investment of $250 each." Steven L. Kent, *The Ultimate History of Video Games: From Pong to Pokemon and Beyond . . . the Story Behind the Craze That Touched Our Lives and Changed the World* (New York: Three Rivers Press, 2001). Matt Fox, *The Video Games Guide: 1,000+ Arcade, Console and Computer Games, 1962–2012* (Jefferson, NC: McFarland, 2013).

3. Mike Snider, *Interview: 'Space Invaders' Creator Tomohiro Nishikado,* May 6, 2009, http://content.usatoday.com/communities/gamehunters/post/2009/05/66479041/1# .VroFTjYrLVo; Henry Allen, "Galaxy of Wars," *Washington Post,* September 2, 1980, https://www.washingtonpost.com/archive/lifestyle/1980/09/02/galaxy-of-wars /ea315a08-a9af-41c9-9666-230d2acbc7e2/.

4. Martin Amis, *Invasion of the Space Invaders* (London: Hutchinson, 1982), 14; Glenn Collins, "Children's Video Games: Who Wins (or Loses)?," *New York Times,* August 31, 1981, http://www.nytimes.com/1981/08/31/style/children-s-video-games -who-wins-or-loses.html.

5. Kent, *The Ultimate History of Video Games;* Mihaly Csikszentmihalyi, "The Pursuit of Happiness: Bringing the Science of Happiness to Life," accessed February 8, 2016, http://www.pursuit-of-happiness.org/history-of-happiness/mihaly -csikszentmihalyi/.; Amis, *Invasion of the Space Invaders,* 20; Mark O'Connell, "The Arcades Project: Martin Amis' Guide to Classic Video Games," *The Millions,* February 16, 2012, http://www.themillions.com/2012/02/the-arcades-project-martin-amis -guide-to-classic-video-games.html.

6. Amis, *Invasion of the Space Invaders,* 56–57; Chris Morris, "Five Things You Never Knew About Pac-Man," CNBC, March 3, 2011, http://www.cnbc.com/id/41888021; "The Making of Pac-Man," *Retro Gamer,* January 27, 2015, http://www.retrogamer .net/retro_games80/the-making-of-pac-man/; Jaz Rignall, "Top 10 Highest-Grossing Arcade Games of All Time," *US Gamer,* January 1, 2016, http://www.usgamer.net /articles/top-10-biggest-grossing-arcade-games-of-all-time.

7. For these and more facts about Atari's success, see Jimmy Russell, *101 Amazing Atari 2600 Facts* (Luton: Andrews UK Limited, 2012). See also R. J. Lavallee, *IMHO (In My Humble Opinion): A Guide to the Benefits and Dangers of Today's Communication Tools* (Boston: bent spoon Multimedia, 2009).

CHAPTER 16: AOL PULLS 'EM IN

1. CompuServ, "Things to Do. People to See. Places to Go," *Popular Science* 235, no. 2 (1989) : 7; CompuServe, "He Was a Sales Force of One. Until He Got CompuServe. Now He's a Sales Force to Be Reckoned With," *Popular Science* 243, no. 3 (1993) : 17.

2. Alec Klein, *Stealing Time: Steve Case, Jerry Levin, and the Collapse of AOL Time Warner* (New York: Simon & Schuster, 2004), 10.

3. Robert D. Shapiro, "This Is Not Your Father's Prodigy," *Wired*, June 1, 1993, http://www.wired.com/1993/06/prodigy/.

4. Ibid.

5. Kara Swisher, *Aol.com: How Steve Case Beat Bill Gates, Nailed the Netheads, and Made Millions in the War for the Web* (New York: Times Books, 1998), 89.

6. Ibid., 94.

7. Ibid., 97.

8. Keith Wagstaff, "AOL's Longest-Running Employee on the History of AOL Chat Rooms," *Time*, July 6, 2012, http://techland.time.com/2012/07/06/aols-longest -running-employee-on-the-history-of-aol-chat-rooms/.

9. Caitlin Dewey, "A Complete History of the Rise and Fall—and Reincarnation!—of the Beloved '90s Chatroom," *Washington Post*, October 30, 2014, https://www .washingtonpost.com/news/the-intersect/wp/2014/10/30/a-complete-history-of-the -rise-and-fall-and-reincarnation-of-the-beloved-90s-chatroom/.

10. EJ Dickson, "My First Time with Cybersex," *The Kernel*, October 5, 2014, http:// kernelmag.dailydot.com/issue-sections/headline-story/10466/aol-instant-messenger -cybersex/.

11. Ibid.

12. Herbert N. Foerstel, *From Watergate to Monicagate: Ten Controversies in Modern Journalism and Media* (Westport, CT: Greenwood Press, 2001), 226.

13. Walter S. Mossberg, "Prodigy Has Lots of Promise, but AOL May Be the Prodigy," *Wall Street Journal*, October 8, 1992, http://www.wsj.com/articles/ SB1004030142121986760.

14. Paul Farhi, "AOL Gets Its Message Out in 'Mail,'" *Washington Post*, December 17, 1998, http://www.washingtonpost.com/wp-srv/style/movies/features/aolinmail.htm.

15. Brian McCullough, "Those Free AOL CDs Were a Campaign for Web Domination. It Worked," *Mashable*, August 21, 2014, http://mashable.com/2014/08/21/aol-disc -marketing-jan-brandt/#XiWBGcICeaq3; Jan Brandt, "How Much Did It Cost AOL to Distribute All Those CDs Back in the 1990s?," *Quora*, December 27, 2010, https:// www.quora.com/How-much-did-it-cost-AOL-to-distribute-all-those-CDs-back-in -the-1990s.

16. Rob Tannenbaum and Craig Marks, *I Want My MTV: The Uncensored Story of the Music Video Revolution* (New York: Penguin, 2011), 140.

17. Klein, *Stealing Time*, 247.

18. Swisher, *Aol.com*, 280.

19. William Forbes, *Behavioural Finance* (West Sussex, UK: Wiley, 2009), 158.

20. Klein, *Stealing Time*, at 167.

21. Complaint, *SEC v. Kelly*, 817 F.Supp.2d 340 (S.D.N.Y. 2011) (08 Civ. 04612), 2008 WL 2149270, at *2.

22. Steven Levy, "Dead Man Walking?," *Newsweek*, January 21, 1996, http://www .newsweek.com/dead-men-walking-176866.

CHAPTER 17: ESTABLISHMENT OF THE CELEBRITY-INDUSTRIAL COMPLEX

1. Edwin Diamond, "Why the Power Vacuum at Time Inc. Continues," *New York*, October 23, 1972.

2. Alan Brinkley, *The Publisher* (New York: Alfred A. Knopf, 2010); David L. Larsen, *Telling the Old, Old Story: The Art of Narrative Preaching* (Grand Rapids, MI: Kregel Publications, 1995).

3. Steve M. Barkin, *American Television News: The Media Marketplace and the Public Interest* (Armonk, NY: M. E. Sharpe, 2003).

4. Edwin Diamond, "People Who Need People," *New York*, January 31, 1994.

5. David E. Sumner, *The Magazine Century: American Magazines Since 1900* (New York: Peter Lang, 2010).

6. Donald M. Wilson, *The First 78 Years* (Bloomington, IN: Xlibris Corporation, 2004).

7. Based on media kits visited in February 2016.

8. Ellis Cashmore, *Celebrity Culture* (New York: Routledge, 2006).

9. Karen Armstrong, *Fields of Blood: Religion and the History of Violence* (New York: Knopf, 2014).

10. Chris Rojek, *Celebrity* (London: Reaktion Books, 2001). "Are Celebrities Bigger than Religion?" Stuff, last modified November 9, 2009, http://www.stuff.co.nz /entertainment/celebrities/2851918/Are-celebrities-bigger-than-religion.

11. Donald Horton and Richard Wohl, "Mass Communication and Parasocial Interaction: Observations on Intimacy at a Distance," *Psychiatry* 19 (1956).

CHAPTER 18: THE OPRAH MODEL

1. Roger Ebert, "How I Gave Oprah Winfrey Her Start," in *Roger Ebert's Movie Yearbook 2007* (Kansas City, MO: Andrews McMeel, 2007), 830.

2. It is then no surprise that it didn't take long for Oprah's local morning show to surpass *Donahue* in the ratings. Eventually, Oprah would become so popular that Donahue would relocate to New York and change his time slot to avoid competing with Oprah's show. General information about Oprah draws from Kitty Kelley, *Oprah: A Biography* (New York: H. B. Productions, 2010), 1–8.

3. In 1970, the FCC adopted the Prime Time Access Rule, which was implemented during the 1971–1972 television season in order to increase the level of competition and diversity in programming. At the same time, the FCC adopted the Financial Interest and Syndication Rules, which prohibited broadcast network ownership of syndication arms. Consequently, existing syndication divisions had to be spun off as new, independent companies. As a result of this regime, Oprah had the choice either to sell rights to her show to the ABC network, which would then sell it into syndication and keep the profits, or to run her show as a "first-run" syndicate with King World Productions, an independent syndicator of television programming. As mentioned, Oprah would choose the latter on advice from Ebert.

4. Eva Illouz, *Oprah Winfrey and the Glamour of Misery: An Essay on Popular Culture* (New York: Columbia University Press, 2003).

5. Richard Zoglin, "Oprah Winfrey: Lady with a Calling," *Time,* August 8, 1988, 62–64.

6. Bill Zehme, "It Came from Chicago," *Spy,* December 1986, 31.

7. Barbara Grizzuti Harrison, "The Importance of Being Oprah," *New York Times Magazine,* June 11, 1989.

8. In fact, Oprah inspired a series of tabloid talk shows that would produce the noun "oprahization," which is the "increased tendency for people to publicly describe their feelings and emotions and confess their past indiscretion." "Oprahization," Word Spy, http://wordspy.com/index.php?word=oprahization. An overview of the described Rivera episode, titled "Teen Hatemongers," can be found at "Geraldo Rivera's Nose Broken in Scuffle on His Talk Show," *New York Times,* November 4, 1988, http://www.nytimes.com/1988/11/04/nyregion/geraldo-rivera-s-nose-broken-in-scuffle-on -his-talk-show.html. Incidentally, Geraldo used to be an amateur boxer.

9. Additional information about the tabloid talk show format can be found at Joshua Gamson, *Freaks Talk Back: Tabloid Talk Shows and Sexual Nonconformity* (Chicago: University of Chicago Press, 1998), 220.

10. See Linda Kay, "My Mom and Oprah Winfrey: Her Appeal to White Women," in *The Oprah Phenomenon,* ed. Jennifer Harris and Elwood Watson (Lexington: University Press of Kentucky, 2007), 58; and Laurie L. Haag, "Oprah Winfrey: The Construction of Intimacy in the Talk Show Setting," *Journal of Popular Culture* 26 (1993): 115–22.

11. Oprah is further quoted as explaining that she hoped to help individuals come "to the awareness that, 'I am Creation's son. I am Creation's daughter. I am more than my physical self . . . ultimately I am Spirit come from the greatest Spirit. I am Spirit." For more on this analysis, see Kathryn Lofton, *Oprah: The Gospel of an Icon* (Berkeley: University of California Press, 2011), 4.

12. Kelley, *Oprah: A Biography,* 3.

13. Susan Mackey-Kallis is a communications professor at Villanova University and is quoted in Susan Berfield, "Brand Oprah Has Some Marketing Lessons," *Bloomberg Business,* May 19, 2011, http://business.time.com/2011/05/24/how-oprah-winfrey -implicitly-endorses-consumerism-and-materialism. Noted in the article is how Winfrey's message of consumerism is genuine, as opposed to ironic.

14. Tarini Parti, "The 'Oprah Effect': Winfrey's Influence Extends Deep into Politics," Open.Secrets.org: Center for Responsive Politics, May 25, 2011, http://www .opensecrets.org/news/2011/05/the-oprah-effect-winfreys-influence-extends-deep -into-politics/. Garthwaite coauthored a study that explored the impact of celebrity endorsements in the outcome of the 2008 elections. The article reports how Winfrey's "endorsement of President Barack Obama was responsible for 1 million of his votes in the Democratic primary."

15. Kelley, *Oprah: A Biography,* 399.

16. The relevant episode featured sleep expert Dr. Michael Bennett, who highlighted various products that help individuals sleep well. The effect of Winfrey's endorsement continued for months, with sales at five times higher than before. For more information, see M. David Hornbuckle, "The Oprah Effect," *Inc.,* August 4, 2009, http:// www.inc.com/articles/2009/08/oprah.html.

17. As described in *The New York Times,* Winfrey announced her book club "in save-your-soul evangelist mode . . . that she wanted 'to get the country reading.'" For more about the impact of Oprah's Book Club, see Gayle Feldman, "Making Book on Oprah," *New York Times,* February 2, 1997, https://www.nytimes.com/books/97/02/02

/bookend/bookend.html; and D. T. Max, "The Oprah Effect," *New York Times Magazine,* December 26, 1999, 36-41.

18. Oprah started her "Favorite Things" show in 1999, and in 2007 she presented her viewers with her most expensive item. The grand total for that year's "Favorite Things" was $7,200. Kelley, *Oprah.*

19. P. J. Bednarski, "All About Oprah Inc.," *Broadcasting & Cable,* January 23, 2005.

20. Jack Neff, "How to Get Your Brand on 'Oprah,'" *Advertising Age,* June 2, 2008.

21. Statement by Harpo Productions, Oprah's production company, that "tightly controls advance and post-publicity about the praise that gets parceled out."

22. Oprah's website featured information about the Law of Attraction in 2007.

23. Rhonda Byrne, *The Secret* (New York: Atria, 2006).

24. Albert Mohler, "The Church of Oprah Winfrey—A New American Religion?," *Albert Mohler,* November 29, 2005, http://www.albertmohler.com/2005/11/29/the -church-of-oprah-winfrey-a-new-american-religion-2/.

25. Michael Shermer, "The (Other) Secret," *Scientific American,* June 1, 2007.

26. An analysis by two economists at the University of Maryland, College Park, estimated that Winfrey's endorsement was responsible for between 420,000 and 1,600,000 votes for Obama in the Democratic primary based on a sample of states that did not include Texas, Michigan, North Dakota, Kansas, or Alaska.

27. Ben Shapiro, "The Oprah Schnook Club," *Townhall.com,* March 19, 2003, http:// townhall.com/columnists/benshapiro/2003/03/19/the_oprah_schnook_club/page /full.

28. For examples of fan comments, see Carol Costello, "Oprah Getting Backlash from Some Fans for Obama Support," *CNN Political Ticker Blog,* December 14, 2007, http://politicalticker.blogs.cnn.com/2007/12/14/oprah-getting-backlash-from-some -fans-for-obama-support/.

29. *Variety* has recognized *The Haves and Have Nots,* written and directed by Tyler Perry, as OWN's most popular series to date. See Rick Kissel, "Ratings: OWN's 'The Haves and Have Nots' Hits Series Highs," *Variety,* September 23, 2015, http://variety.com/t /the-haves-and-the-have-nots/.

CHAPTER 19: THE PANOPTICON

1. Rob Tannenbaum and Craig Marks, *I Want My MTV: The Uncensored Story of the Music Video Revolution* (New York: Penguin, 2011), 385.

2. Nina Blackwood et al., *VJ: The Unplugged Adventures of MTV's First Wave* (New York: Atria, 2013).

3. David Copeland, *The Media's Role in Defining the Nation: The Active Voice* (New York: Peter Lang, 2010).

4. Tannenbaum and Marks, *I Want My MTV,* 385.

5. Ibid., 389.

6. Ibid., 550.

7. Daniel B. Morgan, *Last Stage Manager Standing* (New York: Page Publishing, 2015).

8. Tannenbaum and Marks, *I Want My MTV,* 551.

9. Jeffrey Ruoff, *An American Family: A Televised Life* (Minneapolis: University of Minnesota Press, 2002), 65; italics added.

10. Ibid., xv.

11. Margaret Mead, panel discussion for *An American Family* (PBS), WNET, 1973.

12. Tannenbaum and Marks, *I Want My MTV,* 551.

13. Ibid., 553.

14. John J. O'Connor, "'The Real World,' According to MTV," *New York Times,* July 9, 1992, http://www.nytimes.com/1992/07/09/arts/review-television-the-real-world -according-to-mtv.html.

15. Matt Roush, "MTV's Painfully Bogus 'Real World,'" *USA Today,* May 21, 1992.

16. O'Connor, "'The Real World,' According to MTV."

17. Meredith Blake, "The Real World: 'This Is the True Story . . . ,'" *A.V. Club,* June 6, 2011, http://www.avclub.com/tvclub/the-real-world-this-is-the-true-story-57041.

18. Jonathan Gray et al., *Satire TV: Politics and Comedy in the Post-Network Era* (New York: NYU Press, 2009), 250; Samantha Murphy Kelly, "The Real World's Big Bullying Problem," *Mashable,* February 10, 2015, http://mashable.com/2015/02/10 /real-world-skeletons-bullying-problem/#kJ_YeAQ5zZqa.

19. Andrew Corbus and Bill Guertin, *Reality Sells: How to Bring Customers Back Again and Again by Marketing Your Genuine Story* (El Monte, CA: WBusiness Books, 2007), 1.

20. Tannenbaum and Marks, *I Want My MTV,* 552.

21. Ruoff, *An American Family,* 120.

22. Annette Hill, *Reality TV: Audiences and Popular Factual Television* (New York: Rout-ledge, 2005), 7.

23. "10 Years of Primetime: The Rise of Reality and Sports Programming," *Nielsen,* September 21, 2011, http://www.nielsen.com/us/en/insights/news/2011/10-years-of -primetime-the-rise-of-reality-and-sports-programming.html.

24. Ginia Bellafante, "The All-Too-Easy Route to Stardom," *New York Times,* October 13, 2007, http://www.nytimes.com/2007/10/13/arts/television/13bell.html?_r=0.

25. Amaya Rivera, "Keeping Up with the Kardashians: Season 1," *PopMatters,* Octo-ber 15, 2008, http://www.popmatters.com/review/keeping-up-with-the-kardashians -season-1/.

26. Elizabeth Currid-Halkett, "How Kim Kardashian Turns the Reality Business into an Art," *Wall Street Journal,* Nov. 2, 2011, http://blogs.wsj.com/speakeasy/2011/11/02 /how-kim-kardashian-turns-the-business-of-self-promotion-into-an-art/.

PART V: WON'T BE FOOLED AGAIN

1. Iain Rodger, "1999: The Year of the Net," *BBC News,* December 30, 1999, http:// news.bbc.co.uk/2/hi/business/574132.stm; James A. Martin, "New Year's on the Net," *CNN.com,* December 31, 1999, http://www.cnn.com/1999/TECH/computing/12/31 /newyear.net.idg/.

2. "EarthCam's *Webcast of the Century* Provides the Most Comprehensive Coverage of the Biggest Web Celebration in History—From Times Square and Around the World," *EarthCam.com,* December 20, 1999, http://www.earthcam.com/press/pr -rel_122099.htm.

3. Jeff Jarvis, "The Dinosaurs Whine," *Buzz Machine,* January 31, 2006, http:// buzzmachine.com/2006/01/31/the-dinosaurs-whine/.

4. In 1999, television producer Michael Davies attempted to revive *The $64,000 Question* for ABC, but abandoned the effort to work on an American version of the British game show *Who Wants to Be a Millionaire?* See David Baber, *Television Game Show Hosts: Biographies of 32 Stars* (Jefferson, NC: McFarland, 2008).

5. Lawrence Lessig, *The Future of Ideas* (New York: Random House, 2001).

CHAPTER 20: THE KINGDOM OF CONTENT

1. In fact, Microsoft's performance was so strong that company shares soared from $2.375 per share to $136.375 per share. For more information about Microsoft's performance in 1996, see Lawrence M. Fisher, "Microsoft Proves Even Stronger than Wall Street Had Expected," *New York Times,* October 22, 1996, http://www.nytimes.com/1996/10/22/business/microsoft-proves-even-stronger-than-wall-street-had-expected.html.

2. While the full text of the essay is no longer available on the Microsoft website, a copy of the text can be found as reproduced by Wayback Machine (Internet Archive) at Bill Gates, "Content Is King," January 3, 1996, http://web.archive.org/web/20010126005200/http://www.microsoft.com/billgates/columns/1996essay/essay960103.asp.

3. "Content Is King."

4. The satellite campus, known as "Red West," ultimately shifted its focus back to developing "ubiquitous, utilitarian" products with the eventual failure of MSN. As a result, programmers would instead create practical "services" such as Expedia. See Amy Harmon, "More Geek, Less Chic; After a Tryout at Microsoft, the Hip Gives Way to the Really Useful," *New York Times,* October 13, 1997, http://www.nytimes.com/1997/10/13/business/more-geek-less-chic-after-tryout-microsoft-hip-gives-way-really-useful.html?pagewanted=all. For an overview of Microsoft's efforts to develop multimedia-based products, see Denise Caruso, "Microsoft Morphs into a Media Company," *Wired,* June 1, 1996, http://www.wired.com/1996/06/microsoft-6/.

5. Stephen Manes, "The New MSN as Prehistoric TV," February 4, 1997, http://www.nytimes.com/1997/02/04/science/the-new-msn-as-prehistoric-tv.html. According to Harmon, Microsoft only had 2.3 million subscribers, which is minimal in light of the fact that MSN was already preinstalled on the millions of personal computers Microsoft sold.

6. Information about the partnership between Microsoft and NBC can be found at Michael Dresser, "Microsoft, NBC to Offer News Joint Venture Plans 24-Hour News on Cable, On-line Internet Service," *Baltimore Sun,* December 15, 1995, http://articles.baltimoresun.com/1995-12-15/business/1995349021_1_microsoft-cable-nbc-executives; and Megan Garber, " 'The Revolution Begins Here': MSNBC's First Broadcast, July 1996," *The Atlantic,* July 16, 2012, http://www.theatlantic.com/technology/archive/2012/07/the-revolution-begins-here-msnbcs-first-broadcast-july-1996/259855/.

7. Information about the first issue of *Slate* can be found at "Inaugural Issue of Slate, New Interactive Magazine from Microsoft and Editor Michael Kinsley, to Debut Online Today," Microsoft News Center, June 24, 1996, http://news.microsoft.com/1996/06/24/inaugural-issue-of-slate-new-interactive-magazine-from-microsoft-and-editor-michael-kinsley-to-debut-online-today/.

8. General information about the growth and impact of Google comes from Steven Levy, *In the Plex: How Google Thinks, Works, and Shapes Our Lives* (New York: Simon & Schuster, 2011), 94.

9. Battelle chronicles the success of Google in John Battelle, *The Search: How Google and Its Rivals Rewrote the Rules of Business and Transformed Our Culture* (New York: Portfolio, 2005).

10. The academic piece written by Brin and Page served as a presentation of Google as "a prototype of a large-scale search engine which makes heavy use of the structure present in hypertext." See Sergey Brin and Lawrence Page, "The Anatomy of a Large-

Scale Hypertextual Web Search Engine," paper presented at the Seventh International World-Wide Web Conference, Brisbane, Australia, April 14–18, 1998.

11. Battelle, *The Search,* 111.

12. Dan Gillmor, "To Be an Online Company, First Throw Out Old Rules," *St. Louis Post-Dispatch,* February 24, 1997, 123.

13. For additional information about GoTo and general criticism of the model, see Laurie J. Flynn, "With Goto.com's Search Engine, the Highest Bidder Shall Be Ranked First," *New York Times,* March 16, 1998, http://www.nytimes.com/1998/03/16/business/with-gotocom-s-search-engine-the-highest-bidder-shall-be-ranked-first.html; "Rankings for Sale: Payola on the Information Highway? Or Payments for Good Shelf Space?," *From Now On: The Educational Technology Journal* 10 (2001), http://www.fno.org/apr01/payola.html.

14. Brin and Page, "The Anatomy of a Large-Scale Hypertextual Web Search Engine."

15. For a description of the term "Googley," see Sara Kehaulani Goo, "Building a 'Googley' Workforce," *Washington Post,* October 21, 2006.

16. A more detailed description of Google's AdWords can be found at "How AdWords Works," Google Support, February 21, 2016, https://support.google.com/adwords/answer/2497976?hl=en. For additional information about AdWords success, see Peter Coy, "The Secret to Google's Success," *Bloomberg Business,* March 5, 2006; Steven Levy, "Secret of Googlenomics: Data-Fueled Recipe Brews Profitability," *Wired,* May 22, 2009.

17. Douglas Edwards, *I'm Feeling Lucky: The Confessions of Google Employee Number 59* (New York: Houghton Mifflin Harcourt, 2011), 190.

18. Levy, "In the Plex," 94.

CHAPTER 21: HERE COMES EVERYONE

1. Rebecca Mead, "You've Got Blog: How to Put Your Business, Your Boyfriend, and Your Life Online," *The New Yorker,* November 13, 2000, 102. Mead's story was published in the collection *We've Got Blog: How Weblogs Are Changing Our Culture* (New York: Basic Books, 2002).

2. See Clay Shirky, *Here Comes Everybody: The Power of Organizing Without Organizations* (New York: Penguin, 2008).

3. Shirky, *Here Comes Everybody: The Power of Organizing Without Organizations,* 55.

4. Jorn Barger, one of the early webloggers, first used the term to capture the concept of "logging the web," or "collecting interesting things from around the world and writing about them on the internet." See Ogi Djuraskovic, "Robot Wisdom and How Jorn Barger Invented Blogging," *firstsiteguide.com,* March 20, 2015, http://firstsiteguide.com/robot-wisdom-and-jorn-barger/.

5. Rick Levine, Christopher Locke, Doc Searls, and David Weinberger, *The Cluetrain Manifesto: The End of Business as Usual* (Cambridge, MA: Perseus, 2000), 76. The book was originally published on the web in March 1999.

6. David Weinberger, "What Blogging Was," *Joho the Blog,* January 8, 2014, http://www.hyperorg.com/blogger/2014/01/08/what-blogging-was/.

7. Erin Venema developed the word "escribitionist" in 1999 to distinguish between web journal authors and those who kept their diaries on paper. See www.escribitionist.org, a webpage containing a copy of the email in which Venema first used the word.

8. Jimmy Wales, February 7, 2011, answer to "Why does Wikipedia ask for donations rather than having ads?," *Quora,* https://www.quora.com/Why-does-Wikipedia-ask-for-donations-rather-than-having-ads.

9. Virginia Heffernan, *The Medium: The Way We Watch Now* (blog), http://themedium.blogs.nytimes.com//.

10. See Allan J. Kimmel, *Connecting with Consumers: Marketing for New Marketplace Realities* (New York: Oxford University Press, 2010).

11. Jeff Jarvis and John Griffin, "Is Print Doomed?," *Fast Company,* December 1, 2005, http://www.fastcompany.com/54733/print-doomed.

12. Lev Grossman, "You—Yes, You—Are TIME's Person of the Year," *Time,* December 25, 2006, http://content.time.com/time/magazine/article/0,9171,1570810,00.html.

13. Jon Pareles, "2006, Brought to You by You," *New York Times,* December 10, 2006, http://www.nytimes.com/2006/12/10/arts/music/10pare.html?pagewanted=print.

14. See Andrew Keen, T*he Cult of the Amateur: How Today's Internet Is Killing Our Culture* (New York: Doubleday, 2007).

15. See Greg Miller, "Turn On, Boot Up, and Jack In with Timothy Leary's Long-Lost Video Games," *Wired,* October 1, 2013, http://www.wired.com/2013/10/timothy-leary-video-games/.

16. C. W. Nevius interviewed Dave Barry after Barry came to speak at the Commonwealth Club in San Francisco. C. W. Nevius, "Podcasts, Blogs, and Dave Barry," *SFGATE,* January 31, 2006, http://www.sfgate.com/bayarea/nevius/article/Podcasts-blogs-and-Dave-Barry-2523537.php.

17. Yochai Benkler, *The Wealth of Networks: How Social Production Transforms Markets and Freedom* (New Haven, CT: Yale University Press, 2006), 5.

18. Shirky, *Here Comes Everybody: The Power of Organizing Without Organizations*, 66.

19. Jeff Jarvis, "My Testimony to Sen. Kerry," *Buzz Machine,* April 21, 2009, http://buzzmachine.com/2009/04/21/my-testimony-to-sen-kerry/.

CHAPTER 22: THE RISE OF CLICKBAIT

1. For a personal recounting of Peretti's challenge to Nike's corporate image, "the ensuing email correspondence with Nike [that] became a global anti-sweatshop event, which made national news in large consuming societies," and the global impact, see Jonah Peretti, "The Nike Sweatshop Email: Political Consumerism, Internet, and Culture Jamming," in *Politics, Products, and Markets: Exploring Political Consumerism Past and Present,* ed. Michele Micheletti (New Brunswick, NJ: Transaction Publishers, 2006), 130–31. For the entire chain of emails exchanged between Peretti and Nike, circulating since January 2001, see "Jonah Peretti's Nike 'Sweatshop' Email," *About .com,* accessed February 19, 2016, http://urbanlegends.about.com/library/blnike.htm.

2. These quotes from Peretti were drawn from an interview by Tim Wu. April 4, 2012. Approximately "11.4 million people received the Nike Sweatshop Email" and "over a three-month period, [Peretti] received 3,655 inquiries." Peretti, *Politics, Products, and Markets,* 132. To read more about how the email spread so quickly and to read some of the inquiries Peretti received, see Peretti, "The Nike Sweatshop Email," in *Politics, Products, and Markets.*

3. Nicola Bednarek, ed., *Fresh Dialogue 8: Designing Audiences/New Voices in Graphic Design* (New York: Princeton Architectural Press, 2008); Greg Holden, *Internet Baby-*

lon: Secrets, Scandals, and Shocks on the Information Superhighway (New York: APress Media, 2004). To learn about Duncan Watts's theories, see Duncan J. Watts, *Six Degrees: The Science of a Connected Age* (New York: W. W. Norton, 2004).

4. "forget-me-not-panties," *Panchira Corp.,* 2005, http://www.forgetmenotpanties .com/. "The forget-me-not-panty site won for getting the most unique users, some 615,000 in the three weeks. Over the competition, it pulled in many times that, more than 20 million total visitors." Heidi Dawley, "Alas, at Last, the forget-me-not-panty," *Media Life Magazine,* December 5, 2005, http://www.medialifemagazine.com/alas -at-last-the-forget-me-not-panty/. To read more about the Eyebeam workshops, see "Contagious Media Showdown—Workshops," *Eyebeam,* http://eyebeam.org/events /contagious-media-showdown-workshops. See also "Unfair Results at Contagious Media Showdown?," *Google Blogoscoped,* May 21, 2005, http://blogoscoped.com /archive/2005-05-21-n39.html.

5. To read all twenty-three points, see Jonah Peretti, "Notes on Contagious Media," 160–61, http://www.cultura.gov.br/documents/10877/35301/9-peretti.pdf/684f6ada -4479-4bed-a3a0-f434837f3e6b. Joe Karaganis, *Structures of Participation in Digital Culture* (New York: Social Science Research Council, 2007). Felix Salmon, "BuzzFeed's Jonah Peretti Goes Long: The Media Mogul (Twice Over) on Being Both Contagious and Sticky," *A Media Corporation,* https://medium.com/matter /buzzfeeds-jonah-peretti-goes-long-e98cf13160e7#.sjme15us5.

6. For the full *LA Weekly* critique of *The Huffington Post,* see Nikki Finke, "Celebs to the Slaughter," *LA Weekly,* May 12, 2005, http://www.laweekly.com/news/celebs-to -the-slaughter-2139949. For other highlights from early critiques, see Liz C. Barrett, "Top 5 UNENTHUSIASTIC HuffPo Reviews of 2005," *Columbia Journalism Review,* May 10, 2010, http://www.cjr.org/behind_the_news/top_5_unenthusiastic _huffpo_re.php. Richard A. Gershon, *Digital Media and Innovation: Management and Design Strategies in Communication* (Los Angeles: SAGE Publications, 2016). The editors of *The Huffington Post, The Huffington Post Complete Guide to Blogging* (New York: Simon & Schuster, 2008). Kerric Harvey, ed., *Encyclopedia of Social Media and Politics* (Los Angeles: SAGE Publications, 2013).

7. Bill Gueskin, Ava Seave, and Lucas Graves, "Chapter Six: Aggregation," *Columbia Journalism Review,* May 10, 2011, http://www.cjr.org/the_business_of_digital _journalism/chapter_six_aggregation.php. For additional statistics on and details about *The Huffington Post's* growth, see Michael Shapiro, "Six Degrees of Aggregation: How The Huffington Post Ate the Internet," *Columbia Journalism Review,* June 2012, http://www.cjr.org/cover_story/six_degrees_of_aggregation.php.

8. As quoted in Joseph Turow, *The Daily You* (New Haven, CT: Yale University Press, 2011), 117. Nate Silver, "The Economics of Blogging and The Huffington Post," *New York Times,* February 12, 2011, http://fivethirtyeight.blogs.nytimes.com/2011/02/12/the -economics-of-blogging-and-the-huffington-post/; Bill Keller, "All the Aggregation That's Fit to Aggregate," *New York Times Magazine,* March 10, 2011, http://www.nytimes .com/2011/03/13/magazine/mag-13lede-t.html?_r=0; Mike Friedrichsen and Wolfgang Muhl-Benninghaus, eds., *Handbook of Social Media Management: Value Chain and Business Models in Changing Media Markets* (New York: Springer Heidelberg, 2013).

9. Keith J. Kelly, "Huffington Post Turns 10—but Its Profits Are Still a Mystery," *New York Post,* May 5, 2015; "AOL Agrees to Acquire The Huffington Post," *Huffington Post,* February 7, 2011, http://www.huffingtonpost.com/2011/02/07/aol-huffington-post _n_819375.html.

10. Doree Shafrir, "The Truth About Perez Hilton's Traffic," *Gawker,* July 10, 2007, http://gawker.com/276369/the-truth-about-perez-hiltons-traffic.

11. Elizabeth Day, "Mr Gossip Steps into the Real World," *The Guardian,* September 30, 2007, http://www.theguardian.com/media/2007/sep/30/digitalmedia.fashion. Perez Hilton interview by Dan Avery, *Big Words,* December 8, 2001; Jacquelynn D. Powers, "Bringing Miami Spice to the Celebrity Dish," *Ocean Drive Magazine,* http://www.siqueiros.com/oceandrive/hybrid/archives/2006_11/cover/index.html; Colleen Raezier, "How the Media Legitimized Perez Hilton, Cyber-Bully Extraordinaire," *NewsBusters,* September 22, 2009, http://www.newsbusters.org/blogs/colleen-raezler/2009/09/22/how-media-legitimized-perez-hilton-cyber-bully-extraordinaire; "Perez Hilton US Media Kit," *Perez Hilton,* http://perezhilton.com/mediakit/US/; Will Wei, "WHERE ARE THEY NOW? Creators of 'Lonelygirl15' Turned Web Series into a Multi-Million Dollar Company," *Business Insider,* July 20, 2010, http://www.businessinsider.com/where-are-they-now-creators-of-lonelygirl15-turned-web-series-into-a-multi-million-dollar-company-2010-7.

12. Jon Morrow, "Why I Quit Blogging (and What to Do if You're Struggling)," *Guest Blogging,* http://guestblogging.com/quit-blogging/; David Weinberger, "This Blog Has Gone Spamtacular," *Joho the Blog,* October 4, 2015, http://www.hyperorg.com/blogger/category/blogs/.

13. Michael A. Banks, *Blogging Heroes: Interviews with 30 of the World's Top Bloggers* (Indianapolis: Wiley Publishing, 2008); Marta Cantijoch, Rachel Gibson, and Stephen Ward, *Analysing Social Media Data and Web Networks* (New York: Palgrave Macmillan, 2014); Paul Boutin, "Twitter, Flickr, Facebook Make Blogs Look So 2004," *Wired,* October 20, 2008, http://www.wired.com/2008/10/st-essay-19/.

CHAPTER 23: THE PLACE TO BE

1. Alan J. Tabak, "Hundreds Register for New Facebook Website," *The Harvard Crimson,* February 9, 2004.

2. George Beahm, *The Boy Billionaire: Mark Zuckerberg in His Own Words* (Chicago: Agate Publishing, 2012), 42.

3. Henry Blodget, "The Maturation of the Billionaire Boy-Man," *New York,* May 6, 2012; David Kirkpatrick, *The Facebook Effect: The Inside Story of the Company That Is Connecting the World* (New York: Simon & Schuster, 2010).

4. Jack Goldsmith and Tim Wu, *Who Controls the Internet?: Illusions of a Borderless World* (Oxford, UK: Oxford University Press, 2006), 17–18.

5. Erin E. Buckels et al., "Trolls Just Want to Have Fun," *Personality and Individual Differences* 67 (2014), 1.

6. Max Chafkin, "How to Kill a Great Idea!," accessed February 22, 2016, http://www.inc.com/magazine/20070601/features-how-to-kill-a-great-idea.html.

7. David Kirkpatrick, "I Get By with a Little Help from My Friends of Friends," *Fortune,* October 13, 2003.

8. Shirin Sharif, "All the Cool Kids Are Doing It," *The Stanford Daily,* April 30, 2004, A4.

9. Emily Rotberg, "Thefacebook.com Opens to Duke Students," *The Chronicle Online,* April 14, 2004; Shirin Sharif, "All the Cool Kids Are Doing It," *The Stanford Daily,* April 30, 2004, A4.

10. Kirkpatrick, *The Facebook Effect: The Inside Story of the Company That Is Connecting the World,* 175.

11. Seth Fiegerman, "Friendster Founder Tells His Side of the Story, 10 Years After Facebook," *Mashable,* February 3, 2014, http://mashable.com/2014/02/03/jonathan-abrams-friendster-facebook/#b9wfGLedTiqV.

12. Danah Boyd, "White Flight in Networked Publics? How Race and Class Shaped American Teen Engagement with MySpace and Facebook," *Race After the Internet*, eds. Lisa Nakamura and Peter A. Chow-White (New York: Routledge, 2011).

13. Amy Lee, "Myspace Collapse: How the Social Network Fell Apart," *Huffington Post,* June 30, 2011, http://www.huffingtonpost.com/2011/06/30/how-myspace-fell-apart_n_887853.html.

14. Fred Vogelstein, "The Wired Interview: Facebook's Mark Zuckerberg," *Wired,* June 29, 2009, http://www.wired.com/2009/06/mark-zuckerberg-speaks/.

15. Zeynep Tufekci, "Grooming, Gossip, Facebook and Myspace," *Information, Communication & Society,* 11 (2008), 546, doi: 10.1080/13691180801999050.

16. Larry Dignan, "Facebook's IPO: Massive Valuation Brings Business Model Scrutiny," May 16, 2012, http://www.cnet.com/news/facebooks-ipo-massive-valuation-brings-business-model-scrutiny/.

17. Brad Smallwood, "Making Digital Brand Campaigns Better," October 1, 2012, https://www.facebook-studio.com/news/item/making-digital-brand-campaigns-better.

18. Christina Sagioglou and Tobias Greitemeyer, "Facebook's Emotional Consequences: Why Facebook Causes a Decrease in Mood and Why People Still Use It," *Computers in Human Behavior* 35 (June 2014).

CHAPTER 24: THE IMPORTANCE OF BEING MICROFAMOUS

1. All quotes from Rex Sorgatz from author email interview beginning January 12, 2016.

2. Rex Sorgatz, "The Microfame Game," *New York,* June 17, 2008.

3. James Ulmer, *James Ulmer's Hollywood Hot List: The Complete Guide to Star Ranking* (New York: St. Martin's Griffin, 2014).

4. Misha Kavka, *Reality TV* (Edinburgh: Edinburgh University Press, 2012), 166.

5. Gareth Palmer, "The Undead: Life on the D-List," *Westminster Papers in Communication and Culture,* 2 (2005), 40, discussing Anita Biressi and Heather Nunn's argument over reality TV.

6. David Weinberger, *Small Pieces Loosely Joined: A Unified Theory of the Web* (Cambridge, MA: Basic Books, 2008), 104.

CHAPTER 25: THE FOURTH SCREEN AND THE MIRROR OF NARCISSUS

1. Taylor Glascock, "Hipster Barbie Is So Much Better at Instagram than You," *Wired,* September 3, 2015, http://www.wired.com/2015/09/hipster-barbie-much-better-instagram/.

2. Jenna Garrett, "Hipster Barbie Quits the Internet, Leaving Us Without a Hero," *Wired,* November 4, 2015, http://www.wired.com/2015/11/socality-barbie-quits/.

3. "How to Grow Your Instagram," *The Miller Affect,* http://themilleraffect.com/grow-your-instagram/.

4. Hannah Ellis-Petersen, "Instagram Users Turn Flash into Cash, as Companies Eye New Advertising Market," *The Guardian,* November 27, 2014, http://www.theguardian.com/technology/2014/nov/27/instagram-users-earn-income-advertising-brands.

5. James Franco, "The Meanings of the Selfie," *New York Times,* December 26, 2013, http://www.nytimes.com/2013/12/29/arts/the-meanings-of-the-selfie.html?_r=0.

6. Laura Donovan, "This Instagram Star Is Calling B.S. on the Industry That Made Her Famous," *ATTN,* November 2, 2015, http://www.attn.com/stories/3966/why-essena-oneill-quit-social-media.

7. Mahita Gajanan, "Young Women on Instagram and Self-esteem: 'I Absolutely Feel Insecure,'" *The Guardian,* November 4, 2015, http://www.theguardian.com/media/2015/nov/04/instagram-young-women-self-esteem-essena-oneill.

CHAPTER 26: THE WEB HITS BOTTOM

1. Jonah Peretti, "Notes on Contagious Media," in *Structures of Participation in a Digital World,* ed. Joe Karaganis (New York: Social Science Research Council, 2007), 160.

2. Ibid., 161.

3. Ben Cohen, "John Peretti Can Laugh at 'The Wolf of BuzzFeed' Because He Is Worth $200 Million," *The Daily Banter,* April 4, 2014, http://thedailybanter.com/2014/04/jonah-peretti-can-laugh-at-the-wolf-of-BuzzFeed-because-he-is-worth-200-million/.

4. Ben Cohen, "Buzz Feed Takes Journalism to New Low with Jurassic Park GIF Version of Egyptian Revolution," *The Daily Banter,* July 9, 2013, http://thedailybanter.com/2013/07/buzz-feed-takes-journalism-to-new-low-with-jurassic-park-gif-version-of-egyptian-revolution/.

5. *Columbia Journalism Review,* Twitter, September 28, 2012, https://twitter.com/cjr/status/251772260455706624.

6. Mark Manson, "In the Future, Our Attention Will Be Sold," December 4, 2014, http://markmanson.net/attention.

7. James Bennett, interview with Eric Schmidt, *Washington Ideas Forum,* October 1, 2010, http://www.theatlantic.com/technology/archive/2010/10/googles-ceo-the-laws-are-written-by-lobbyists/63908/.

8. Gregor Aisch, Wilson Andrews, and Josh Keller, "The Cost of Mobile Ads on 50 News Websites," *New York Times,* October 1, 2015, http://www.nytimes.com/interactive/2015/10/01/business/cost-of-mobile-ads.html?_r=0.

9. Marco Arment, "The Ethics of Modern Web Ad-blocking," *Marco.org,* August 11, 2015, https://marco.org/2015/08/11/ad-blocking-ethics.

10. Ashlee Vance, "This Tech Bubble Is Different," *Bloomberg Businessweek,* April 14, 2011, http://www.bloomberg.com/bw/magazine/content/11_17/b4225060960537.htm.

11. James Williams, "Why It's OK to Block Ads," *Practical Ethics* (blog), University of Oxford, October 16, 2015, http://blog.practicalethics.ox.ac.uk/2015/10/why-its-ok-to-block-ads/.

12. Heidi Moore, "BuzzFeed Announces $19.3m in Funding As It Transforms Internet Advertising," *The Guardian,* January 3, 2013, http://www.theguardian.com/media/2013/jan/03/buzzfeed-new-funding-transforms-advertising.

13. Andrew Sullivan, "Guess Which Buzzfeed Piece Is an Ad," *The Dish* (blog), February 21, 2013, http://dish.andrewsullivan.com/2013/02/21/guess-which-buzzfeed-piece-is-an-ad/.

CHAPTER 27: A RETREAT AND A REVOLT

1. Tim Wu, "Netflix's War on Mass Culture," *New Republic,* December 4, 2013, https://newrepublic.com/article/115687/netflixs-war-mass-culture.
2. Netflix, Inc. Earnings Conference Call, interview with Reed Hastings, *Thomson Reuters,* January 22, 2014, http://files.shareholder.com/downloads/NFLX/0x0x720548/ea656605-6780-4844-9114-3985aaabeaa4/NFLX-Transcript-2014-01-22T22_00.pdf.
3. "Netflix Declares Binge Watching Is the New Normal," *PRNewswire,* December 13, 2013, http://www.prnewswire.com/news-releases/netflix-declares-binge-watching-is-the-new-normal-235713431.html.
4. Damon Lindelof, "Mourning TV," *New York Times,* November 11, 2007, http://www.nytimes.com/2007/11/11/opinion/11lindelof.html?_r=0.
5. Andrew Romano, "Why You're Addicted to TV," *Newsweek,* May 15, 2013, http://www.newsweek.com/2013/05/15/why-youre-addicted-tv-237340.html.

CHAPTER 28: WHO'S BOSS HERE?

1. Matthew Panzarino, "Apple's Tim Cook Delivers Blistering Speech on Encryption, Privacy," *TechCrunch,* June 2, 2015, http://techcrunch.com/2015/06/02/apples-tim-cook-delivers-blistering-speech-on-encryption-privacy/.
2. Ibid.
3. Tim Cook, "Apple's Commitment to Your Privacy," *Apple,* http://www.apple.com/privacy/.
4. Robin Anderson, *Consumer Culture and TV Programming* (Boulder, CO: Westview Press, 1995).
5. Richard Serra and Carlota Fay Schoolman, "Television Delivers People," *Persistence of Vision—Volume 1: Monitoring the Media* (1973), video.
6. Farhad Manjoo, "What Apple's Tim Cook Overlooked in His Defense of Privacy," *New York Times,* June 10, 2015, http://www.nytimes.com/2015/06/11/technology/what-apples-tim-cook-overlooked-in-his-defense-of-privacy.html?_r=0.
7. Lev Grossman, "Inside Facebook's Plan to Wire the World," *Time,* December 15, 2014, http://time.com/facebook-world-plan/.
8. iOS Developer Library, "What's New in Safari," *Apple,* https://developer.apple.com/library/ios/releasenotes/General/WhatsNewInSafari/Articles/Safari_9.html.
9. Joshua Benton, "A Blow for Mobile Advertising: The Next Version of Safari Will Let Users Block Ads on iPhones and iPads," *NiemanLab,* June 10, 2015, http://www.niemanlab.org/2015/06/a-blow-for-mobile-advertising-the-next-version-of-safari-will-let-users-block-ads-on-iphones-and-ipads/.
10. Randall Rothenberg, "Ad Blocking: The Unnecessary Internet Apocalypse," *Ad Age,* September 22, 2015, http://adage.com/article/digitalnext/ad-blocking-unnecessary-internet-apocalypse/300470/.
11. David Chavern, "Opinion: Ad Blocking Threatens Democracy," *Digiday,* January 12, 2016, http://digiday.com/publishers/opinion-ad-blocking-disastrous-effect-healthy-democracy/.
12. Avram Piltch, "Why Using an Ad Blocker Is Stealing," *Tom's Guide,* May 22, 2015, http://www.tomsguide.com/us/ad-blocking-is-stealing,news-20962.html.
13. Marco Arment, "Introducing Peace, My Privacy-Focused iOS Ad Blocker," *Marco.org,* September 16, 2015, https://marco.org/2015/09/16/peace-content-blocker.

14. James Williams, "Why It's OK to Block Ads," *Practical Ethics* (blog), University of Oxford, October 16, 2015, http://blog.practicalethics.ox.ac.uk/2015/10/why-its-ok-to -block-ads/.

15. Michael Wolff, "Ad Blockers Impair Digital Media," *USA Today,* September 13, 2015, http://www.usatoday.com/story/money/columnist/wolff/2015/09/11/wolff-ad -blockers-impair-digital-media/72057926/.

INDEX

A&E, 328, 331
ABC (American Broadcasting Company),
    97*n*, 129, 136, 162, 210, 229, 267,
    365*n*, 373*n*, 376*n*
Abrams, Jonathan, 293, 297
Adams, David, 99
Adams, John, 159, 352*n*
Adams, Samuel Hopkins, 32, 33–5
adblockers, 337–8
advertising, 7, 24–6, 50, 70–1, 73–4, 83,
    117, 122, 155–6, 159
  backlash against, 147–50, 341
  channel surfing's effect on, 178–80
  to children, 161–2
  and choice, 77–8, 119–20
  collapse of, 75
  counterculture's effect on, 166–9
  deceptive, 78, 79–80
  "direct mail," 31
  disenchantment with, 74–81
  on Facebook, 296–7, 299–300
  of food, 133
  Freud's influence on, 56–7
  Google and, 258–9, 262–6
  by government, 38–50
  Hitler's work in, 111
  internal critics of, 75–6

motivation research on, 132–4
in newspapers, 11–18
online, 189, 200, 201, 208–9, 264,
    267, 283–4, 323–4, 329
patent medicine's influence on,
    28–30
post–World War I, 51–2
power to drive sales by, 139–40
public disenchantment with, 35
in public schools, 3–5, 342
on radio, 86–94, 98, 103
"reason why," 54, 80, 131
religion and, 71
spending on, 70, 76, 130–1
targeted, 53, 60, 64
television and, 130–1
ubiquity of, 71–2
women as target of, 53, 59–64
*see also specific agencies, campaigns,
    and products*
Advertising, Its Principles and Practice
    (textbook), 60
"advertorial," 325–6
AdWords, 264, 265, 266, 267, 329
Affordable Care Act (2010), 38
African Americans, 91, 156, 157, 171
Alda, Alan, 165, 226

Allen, Gracie, 102
Allen, Robert C., 360*n*
Allen, Steve, 135
Allies, 107, 121
All in the Family (TV show), 164, 165
All Things Considered (radio show), 163
Alpert, Richard (Ram Dass), 151–2
AltaVista, 258
Amazon, 201, 321, 323, 340
AM Chicago (TV show), 227, 228
American Academy of Pediatrics, 54
American Family, An (TV show), 240–1,
    242, 244, 245
American Idol (TV show), 247, 248
American Tobacco Company, 65, 66, 69,
    134
America Online (AOL), 186, 198, 199,
    200, 202–6, 207–13, 215, 260, 264,
    281, 284, 291, 292–3, 294, 297, 306,
    321
America's Answer to the Hun (film), 45
Amis, Martin, 193, 195, 196
Amos 'n' Andy (radio show), 87–93, 96,
    99, 100, 104, 118, 137, 194, 244,
    331
Anacin, 131, 139, 179, 263
Anderson, Robin, 336
André, John, 15
Androids, 300*n*, 310, 311*n*, 338
anti-Semitism, 112, 113
AOL–Time Warner, 321
    see also America Online; Time
    Warner
Apple, 79, 119, 144, 180, 192*n*, 199*n*,
    310, 311*n*, 321, 335, 336–9
Apple II, 197, 198–9
Arcangel, Cory, 279
Arment, Marco, 324
Armstrong, Karen, 223
Armstrong, Lance, 236
ARPANET, 183
"Arrow Man" campaign, 157
Article III Groupie (anonymous poster),
    287
Asquith, Herbert, 37
As the World Turns (TV show), 239
AT&T, 97*n*, 208*n*, 213
Atari, 192, 196–7, 371*n*
Atlantic, 75, 321

attention:
    ability to ignore and, 19–20
    capturing of, 9
    as commodity, 6
    and human freedom, 119–20
    neuroscience of, 19–21
    "peak," 129–30
    quality of, 125
    religion as early claimant on, 26–7
    transitory vs. sustained, 125
    zones of, 94
Attention Deficit Disorder, 194
attention industry, 5–6, 215
    Internet's effect on, 274–5
    as new norm, 5–6
    race to the bottom in, 16–17
    revolts against, 7, 22–3, 151–69
    rise of, 11–23
    television's place in, 134–6
    triggers for, 21
    see also advertising
attention span, 6–7
Auden, W. H., 102
audience fragmentation, 175, 270–1
Audimeter, 104, 105
Aunt Jemima, 28
A.V. Club, The, 243
Aylesworth, Merlin H., 360*n*

Babes (TV show), 177
Baer, Ralph, 191, 192, 196, 371*n*
Baldwin, Billy, 128
Ball, Lucille, 128
Baltimore Sun, 284
Barbie (doll), 161
Barger, Jorn, 378*n*
Barlow, John Perry, 291–2
Barnouw, Erik, 91, 150
Barry, Dave, 274
Barthes, Roland, 224
Barton, Bruce, 71
Bartos, Rena, 178
Bates, Ted, 226
Battelle, John, 258–9, 260, 264*n*–5*n*
BBC, 101, 102, 117, 251, 267
Beatles, 158, 160
Beat the Clock (TV show), 139, 142
behavioral science, 56–7
Behaviorist Manifesto (Watson), 56–7

Behrman, S. N., 51
Belgium, 38, 41, 46, 50, 110
Belief (TV show), 236
Belmont, Alva, 63–4
Benkler, Yochai, 274, 287
Bennett, James Gordon, 15–16
Bennett, Michael, 374*n*
Benny, Jack, 102
Benson-Allott, Caetlin, 145
Benson & Hedges, 167
Berle, Milton, 123–4, 128
Berlow, Myer, 208–9, 210
Bernays, Edward, 49–50, 56, 66, 67–9, 100,
    103, 122, 174, 356*n*, 361*n*
BET (Black Entertainment Television),
    175, 236
Beverly Hillbillies, The (TV show), 162
Beverly Hills, 90210 (TV show), 239
Bezos, Jeff, 170
"Big Brother" advertisement, 180
Big Sister (radio show), 102
billboards, 22, 23
"Billie Jean" (song), 179
Biltmore Agreement, 103*n*
binge watching, 330–1
Bird, Drayton, 24
Birth of a Nation, The (film), 89
Bismarck, Otto von, 38
Bissell Carpet Sweeper, 25, 348*n*–9*n*
Blackberry, 308–10
blackpeopleloveus.com, 280
blogs, 268–73, 274, 285–8, 306, 322
Blue Book report (FCC), 101*n*
Boing-Boing (blog), 270, 271
Bok, Edward, 33*n*
Bolt, Beranek and Newman (BBN), 183,
    185
Booth, Charles, 369*n*
Bored at Work Network (BWN), 267
Bowen, Michael, 153
Boyd, Danah, 298
Brandeis, Louis, 48–9
brand elasticity, 155
Brandenburg v. Ohio, 353*n*
branding, 53, 57–9, 60, 62, 64, 72, 78–9,
    80, 131, 155–6, 298, 300
Brandt, Jan, 206
Bravo, 175, 369*n*–70*n*
Breaking Bad (TV show), 333

Breakout (video game), 192
Brennan, Edward, 201
Brin, Sergey, 258, 259, 260–1, 262, 265, 338,
    377*n*
Brinkley, Alan, 218–19
Broadcasting, 88
Brothers, Joyce, 137
Bryan, William Jennings, 114
Buggles, 237
Bunim, Mary-Ellis, 239–40, 241, 242, 243,
    248
Burgess, Ernest W., 369*n*
Burnett, Leo, 131–2, 167
Burns, George, 102
Burrows, Stephen, 220
Burton, Richard, 220
Bush, George W., 281
Bushnell, Norman, 192, 196, 371*n*
Business Week, 75
Büyükkökten, Orkut, 293–4
BuzzFeed, 318–21, 325–6, 327

cable television, 174–6, 177–8
Cadillac, 53, 58, 59, 72, 75, 78, 131, 138
Calvin Klein, 179
Camel cigarettes, 69, 78, 79, 126
Camel News Caravan (TV show), 126, 206
Canadian Broadcasting Company, 161
capitalism, 9, 168
Carnival Cruise Line, 300
Carr, Nicholas, 326
Case, Steve, 198, 202, 205, 209
Catholicism, Catholics, 39, 58, 71, 75, 118
CBS (Columbia Broadcasting System), 88,
    95, 96–8, 99, 101–3, 104, 105–7, 118,
    124, 126–9, 135, 136–9, 140–1, 142,
    143, 148, 162, 163, 164–5, 175, 200,
    210, 221, 228, 239, 271*n*, 284, 286,
    301, 361*n*, 365*n*
    "Tiffany Network" strategy of, 100–1,
    126
CBS Evening News, The, 126, 341
celebrity, 63–4, 137, 215–16, 217–26, 244–6,
    281–2, 284, 286, 303, 304, 305, 306,
    307, 312, 314
Century of the Self, The (documentary
    series), 56
Chamberlin, Edward, 78
Channels, 178

channel surfing, 178, 180

Chaplin, Charlie, 63

Charlie Brown Christmas, A (TV special), 163–4, 368n

Charlie's Angels (TV show), 221

Chase, David, 332

Chase, Stuart, 73–5, 78

chat rooms, 202–3, 204, 206, 292

check-in impulse, 186–8, 205, 308, 339

Chéret, Jules, 18–19, 21, 22

Chiang Kai-shek, 219

Chicago School of Sociology, 170–1

Children's Corner, The (TV show), 161

choice, 119–20, 156, 160, 177, 180

Chomsky, Noam, 68, 271n

Christianity, Christians, 26, 118n, 230, 234, 235

Chrysler, 58, 75, 134

Churchill, Winston, 219

cigarettes, 58, 65–9, 78, 79–80, 126, 131–2, 134, 153, 355n, 356n

Claritas, 171, 173, 174

Clark, Dick, 251

Clark Stanley's Snake Oil Liniment, 27–9, 30, 33, 35, 36

clickbait, 282–3, 284, 310–11, 318, 322

Clicquot Club Eskimos, 86, 89

Clinton, Bill, 270, 282

Clinton, Hillary, 235

Clooney, George, 305

Cluetrain Manifesto, The (Locke, Searls, Weinberger, and Levine), 269

cluster analysis, 171–4

Clustering of America, The (Weiss), 369n

CNN, 161, 176, 201, 251–2, 257, 267

Coca-Cola, 4, 53, 58, 72, 78, 155, 156, 157, 164, 169, 173, 179n, 180, 209, 370n

Cohen, Ben, 320

Colburn, David, 210

Cold War, 143

Colgate, 85–6

Colgate Comedy Hour (TV show), 123

Colgate-Palmolive, 360n

Collier's Weekly, 33–5, 36

Columbia Journalism Review, 283, 320

Columbia University, 75, 81, 85, 138, 139
    Department of Biologic Chemistry at, 359n

Comcast, 321

commercial breaks, 136, 263
    public annoyance at, 145–6

Committee on Public Information (CPI; Creel Committee), 43, 44, 45, 46, 47, 49, 56, 149, 352n

Commodore PET, 198–9

Commodore 64, 197

Compaq computers, 260

CompuServe, 198, 200, 202, 207

computers, 170, 181, 192, 196–7
    personal, 185, 198–9
    see also Internet

Computerworld, 189

Condé Nast, 326

conditional indifference, 174

Confessions of an Advertising Man (Ogilvy), 363n

Congress, U.S., 35, 43, 103, 149

Conquest of Cool, The (Frank), 168

Constitution, U.S., 48

consumerism, 54, 75–6, 130–1, 159, 231

consumer movement, 74–5, 76–7

Consumers' Research General Bulletin, 74–5

contagious media, 280–1

"Contagious Media Showdown" web contest, 280

"Content Is King" (Gates), 255

Cook, Tim, 335, 336, 337

Coolidge, Calvin, 63, 71

Coppard, George, 41

copywriters, 52, 71

Correll, Charles, 87

Cosby Show, The (TV show), 176

Couric, Katie, 278

Cowan, Louis G., 137, 138

Cox, H. C., 88

Crawford, Jesse, 88

Creel, George, 43–5, 46, 94, 109, 127, 352n

crime reporting, 15

Crispin, Mark, 189

Crosby, Bing, 100

"Cross of Gold" speech (Bryan), 114

crowd psychology, 113–16

Csikszentmihalyi, Mihalyi, 194

Currid-Halkett, Elizabeth, 249

Cusack, John, 282

Cutler, Jessica, 287

cybersex, 203–4

cyberspace, 203, 291–2

Daily Banter, The (journalism site), 320
Daily Kos (blog), 287
Daily Mail, 321
Damon, Matt, 223
Daniels, Draper, 167
Darkie toothpaste, 88, 360*n*
David, Larry, 282
Davies, Michael, 376*n*
Day, Benjamin, 11–13, 14–15, 18, 92, 140, 190, 347*n*
D-Dog (British Lancaster bomber), 107
Deadliest Catch, The (TV show), 247
Dean, Howard, 270
Dean, Randy, 202
Debs, Eugene, 46–7, 48, 352*n*–3*n*
Debs v. U.S., 352*n*
Deep End of the Ocean, The (Mitchard), 232
Defense Advanced Research Projects Agency (DARPA), 185
demand engineering, 53–6, 62, 64, 67–8, 78, 132
Democratic Party, Democrats, 114, 235, 281, 375*n*
Dennis v. United States, 127*n*
Denton, Nick, 287
Depression, Great, 74, 76, 81
Deutsche Arbeiterpartei (DAP; German Workers' Party), 112
Diana, Princess of Wales, 305
DiCaprio, Leonardo, 223
Dichter, Ernest, 133–4, 147, 148, 174, 309, 364*n*
Dickson, EJ, 203–4
Diet Coke, 173, 262
Digital Equipment Corporation (DEC), 188, 190
Diller, Barry, 176, 177
"dinosaur effect," 164
Discovery Music Network, 238*n*
"disenchantment effect," 23, 238
Disney, 161
Dixon, Chris, 299
doctors' endorsements, 66, 79
Dodge Motors, 58, 59, 75
Donahue, Phil, 227, 229, 373*n*
Donkey Kong (video game), 195
Dorsey, Jack, 306
dot-com crash, 264
dot-coms, 210–11

Dotto (TV show), 139, 148–9
Dough-Re-Mi (TV show), 139
Dove soap, 233
Doyle, Arthur Conan, 37, 42
Doyle Dale Bernbach, 225
Do You Trust Your Wife? (TV show), 142
Dr. Shoop's Restorative, 28, 29–30, 31, 349*n*
Drudge Report (blog), 270, 281
Dr. Yes: The Hyannis Affair (TV show), 175
Duchamp, Marcel, 135
Duke University, 294, 366*n*
Duran Duran, 237

Ebert, Roger, 227–8, 373*n*
Ed Sullivan Show, The (TV show), 129, 160, 164, 270
Education Funding Partners (EFP), 3–4
Edwards, David, 243
Edwards, Douglas, 264
Effective Direct Advertising (Ramsay), 60
Elder, Robert, 104, 105
Eliot, T. S., 76
Elixir of Life, 29
Ellul, Jacques, 41, 48, 146, 148, 363*n*
email, 183–5, 204–5, 279, 308–9, 310
  check-in impulse and, 186–8, 205, 339
  spam, 188–90
Entertainment Tonight (TV show), 226
Ephron, Nora, 205
EPIC (Electronic Privacy Information Center), 335, 336
Espionage Act (1917), 46, 47, 48, 352*n*
ESPN (Entertainment and Sports Programming Network), 15, 175, 331
Esquire, 218, 241, 245
eToys, 260
Excite, 258
Expedia, 377*n*
Expedition Robinson (TV show), 243–4
Eyebeam, 279, 280, 281

Facebook, 18, 186, 211, 288, 290, 291, 293, 294–302, 307, 311, 312, 316, 317, 318, 319, 322, 325, 327, 329, 336, 337, 343
Facemash (website), 290
"Face of Garbo, The" (Barthes), 224
fame, 303–4, 307, 315
Famous Players, 63
Farrow, Mia, 220

Febreze, 78
Federal Communications Commission (FCC), 100, 101*n*, 373*n*
Federal Radio Commission (FRC), 361*n*
Federal Trade Commission (FTC), 69, 73, 79, 80, 81, 265*n*, 359*n*
Feminine Mystique, The (Friedan), 147*n*
film industry, 45–6, 194, 224
films, propaganda, 45–6
Financial Interest and Syndication Rules, 373*n*
Fincher, David, 328–9
Fireside Theater (TV show), 123
First Amendment, 122, 127, 141, 353*n*
first mover advantage, 124
Flagg, James Montgomery, 352*n*
flame wars, 206
Flash-Matic, 145
Flickr, 288
flow state, 194
focus groups, 133
Folies-Bergère, 21
Fontana, Tom, 332
food advertising, 133
Food and Drug Administration, U.S. (FDA), 33, 80
Food and Drugs Act (1906), 35, 36, 80
Forbes, William, 211
Ford, Henry, 53
Fortune, 93, 293, 355*n*
"Four Minute Man" program, 45
Fox Broadcasting Company, 176, 177
Fox Network, 176–7, 239
Fox News Channel, 176–7, 257, 320, 370*n*
Franco, Francisco, 103, 219
Franco, James, 313–14
Frank, Thomas, 155, 168
Frankfurt School, 154
Frauenfelder, Mark, 270
FreePC, 260
free will, 186
Fregin, Doug, 308, 309
Freston, Tom, 237, 238, 242, 249
Freud, Sigmund, 49, 56–7, 113–14, 115, 292
Friedan, Betty, 147*n*
Friendly, Fred, 126, 141, 142, 162, 177, 178
Friendster, 293, 294, 295, 297
Frost, Robert, 135

Funkwarte (Radio Guard), 108, 118
Future of Ideas, The (Lessig), 253

Game of Thrones (TV show), 331, 333
"Gangnam Style," 319
Garbo, Greta, 224
Garthwaite, Craig, 231
Gates, Bill, 255–6, 290
Gault, Robert Harvey, 366*n*
Gawker (blog), 287
Geldof, Bob, 243
General Electric (GE), 58, 200, 360*n*
General Motors, 59, 209, 212
GEnie (General Electric Network for Information Exchange), 198, 200, 206
geodemography, 171–4
Geritol, 138
German Radio Division, 118
German Workers' Party (Deutsche Arbeiterpartei; DAP), 112
Germany, 37–8, 39, 40–1, 42, 43, 46, 50, 110, 112, 113, 352*n*
Germany, Nazi, 42, 44, 107, 108–9, 113, 115–19, 120–1, 154, 271
Get a Life (TV show), 177
Gibson, William, 198
Gies, William J., 359*n*
Gilbert, Craig, 240, 245
Gilder, George, 331
Gillette, 86
Gilligan, Vince, 333
Gilligan's Island (TV show), 334
Girard, René, 315
Gizmodo (blog), 287
Gladwell, Malcolm, 162
Glaser, Milton, 166
Glass, Noah, 306
Glatzer, Ross, 201
Goebbels, Paul Joseph, 109, 116–17, 120, 127
Goodfellow, Louis Deal, 366*n*
Google, 18, 211, 258–9, 260, 261–6, 267, 272, 274, 283, 291, 293, 295, 296, 297, 299, 300, 301, 305, 310, 311*n*, 323, 325, 329, 336, 337, 338, 339, 377*n*
Gosden, Freeman, 87–8
Gospel of Wealth, 234
gossip blogs, 285–6

GoTo.com, 260, 262, 264, 264*n*–5*n*

Gould, Jack, 142

Great American Dream Machine, The
(variety show), 163

"Great American Fraud, The" (Adams),
33–5

Great Britain, 5, 37–8, 39–43, 44, 46, 47,
48, 50, 53, 63, 102, 107, 109–10, 117,
118, 121, 347*n*

Great Depression, 74, 76, 81

Great Gatsby, The (film), 220

Great Refusal, 154, 180, 274

Green, Tyler, 294

Green Acres (TV show), 162

Greene, Mean Joe, 180, 370*n*

Grey, Charlotte, 13

Griffith, D. W., 89

Grind, The (TV show), 246

Groening, Matt, 176

Gross, Bill, 259–61, 263, 264*n*–5*n*

gross ratings points (GRP), 140

Grumpy Cat, 319

Guiding Light (radio show), 360*n*

Guinea Pigs No More (Matthews), 77

Gunsmoke (TV show), 142, 148

Gunther, John, 354*n*

Haag, Laurie, 230

Habermas, Jürgen, 15, 347*n*

Hadamovsky, Eugen, 118

Halberstam, David, 99–100, 101, 129, 141–2

Hale, Ruth, 68

halitosis, 54–5, 62

Hall, Brad, 282

Hall, Fred A., 13

Hamburger Hamlet, 227–8

Hammerbacher, Jeff, 324

Hand, Learned, 48

Handler, Milton, 81

H&R Block, 200

Hanfstaengl, Ernst, 113, 115

Hanks, Tom, 205

Harley-Davidson, 78

Harper's, 31, 222

Hart, Dorothy, 103–4

Harvard University, 113, 151, 289, 290, 291,
293, 294, 295

Hastings, Reed, 329

"hate" films, 45

Haves and Have Nots, The (TV show), 236,
375*n*

Hawley & Hazel Chemical Company, 360*n*

Hawthorne effect, 241

Hay, Bill, 89, 360*n*

HBO, 258, 328, 331, 332

headline optimization, 319

Hearst, John Randolph, 103–4

Heck, Alfons, 115

Hee Haw (TV show), 162

Heffernan, Virginia, 272–3

Heinz, 58

Heiskell, Andrew, 217–18, 219, 221

Hermès, 78, 79

Herrera, Monica, 179*n*

Herschel, John, 17

Hertz Rent-a-Car, 226

Hidden Persuaders, The (Packard), 146–8

Hilgemeier, Eddie, 148–9

Hill, George Washington, 65–6, 67, 69, 79,
80, 134, 355*n*

Hill, Percival, 65

Hilton, Nicky, 285

Hilton, Paris, 243, 247, 248, 285

"Hipster Barbie," 313

Hitler, Adolf, 50, 103, 106, 107, 108, 109–13,
117, 120, 219
as public speaker, 112–13, 115–16

Hitler Myth, The (Kershaw), 118*n*

Hofbräuhaus hall, 113

Hollingshead, Michael, 152

"Hollow Men, The" (Eliot), 76

Holmes, Oliver Wendell, 47, 48

HomeGrocer.com, 211

Hooper Ratings, 105

Hoover, Herbert, 86, 87

Hopkins, Claude C., 24–5, 28, 29–30,
31–2, 33, 34, 35, 36, 52, 54, 55–6, 58,
60, 66, 67, 69, 70, 72, 85, 86, 131, 166,
348*n*–9*n*, 350*n*, 355*n*

Horton, Donald, 224

"Hot or Not" (website), 290

Hourihan, Meg, 268

Houseman, John, 102

House of Cards (web series), 328–9, 330, 333

Howdy Doody Show, The (TV show), 161

Huffington, Arianna, 281, 282

Huffington Post, The, 281–4, 285, 286, 288,
298, 300, 318, 321

Hulu, 330
Hunt, Bertha, 356n
Huntley-Brinkley Report, The (TV show),
    127

IBM, 183, 200, 201
Idealab, 260
If Loving You Is Wrong (TV show), 236
"I ♥ NY" campaign, 166
I Love Lucy (TV show), 128, 130, 137, 175,
    271, 301, 331, 334
individualism, 168, 171
infomercials, 232–3
information overload, 19–20
Inside North Vietnam (TV show), 162–3
Instagram, 311–17, 327
Instapundit (blog), 270
Institute for Motivational Research, 147
intentional traffic, 259
International Advertising Association, 76
International Federation for Internal
    Freedom, 151–2
Internet, 21, 72, 183–5, 186, 188, 199, 204,
    206, 210n, 211, 212, 213, 246, 251–3,
    267–75, 276–88, 289, 291–302,
    303–4, 312, 322, 328, 330, 335, 341
    content on, 255–66
    online advertising and, 189, 200, 201,
        208–9, 264, 267, 283–4, 323–4, 329
Interpretation of Dreams, The (Freud), 56
iOS 9 operating system, 337
iPads, 336, 337
Ipana Troubadours, 86
iPhones, 249, 300n, 310, 311, 336, 337, 338
iTunes, 321
Iwatani, Toru, 195–6

Jackson, Michael, 179, 237
James, William, 7, 94, 344, 348n
Japan, 19n, 192–3
Jarvis, Jeffrey, 252, 273, 275, 321
Jenner, Bruce (Caitlyn), 248
Jenner, Kendall, 248
Jenner, Kylie, 248
Jepson, Helen, 355n
Jersey Shore (TV show), 244, 247
Jewett, Helen, 15
Jews, Judaism, 26, 93, 113
J. Fred Muggs (chimpanzee), 135

Jobs, Steve, 192n, 338
Johansson, Scarlett, 223, 305
joint attention, 115
Jolie, Angelina, 223
Jolly Green Giant, 131
Journal of Commerce, 11
Joyce, James, 270
Julius Caesar (Shakespeare), 102
Jung, Carl, 132
Jungle, The (Sinclair), 35
Just Plain Bill (radio show), 102
J. Walter Thompson Company, 53, 56, 57,
    62, 63, 70, 178, 201
    Women's Editorial Department at, 61,
        62–3, 64, 69, 171–2, 357n

Kaiser, the Beast of Berlin, The (film), 45–6
Kardashian, Khloé, 248
Kardashian, Kim, 232, 247–8, 313, 314
Kardashian, Kourtney, 248
Kardashian, Kris, 248
Kardashian, Rob, 248
Kardashian, Robert, 248
Kay, Linda, 230
Keeping Up with the Kardashians (*KUWTK;*
    TV show), 247–9
Keller, Bill, 283–4
Kelley, Kitty, 232
Kellogg's, 131, 161
Kennedy, John C., 349n
Kennedy, John F., 220
Kennedy, Robert F., 240
Kershaw, Ian, 118n
Kickapoo's Indian Sagwa, 28, 29
Kidd, James W., 29
King, Gayle, 233
King World Productions, 373n
Kipling, Rudyard, 40–1
Kirchenkampf ("church struggle"), 118n
Kitchener, Herbert, 37–8, 39–40, 42, 46,
    63, 323
Klauber, Ed, 103
Klum, Heidi, 282
Kohl, Herb, 204
Korean War, 164
Kottke.org, 270
Kraft, 58
Krieger, Mike, 311
Ku Klux Klan, 89, 227

labeling rules, 35
Ladies' Home Journal, 31, 33*n*
Lanier, Jaron, 326
Lansdowne, Helen, *see* Resor, Helen
    Lansdowne
La Palina cigars, 86, 95–6
La Palina Hour (radio show), 86
Lasker, Albert, 52, 65–6, 67, 69, 70, 79, 80,
    357*n*
Lavandeira, Mario Armando, Jr., 285
LA Weekly, 282
Lawler, John, 13–14
Lawler, Mary, 13–14
"Law of Attraction" doctrine, 234–5
Lawrence Welk Show, The (TV show), 164
Lazaridis, Mihalis "Mike," 308, 309
League of Women Shoppers, 75
Leary, Timothy, 151–5, 156, 158, 159, 165,
    168, 274
Le Bon, Gustave, 113, 115
Lenin, Vladimir, 117
Lennard, Natasha, 271*n*
Lerer, Ken, 281, 282, 285
Lerner, Max, 117–18
Lessig, Lawrence, 253, 269, 275, 288
Levy, Steven, 212, 265
Lewinsky, Monica, 247
Lewis, Jerry, 205*n*
LeWitt, Sol, 281
Liebling, A. J., 218
Life, 164, 217, 219, 355*n*
Life After Television (Gilder), 331
*Life and Adventures of the American
    Cowboy, The* (Stanley), 27–8
Liggett & Myers Tobacco Company, 142
"like" button, 300
Lindelof, Damon, 331
LinkedIn, 293
Lippmann, Walter, 47–8, 49, 56, 149–50,
    153
Liquozone, 31, 32, 33, 34, 36, 54, 350*n*
Listerine, 54–5, 62
"Little Albert" experiment, 57
Live Aid, 243
"Live–Give" campaign, 158
Lohan, Lindsay, 248
Lombroso, Cesare, 63
London, Jack, 350*n*
Lonelygirl15 (YouTube poster), 286

Longworth, Alice Roosevelt, 64
"Lookalike Audience," 300*n*
Lopez, Vincent, 88
Lord & Thomas, 52, 53, 55, 66, 70, 89, 355*n*
Lost (TV show), 331
Loud family, 240, 241, 245
Louis-Dreyfus, Julia, 282
Louis Vuitton, 78
Luce, Henry, 63, 217, 218, 219, 220, 221
Lucky Strike, 58, 65–9, 79–80, 134, 153,
    355*n*, 356*n*
Ludendorff, Erich, 50
Lukasik, Stephen, 185–6
Lycos, 258, 264
Lydia Pinkham's Herb Medicine, 28

Mackey-Kallis, Susan, 231
MacLeish, Archibald, 102
MacManus, Theodore, 58–9, 60, 75, 131,
    300
Madel, Jerry, 165
Mad Men (TV show), 52, 328
Magellan, 258
Magnavox Odyssey, 191, 192, 196, 371*n*
mail-order catalogues, 31
Mander, Jerry, 129–30, 160, 165, 168, 363*n*
M&M's, 131
Manners, Lady Diana, 64
Man Nobody Knows, The (Barton), 71
Manson, Mark, 322
Marcuse, Herbert, 154, 156, 158, 159–60,
    165, 168, 203, 269, 301
Marlboro Man, 131–2, 139, 157, 167
Married . . . with Children (TV show), 176,
    177
Martin, Liam, 313
Marx, Karl, 22, 76, 121, 154
Mary Tyler Moore Show, The (TV show),
    164, 165
mascots, 131
M*A*S*H (TV show), 164, 165
Mashable, 320
Masses Publishing Co. v. Pattern, 353*n*
"Mass Hoax, The" (Eyebam workshop),
    280
mass production, 53, 57–8, 78
Match.com, 293, 296
Mattel, 161
Maule, Frances, 61, 64

McCann Erickson, 53, 169
McCarthy, Joseph, 127
McCracken, Grant, 330
McDonald, E. F., 144–5, 366*n*
McGuinness, Peter, 356*n*
McLuhan, Marshall, 151, 152–3, 156, 164, 339
Mead, Margaret, 135, 241
Mead, Rebecca, 268
Media Rights Capital, 328
Meetup.com, 293
Megnut.com, 268, 270
Mein Kampf (Hitler), 110, 111
Mercury Theatre on the Air (radio show), 102
Metropolitan Opera, 66, 355*n*
Meyers, Cynthia B., 360*n*
Mickey Mouse Club, 161
microfame, 303–7
"Microfame Game, The" (Sorgatz), 304
Microsoft, 208, 255, 256–8, 272, 321, 333, 377*n*
Microsoft Windows, 198, 255, 256
Mies van der Rohe, Ludwig, 70
Millay, Edna St. Vincent, 76
Miller, Amanda, 313
Miller, Mark Crispin, 39
Millman, Robert, 193
Ministry of Public Enlightenment and Propaganda, 116, 118, 120
    National Radio Division of, 109
mirror neurons, 125
Mister Rogers' Neighborhood (TV show), 161–2
MIT, 104, 276, 279, 290*n*
Mitchard, Jacquelyn, 232
Mohler, Albert, 234–5
Monkees, The (TV show), 239
Monroe, Marilyn, 221
Montgomery Ward, 31
Morning Courier and New York Enquirer, 11, 16
Morning Herald, 15–16
    see also New York Herald
Mossberg, Walter, 204
mouthwash, 54–5, 78
movies, 83, 124–5
movie theaters, advertising in, 92
Mr. Personality (TV show), 247

"MSN 2.0," 256–7, 377*n*
MSNBC (Microsoft-NBC), 257
MTV, 174, 177, 179, 208, 237–40, 241–3, 246, 247
muckraking, 32–6
Mulcahey, Katie, 356*n*
Münsterberg, Hugo, 124
Murdoch, Rupert, 176, 177, 370*n*
Murray, Jonathan, 239–40, 241, 242, 243, 248
Murrow, Edward R., 106–7, 126–7, 142–3, 160–1, 165, 365*n*
Music Boulevard, 210, 211
Mussolini, Benito, 44, 63, 103, 127, 219
Myers, David, 187
My Favorite Husband (radio show), 128
My Life in Advertising (Hopkins), 348*n*
MySpace, 294, 295, 297–8

Namco, 195
nanotargeting, 297, 299
Nardroff, Elfrida von, 139
National Enquirer, 219, 220, 225
National Football League (NFL), 136, 239
National Laboratories, 73
"national moments," 117, 118
National Public Radio (NPR), 102, 163, 184
National Socialist Party, 117
National Woman's Party, 63
NBC (National Broadcasting Company), 88, 89, 91, 92, 96–9, 100, 101, 102, 103, 107, 118, 123–4, 126, 127–9, 134–6, 138, 141, 145, 150, 161, 162, 175, 176, 228, 257, 271*n*, 360*n*, 365*n*, 366*n*
Nelson, Ted, 193
Nelson's Column, 40
Netflix, 213, 328–31, 340
Net Neutrality, 210*n*
network effect, 291
NetZero, 260
Neuromancer (Gibson), 198
New Republic, 47, 51, 52
News Corporation, 297
news coverage:
    on radio, 103, 105–7
    on television, 126–9
Newspaper Association of America, 337
newspapers, 5, 11–18, 84, 103*n*, 268–9, 283–4, 301, 309

New York, 178, 179, 217, 304
New York *Daily News,* 128, 149
New Yorker, 90, 91, 147, 218, 268, 321
New York Evening News, 356n
New York Herald, 16–17
New York Herald Tribune, 142
New York Observer, 304
New York Philharmonic, 102
New York Post, 285
New York State, 14, 151, 208
New York Sun, 12–15, 16, 17–18, 32, 91, 92,
    140, 201, 284
New York Times, 11, 12, 68, 72, 101, 103, 127,
    135, 142, 174, 175, 193, 218, 220, 222,
    226, 242, 248, 256, 260, 272–3, 283,
    285, 287, 304, 324, 326, 330n, 336,
    356n, 374n
New York Times Magazine, 229
New York Transcript, 15
New York University, 170
Nielsen, Arthur Charles, 105, 123, 141,
    264
Nielsen, George, 170
Nielsen Drug Index, 105
Nielsen Food Index, 105
Nielsen ratings, 104–5, 123, 128, 134, 146,
    273
Nieman Lab, 337
Nies, Eric, 246
Nike, 30, 276–8, 279, 280, 379n
"900 Inter@ctive Pager, The," 308–9
Nintendo, 279
Nishikado, Tomohiro, 192–3
Nixon, Richard, 228
Norcia, Steve, 173
North Dakota, 375n
Northwestern University, 366n
    Kellogg School of Management at, 231
"Notes on Contagious Media" (Peretti),
    280–1
Nuremberg rallies, 115–16
Nussbaum, Emily, 330n
NYPost.com, 323

O, The Oprah Magazine, 233
Obama, Barack, 223, 235, 306, 309, 375n
O'Connor, John J., 242
Ogilvy, David, 22, 23, 25, 70, 130, 363n
Old Dutch Cleanser, 62

Olivier, Laurence, 226
Omni, 196
100,000,000 Guinea Pigs (Kallet), 77
O'Neill, Essena, 316
operant conditioning, 186–7, 194
"Oprah's Favorite Things" program, 232
orange juice, 54, 78
"Order of the White Feather," 351n
organized religions, 26–7
Orkut, 293–4
Osbournes, The (TV show), 247
Oscar Meyer, 133
Osteen, Joel, 234
Oswald, Lee Harvey, 220, 240
Oswald, Marina, 220
Our Master's Voice (Rorty), 75–6
OWN (Oprah Winfrey Network), 235–6,
    375n
Oxford Dictionary, 312, 330n
Oz (TV show), 332

Packard, Vance, 146–8, 153
Pac-Man (video game), 195–6, 311
Page, Larry, 259, 260–1, 262, 263, 265, 297,
    338, 377n
pagers, 308–9
Pagesixsixsix.com, 285
paid endorsements, 63–4
Painted Dreams (radio show), 360n
Paley, "Babe" Cushing Mortimer, 128
Paley, Samuel, 96
Paley, William S., 95–8, 99–100, 101–4,
    105–6, 124, 126, 127–9, 134, 136–7,
    138, 140–1, 142, 143, 164, 165, 175,
    234, 361n, 365n
Palmer, Gareth, 305
"para-social interaction," 224
Pareles, Jon, 273
Park, Robert E., 369n
Parliamentary Recruiting Committee, 40
Parsons, Charlie, 243, 244
patent medicines, 28–30, 42, 52, 54, 60, 63,
    66, 69, 71, 78, 80, 147
    backlash against, 31–6
Pavlov, Ivan, 57
PBS, 240
"peak attention," 129–30
Peanuts (comic strip), 368n
Pears' soap, 63

People, 219–22, 224, 225, 226, 228, 284, 305, 314, 321
"people meters," 105
Pepsi Cola Company, 152, 155–8, 160, 163, 165–6, 168, 172, 179
"Pepsi Generation" campaign, 156–7
Pepsodent, 55–6, 85–6, 88–90, 92, 96, 104, 359*n*
Peretti, Chelsea, 280
Peretti, Jonah, 267, 276–81, 282, 285, 318, 319, 320, 321, 325–6, 379*n*
Perez Hilton (blog), 285–6
"Perfect Song, The" (song), 89
Perry, Katy, 306
Perry, Tyler, 375*n*
Pershing's Crusaders (film), 45
personal computers, 185, 198–9
Peter Pan (musical), 135
Pew, 349*n*
pharmaceutical industry, 80
Philadelphia Inquirer, 204
Philco Television Playhouse (TV show), 123
Phil Donohue Show, The (TV show), 227, 373*n*
Philip Morris, 128, 131, 166–7
Phillips, Irna, 93–4, 239, 360*n*
Pickford, Mary, 63
Pictorial Arts Division, 46
Pillsbury, 93
Pillsbury Doughboy, 131
Pinkham, Lydia, 356*n*
Pittman, Bob, 208, 209, 210, 211, 212, 237, 238
Playboy, 221
Playboy Channel, 175
Playboy Enterprises Inc., 175
Playstation, 326
Polaroid, 225–6
"political religion," 118
Polley, Eugene, 145
Pompeii, 26
Pond's cold cream, 63–4, 167, 168
Pong (video game), 192
Pontiac, 232, 233
"poor Edna" series, 62
PopMatters, 248
populism, 112
Portlandia (TV show), 332

posters, 18–19, 20–2, 28, 111, 124
backlash against, 22–3
in World War I, 40, 46
Post Office, U.S., 31, 172
"Potential Ratings in ZIP Markets" system (PRIZM), 172–4, 175, 271, 297
Pottasch, Alan, 155, 156–7
Powell, Kevin, 244–5
Presley, Elvis, 129
Prime Time Access Rule, 373*n*
Printer's Ink, 50, 59, 86
Prius, 326
privacy, 323, 336, 342
Procter & Gamble (P&G), 62, 209, 239
Prodigy, 198, 200–2, 204, 205, 206–7, 208, 213
"Project Confidence," 209–12
"Project Pigeon," 187*n*
propaganda, 5–6, 38–50, 53, 59, 68, 83, 120–1, 122, 127, 146, 148, 159
films, 45–6
Hitler's approach to, 110–11
Nazi use of, 116–19
Propaganda (Bernays), 66, 100, 122
psychedelic drugs, 152
Psychopathology of Everyday Life, The (Freud), 56
public broadcasting, 161–3
Public Broadcasting Laboratory (TV show), 162–3, 177
public interest shows, 96–7
public opinion, 15
manufacturing of, 47–8
Public Opinion (Lippmann), 47–8
public relations, 49, 110, 122
public schools, advertising in, 3–5, 342

Queen for a Day (TV show), 305
Queer Eye for the Straight Guy (TV show), 369*n*–70*n*
quiz shows, 137–9
quiz show scandal, 148–9

radio, 83, 86–94, 95–6, 121, 124, 142, 144, 181, 259, 283
advertising on, 86–94, 98, 103
audience ratings and, 104–5
business model of early, 96–7
college, 163

daytime, 93–4
government use of, 117
Nazi uses of, 108–9, 116–19
news coverage on, 103, 105–7
Nielsen ratings for, 104–5
Paley and, 95–106
programming for, 101–2
Radio Act (1927), 361n
Radio Broadcasts, 96
Radio Free Europe, 121
Radio Guard (Funkwarte), 108, 118
Radio Moscow, 117
"Rally of Freedom" (1935), 116
Ram Dass (Richard Alpert), 151–2
Ramsay, Robert E., 60
RCA (Radio Corporation of America), 92, 98, 124, 360n
"Reach for a Lucky" campaign, 69, 79–80, 153
Reader's Digest, 126
Real Housewives, The (reality TV franchise), 244, 247
Reality in Advertising (Reeves), 131n
reality television, 241–2, 244–9, 252, 305
Real World, The (TV show), 241–3, 244, 245, 246, 247
recognition, politics of, 171–2, 174
Recruiting Committee (Britain), 39–40
Reddit, 319, 322
Redford, Robert, 305
Red Scare, 127
Reeves, Rosser, 131, 139
Reichsfunk-Gesellschaft, 109
Reith, John, 101
"Rejection Line" (website), 280
religion, 26–7, 215–16
remote control, 145–6, 177, 178, 180
Remote Control (TV show), 239
Republic.com 2.0 (Sunstein), 271n
Research in Motion, 309, 310
Resor, Helen Lansdowne, 60–1, 63, 70
Resor, Stanley B., 56, 57, 61, 63, 70, 78
Revlon, 137, 138, 139
Reynolds, Glenn, 207
Rhine, Joseph Banks, 366n
Riefenstahl, Leni, 44, 116
RIM 900, 308–9
Rinso, 102
Rise of the Goldbergs, The (radio show), 92

Rivera, Geraldo, 229
R. J. Reynolds Company, 126
Robbin, Jonathan, 170, 369n
Robot Wisdom (blog), 270
Rogers, Fred, 161–2
Rojek, Chris, 224
Rolling Stone, 218
Rolling Stones, 160
Rolls-Royce, 65
Romano, Andrew, 332–3
Roosevelt, Franklin D., 75, 80, 106n, 219, 352n
Roosevelt, Theodore, 35, 64
Rorty, James, 75–6
Rose, Jessica, 286
Rosenbaum, Steve, 257
Rothafel, Samuel "Roxy," 86
Ryan, Meg, 205

Safari, 337
Safire, William, 220–1
St. Mark's Place (proposed TV show), 239
Salon, 271n, 283, 284
Sam 'n' Henry (radio show), 87n
    see also *Amos 'n' Andy*
Sanders, M. L., 42
Sanders Associates, 191
Sarandos, Ted, 328–9
Sarnoff, David, 96, 98–9, 100, 103, 104, 124, 126, 129, 134, 135, 150, 364n
Sarnoff, Lizette, 104
Saturday Evening Post, 110
Saturday Night Live (TV show), 239, 285
Savage, Fred, 305, 306
Schlesinger, Arthur M., Jr., 282
Schlink, Frederick, 73–5, 78
Schmidt, Eric, 323
Schober, Joe, 203
scientific advertising, 52–4, 57, 61, 70
Scientific Advertising (Hopkins), 51–2
Scientific American, 235
Scott, Ridley, 180
Scott, William, 14
Seacrest, Ryan, 248
search engines, 258–66, 272
Sears, 31, 200, 201, 205
Sears, Richard, 31
Secret, The (Byrne), 234, 235
Securities and Exchange Commission, 212

Sedition Act (1918), 46
See It Now (TV show), 126–7, 142, 164
Seinfeld (TV show), 282
"selfies," 312
selfie sticks, 315
Selfish (Kardashian), 248
Selter, Jen, 314
Serra, Richard, 336
Sesame Street (TV show), 158, 161, 162, 164, 177
Shakespeare, William, 102
Shapiro, Ben, 235
sharing, 271–2, 319–20
Shark Tank (TV show), 247
Shermer, Michael, 235
Shields, Brooke, 179
Shirky, Clay, 269, 274–5, 287
shopping, online, 201–2, 213
Showtime, 331
Shredded Wheat, 62
Siemering, Bill, 163
Silicon Valley, 188, 262, 335
Silverman, Fred, 163, 164–5, 174, 239, 243
Simple Life, The (TV show), 243
Simpson, Ashlee, 285
Simpson, O. J., 226, 248
Simpsons, The (TV show), 176, 177
Sinclair, Upton, 35
Site, The (TV show), 257
$64,000 Question, The (TV show), 137–9, 142, 149, 252, 376n
60 Minutes (TV show), 164, 221
Skinner, B. F., 186–7, 188
Skipper, John, 331
Slashdot.org, 270, 271
Slate, 257, 265n, 283, 284, 321
slave trade, 14
Smallwood, Brad, 300
smartphones, 309, 310–11, 312, 314
Smith, Al, 87
Smith, Douglas, 31, 32, 34
Smith, Kenneth, 88
Smith, Ralph Lee, 177
Smokey Bear ads, 122
smoking, 131–2, 167
Snake Oil Liniment, 27–9, 30, 33, 35, 36
Snapchat, 319
Snow Crash (Stephenson), 198
soap operas, 91, 93–4, 239, 244

Socality Barbie, 313
social media, 6, 7, 41, 186, 207, 271–3, 291–2, 298–9, 304, 315–16, 321, 323
SocialNet, 293
Social Network, The (film), 328
social networks, 288, 293–4, 311–12, 318, 322
Sony, 326
Sopranos, The (TV show), 331, 332
Sorgatz, Rex, 303–4, 306, 307
Soviet Union, 42, 109, 117, 121
Space Invaders (video game), 193–4, 195, 196, 311
Space War! (video game), 192
spam, 188–90, 211
speech, freedom of, 48–9
Speer, Albert, 109, 115
Spielberg, Steven, 260
Spiers, Elizabeth, 287
sponsorships, 86–7, 92, 96, 136, 140
sports, 135–6, 239
Springer, Jerry, 229–30
Sprint, 209
Sprite, 297
Spy, 228–9
Squirt, 169
Stafford, Tom, 187–8
Stalin, Joseph, 121, 219
Stanford Daily, 294
Stanford Research into Tobacco Advertising, 355n
Stanford University, 183, 294
Stanley, Clark, 27–9, 30, 31, 33, 36, 349n
Stanton, Frank, 100
Star Wars (film), 193, 194
Stegner, Wallace, 170
Stempel, Herb, 138, 149
Stephenson, Neal, 198
Stern, Howard, 229, 244–5
Stole, Inger L., 81
Stolley, Richard, 219–20, 222, 225
Stone, Biz, 306
Stunden der Nation, 118
Subaru, 332
subliminal messages, 147
suffrage movement, 61, 62
Sullivan, Andrew, 271, 326
Sullivan, Ed, 128, 142
Sullivan, "Little Tim," 355n–6n

Sullivan Ordinance, 355*n*–6*n*

Sunstein, Cass, 271*n*

Super Bowl, 90, 136, 179–80, 263

Super Mario Brothers (video game), 279

Supreme Court, U.S., 47, 48–9, 79, 127, 352*n*–3*n*

Survivor (TV show), 243–4

Swan, The (TV show), 252

Swartz, Aaron, 290*n*

Swayze, John Cameron, 126

Swift and Company, 51

Swisher, Kara, 202

Systrom, Kevin, 311

TaB, 173

Talking Points Memo (blog), 287

targeting, 53, 60, 64, 325

Tartaroff, 85

Taylor, Elizabeth, 220, 225

Taylor, Frederick, 170

Taylor, Philip, 42

Taylor v. Mississippi, 127*n*

Technorati, 288

TED (Technology, Entertainment, Design) conference, 259–60

Teddy Antiperspirant foot powder, 111

Telecom Act (1996), 208*n*

television, 7, 83, 94, 121, 123–9, 160–2, 168, 174–5, 181, 190, 191, 196, 199, 228, 252–3, 257, 263, 274, 283, 309, 336, 340

    backlash against commercial, 145–50

    celebrity and, 137, 224–5, 244–6

    children's, 161–2

    "grazing" on, 178

    magazine format in, 136

    news coverage on, 126–9, 176–7

    peak attention and, 129–30

    prime-time, 134–5, 140

    quiz show scandal and, 148–50

    quiz shows on, 137–9

    ratings and, 140–1

    reality, 241–2, 244–9, 252, 305

    self-imposed censorship in, 142–3

television commercials, 130–1, 136, 178, 263

Telmex, 213

Templin, Walter, 85, 86, 87, 88, 89, 92, 360*n*

testimonials, 63–4, 66, 79

Tetris (video game), 311

Texaco Star Theater (TV show), 123–4

Texas Instruments, 185

Theory of Monopolistic Competition, The (Chamberlin), 78

Thriller (music video), 237, 238

Thuerk, Gary, 188–90

Tic-Tac-Dough (TV show), 139

"Tiffany Network" strategy, 100–1, 126

Time, 55, 63, 106, 138, 144–5, 218–19, 220, 221, 228, 273, 284, 355*n*

Time-Life Inc., 217, 218, 219, 220, 221, 222, 225

Time Warner, 196, 205*n*, 208, 213, 321

TMZ, 285

Toast of the Town, The (TV show), 128

    see also Ed Sullivan Show, The

Tobaccowala, Rishad, 283

Today's Children (radio show), 93, 360*n*

Today show (TV show), 135, 136*n*, 278

Toffler, Van, 239

Tomlinson, Ray, 183, 184–5

Tonight show (TV show), 135, 136*n*

Tony the Tiger, 131

toothpaste, 54–6, 78, 85, 88–90, 139

"Torches of Freedom" parade, 68

Toulouse-Lautrec, Henri de, 22

Toyota, 326

tracking technologies, 300–1, 323, 325, 337, 338

Travolta, John, 235

Triumph of the Will (film), 44

trolls, 16, 189–90, 292–3

Tufekci, Zeynep, 298–9

Tugwell, Rexford, 75, 80, 81

Tugwell Bill, 80–1

24 (TV show), 330*n*

Twenty One (TV show), 138, 139, 149

Twitter, 186, 288, 303, 304, 305–7, 311, 312, 317, 318, 319, 327, 329

Tye, Larry, 356*n*

Ulmer, James, 305

Ulmer Scale, 305

Uncle Sam, 46, 352*n*

Uncle Tom's Cabin (Stowe), 91

Understanding Media (McLuhan), 151

Upworthy, 320

USA Today, 45, 242
Us Weekly, 226

Valentino, Rudolph, 224
Vanderbilt, Gloria Morgan, 64, 220
Van Doren, Charles, 138, 149, 244, 304
Vanilla Ice Goes Amish (TV show), 252
variable reinforcement, 187–8
VAX T-series, 188
Veach, Eric, 263
Venema, Erin, 378*n*
video games, 191–7, 198
"Video Killed the Radio Star" (song),
    237
Video Music Awards (1992), 244–5
Vietnam War, 163, 193, 217
Vin Mariani, 21
viral lift, 319–20
viral media, 318–19
Virgin Galactic, 119
Virginia Slims, 167
virtual sex, 203–4
Vogue, 128, 263, 356*n*
Voice of Experience, The (radio show), 102
Volksempfänger ("people's receiver"), 108,
    118
Volksgemeinschaft (people's community),
    109, 117, 120
von Meister, William, 200

Wales, Jimmy, 272
"walled garden" strategy, 210–11, 212, 260
Wall Street Journal, 11, 101, 204, 356*n*
Ward, Aaron Montgomery, 31
Warhol, Andy, 246, 307
Warner-Amex, 174
Warner Communications, 196
War of the Worlds (radio program), 102
war-will, 44, 48
Washington, George, 352*n*
Washington Post, 68, 114, 193, 205, 283, 287,
    321, 356*n*
Watson, John B., 56–7, 186, 354*n*
Watts, Duncan, 279–80
Weaver, Sylvester "Pat," 134–6, 137, 141, 150,
    175, 263, 364*n*
Webby Award, 279
Weinberger, David, 269, 286–7, 307
Weiss, Michael, 172, 369*n*

Weiss, Rob, 203
Welles, Orson, 102, 146
Wells, H. G., 102
Wells, Mary, 166, 167
Wells, Rich, Greene, 166–7
Wesley, John, 26
Westinghouse, 360*n*
Wheeler-Lea Amendment, 359*n*
whisper (scare) campaigns, 62
Whitney v. California, 48–9, 353*n*
"Who Needs People?" (Safire), 220–1
Who Wants to Be a Millionaire? (TV show),
    138*n*, 252, 376*n*
"Why We Are Anti-Semites" speech
    (Hitler), 113
Wife Swap (TV show), 247
Wikipedia, 258*n*, 272, 286, 322
Wiley, Harvey Washington, 35
Williams, Evan, 306
Williams, James, 324–5, 338
Willingham, Calder, 125–6
Wilson, Donald M., 221
Wilson, Samuel, 352*n*
Wilson, Woodrow, 43–4, 47, 352*n*
Wilson and the Issues (Creel), 43–4
Winfrey, Oprah, 227–9, 230–6, 270, 373*n*,
    374*n*, 375*n*
Winn, Marie, 148, 149
Wired, 201, 259, 265, 287–8
Wired Nation, The (Smith), 177
Wisdom (TV show), 135
Wisner, George, 13, 14
Wohl, Richard, 224
Wolff, Michael, 209, 338, 340
Wolves of Kultur (film), 45
women, 75, 76, 93–4, 134, 167, 171–2, 175,
    195, 218
    as advertising target, 53, 59–64
    smoking by, 67–8
Wonder Bread, 102
Wonkette (blog), 287
Wood, David, 284
Wood, Robert, 164
Woodbury, John, 60
Woodbury soap, 60–1
Woodroff, Louis, 105
Woodward, Helen, 75
World Cup (2014), 319
World's Fair (Chicago; 1893), 27

World War I, 37–44, 76, 94, 109–10, 121, 130
World War II, 106–7, 175, 187*n*
Wozniak, Steve, 192*n,* 199*n*
Wright, Frank Lloyd, 135
Wright Brothers, 14, 189
WS Crawford, 53

Yahoo!, 213, 258, 262, 264, 265*n,* 339
Yates v. United States, 127*n*
You Are Not a Gadget (Lanier), 326
You Do What You're Told (CBS pamphlet), 98
Young & Rubicam, 134

Your Money's Worth (Chase and Schlink), 74, 76
Your Show of Shows (TV show), 123
youth movement, 154, 156–7
YouTube, 272, 286, 316, 325, 327, 329, 341
You've Got Mail (film), 205

Ze Frank, 279
Zenith Foundation, The (radio show), 366*n*
Zenith Radio Company, 144–6, 178, 366*n*
Zone Improvement Plan (ZIP) codes, 172
Zuckerberg, Mark, 289–91, 293, 294, 296, 297, 298, 307, 311, 312, 336, 339

World War I, 37–44, 76, 94, 109–10, 121, 130

World War II, 106–7, 175, 187*n*

Wozniak, Steve, 192*n,* 199*n*

Wright, Frank Lloyd, 135

Wright Brothers, 14, 189

WS Crawford, 53

Yahoo!, 213, 258, 262, 264, 265*n,* 339

Yates v. United States, 127*n*

You Are Not a Gadget (Lanier), 326

You Do What You're Told (CBS pamphlet), 98

Young & Rubicam, 134

Your Money's Worth (Chase and Schlink), 74, 76

Your Show of Shows (TV show), 123

youth movement, 154, 156–7

YouTube, 272, 286, 316, 325, 327, 329, 341

You've Got Mail (film), 205

Ze Frank, 279

Zenith Foundation, The (radio show), 366*n*

Zenith Radio Company, 144–6, 178, 366*n*

Zone Improvement Plan (ZIP) codes, 172

Zuckerberg, Mark, 289–91, 293, 294, 296, 297, 298, 307, 311, 312, 336, 339